General Belisarius: Soldier of Byzantium

General Belisarius: Soldier of Byzantium

The Life of Belisarius

Lord Mahon
(Philip Henry Stanhope)

With a Short Biography of Belisarius
by S. G. Goodrich

General Belisarius: Soldier of Byzantium
The Life of Belisarius
by Lord Mahon
(Philip Henry Stanhope)
With a Short Biography of Belisarius by S. G. Goodrich

First published under the title
The Life of Belisarius

Leonaur is an imprint of Oakpast Ltd
Copyright in this form © 2014 Oakpast Ltd

ISBN: 978-1-78282411-4 (hardcover)
ISBN: 978-1-78282-412-1 (softcover)

http://www.leonaur.com

Publisher's Notes

The views expressed in this book are not necessarily those of the publisher.

Contents

Preface	7
Note to the Second Edition	9
The Beginning	11
Causes of Hostility	26
Conquest of Africa	47
Reign of Theodoric	94
Active Preparations	122
Chosroes, or Nurshirvan, King of Persia	179
Italy After the Departure of Belisarius	207
Conspiracy to Murder	253
Belisarius: A Short Biography	291

Belisarius

Preface

The events related in the following pages fall within the scope of Gibbon, in his justly celebrated history, and had he treated of them with that fullness of detail which distinguishes some other portions of his work, any further attempt to record them would be both unnecessary and presumptuous.

But, although the space he has allotted to them is well proportioned to his general limits and design, yet he has dwelt so lightly on several important transactions, has omitted so many circumstances, and has merely alluded to so many others not unworthy of attention, that this interesting period may, perhaps, be thought to require a more particular narrative.

A careful consideration of the original authorities has also led me in some cases to new conclusions; and thus, for instance, the mendicity and loss of sight of Belisarius, which every writer for the last century and a half has treated as a fable, may, I conceive, be established on firm historical grounds. An ancient and authentic testimony to that effect is now brought forward, which, though already printed, has hitherto been overlooked in the examination of this question.

I could not discover any fresh historical manuscripts relating to my subject in the Royal libraries of Paris or Madrid. Having some years ago read Joinville's *Histoire de St. Louis*, with the notes of Ducange, I happened to recollect that an unpublished life of Belisarius is quoted by the latter, and with this clue I found the work at Paris, in a volume containing several other treatises, and marked 2,909 in the *Catalogue of Greek Manuscripts*.

It proved, however, to be a poem of no greater antiquity than the fourteenth century, written in the same metre as the *Chiliads of Tzetzes*, and nothing more than a professed fiction, merely selecting Belisarius as the hero of some fabulous achievements, and having of

course no better claims to credit than Marmontel's romance.[1]
December, 1828.

---

[1] A fuller account of this *Manuscript*, which relates a fabulous conquest of England by the Greeks, was communicated by me to the Society of Antiquaries, in November 1832, and will be found printed in the *Archaeologia*, vol. xxv.

Note to the Second Edition

In sending forth this new edition after an interval of almost twenty years, I have not made either any alteration from, or any addition to, the first; But I am desirous of noticing two most able essays, which, in reference to my work, have proceeded from different quarters, on the much debated question of the mendicity and loss of sight of my hero.

The first of these essays is from no less an authority than M. von Hammer, the justly celebrated Oriental scholar and historian, and appeared in the *Jahrbücher der Literatur* of Vienna, in 1832. M. von Hammer, in a most courteous style, and after several unmerited compliments to my work in general, expresses his disbelief of the popular story which I have maintained, founding his disbelief especially on the fact that Marcellinus, whom he blames me for not having consulted on the question, is wholly silent as to the alleged beggary and blindness.

In writing to M. von Hammer soon afterwards, I took the liberty to express my surprise at this statement, on the ground that the *Chronicle of Marcellinus*, as printed in *Father Sirmondi's Collec*tion, has its latest entry under the date of *a.d.* 558, and could not, therefore, possibly contain any allusion to an event which must have occurred in, or after, *a.d.* 563. M. von Hammer honoured me with a reply dated July 3, 1832, in which he observes that his statement had been incorrectly printed, and that, instead of Marcellinus, he intended to say Malala. In that case, however, his former charge against me, of having failed to consult this author, must surely fall to the ground; since on reference to the passage in my work of the first edition, and of the present), it will be seen that the case of Malala is very fully discussed. I have there shown that the part of *Malala's Chronicle*, which, from the date, might be supposed to contain the account of Belisarius as reduced to want and deprived of sight, has, unfortunately, perished from a failure of the manuscript,—that it is now impossible to ascertain whether Malala did or did not make that statement—but that there is some slight reason for supposing that he did.

In another passage of the same essay, M.. von Hammer informs us, (by the aid of an Oriental work, *Hadschi Chalfa*, on Roumeli and Bosnia), that Germania, the birthplace of Belisarius, may be identified with the present Tschirmien or Tschermen, a town not fen distant from the line of road between Constantinople and Adrianople, and about one day's journey from the latter, he adds:

> The name of Belisarius, is Illyrian (or Sclavonic), and denotes the *White Prince* (Beli-Tzar). Since Lord Mahon, in a note only a few pages further, rightly explains Belgrade as Beli-grad, the '*White City*,' we are surprised that the '*White Prince*' should have escaped his notice.

The justice of this animadversion upon me from this eminent critic, and the fault of omission which I have here committed, I am bound most fully to acknowledge.

The second essay to which I wish to call attention, is published in *Blackwood's Magazine*, No. ccclxxix., and comes from the pen of a British traveller, who dates "Athens, March 20, 1847," and speaks of his four-and-twenty years' intimate acquaintance with the East." A wholly new theory is there propounded. A most ingenious attempt is made to deduce the narrative of the beggary and blindness of Belisarius, as a romance of the later writers from the real fate of Symbat, an Armenian noble in the Byzantine service, who married the daughter of the Caesar Bardas, the uncle of the Emperor Michael III. I cannot concur in this train of reasoning, nor yield my own, but I most readily bear my testimony to the great learning, perspicuity, and candour with which the theory is set forth, and the question discussed.

March, 1848.

Chapter 1

The Beginning

At the beginning of the sixth century of the Christian Era, the Empire of Constantinople was beset with enemies and sinking to decay. The tide of barbarian invasion had lately overwhelmed one half of the ancient provinces of Rome, and these conquests, both by their effect and their example, threatened speedy downfall to the rest. The emperors became either hated from their reforms, or despised from their incapacity, and in either case their fate was the same. Frequent insurrections wasted the resources of the State, and deprived the government of all energy and enterprise; while the armies, turbulent and feeble, had thrown off the restraints of military discipline.

It is the purpose of my narrative, to show how the genius of one man averted these dangers, and corrected these defects; how the tottering empire was upheld; how the successors of Augustus were enabled, for a time, to resume their former ascendancy, and to wrest from the hands of the Barbarians their most important possessions.

Belisarius, as Procopius briefly tells us, was born at Germania, on the confines of Thrace and Illyria.[1]

The name of his birthplace has awakened the patriotic ardour of two learned Germans, who labour with more zeal than success to extort Pannonia from the words of the historian, and to claim the hero as their countryman.[2] Germania is elsewhere mentioned as a city of some importance, and as being in the neighbourhood of Sardica, but

---

1. *Procop. Vandal,* lib. L c. 11. His words are merely transcribed by Theophanes (*Chronograph*).
2. Giphanius (*Comment de Justinian. Imp.*), and his friend Velserus expresses his concurrence in that opinion, (Op. ed. 1682). The chief proof of Giphanius is drawn from the Barbaric name of one of the chargers of Belisarius, as if a horse and his rider were always from the same country!

its precise position is unknown.³ It does not seem improbable that its name may have been derived from the ancient settlement of some German families, and that the forefathers of Belisarius may have been connected in kindred with these strangers.

The exact age of Belisarius is not recorded; but in his first military enterprise, which took place about two years before the accession of Justinian, we find him termed, by Procopius, a lately-bearded stripling.⁴ The same expression is applied by the same historian to Photius at his departure for the Gothic war.⁵ Now the mother of Photius was then thirty-six years of age,⁶ and her son could, therefore, hardly have exceeded twenty. If we suppose this to have been the age of Belisarius at his earliest exploit, and fix his birth twenty years before, (a.d. 505), we shall, I think, approach as nearly to the truth as our imperfect information will allow.

Some modern historians deny Belisarius the advantage of liberal studies, and place his birth amongst the peasants of his province. Yet from two passages in Procopius, which have not hitherto been observed, it may be concluded that he was of noble blood, and inherited a patrimonial fortune. He is mentioned as possessing an estate near Constantinople, in the year before the African expedition, when, having but very lately been appointed to any high or lucrative station, he could hardly have derived from it the means of purchase.⁷ Nor could he have acquired this property by marriage, since his wife's first husband had died poor.⁸ Besides, the Greek word used by Procopius is almost always applied exclusively to that property which descends by hereditary right.⁹

As to the family of Belisarius, we may remark the letter addressed by Pharas, the Herulian prince, to King Gelimer at Papua. The former writes:

> Why should you consider it disgraceful to be a subject of Justinian with Belisarius and myself? Though we also, like you, are

---

3. *Procop. de Ædif. lib.* iv. c. i. With this passage before me, I am surprised that Gibbon "cannot find Germania in any civil or ecclesiastical lists of the province." (Vol. vii., ed. 1820.)

4. (*Pers, lib.* i. c. 12). This expression seems to be copied from Homer, (II. xxiv. 348).

5. *Goth. lib.* i. c. 5.

6. *Hist. Arcan.* c. 4.

7. (*Procop. Goth. lib.* iiL c. 35. This estate seems to have been called Rufinianae, and to have been of great extent. (*Pers. lib.* i. c. 25.)

8. *Hist. Arcan.* c. 2,

9. See Stephanus in *Thes.*

of noble birth, we glory in obeying so magnanimous a sovereign.[10]

Were not these words entirely conclusive, it might be added, that Procopius, in his later libel, says nothing of the parents of Belisarius, though he gladly commemorates those of his wife, as common charioteers, those of the emperor as peasants, and those of the empress as comedians. His animosity would certainly not have forgotten or suppressed a circumstance which his prejudices would consider ignominious to the hero.

That Belisarius held the Christian faith is apparent from his spiritual adoption of Theodosius,[11] and from the religious seal of the emperor, who strictly excluded all pagans and heretics from office.[12]

The first step of Belisarius in his military career was an appointment in the personal guards of Justinian, while yet heir apparent to the throne.[13] Since, at this period, these places were usually bestowed as the rewards of long service, or of some eminent achievement, we may regard the choice of Belisarius as a proof of his early promise. At Constantinople no opportunities could arise for military fame, and history is silent on his actions, until we find him promoted to the command of a squadron in the Persian war. But before we follow Belisarius to the banks of the Euphrates, it will be proper to examine the composition of the Byzantine armies, and the frontiers, administration, and resources of the Byzantine empire at this time. Such information, though most essential, is not easily obtained: it is passed over by the contemporary writers as generally known, and can only be gathered from their short and scattered allusions.

After the conquest of Italy by the barbarians and the disuse of its language, it might have been expected that the subjects of Constantinople would no longer call themselves Romans. But this title was too glorious to be so readily relinquished. In every succeeding age the rabble of Greek armies still boasted of their kindred with the ancient legions; and the name of Romania was applied to the varying limits of the Byzantine territory, until it has settled on Thrace, to which they were latterly confined.[14] At the accession of Justinian, however, the boundaries of his empire were nearly the same as those of the Otto-

---

10. *Procop. Vandal, lib.* ii. c. 6.
11. *Vandal lib.* i. c. 12.
12. John Malala, vol. ii.
13. *Procop. Pers.* lib. i. c. 12.
14. See John Malala (vol. ii.) for the early use of this term.

man at present.

Its northern frontier in Europe was marked by the Danube; and some castles beyond that river were maintained rather to secure the passage than with any view of ulterior possessions. From the Save the line of frontier turned inwards to the south, meeting the Adriatic below Epidaurus, [15] and bounding the Gothic province of Dalmatia. The whole territory between Thermopylae and the Danube was termed, in its eastern portion, Thrace, in its western, Illyria, or, more properly, Illyricum;[16] and the two Moesias, which are seldom mentioned in this age, appear to have become mere subordinate divisions of these provinces.

Thus, therefore, both Thrace and Illyria must always be understood at this period as extending to the Danube. [17] The northern districts had suffered most severely from barbarian inroads during the preceding century, and their desolation was witnessed by Priscus, when proceeding on his embassy to Attila. He says:

> We found the city of Naissus nearly subverted by the enemy, and forsaken by all its inhabitants, except a few sick wretches, who had crept beneath the ruins of the churches for shelter. As we travelled onwards, we saw the banks of the river thickly strewed with the bones of the slain.—Excerpt. *Legat.*

Some relief and repose was, however, afforded to these unhappy provinces when the emperors yielded their claims on Noricum and Pannonia to Theodoric the Great. The Ostro-Goths thenceforward served as a shield and bulwark to the Thracian and Illyrian lines. But the victories of the Romans in Italy under Belisarius proved fatal to their security on this frontier. The Goths withdrew their troops for domestic defence, new hordes of barbarians rushed in to occupy their place, and the Romans found it necessary to fortify the passage of the Danube with numerous entrenchments, and to guard it with unremitting care. The key of their position was Singidunum, or Belgrade, advantageously situated at the confluence of the Danube and the Save;

---

15. That Epidaurus was a Gothic city may be presumed from *Procop. Goth. lib.* i. c. 7.
16. This province was called by the ancients sometimes Illyricum and sometimes Illyris; but Illyria may be used, as more familiar to a modern ear. (D'Anville, *Geograph. Anc.* vol. i.)
17. This conclusion may be drawn from *Goth. lib.* iv. c. 18. and *De Ædif. lib.* iv. c. 7, where the Roman troops in Thrace and Illyria are said to defend the passage of the Danube. See also Wesseling's *Itineraria*. In all the fifteen books of Procopius, I do not believe that the name of Moesia more than once occurs.

it had been laid in ashes by the Huns, but was rebuilt and strengthened by Justinian.[18] From thence to the Euxine, the southern bank was bristled with upwards of sixty fortresses, each was provided with an adequate garrison, and an officer appointed to the general inspection and control of all.[19]

Such precautions, added to the want of boats, kept the barbarians in check during summer, but the severity of the winters often enabled them to effect their passage on the ice.[20] Having once crossed the great river, they without further hindrance swept over the open country, outstripped the march, or repulsed the attacks of the forces sent against them, and returned homewards, laden with their spoil. It is true that above five hundred forts are pompously set forth as having been constructed or repaired by Justinian; but their very number is the most convincing proof of their weakness, and in most cases they probably consisted of only a single tower. By their means the approach of the enemy might be discerned from afar, and the peasants, crowding within them, might securely await the passage of barbarians, impatient of delay and ignorant of sieges.

The inefficiency of these forts in withholding the progress of invaders is also manifested by the need of other special bulwarks for the Grecian provinces and Byzantine capital. The defile of Thermopylae was carefully fortified; and, in case its entrenchments should be broken through, another line across the isthmus of Corinth defended the Peloponnesus. But the protection of Constantinople was far more costly and laborious, because far less assisted by nature. Besides its immediate ramparts, the Emperor Anastasius built, and Justinian strengthened, the celebrated *Makron Teichos*, or Long Wall, extending from the Propontis to the Euxine.[21] Its distance from the capital was forty miles, its length threescore; it was flanked with numerous towers, and guarded by a constant garrison.—Such plans for national fortifications have been often tried, yet in no country from Scotland to China, have they ever proved effectual; they are found either too limited for restraint, or too extensive for defence.

From the Bosphorus, the Roman Empire stretched for several

---

18. Procop. *De Ædif. lib.* iv. c. 5. This city is called Singedon by the Byzantine writers. The Sclavonic name of Beli-Grad (White City) began to prevail before the year a.d. 959. See a memoir by D'Anville in the *Acad, des Inscript.* vol. xxviii.
19. Compare *Procop. Goth. lib. iii.* c. 14. and De Ædif, lib. iv. c. 5, 6, & 7.
20. *Agathias, lib.* v.
21. Compare Evagrius, *Hist. Eccles. lib.* iii. c. 38, and *Procopius de Ædif. lib.* iv. c. 9. See also a note of Ducange to the *Paschal Chronicle*.

hundred miles along the coast of Asia, till the town of Rhizaeum, below Trebizond.[22] Here the line of frontier turned round the wild mountains of the Zani, and proceeded southwards, comprehending the cities of Theodosiopolis [23] and Dara, and following the course of the Nymphaeus till its junction with the Tigris,[24] and of the Aborrhas, till it met the Euphrates at Circesium.[25] Beyond the latter river the Persian and Byzantine territories were separated by a wide and inhospitable desert, inhabited only by some roving tribes of Arabs, who declared themselves the allies of either party, whenever they found a favourable opportunity for plundering the other. The Roman provinces of Syria, Palestine, and Egypt, often felt and always feared their rapine; and even the fear of it proved fatal to industry and cultivation. The rugged and almost inaccessible chain of mountains in the south of Asia Minor bore at this time the name of Isauria, which had formerly been applied to only one of its districts.

Its inhabitants displayed the common character of mountaineers—impatience of control and recklessness of danger; and became by turns the most destructive enemies and most valiant soldiers of the Empire. Their flying parties laid waste the open country from Ephesus to Antioch, and made even the inmate of cities tremble within his walls. Often defeated, but never subdued, they enriched themselves either by these predatory visits, or by a yearly tribute of five thousand pounds weight of gold as the price of their tranquillity; and this system had continued for a great number of years(474-491), when their countryman Zeno ascended the Imperial throne.[26] The great favour and indulgence shown them in this reign naturally produced their disaffection in the next, and they rose against Anastasius in a general rebellion, which could not be disregarded or forgiven, like their former hasty inroads.

The long and bloody war which ensued brought about their thorough subjection; and under Justinian they formed the flower of the Roman armies. But Asia Minor had suffered from their havoc as severely as the East from the Saracens, or Thrace and Illyria from the

---

22. That Rhizaeum was the frontier town appears from *Goth. lib. iv. c. 2*, and *Pers. lib. ii. c. 29*.
23. *Procop. Pers. lib. i. c. 10*.
24. *Ibid. c. 21*.
25. *Ibid. lib. ii. c. 5*. We must understand the Aborrhas, instead of the Tigris, in the ancient negotiations of Peter. (Excerpt *Legat*.)
26. Evagr. *Hist. Eccles. lib. iii. c. 35*. See also Ammian. *Marcellin. lib. xiv. c. 2*. And *Marcellin. Chronic*, ap. Sirmond. *Op*. vol. ii.

barbarians of the Danube; and when to these we add the frequent expeditions of the Vandals in the Ægean Sea, it will be perceived, that scarcely any Roman district had of late been free from desolation, and that the real strength of the empire at the accession of Justinian by no means corresponded to the number and extent of its provinces.

It is remarkable, that as the territory of the Romans in this age nearly approached to that of the Turks at present, so the troops appointed for its defence, under each, were precisely the same. The number of one hundred and fifty thousand men was fixed both by Justinian and by Solyman;[27] but in the latter case, this force was real and effective, and in the former, little more than an empty sound, which served to please the vanity, or allay the apprehensions, of the people. Not one half the number were certainly ever enlisted; they were barely sufficient to garrison the frontiers; and an army of fifteen or twenty thousand men for active operations, could not be mustered without great difficulty and delay. In the annals of this age, we are often astonished at the smallness of the means with which the most mighty wars are undertaken and waged, whilst, in the foregoing century, the Byzantine empire could send forth an expedition of one hundred thousand men.[28]

The chief root of this evil was the negligence and weakness of Justinian, who often allowed the officers to supply the rations of the army, and the paymasters to levy the taxes for its maintenance. Thus, it manifestly became the interest of both these classes, to keep the number of the soldiers far below their returns to the. government, and to permit frequent furloughs from the most important posts, and on the most trifling occasions. Justinian endeavoured to restrain these abuses by an edict, but they were inherent to the very nature of his military system.[29]

The Roman troops at this period no longer bore the slightest resemblance to those of Scipio or of Caesar. The very name of legions was disused. From the foolish vanity of commanding a greater number of these squadrons, successive emperors had diminished them in size, until from six or seven thousand men they dwindled to as many hundreds. Thus, in the fourth century, we find the defence of a single city committed to seven legions. In the fifth, that name is applied to a body of twelve hundred, and to another of only eight hundred men,

---

27. *Agathias, lib. v.* Robertson's forty-fifth note to the first volume of Charles V.
28. *Procop. Vandal, lib. i. c.* 6.
29. Compare *Justinian. Cod. lib. i.* tit 27. *Procop. Goth. lib. iii* c. 1. and *Agathias, lib. v.*

and in the time of Belisarius it had altogether disappeared.[30] It was not uncommon at this period to divide the troops according to their birth-place or nation; and thus, for example, the Isaurians, instead of being draughted into the other squadrons of the empire, marched beneath a separate standard. This policy, the first germ of the feudal system in the middle ages, destroyed all unity of feeling among the troops as brother Romans, and all unity of discipline as fellow soldiers, and rendered them more like an assemblage of allies than the army of a single power.

The flower of the forces consisted of the *doryphori* or guards, who were attached, not merely to the person of the emperor, but to that of every general or officer of distinction, and who, in either case, were highly honoured and carefully selected. This post was conferred on those most distinguished for strength and stature, even from amongst the captives made in war, and was often assigned to veterans as the reward of some eminent exploit.[31] A larger pay was bestowed on them than on the other soldiers; their arms were more complete; and their chargers (they were always horsemen) were equally fitted for close combat or long journeys. The best officers of this century were trained amongst these troops. Besides their general oath of fidelity to the state, they bound themselves by a particular obligation to their chief or patron,[32] and were termed his household,[33] a phrase analogous to that of *maison militaire* in modern France.

Those of the emperor bore the name of the schools, and amounted only to three thousand five hundred soldiers, till Justinian added two thousand to their number. Yet they were never so weak as in his reign. Under former governments, when each guardsman was chosen for merit, they formed a band of iron veterans, a last resource against barbarian invaders, and their disciplined valour might have triumphed over tenfold antagonists. It was the emperor Zeno who first broke through the ancient order, by granting this promotion to many of his Isaurian countrymen, more remarkable for attachment to his person than for their service to the state. But in the latter years of Justinian the tide of corruption overflowed all bounds. Commissions in the schools were exposed to public sale, the highest bidder was esteemed the bravest soldier,

---

30. Ammian. *Marcellin. lib. xix.* c. 2. See a *Memoir by Le Bean* in the *Acad. des Inscript.* vol. xxv.
31. *Procop. Goth. lib. iv.* c. 29. *Hist. Arcan.* c 24.
32. *Procop. Vandal lib. ii.* c. 8.
33. *Oikia. Goth. lib. i.* c 18. &c.

and these posts were eagerly purchased by unwarlike citizens, desirous of exemption from civil duties without incurring military dangers.

Thus the hardy veterans, the Armenian and Isaurian mountaineers, were replaced by lazy townsmen unable to wield their own weapons; and thus it will be seen in the sequel, that when the barbarians had forced the Long Wall and were advancing to the capital, these troops could make no effort for its rescue, and scarcely surpassed in courage or exertion the terrified crowd of women and of children.[34]

In the days of the ancient Republic the chief strength of the legion consisted of its foot soldiers, and in comparison with them the cavalry was neglected and despised. In fact, it is to the deficiency of the Romans in this branch of military service that Polybius ascribes their frequent reverses in the second Punic war.[35] The barbarians of the north, on the contrary, considered horsemen the most honourable;[36] and the Imperial mercenaries soon spread amongst the Romans a prejudice so agreeable to the decline of military vigour. Accordingly, in the reign of Justinian, all the best troops were mounted, and the infantry had dwindled to a small and subordinate band. It is true, that on one occasion (the African expedition) we find them exceed the cavalry in numbers, but this may probably be ascribed to the cost and difficulty of transporting horses on so long a voyage.

In most cases the foot soldiers were not merely inferior in number at the outset of each campaign, but, as Procopius tells us, they often diminished during its progress, because the capture of horses from the enemy enabled them to join the more popular and easy service. Their officers seldom condescended to share their fatigues, but looked upon their rank as a privilege to ride, and it will readily be imagined how hurtful an effect this example produced upon the subalterns.[37] Like most men, when unjustly contemned, they soon sunk to the level of their reputation; and it was only by the care of Belisarius, that they in some degree retrieved it. The same principle of indolence and relaxation, which transformed the Byzantine troops to horsemen, also induced them to lay aside the weighty weapons of their forefathers.

Their chief reliance in this age was placed upon the bow; and as archers they were less expert than the Persians,[38] but more so than the

---

34. The testimony of Agathias (*lib. v.*) confirms that of the secret historian (c 24).
35. *Hist. lib. iii* c 117.
36. See a remarkable instance of this feeling in the *Excerpt Legat.*
37. *Procop. Goth. lib. i.* c. 28.
38. *Pers. lib. i.* c. 18.

Goths.[39] For close combat every soldier was provided with a sword, and this was the only weapon which the guards retained when stationed in a peaceful city.[40] In the field the guards appear to have been distinguished by the special use of the lance. Each horseman bore a shield, and his person was still further protected by greaves, a cuirass, and a helmet.[41]

The declining strength and spirit of the Roman soldiers had introduced the use of Barbarian mercenaries at a very early period; and it was observed, even in the reign of Tiberius, that the vigour of the armies was drawn from foreigners alone.[42] But this dangerous resource was at first confined to narrow bounds, most of these levies being compelled to adopt the discipline and follow the ranks of the legions; and the subsequent error, of permitting them to form in separate squadrons, and to out-number the native troops, was glaring and fatal. Under Justinian it was thought prudent to distrust, but necessary to employ, them. These auxiliaries were obtained either by a public treaty with the nation to which they belonged, or by the allurements held out to private ambition. In the former case they served only for a particular period, in the latter they were considered as permanent troops of the empire, and in either they bore the name of federates.[43] Amongst the foremost of these, were the Massagetes or Huns, dwelling to the northward of the Caucasus: they were remarkable for their skill in horsemanship and archery.[44]

The Heruli were likewise mounted, and, being almost unencumbered with defensive armour, were extremely useful as light cavalry; but they are represented by Procopius as the most drunken and deceitful of all the barbarian tribes.[45] A part of the country beyond the Danube was their native seat, they had often desolated the Roman provinces with their incursions, and had rendered tributary to them even the aspiring nations of the Lombards; but, at the accession of

---

39. *Goth, lib. i.* c. 27.
40. *Vandal. lib. ii.* c. 28.
41. Compare the description of Procopius (in *Praef.*) with the complaints of Vegetius (*lib. i.* c 20), which however are applied chiefly to the infantry.—The usual arms, with their half barbarous names, are enumerate in the eighty-fifth novel of Justinian.
42. Tacit. *Annal. lib. iii.* c. 40.
43. See *Procop. Vandal, lib. i.* c. 11. and the one hundred and sixteenth novel of Justinian.
44. *Procop. Pers. lib. i.* c. 10. *Goth. lib. ii.* c. 1; lib. iv. c. 5. He seems to adopt the name of Massagetes in imitation of Herodotus.
45. *Vandal. lib. ii.* c. 4.

Justinian, their pre-eminence had greatly declined.[46] Any of these barbarians, when joining a Byzantine army, marched under their own national banner, were commanded by their own officers, and commonly adhered to the military regulations of their countrymen.

It was only with great difficulty, and through some severe examples, that Belisarius succeeded in rendering them in some degree amenable to the laws of Roman discipline. The inefficiency of such mingled and discordant forces, and the difficulty of uniting them to one common end, have been felt in every age;[47] and nothing tends more strongly to enhance the conquests of Belisarius, than to view a structure so extensive raised from such slender materials.

In the reign of Constantine the Great, the Roman troops had been ranked in two classes: the *Limitanei*, who guarded the frontiers; and the *Comitatenses*, who attended the sovereign and undertook any military enterprise. But this distinction appears soon to have become nominal and empty; and though some faint trace of it may still be found in the edicts of Justinian, none appear in the records of his wars.[48] The system of pay at this latter period was founded on judicious policy, and might perhaps be advantageously applied in modern times. A small stipend was allowed to the newly levied soldier, but it gradually increased according to his term of service; and the veteran was enabled, not merely to live in opulence, but to bequeath some money to his heirs. A gift to each soldier, of five pieces of gold, was also usually made once in as many years; but Justinian altogether suppressed this indulgence, at the very period when the victories of the Roman army seemed most to deserve his liberality.[49]

The troops might have borne the loss of their donative; but the avarice and negligence of the emperor, in withholding their regular pay, loosened the only tie by which military obedience can be secured, or even claimed. Such arrears, which we find constantly recurring the annals of this reign, counteracted the efforts of Belisarius for the restoration or maintenance of discipline, while the disaffection of the soldiers as displayed, sometimes in loud complaints, and sometimes in secret conspiracies. Large bodies deserters enlisted in the Persian

---

46. *Goth. lib. ii.* c. 14.
47. See the judicious remarks of Polybius, (*lib. i.* c. 65). The lawless and undisciplined state of the Roman armies, at this time, is incidentally admitted by Procopius. (*Vandal, lib. i.* c. 21.)
48. *Justinian. lib. i.* tit.
49. *Hist. Arcan.* c. 24.

and Gothic ranks, from no other ground;⁵⁰ and the remainder were reduced to a state of poverty which compiled them to plunder the provincials, and which thereby impaired both their good order and their popularity.

Such was the state of the Byzantine Empire at accession of Justin the First, (*a.d.* 518). By birth an Illyrian peasant, by profession a soldier, Justin had distinguished himself in the Isaurian war, and had gradually attained the post of commander to the Imperial Guards. Already in the dotage of his faculties, he had long survived the military daring to which he owed his reputation and his rise. His education had, of course, been neglected, and his ignorance was such, that his signature could only be obtained by means of a wooden case, which directed his pen through the four first letters of his name. ⁵¹

Unpractised in business, yet jealous of authority, he was equally unable to reign or to resign. From the very first, the chief administration of affairs devolved on Justinian, his nephew and intended heir, whom he was reluctantly compelled to raise up from office to office, and at length to acknowledge as his partner on the throne. His death, (August *a.d.* 527), after a languid reign of nine years, and a life of nearly fourscore, left Justinian sole sovereign, in name as well as in fact.

In comparing the new emperor with his illustrious contemporaries at Ravenna and at Ctesiphon, it may be remarked that their very unequal merit has been almost equally rewarded by fame. The memory of Justinian is adored by the civil lawyers, Theodoric yet lives in the rustic songs and legends of his countrymen, and the Eastern historians celebrate Nushirvan as the greatest and most glorious of their sovereigns. By their absolute power, all three possessed the means, by the length of their reigns the leisure, for effecting any plans of conquest or reform.

Yet it will be found, that while the Kings of Persia and of Italy were indebted to their own achievements for renown, the Roman emperor only shines as a general or legislator through the borrowed

---

50. *Pers. lib. ii.* c. 7. *Goth. lib. iii.* c. 11, &c.
51. *Hist. Arcan.* c. 6, and a cautious but decisive hint in the public history. (*Vandal, lib. i.* c. 9.) The story of the frame is repeated by the Valesian fragment, but foolishly applied to Theodoric the Great, who was of royal birth, and had received a liberal education at Constantinople, under the care of the Emperor Leo. The panegyric of Ennodius on his studies could never have been addressed to a wholly illiterate monarch; and Le Beau has shown that a strong collateral proof of his knowledge may be drawn from Cassiodorius (*Var. lib. ii. ep.* 15). The testimony of Theophanes is positive to the same effect, but his general inaccuracy deprives it of weight.

light of Belisarius and Tribonian. His mind was essentially feeble, and bore the appearance of fickleness and inconsistency, because it could form no opinions of its own, and was compelled to lean on others for direction and support. To him the last adviser always seemed the wisest, and the absent always in the wrong. From hence proceeded his fears and suspicions with regard to Belisarius, often checked by the aspect of the hero, but constantly reviving in his absence, and which no length of service, no trial of fidelity, were sufficient to destroy.

The religion of Justinian was sincere and fervent, but, as commonly happens to a weak understandings was less fruitful of virtues than of rites and forms. While he carried his fasts and vigils to the utmost extent of monkish self-denial, he directed the assassination of Vitalian, to whom he had lately sworn upon the Eucharist the friendship of a brother.[52] His persecutions of all heretics, all Jews, and even of the small remnant of Pagans, and the desolation of Palestine, by goading the Samaritans into revolt,[53] may be partly excused by the intolerant spirit of the age, but certainly outstripped it in fierceness, and appear ridiculous as well as hateful, since this scourge of heretics became, in his dotage, a heretic himself.

The defect of his judgment in business may be compared to the false colouring of an unskilful painter, by which all the parts of a landscape seem equally removed. In aiming at different objects, he did not consider their relative importance, but pursued the slightest with the same zeal and energy as the most momentous. The building of a church at Constantinople, or the restoration of the Catholic faith in Africa, the acquisition of a kingdom, or the repairs of a fortress, all occupied precisely the same space in his little mind. Ambitious of uniting the fame of an architect with that of a conqueror, he lavished in splendid fabrics at home the sums by which his foreign armies should have been recruited and maintained.

While these favourite edifices wrung from an exhausted people its resources for defence, the distant armies were too often deprived of pay, pinched with want, or from the delay of reinforcements overwhelmed by the superior numbers of the enemy. No sooner had the emperor sent an expedition from Constantinople, than he seemed to

---

52. See Victor Tunnunensis ap. *Canis. Antiq. Lect* 1725, vol. i.; and Alemanni *Not. Hist.* Vitalian was a chief of barbarian parentage, and had made himself very popular by a rebellion against Anastasius, in support of the orthodox faith. He was therefore received with open arms by Justin and Justinian, but it is difficult to forgive a subject who can raise an army of sixty thousand men.

53. *Eutychius Annal.* Vol. ii. p. John Malala, vol. ii.

have dismissed it likewise from his thoughts. His predecessor, Anastasius, though diminishing the public burthens, had amassed and bequeathed a sum of no less than three hundred and twenty thousand pounds weight of gold;[54] and the accumulated treasures of the Goths and Vandals were poured before the throne of Justinian. But all these resources were insufficient to supply his prodigality; heavy taxes were imposed, old arrears were claimed, offices put to sale, charities suppressed, private fortunes seized; in short, every act of rapacity, injustice, and oppression, was practised by his ministers, and meanness was called in to support magnificence.[55]

It may be observed, that greater evils commonly result to a state from the weakness than from the vices of its sovereign, since his incapacity rears and fosters a thousand subordinate oppressors whom a more active tyranny restrains. The subjects of Justinian, finding themselves injured and impoverished in his reign, viewed him with detestation as the cause of their calamities. Yet their angry invectives should not blind us to his real merits. His private life deserves the praise of temperance, study, and devotion; he appeared easy of access, and courteous in demeanour; and his temper was naturally gentle and forgiving. If he was prone to suspect, he was, however, slow in punishing. His earnest desire of fame, though often degenerating into petty vanity, was yet the spring of many noble undertakings; nor can posterity forget how greatly he promoted and encouraged the compilation of the Roman jurisprudence.

His discernment of military merit has been justly praised; and he might have secured both the attachment and the welfare of his subjects, had his choice of ministers been equally happy. His principal favourites were Tribonian and John of Cappadocia. The former was a man of commanding talents and deep learning, but he is accused by his contemporaries of the utmost corruption in administering the laws. The latter, dissolute and cruel, a scoffer at religion, rapacious for the profit of the emperor and for his own, crushed the people by the weight of his exactions, and was at length dismissed, not for his notorious plunder, but for an alleged conspiracy. The charges against him may perhaps have been exaggerated, from the usual readiness of man-

---

54. *Hist. Arcan.* c. 19.
55. The rapacious prodigality of Justinian might be proved, even from the flatteries addressed to him. Thus, for instance, in one place he is praised for his noble contempt of money (*Procop. De Ædif. lib. v.* c. 5). The testimony of Evagrius is calm and strong (*Hist. Eccles. lib. iv.* c. 30).

kind to trample on the fallen; yet they are countenanced by the strong and universal hatred displayed against him in the sedition of Nika.

But it was the Empress Theodora who ruled with the most absolute power over the mind of her husband, and therefore over the administration of the state. Her youth had been spent on the public stage, and in the most unrestrained pursuit of pleasure; and the first act of Justinian, on ascending the throne, was to contract a marriage which would have disgraced the meanest of his subjects. Dismissing her lovers, the fair comedian was allowed to regulate the faith and to wield the destinies of provinces. Her anger was capricious, her resentment deep and bloody, and her avarice boundless. The character of Theodora formed a singular contrast to that of Justinian; and it will be seen, in the sequel, how severely Belisarius suffered from the stern passions of the one and yielding weakness of the other.

CHAPTER 2

Causes of Hostility

During nearly the whole reign of Anastasius, at Constantinople, the throne of Persia was held by Kobad,[1] seventeenth of the Sassanides. The warfare which the emperor waged against him had been most disastrous to the Romans. Amida had been shamefully lost, in spite of the heroic efforts of its citizens, and still more shamefully recovered, by a ransom to the victors. An army of fifty-two thousand men, the greatest ever sent forth in this century by the Byzantine government, had been entrusted to the command of some worthless favourites: they were overthrown in several pitched engagements, and still more frequently fled without hazarding a blow.[2]

Thus the name of the Romans, in this quarter, became degraded and despised; their spirit was broken; and they might perhaps have been driven from Asia, had not Kobad, at this juncture, been suddenly called elsewhere by the invasion of some Northern hordes. Embarrassed by these new and formidable enemies, he agreed to a truce with the Romans; which, though concluded at first for only seven years, had been prolonged till the reign of Justin. Some causes of complaint, on both sides, had, however, since arisen. An ancient treaty enacted, that neither should build additional fortresses near the common frontier; yet, by order of Anastasius, the open town of Dara[3] was surrounded

---

1. As usual, this name has been disfigured by the Greeks. Procopius makes it Cabades, and Count Marcellinus Choades. The name of Cabades was afterwards applied to a sort of military dress in use among the Greeks, and borrowed from the Persians (*Tzetzes, chil. xii. v.* 793).
2. The numbers of these troops are given by Josué Stylites (ap. Assemanni. *Bibliot Orient* vol. i.) and their operations detailed by Procopius (*Pers. lib. i.* c. 6), and John Malala (*vol. ii.*).
3. See Procop. *De Ædif. lib. ii.* c. 1. and Assemanni *Bibliot. Orient*, vol. i. In the course of reading, I have found three different derivations for, (continued next page),

with lofty ramparts, and became the strongest bulwark of the Romans in the East. On the other hand, the gates or defiles of Caucasus, which commanded the passage of these mountains, and restrained the barbarians beyond them, were usurped by the Persians. [4] Yet these mutual injuries served, in some degree, to balance each other, and might have failed in producing a renewal of the war, had they not been envenomed by a separate and more recent injury.

Kobad shared the fate of most monarchs: he hated his natural heir, and was attached to his youngest sons, perhaps only as viewing in them the future enemies of the elder. He had formed the plan of breaking through the customary order. and of naming for his successor his third son, afterwards celebrated under the name of Chosroes by the Greeks, and of Khosrou or Nushirvan by the Persians. As a first step to this exaltation, the king deemed it desirable that Chosroes should be adopted by the Roman emperor, and, by this high though fictitious kindred, become more distinguished in the public estimation. This proposal, which included an offer of friendship and alliance, was joyfully received by Justin and his nephew; and they were about to close with it, when Proclus, one of their most trusted ministers, withheld them. He set forth to them, that, by adoption, Chosroes would acquire the rights of a son to Justin, and might therefore urge his claim to the empire, in preference to Justinian. This groundless fear (for what Byzantine subject would have acknowledged the claim of a Magian?) prevailed over the considerations of sound policy.

Unwilling to grant, and yet afraid to deny, the two princes endeavoured to elude the difficulty by refusing a civil but offering a military adoption. The last, it seems, was reserved for barbarians, and considered less honourable than the former.[5] But this answer was heard with indignation by the Persian ambassador; the conferences were broken off in mutual displeasure; and Nushirvan, who, in full confidence of a speedy invitation, had already advanced to the banks of the Tigris, returned homewards, brooding over future projects of revenge.

It was on these grounds, and in the latter part of Justin's reign, that

---

the name of Dara; the one in Evagrius (*Hist. Eccles. lib. iii.* c. 37), the second a very absurd one in Aimoin (*De Gest. Franc, lib. ii.* c. 5), and the last in the *Paschal Chronicle*.
4. These gates are described by Pliny, *Portae Caucasiae magno errore multis Caspiae dictae, ingens naturae opus, montibus interruptis repente* (*Hist. Nat. lib. vi.* c. 11). For their present state, see D'Anville (*Geograph. Anc.* vol. ii..)
5. Consult a memoir on the ancient military adoption in the *Acad. des Inscript.* (vol. xxi.). An instance of it was given by Theodoric the Great, who adopted the King of the Heruli (Cassiod. *Var. lib. iv.* ep. 2).

Kobad renewed the war; and his first enterprise was the invasion of Iberia. This country was governed by its native princes, but had long been tributary to the Persians. Its inhabitants, zealous Christians since the time of Constantine, had yet never swerved from their alliance to a Magian, until the persecuting zeal of Kobad, precisely at this time, changed religious into political adversaries. They disclaimed his authority, and besought the protection of the emperor, who promised them large reinforcements, but sent only a handful of soldiers. Meanwhile Kobad, disabled by old age from leading his troops in person, dispatched a powerful army against the Iberians, headed by a *varisa* or governor of a Persian province.[6] All resistance was overborne by his superior numbers; the whole country was subdued; and Gurgenes, its prince, found it necessary to withdraw, as a helpless exile, to Constantinople. During this more important warfare, some petty hostilities took place on the Armenian frontier, which are only memorable as first raising to historical notice the great captain of that age.

Belisarius, who had now attained the command of a squadron, performed his earliest recorded achievement, jointly with another Roman officer, named Sittas, by an inroad into Persarmenia. They ravaged a large extent of country, and brought back a considerable number of prisoners. On a second incursion, however, they were less fortunate, being suddenly attacked and overthrown by some Persians under Narses.[7] Yet we may conclude that the personal conduct of Belisarius, on the last occasion, was not only free from blame, but even entitled to praise, since we find him, immediately afterwards, promoted to the post of Governor of Dara, and commander of the forces stationed in that city. The fates of his first antagonist and colleague may also excite some interest. Narses soon afterwards deserted to the Romans, with his two brothers, and served against the Goths in Italy, but must not be confounded with the celebrated eunuch of that name.[8] Sittas advanced his fortune by a marriage with a sister of the Empress Theodora,[9] appointed to a command in Armenia, where he fell in battle.[10]

---

6. Procopius tells us only that *varisa* was a Persiain dignity, but I think that I may infer its identity with the *Vitaxa* of Ammianus Marcellinus.

7. The date of these incursions is not given by Procopius, but, as he places the death of Justin so shortly afterwards, they can hardly be fixed earlier than a.d. 525. (*Pers. lib. i.* c. 12.)

8. *Procop. Pers. lib. i.* c. 15.

9. John Malala, vol. ii.

10. *Procop. Pers. lib. ii.* c. 3. He must not be confounded with the Sittas of Theophylact Simocatta. (*lib. iv.* c 15.)

It was at Dara that Belisarius chose for his secretary Procopius, afterwards the historian of his times. This writer, born at Caesarea, in Palestine, was. a lawyer in the early part of his career, and a senator, or perhaps a prefect at its close.[11] With regard to his religion, there is strong reason to believe that he held the Christian faith.[12] He attended Belisarius throughout his campaigns till his last return from Italy, and declares himself to have been an eye-witness of almost every transaction he relates.

His narrative happily combines the judgment of a statesman, with the spirit of a soldier, but its chronology is broken, and its interest impaired by the division of his books, (two Persian, two Vandal, and four Gothic,) according to the countries and wars. As these writings afforded but few opportunities to introduce the name of the unwarlike emperor with praise, six books of Edifices were added by Procopius, wherein he pours forth all the flatteries which thirst for promotion can inspire.

On considering the value of his testimony as an historian, the only apparent drawback is presumed partiality to his master. But, against this feeling, there are in his case two distinct securities. His work was written at a period when Belisarius had been recalled from active employment, and had suffered beneath the Imperial suspicion and displeasure, and it was written for presentation, not to the victorious general, but to the jealous monarch. Secondly, it is evident from the book of *Anecdotes*, or *Secret History*, which Procopius afterwards compiled, that was, in fact, a private enemy and accuser of Belisarius, having probably been disappointed in the payment for his services. It was, therefore, neither his interest nor his inclination to set forth the achievements of Belisarius in too favourable colours, to give them higher praise than their recent and well-known merit imperiously demanded.[13]

Several modern critics have doubted whether Procopius be really the writer of the *Secret History*, and have endeavoured to decry its testimony altogether, but their judgment appears to be misled by their

---

11. The senatorial rank of Procopius appears from Hist. Arcan. c. 12, but his identity with Procopius, Prefect in *a.d.* 562, is only a conjecture. (Hanckius De Script B. P. i c. 5. sect 17.)

12. Observe his distinct profession of Christianity (*Pers. lib. ii* c. 13. *De Ædif lib. v.* c 7-), and weigh the decided opinion of Hanckius (P. i. c. 5, sect 5) and Fabricius (*Bibliot Graec.* vol. vi.).

13. As to direct panegyric, Procopius hardly bestows so much on Belisarius as on the obscure and now forgotten Chilbudius Compare *Goth. lib.iii.* c i and 14.

too partial admiration of Belisarius or Justinian.[14] Their arguments only tend to show what might have been presumed, that this libel was not openly acknowledged or generally circulated. The degree of credit which it deserves is, however, allowed on all hands to be small. What reliance can be placed upon an author, who seriously believed Justinian an incarnate demon, and asserts of the conqueror of Africa and Italy that he was universally despised as a traitor, and scoffed at as a fool?[15]

Such unmeasured accusations only recoil on the accuser; and Procopius little thought, whilst labouring to blacken the memory of others, how deep a stain he was imprinting on his own. But the want of authentic memoirs forbids us to cast away the lampoon, and in weighing and selecting its assertions, we should, I think, be mainly guided by their publicity. We may trust those specific charges, which must, if true, have been generally known, and which, therefore, if false, could hardly have been brought forward by a contemporary. According to this test, many very serious accusations against Belisarius may be looked upon as sufficiently established. When, on the other hand, the *Secret History* relates, for example, a private conversation between Antonina and the empress, which each had a strong interest in concealing,[16] or an equally secret, and still more improbable scene, in a subterranean chamber at Carthage,[17] I have no hesitation in rejecting its authority.

Soon after Belisarius had assumed the command at Dara, the death of Justin left his nephew in full possession of the throne. The new emperor perceived the importance of strengthening and securing the fortifications which Anastasius had constructed at Dara. The impregnable city of Nisibis, once the bulwark of the Romans in the East, and which had stood three sieges against Sapor, had been surrendered to Persia by the treaty of Jovian.[18] Being only fifteen miles from that fortress, Dara served, in some measure, to supply its place and diminish its importance, and, above all, it promised great advantages in case of an invasion, by delaying the progress of the hostile army. Fully impressed with these considerations, Justinian directed Belisarius to build a castle on the frontier, within three miles of Dara, as a defence and bulwark

---

14. See a memoir in the *Acad. don Inscript.* (vol. xxi.) Marmontel, in his preface to Bélissaire, and La Mothe he Vayer. (*Œuvres*, vol. viii.)
15. *Hist. Arcan.* c. 5, and 12. The expressions respecting Belisarius are still stronger than I have rendered them.
16. *Hist. Arcan.* c. 3. Gibbon, vol. vii.
17. *Hist. Arcan.* c 1. Gibbon, vol. vii.
18. Ammian. *Marcellin. lib. xxv.* c 8. Agathias, *lib. iv.*

to its ramparts.

Belisarius showed great activity in fulfilling these orders, he selected a convenient site at Mindon,[19] and by the multitude of workmen the walls had already risen to some height above the ground, when he received a haughty mandate from the Persians, requiring him to stop short in this undertaking, and case of refusal threatening an attack. It appears that there then existed some agreement between both parties on this frontier to refrain from those petty, yet ruinous incursions, which add nothing either to the advancement or the glory of the war, and are only productive of mutual devastation. The Persians, however, were determined that this interval of quiet should not be employed in preparing fresh obstacles for them to overcome.

Their demand was referred to Justinian by the Roman general, and the emperor, far from allowing the building to be discontinued, sent reinforcements to Belisarius, and desired him to withstand all aggression to the utmost. The Byzantine Army stationed itself for the defence, the Persian advanced for the destruction, of the castle, and a long and well-contested engagement ensued. It was at last decided against the Romans, many of their bravest soldiers were slain or taken prisoners, and the remainder were driven back within the walls of Dara.

The victorious Persians proceeded without further hindrance to raze the unfinished and forsaken fortress to the ground, and then returned in triumph to Nisibis, their former station.[20] The conduct of Belisarius in the skirmish of Mindon is not mentioned, but we find the same collateral evidence as in his Persarmenian expedition, to prove that it was not unworthy of his fame. Within a few months from this time, he was named commander-in-chief on the whole line of Asiatic frontier, with the high title of general of the East, and these honours never could so closely have followed his defeat had it been in the slightest degree attributable to his want of skill, of courage, or of personal exertion. From this period, the actions of his life assume a national and historical importance, instead of claiming interest only as the first steps of a celebrated man. We have endeavoured to explore the fountain, we may now embark in the stream, and follow the current of the river.

---

19. Procop, *Pers. lib. i.* c. 13. I suspect that, instead of Mindon, we should read Mygdon, which was the name of the river on which Nisibis was built, and which might easily be applied to a village near its banks.

20. No date is assigned by Procopius for the skirmish of Mindon, but from the series of events between the accession of Justinian and the Battle of Dara, of which we know the precise times, it must in all likelihood have taken place in a *a.d.* 528.

In his new appointment, Belisarius continued to fix his headquarters at Dara, and earnestly applied himself to raise and collect an army. For this purpose, he appears to have traversed the neighbouring provinces in person, and at last succeeded in mustering five and twenty thousand men, but the discipline of these forces was relaxed, and their spirit broken by their former reverses. On returning to Dara, the general was joined by Hermogenes, the Master of the Offices,[21] who, in some degree, shared his authority, but whose chief object in advancing to the frontier was, if possible, to conclude a peace. negotiations were resumed, and their lingering left Belisarius inactive during many months, without having either to undertake or to repel any military enterprise.

It was hoped that the old age of Kobad might incline him to tranquillity, and his ambition be satisfied with the conquest of Iberia. But in the midst of these parleys, (*a.d.* 530), news suddenly reached the Roman general that an army of forty thousand men was marching against him. These troops comprised the *phalanx* of ten thousand Immortals,[22] the flower of the Persian Army, and were commanded by Firouz, who held the office of *mirranes*, or *generalissimo* in that country.[23] His confidence of victory was founded as much on his superiority of numbers, as on the recent experience of Roman degeneracy, and he announced his approach by the arrogant message that a bath should be ready next evening for his refreshment at Dara. Belisarius only replied by his preparations for battle. In front of the city, towards the side of Nisibis, he had drawn a deep trench, turning inwards at the sides, and then again extended in lines parallel to the first, nor was it devoid of intervals or bridges at regular distances to afford a passage for the Byzantine soldiers. Behind these lines the troops were marshalled in order, the cavalry at the wings, and the infantry under the personal command of Belisarius, in the centre.

It was not long before the Persian Army appeared upon the plain, but the *mirranes* viewing the advantageous, position of the Romans,

---

21. The Master of the Offices was one of the chief officers of State. He extended his control over the palace, the posts, the arsenals, and the foreign embassies. See Cod. *Justinian, lib. i.* tit 31 , and Cassiod. *Var, lib. vi.* form. 6.

22. For the Immortals, see Herodotus (lib.vii. c, 83), and Diodorus Siculus (*lib. xi.* c 7). The Emperor Michael Ducas afterwards instituted a similar body of Immortals in the Roman Army. (Nicephor. *Bryenn. lib. iv.* c. 4).

23. I think I may venture to assert that the Mirranes of Procopius is the same as the Merenes of Ammianus Marcellinus (*lib. xxv.* c. 1). In the latter place, Gibbon mistakes the office for the name of the general (vol. iv.).

deferred his attack till the ensuing day. Meanwhile, the two armies were amused by the aspect, and interested by the augury of a single combat, which was challenged by the Persian, but gained by the Roman champion. Next morning, the Persians drew a reinforcement of ten thousand men from the garrison of Nisibis, thus increasing their army to double the number of the Roman. Belisarius, doubtful of victory determined, if possible, to avoid an engagement. He despatched a letter to the *mirranes*, complaining of his aggression at a time when negotiations were in progress, and when hopes of peace might be reasonably entertained.

In his answer, Firouz, according to the common practice to excuse by imputing perfidy, complained that no reliance could be placed on the professions or even the oath of a Greek.[24] Thus disappointed, Belisarius commanded that the letters which had passed between them should be affixed to the standards, and borne in the brunt of battle, as appeals to Heaven, and testimonies of his own pure and peaceful intentions. A similar measure was once resorted to by the Huns of Sogdiana, and by the Turks on the field of Warna,[25] and it seems well fitted to cheer the soldiers by the expectation of divine support. Nor did Belisarius fail, as was customary in this age, to address his troops in public; he exhorted them not merely to obtain a present victory, but so effectually to humble the presumption of the Persians that they never again might venture to invade the Roman territories. The *mirranes* had delayed his attack till noon, in hopes of finding the Byzantine Army, with whose usual hour for meals he was acquainted, faint and exhausted from hunger.[26] He stationed the Immortals in his rear as a reserve, and determined to engage with only half the remainder at a time, so that his squadrons might relieve each other by rotation.

The battle began by a mutual discharge of arrows, so numerous, says Procopius, as to darken the air. In this distant warfare the Persians were greatly assisted by the constant succession and exchange of reinforcements, which was in some degree counterbalanced by the disadvantage of the wind blowing towards them and diminishing the speed and effect of their missiles. When the quivers were emptied,

---

24. We may gather from Liberatus, that in this age the "*Graecorum juraments*" were proverbially false. (Breviar).
25. For the instance of the Huns, see Procopius (*Pers. lib. i. c.* 4), and for the Turks, Tindal's *Cantemir* (book ii.).
26. The Roman soldiers usually dined at mid-day and the Persian in the evening. Compare Procopius *Pers. lib. i.* c. 14; and *lib. ii.* c. 18.

the two armies came to closer combat, and the encounter was long and obstinate. At length the left wing of the Imperial forces began to yield, and the Persians were already commencing a pursuit, when some Herulian horse, under Pharas,[27] judiciously stationed by Belisarius behind a hill, rushed forward with so unexpected and vigorous a charge as to turn the tide of victory against the Barbarians. It was in vain that the *mirranes* despatched to their succour the whole battalion of Immortals. After a valiant resistance they also became involved in the rout, and the victory of the Romans was complete.

Throwing aside their weighty bucklers the vanquished fled in every quarter, but left the royal standard in the hands of the Romans,[28] and eight thousand men dead upon the field. Their loss would probably have been still more considerable had not their flight been undisturbed from the prudent apprehension of Belisarius lest the tumultuous disorder of his troops in pursuit should encourage and enable the enemy to rally. This victory, the first gained over the Persians by the Imperial armies for a long succession of years, produced a great moral effect, and decided the fate of the campaign. The Persians did not dare to encounter the Romans in any pitched engagement, and in the slight skirmishes which sometimes took place, the latter maintained their new and unwonted superiority.

The tidings of this battle sunk deep into the mind of Kobad. He beheld himself baffled by a nation which he had hitherto despised as weak, and still hated as hostile. Some of his best troops had fallen, and the remainder were scattered and disbanded. Above all, they had lost that confidence of success, which, in soldiers, is the surest means to its attainment, whilst, in general, it is the common forerunner of rashness and defeat. Inflamed with disappointment and anger, Kobad deprived the *mirranes* of the golden fillet for his hair, which was worn in Persia as a most distinguished honour by special permission of the king. In this custom we may, perhaps, discover the earliest germ of those orders of knighthood, which now in almost every civilised nation reward the merit of the subject, or the favour of the sovereign. The institution is clearly the same, whether the emblems be worn on the bead or on the breast. Should this conjecture be well founded, such orders have undergone a singular vicissitude in returning, as an imitation from the

---

27. Pharas or Faras, was a Barbaric word. See Paul Warnefrid (*lib. ii.* c. 9), and the Lombard Code (*lib. iii.* tit 13, ap. *Lindenbrogiom*). As a name, it teems to imply noble birth.

28. John Malala, vol. ii.

Europeans, to the very country whence they were first derived.[29]

In deliberating on his plans for the next campaign, Kobad was guided by the experience of Almondar, the aged prince of the Arabs at Hira,[30] who for the last fifty years had carried on a predatory warfare against the Romans with spirit and success. Each of his frequent inroads through the provinces between Egypt and Mesopotamia had been marked by the burning of the houses, and captivity of the inhabitants, yet each remained unpunished from the caution and quickness of his movements. This veteran chieftain advised the Persian monarch to avoid the beaten track of Amida or Nisibis, and to invade the Roman territories for the first time on the side of Syria. Here his approach would be unexpected, and therefore his progress easy, and he might hope to reduce the city of Antioch, which its luxury rendered both alluring and defenceless.

According to this counsel, (*a.d.* 531), Kobad dispatched an army consisting of fifteen thousand chosen Persian horse, headed by Azarethes, and of a larger but less disciplined body of troops under Almondar. These two generals began their operations very early in the year. They passed the Euphrates below Mesopotamia, and proceeded along the southern bank through the vast deserts which divided them from the imperial frontier. To these deserts the Romans had always trusted as to the securest bulwark,[31] and the aggression of the Persians in this quarter filled them with surprise and dismay. There was no force in readiness to repel or even to delay the barbarians; they continued to advance without difficulty, and were already at Gabbula, within sixteen miles from the city of Chalcis, and little more than one hundred from Antioch, when the promptitude of Belisarius changed the aspect of affairs. He was at Dara when he received the first news of the Persian invasion.

For a short time he was doubtful what course to pursue, lest by drawing his troops from his actual station he should leave it open to the attacks of Kobad with another army. Perceiving, however, how pressing was the danger of Syria, he placed only some slight garrisons in the Mesopotamian cities, and immediately set off at the head of

---

29. The Lion and Sun are said to have been used as the Persian arms, so far back as *a.d.* 1244, but the order itself is of very recent date. (Malcolm's *History of Persia*, vol. ii.)

30. See Evagrius *Hist. Eccles. lib. iv.* c. 12; and D'Anville *Geograph. Anc.* vol. ii. An account of the dynasty is given by Herbelot, *Bibliot Orient.*

31. See the remarks of Montesquieu on the Persian frontier. (*Esprit des Loix, lib. ix.* c. 4.)

twenty thousand men. [32] With forced marches he reached the shore of the Euphrates, crossed that river at Barbalissus, and succeeded in arriving at Chalcis before the troops of Azarethes and Almondar. He now presented a firm front against them, and checked their further progress, unless they should hazard a battle. His vanguard, led by Sunica, surprised and attacked some of their small detachments; it made many prisoners, and sent the remainder headlong to their camp at Gabbula. But as Sunica had acted without orders, Belisarius, who felt the necessity of strengthening and upholding discipline, expressed great displeasure, and would have deprived that officer of his command, had not Hermogenes pleaded in his favour.

The Persian generals were astonished and alarmed by the rapidity of Belisarius, and reflected with anxiety on the consequences of a defeat at such a distance from their frontiers, to which not a single fugitive might escape with the melancholy tale. A victory, on the other hand, would by no means be equally decisive, since Belisarius might then collect his broken forces within the ramparts of Chalcis or of Antioch, and firmly stand a siege until succours should arrive. Moved by these considerations, and disheartened by their great overthrow at Dara, they determined to abandon their enterprise, and to retrace their steps. They accordingly marched back to the Euphrates, and were followed by Belisarius, who made, however, no attempt to harass or come up with them. He perceived that a battle could hardly increase, but might easily forfeit, the advantages bestowed by their voluntary flight, and therefore avoided giving them any opportunity for an engagement. In his pursuit he remained always at one day's distance from them, encamping each night in the station which they had left the morning before.

Such prudent caution, of which all great commanders have felt the necessity,[33] was bitterly reviled as cowardice by the ignorant and therefore presumptuous soldiery, though no one yet ventured to upbraid him in his presence. Retreating in this manner, the Persians arrived opposite the city of Callinicum, where they intended to alter their route by crossing the Euphrates, and proceeding through the deserts

---

32. This general number assigned by Procopius agrees very nearly with the details of John Malala; eight thousand Romans, under Belisarius in person, five thousand Arabs under Arethas, four thousand reinforcements under Sunica, and four thousand more under Hermogenes (*Chronograph.* vol. ii.)

33. Observe, for instance, the policy of Julius Caesar, in never driving a retreating army to despair. (*Dion Cassius, lib. xli.* c22.}

of Mesopotamia to the Tigris. It was not the design of Belisarius to pursue them any further, and he rejoiced in having saved Syria without striking a blow. But the Roman troops, whose confidence had risen from seeing the enemy always give way before them, and whose enthusiasm was kindled by the approaching festival of Easter, could no longer conceal, or moderate their desire, of seizing this last occasion for battle.

The general in a public harangue exclaimed:

> Whither would you urge me? The most complete and most happy victory is to baffle the force of an enemy without impairing our own, and in this favourable situation we are already placed. Is it not wiser to enjoy the advantages thus easily acquired, than to hazard them in the pursuit of more? Is it not enough to have altogether disappointed the arrogant hopes with which the Persians set out for this campaign, and compelled them to a speedy and shameful retreat? Were we to drive them to a conflict, no further benefits could attend us as victors beyond those which we now possess, and our utmost achievement would be putting fugitives to flight. If vanquished, on the contrary, our rashness might lay open the defenceless provinces of the East to the havoc of a new invasion. Remember also that God does not afford the same protection in unprovoked as in necessary dangers. Deprived of refuge in case of defeat, the Persians will fight with all the courage of despair, whilst we, enfeebled by a rigorous fast,[34] wearied with rapid marches, and having by our speed outstripped several of our slower battalions, must enter the field with diminished strength and unequal chances of success.

These remonstrances, however just and reasonable, failed in their effect. The soldiers were set on by several of their officers; their suppressed murmurs grew into clamorous complaints; and they openly taunted the general with the twofold offence of wanting courage and of checking it in others. Unable to withstand, Belisarius, as formerly Spurinna,[35] determined to yield with cheerfulness, and assured his troops that his previous denials had merely been intended to try their earnestness and spirit. Having, through this judicious policy, re-

---

34. The Romans abstained from food on the day preceding Easter Sunday. (Procop. *Pers. lib. i.* c. 18.)
35. *Tacit Hist. lib. ii.* c 18.

gained their confidence and goodwill, he endeavoured to disprove his gloomy forebodings, by his skilful dispositions for the battle. He placed his infantry to the left, near the river; the Arab auxiliaries on a rising ground, to the right; and chose his personal station with the cavalry, in the centre.

On their part, the Persians prepared with resolution for the conflict, which they could not avoid. It was fought, (April 19 a.d. 531), with great fury, and remained very long undecided. The Persians, as better bowmen, far exceeded the Romans in the number of arrows they let fly; but, from the strong helmets and breastplates of the latter, the darts of the first were less frequently fatal. Several charges of cavalry ensued; and already had two-thirds of the day elapsed without any material result, when, at length, a chosen squadron of Persians made a gallant onset upon the Saracens to the right. This charge was met by so feeble a resistance, and followed by so thorough a dispersion of the Arabs, that they were afterwards suspected of treachery; and this imputation is countenanced by the presence of Almondar and their countrymen in the opposite ranks. Thus freed from the right wing, the Persians immediately surrounded the cavalry in the centre, which, being pressed on all sides, and exhausted with fatigue, was but ill able to offer any effectual opposition.

Most of the horsemen, together with a share of the infantry, escaped headlong to some neighbouring islands of the Euphrates; and it was observed, that those who had been the most forward to arraign the doubts of Belisarius, and to demand a battle, were amongst the least courageous and persevering in maintaining it. Belisarius continued to stand firm his original post, till the flight or the slaughter of the cavalry around him compelled him to retreat. With the few attendants left him, he joined a small battalion of infantry which still remained unshaken near the river. Dismounting from his horse, and bidding his guards follow his example, he placed himself in the foremost ranks of the foot, and by this intrepid conduct afforded safety to the runaways; since the Persians forthwith stopped short in their pursuit, to overwhelm the small but heroic band of Belisarius. To hinder its being entirely surrounded, he ordered his soldiers to gather close to the shore of the Euphrates, and, turning from its stream, to present, in every other direction, by their helmets and bucklers, an iron barrier to the enemy.

Thus defended on one side by their position, and on the other by their intrepidity, this slight detachment sustained, during several hours, a brave and unequal contest against all the hostile cavalry. Repeated attempts to break their line were unavailing; and the alarm of the Persian horses, at the clangour of the shields, saved the Romans from the imminent danger of being trampled down. This stubborn conflict was ended only by the approach of night: the baffled Persians withdrew to their camp; and Belisarius, having obtained some boats, embarked with the few survivors of the engagement, and reached an island in the river. Next morning, the imperial forces proceeded to Callinicum, on the opposite bank,[36] from which this memorable battle has derived its name. It was fought on Easter Sunday, the nineteenth of April; and a superstitious historian does not fail to ascribe the Roman overthrow, on this occasion, to the impiety of polluting so holy a festival with bloodshed.[37]

Had the result been different, he would, no doubt, have held it forth as a signal and striking manifestation of the Deity on this sacred day. The Persians, on their part, having plundered the corpses of the slain, and deplored the number of their own, found it expedient, in spite of their victory, to continue their retreat. The greatness of their loss in this battle, may be estimated from the resentment of Kobad, and the disgrace both of Azarethes and Almondar.[38] Nor was it easy to deceive the monarch on this subject; since it is said, that amongst the ancient Persians, each soldier, at the commencement of a campaign, was directed to deposit an arrow, which he resumed at the conclusion; so that, by the number of remaining arrows, the extent of the national disasters might be accurately known.

A few months from this time, the illness and death of Kobad, in his eighty-third year,[38] gave, a new turn to the posture of affairs. The difficulties which he had apprehended in appointing his favourite son Nushirvan as his successor, were removed by the respect of the Persians for his memory, and their obedience to his last commands. Yet the new monarch was by no means secure upon his throne: he suspected the progress of a conspiracy, which soon afterwards broke forth against him, and he perceived the necessity of leisure to strengthen

---

36. Callinicum was called after its founder or rebuilder, Seleucus Callinicus. See a note of Ducange to the *Paschal Chronicle*, and D'Anville, *Geograph. Anc.* vol. ii

37. The disgrace of Azarethes is mentioned by Procopius (*Pers. lib. i.* c. 18), and that of Almondar may be found in Herbelot, who seems, however, to mistake the cause. (*Bibliot. Orient.*)

38. He died on the 13th of September, a.d. 531. See John Malala, vol. ii., and Procopius, *Pers. lib. i.* c 21. According to Malala, he had ascended the throne a.d. 488; but Assemanni prefers the date of a.d. 490. (*Bibliot. Orient*, vol. i.)

and confirm his power. He therefore renewed the negotiations with Justinian, and at last concluded a treaty of peace, to which the presumptuous surname of Eternal was applied.³⁹ It was stipulated, that the generals of the East should no longer fix their headquarters at Dara; that the Persians should keep possession of the gates of Caucasus; and that a subsidy of eleven thousand pounds weight of gold should be contributed by the Romans, to maintain these defiles against the common inroads of the northern barbarians.

The last article may be regarded as nothing but a tribute, under a more specious name. The ratification of these terms was for some time delayed, by the haughtiness of Chosroes and the irresolution of Justinian; yet, as the principal articles were probably agreed upon, the latter was enabled to withdraw Belisarius and the greater part of his troops from the Persian frontier. He already meditated an expedition against the Vandals, and secretly intended the young general of the East for this important command.

In the interval between the Persian and the Vandal wars, (January, 532-June, 553), during which Belisarius resided at Constantinople, he became the second husband of Antonina. His bride was several years older than himself, having been born in the last year of the fifth century,⁴⁰ and was the child of an actress and of a public charioteer. The profession of both was regarded as vile, and the personal character of the former as infamous, yet their fair daughter had contracted an exalted, though not a wealthy, marriage, and became the parent of several children; amongst whom Photius, and the future wife of an officer of distinction, named Hildiger, are particularly mentioned.⁴¹ Antonina seems to have filled a high office in the imperial palace,⁴² and to have thereby enjoyed the rank and honours of Patrician.

Though thus raised above the dangerous profession of her mother, she still adhered to the morals of the stage, and her conjugal infidelities were numerous. Her character was bold and decided; she was careless of peril or fatigue, and equally capable of planning or achieving the most difficult undertakings. Besides her beauty, she was remarkable for a peculiar power of fascination, which she exerted over the Empress

---

39. Evag. *Hist. Ecc. L iv.* c. 13. Justin, in 2nd pref. to Pandects, &c.
40. Procop. *Hist. Arcan.* c. 4. The construction which would make Antonina fifteen years older, seems quite inadmissible.
41 Procop. *Goth. lib. ii.* c 7. Theophanes, inaccurate as usual, calls him Photinus, son-in-law of Belisarius. (*Chronograph.*)
42. This office was nearly answering to Lady of the Bedchamber in modern courts. See Alemanni *Not. Hist.*

Theodora, to whom her office gave her frequent access; and which was still more useful to her in attracting, and ever afterwards holding, the affections of Belisarius. In fact, his submissive and blind attachment to this woman is the chief blot upon his fame.

She repaid his confidence with zealous friendship, she followed him in most of his campaigns, and sometimes even promoted their success by exertions more suitable to her spirit than her sex. But her passions, both of love and aversion, knew no bounds. Her amour with Theodosius cannot plead the excuse of youthful frailty, and the persecuted her son with more than the usual hatred of an adulterous mother. By Belisarius she had an only daughter Joannina, who appears to have been born before the departure of her parents to Africa, since we find her on the point of marriage within sixteen years from that time.[43] Before that embarkation, also, Belisarius had an opportunity to prove his gratitude and discharge his obligations to the emperor, by supporting, nay, even saving, his throne in a most dangerous rebellion. The causes of this extraordinary popular movement will need some previous explanation.

The growing fondness of the Romans for the amusements of the Circus had been deplored by the great satirist and the great historian, whose writings reflect such lustre on the first period of the empire.[44] This passion, which appears to have outlived so many nobler pursuits, and continued in every vicissitude of government, followed the change of capital to Byzantium, bringing discord and confusion in its train. It was probably still further increased, in the fifth century, by the final abolition of the gladiatorian combats;[45] and the only remaining games of the Circus were thenceforward frequented with redoubled ardour. The charioteers were distinguished from each other by the various colours of red, white, blue, and green, intended to represent the seasons;[46] and each colour, or at least the two latter, possessed numerous and devoted partisans.

---

43. Compare Procop. *Hist. Arcan.* c. 5; and *Goth. lib. iii.* c. 30.
44. Juvenal, *Sat x.* 81; and Tacitus *Annal. lib. xiv.* c. 20, lib. xv. c. 36. The Romans viewed even the departure of Nero from their city with regret, dreading an interruption of the public games.
45. There was an edict of Constantine the Great against gladiatorian combats; but it does not seem to have been observed. (Socrates *Hist. Eccles.* lib. i. c 18.) Their abolition is due to the heroic martyrdom of St. Telemachus, in the beginning of the fifth century. (Theodoret *Hist. Eccles. lib. v.* c. 26.)
46. Cassiod. Var. lib. iii. ep. 51. Some curious particulars, relative to the ancient games, may be gathered from this letter

Their mutual animosity was embittered, both by civil and religious prejudices. The Emperor Anastasius had secretly favoured the Greens, Justinian openly protected the Blues; the latter, therefore, became the emblem of loyalty, and the former of disaffection. For some less evident reason, the Blues were looked upon as the party of the established and orthodox Church; and the convenient imputation of heresy, thrown forth against the others, served as a pretext for every act of rapine or oppression. It was in vain that the laws denounced these dangerous factions, since the disgraceful partiality of Justinian inflamed them by complete impunity to the one, and excessive rigour to the other.[47] The results of this policy, at the close of the Persian war, are described as follows, by a discerning eyewitness.[48]

> The adherents of each party are ready to lavish their fortunes, to risk their lives, or to brave the severest sentence of the laws, in support of their darling colour. They attack their antagonists, as if animated by some personal and grievous injury, and though well aware that, if even victorious in the skirmish, they may not improbably be dragged to prison, and condemned to an ignominious punishment. No length of friendship, no closeness of kindred, no precept of religion, can withhold their fury; and however careless of the national honour, they are most keenly alive to the advancement and triumph of their faction. Nor do even women, though debarred from partaking the amusements, avoid the quarrels of the Circus, and their separate choice of a colour often fills their families with discord.[49] Such, in this capital, is the extent to which public folly, or rather madness, has arrived. By these factions, the empire has been shaken as by an earthquake or a deluge. All the youthful libertines of Constantinople assume the dress and ape the zeal, in order to share the privileges of the Blues. To distinguish their comrades, they adopt a Barbaric garb, the long hair and loose garments of the Huns, and during the night they prowl forth in quest of prey. Their licentious or avaricious passions are then indulged without restraint, and no peaceful citizen can safely wear a golden

---

47. In speaking of the partiality of Justinian, Evagrius uses the strongest language. His testimony is confirmed by John Malali (vol. ii.), and the secret historian (c. 7).
48. I have joined and abridged two passages in Procopius. (*Pers. lib.* i. c. 24, and *Hist Arcan.* c. 7.)
49. The words of Procopius seem decisive, as to the total exclusion of ladies from these games.

ornament or appear in the streets after sunset.

A state of society like this could not be permanent, and the gloomy clouds soon gathered to a storm. Justinian perceived the necessity of vigorous measures too late, since, beyond a certain period, they serve rather to exasperate than to deter. By his orders, some ringleaders of each party were put to death, and several more imprisoned. At the celebration of the public games, during the mouth of January,(*a.d.* 532), both parties clamorously demanded the liberation of their captives: they received no answer from the emperor,[50] and they immediately their mutual animosities to forward their common views. That very evening the guards were massacred and the prisons forced, but, as is usual with mobs, the sedition continued to rage long after its first object was attained.

The opportunity of unbounded license was too tempting to be so rapidly relinquished, and the strange union between the Blues and Greens was continued from hatred to the ministers Tribonian and John of Cappadocia. The city was fired, the Cathedral of St. Sophia, a part of the Imperial palace, and a great number of other public or private buildings were consumed, and the watchword of *Nika, Vanquish!* then used by the seditious, has since given a name to the sedition. Every attempt to withstand the rioters proved unsuccessful, and some relics of great reputation, which were displayed in this emergency, failed both in drawing down a miracle from Heaven, and in allaying the fury of the factions. The principal citizens hurried to the opposite shore of the Bosphorus, and the emperor entrenched himself within his palace. He endeavoured to restore tranquillity by the dismissal of his unpopular ministers, and proceeded in person to the Hippodrome, where, with the Gospels in his hand, he made some of those solemn, but vague promises, which seldom miss their effect upon the populace.

On this occasion, however, he was disregarded. A few amongst the Blues acknowledged the authority of their repentant sovereign, but the other party far surpassed and overpowered them, and Justinian fled back for refuge to his palace. Here he greatly added to the dangers of

---

50. Such is the simple and probable account of Malala (vol. ii.) Theophanes gives a long and incredible conversation in barbarous Greek, which he states to have passed between the emperor and his subjects by the voice of a crier. (*Chronograph.*) Gibbon, who somewhat hastily adopts this fable, admits it however to be "the most singular dialogue that ever passed between a prince and his subjects," (vol. vii.) But the authority of Theophanes, till near his own times, is so slight, that we should never trust him more than we can help.

his situation (nothing is so blind as fear) by supplying the rebels with what they had hitherto needed, the name and authority of a leader. The Greens naturally looked with regret to the Emperor Anastasius, their former patron, and with hope to Hypatius, his nephew, who was invested with the dignities of senator and patrician, and had served, though with little distinction, in the Persian wars.[51] His talents seem to have been of the meanest order, but he deserves the praise of never having suffered his ambition to outrun them.

Far from entertaining any views of the throne, to which he might have aspired with some colour of hereditary right, he had, at the very outset of the tumults, hastened to Justinian, and remained in dutiful attendance with some of his senatorial colleagues. Yet the emperor, who still continued to suspect him, commanded his departure from the palace, as if a spy were more to be dreaded than a rival, and although Hypatius himself earnestly represented that the people might compel him to an involuntary usurpation. His honest predictions were fulfilled. Early on the sixth day of the sedition, (Jan. 18, a.d. 532), he was hailed with transport by the people, and in spite of his own entreaties and the tears of his wife, was led to the Fonrum of Constantine and proclaimed emperor. In this hasty ceremony no diadem could be found to crown him, and a gold collar supplied its place, as formerly with Julian. [52]

These tidings were brought to Justinian when holding a council of his most faithful adherents: he was filled with consternation, he proposed to resign the contest, and to embark with his family and treasure for some distant retreat. This pusillanimous design might perhaps have prevailed had it not been withstood by the noble spirit of the empress. For the first and last time the comedian Theodora seemed worthy of her throne, and by her exhortations it was determined to prefer the chance of victory or death to the certainty of exile. None of the troops showed zeal or attachment to this cause, and the only hope of Justinian rested on Belisarius and on Mundus, a Barbarian by birth,[53] who had lately been named Governor of Illyria, but who was then present in the capital. Belisarius undertook to forestall the attack

---

51. See Ducange, *Fam. Aug. Byz.*, and Procop. *Pers. lib. i.* c. 8, 11.
52. Ammian. Marcellin. lib. xx. c. 4.
53. Procop. *Goth. lib. i.* c. 5. The unpopularity of Justinian, even with his own guards, and his sole dependence on his two generals, are admitted by this historian, though his account of the Nika Sedition is extremely cautious and reserved. (*Pers. lib. L* c. 24.) For the life and character of Mundus see John Malala. (vol. ii.)

of Hypatius and surprise his adherents, by a sadden sally against his headquarters in the Hippodrome.

He advanced to the front gates of the palace, and called on the Imperial guards without to open them. But these troops were unwilling to declare for either party, their secret wishes were perhaps in favour of Hypatius, and they prudently delayed their choice that they might not fail to side with the victorious. Accordingly they turned a deaf ear to the commands of Belisarius, and kept the gates resolutely closed. Dismayed at this defection, Belisarius returned to the hall of audience and announced to the emperor, that his very guards had left him, and that the passage was blockaded. He next attempted to issue forth by a postern, at the head of some faithful veterans, but the relics of the conflagration almost hindered his progress. It was with considerable difficulty and danger that he forced his way through the encumbered streets and tottering ruins, and at length found himself in sight of the Hippodrome and of the rebels before it.

Meanwhile a change had taken place in favour of his cause by means of that fickleness of purpose to which all popular assemblies are naturally prone. The Blues had at length perceived, with shame and self-reproach, that their resentment for a slight offence was tending to deprive them of a gracious patron, and to seat an hereditary antagonist upon the throne, and they themselves began to wonder at their own blind folly in leaguing with their bitterest enemies. Such reflections urged them to withdraw from the contest which they had provoked; one by one they slunk away, and within a few hours from his proclamation Hypatius had lost many of his partisans.[54] Still, however, the Greens presented a strong and massy line.

They were dismayed at seeing Belisarius and his soldiers suddenly issue from amongst the smoking ruins, nor did the general allow them time to recover from their consternation. Drawing his sword and commanding his veterans to follow, he charged them with vigour and success. They very far outnumbered his scanty squadron, but many were destitute of weapons, and none of them could vie in equipment with the complete armour of the soldier's. Belisarius pushed his advantage to the utmost; he broke open the front gates of the Hippodrome, and Mundus, who had marched from the palace with another division of troops, and was now at no great distance, rushed forward on hearing the clangour of the conflict, and burst into the Circus on the opposite side. The insurgents then gave way and dispersed in every quarter.

---

54. Pascal *Chronicle*.

Hypatius was dragged from the throne which he had ascended but a few hours before, and thrown into a dungeon with his brother Pompey, where next day both were privately put to death by order of the emperor.[55] As soon as the victory was decided, it would seem that the Blues emerged from their concealment to glut themselves in safety with the blood of their adversaries, and the rage of the soldiers was almost equally merciless and ungovernable. The lowest computation assigns thirty thousand as the number of the slain, of whom probably nine-tenths were cut down as fugitives or suppliants.

This ferocious vengeance, so disgraceful to every one engaged in it, would deeply stain the fame of Belisarius were we to suppose that he did not attempt to check and restrain it by every effort in his power. Of his conduct after completing the victory no account is given, but from his zealous humanity in all like cases, such for instance as the sack of Naples, it does not seem unreasonable to conclude that he was at least as anxious to spare the blood of fellow citizens as of strangers and enemies. This massacre, like all indiscriminate and excessive punishments, produced no moral effect. The games of the Circus were indeed discontinued for several years, but on their renewal the same factions reappeared to distract the peace or endanger the safety of the Empire on many subsequent occasions.[56]

---

55. The order of the emperor is suppressed by the courtly Procopius, but is recorded by Evagrius (*Hist. Eccles. lib. iv.* c. 13.) Jornandes (*De Regn. Success*), &c.
56. See for example Theophylact Simocatta, *lib. viii.* c. 10; and Paul Warnefrid, *lib. iv.* c 37.

CHAPTER 3

Conquest of Africa

The northern coast of Africa, known to the Orientals by the local name of Magreb,[1] and to us by the merited by-word of Barbary, hardly retains a trace of the most formidable rival and most opulent province of the Romans. After the fall of Jugurtha, it had enjoyed a long period of prosperity and peace, disturbed only by a few petty insurrections, such as that of Tacfarinas in the reign of Tiberius, and afterwards by the schism and persecution of the Donatists. Excepting a short and single attack in the reign of Gallienus, it had escaped the sufferings which almost every other portion of the empire had repeatedly undergone from the northern tribes, and at the beginning of the fifth century, the Africans far exceeded all their fellow-subjects in wealth, population and resources.

But though the scourge of invasion had been so long delayed, it fell at length with redoubled violence upon them. During the minority of Valentinian the Third, his mother the Empress Placidia, presided in the councils of Ravenna, Ætius and Boniface were then the two chief pillars of the state, their courage was undaunted, and in that degenerate age surprising, insomuch that, according to the forcible expression of an ancient historian, the last remains of Roman valour seemed to have retreated to their breasts.[2] The former bore with suppressed impatience, the appointment of Boniface as governor of Africa, and availed himself of the weakness of a female reign, to execute a stratagem as disgraceful to himself as pernicious to the empire.

By a false charge of disloyalty he obtained the recall of his rival, by secret letters to Africa he represented this recall as the forerunner of disgrace and death, and at length drove Boniface into the very acts of

---
1. Magreb signifies a country to the west (Herbelot *Bibliot Orient.*)
2. Procop. *Vandal, lib, i.* c. 3. See the observations of Dom. Ruinart (*Hist. Persecut.*)

treason of which he had at first unjustly accused him, Boniface refused to obey the orders of Placidia, and wishing to secure himself from the effects of her resentment, concluded a treaty with the Vandals in Southern Spain.

It is no small proof of the fertility and flourishing state of Africa at this time, that they should so readily have forsaken a certain possession for a new and precarious conquest. The Vandals embarked with their families, (May, a.d. 429), from the province whose name of Andalusia still denotes their former residence, [3] landed on the opposite cape of Ceuta, Their leader was the far-famed Genseric, [4] one of the most able but most lawless and bloody monarchs recorded in history. Of a middle stature, and lamed by a fall from his horse, his demeanour was thoughtful and silent, he was contemptuous of luxury, sudden in anger, and boundless in ambition. Yet his impetuosity was always guided and restrained by cunnings he well knew how to tempt the allegiance of a foreign nation, to cast the seeds of future discord, or to rear them to maturity.[5]

The numbers of the barbarians on their passage to Africa, though augmented by an unwarlike crowd of women and children, contained no more than fifty thousand fighting men. Genseric, however, was well aware that the reputation of powerful forces is often equivalent to their presence, and artfully appointed eighty *chiliarchs*, or nominal chiefs of one thousand soldiers, so as to strike his enemy with greater terror. [6] His progress through the African province was rapid and unopposed, until Boniface, having discovered the artifices of Ætius, and the favourable disposition of Placidia, bitterly repented the effects of his hasty resentment. He endeavoured by promises and persuasion to withdraw his Vandal allies, but he found it far less easy to allay than it had been to raise the storm.

His proposals were haughtily rejected, and both parties had recourse to arms. Boniface was defeated, and forced to seek shelter within the walls of Hippo Regius, so called from having formerly

---

3. Mariana *Hist. Hisp. lib. v.* c. 3.
4. This name is very variously written. He is called Gizeric by the Greeks, Procopius, Evagrius, &c. Gaiseric by Idatius, and Geiseric by Victor Vitensis and Prosper, The real Vandal word was probably Geisreich, *viribus fortibus pollens*, (Grotius *Hist. Goth.*)
5. *Jornandes De Reb. Getic* c. 33. This character is quoted by Lord Byron, as a precedent for his Conrad and Lara. (Notes to Corsair, third *canto*.)
6. See the Vandal chronicle of Isidore, (ed. Undenbrogn.) Idatius, (*ap. Sirmond*, vol. ii.) and Victor Vitensis. (*De Persec. lib. i.* c. 1.) Some vague popular rumours are repealed by Gregory of Tours (*Hist. Franc. lib. ii.* c. 2), and some valuable historical facts collected by Procopius. (*Vandal. lib. i.* c 3.)

been the residence of the Numidian kings,[7] while the Vandals, spreading over the whole extent of the defenceless country, wreaked upon it the most fearful havoc, and scarcely any cities but those of Carthage and Hippo Regius could escape their fury. The latter was by Genseric in person, but he was at length compelled to retreat by a scarcity of which his own devastations were in all probability the cause.

Soon afterwards, Boniface, at the head of some Italian reinforcements and Byzantine auxiliaries, sallied forth from the gates to try the fortune of another battle. It proved as disastrous as the former, and the Roman general, relinquishing all further hope of offensive warfare, and only leaving garrisons in the fortresses, embarked for Ravenna. We may justly feel surprise at his confidence in returning to the court of his injured sovereign. His fatal rashness had cost the empire its most important province, his delusion was an insufficient excuse, his repentance a poor and barren atonement, and Placidia, though she might be constrained to dissemble, could hardly, as a sovereign or a woman, be expected to forgive.

He was however, received with smiles and professions, but shortly after his return fell in conflict by the spear of his rival. His son-in-law, Count Sebastian, succeeded to his power, and the adventures of this brave but unfortunate man, were they less briefly recorded, might furnish singular materials for romance. During several years he ruled in the palace of Ravenna, till Ætius, who had fled to the Huns from the indignation of his sovereign, found means to resume his former ascendancy, and forced Sebastian in his turn to become an exile. Attended by a numerous train he proceeded to Constantinople, a retreat which the persevering hatred of his enemy at length compelled him to abandon. He then directed his course to Spain, and seized on the city of Barcelona, which he vainly endeavoured to maintain.

Being driven from thence by the King of the Visigoths, he sailed to Africa as a last resource, with the view of offering his services to Genseric. This crafty tyrant suspected his designs, and dreaded his abilities, and having precipitately returned from a distant expedition, at the news of his landing, very quickly sacrificed him either by fraud or

---

7. Some remains of Hippo may still be traced in the neighbourhood of Bona, and Dr. Shaw was shown the site of the convent of St. Augustine by the Moors, who have, as he remarks, an interest in keeping up this profitable tradition. (*Travels in Barbary*, ed. 1738.) According to his conjecture, the modern name of Bona is a corruption from Hippona, but Marmol explains it is a Latin compliment to the goodness of the soil. (Vol. ii. ed. 1667)

force as a victim to his jealousy.⁸

The retreat of Boniface from Africa seemed to leave that country at the mercy of the Vandals, but they were less fitted for sieges than for battles, and Carthage continued to withstand them. That capital, which had risen from its ruins at the command of Julius Caesar, and been embellished by Diocletian,⁹ appears to have regained no inconsiderable share of its former opulence and pride, and might be considered at this time as the second city of the West. Under these circumstances, Genseric thought it prudent to conclude a treaty with the Emperor Valentinian, by which he yielded a share of his conquests, and pledged himself to a yearly tribute for the rest. ¹⁰His object was perfidy, and he attained it. lie surprised Carthage in the midst of peace, ten years from his first landing, (a.d. 439), and the whole Roman province of Africa now acknowledged him as king. He next applied himself to confirm and uphold his power, and rewarded the attachment of his barbarian soldiers by an arbitrary distribution of forfeited estates.

The allegiance of the native inhabitants was secured, not by affection but by terror. No fault escaped the vengeance, no treasure the rapacity of Genseric. Born a Catholic, he had afterwards embraced the Arian doctrines, held by the greater part of his followers, and now availed himself of his extensive sway to persecute his former brethren with all the malignant zeal of an apostate. In order to prevent the imperial forces in any fresh invasion from again retaining a footing in the country by the number of fortresses, he razed nearly all the African rampart, except those of the capital and Hippo Regius, which on the contrary he appears to have strengthened and repaired.¹¹

It may be remarked, that the same plan was adopted by the great cardinal Ximenes, with regard to the kingdom of Navarre, and that in the opinion of a most judicious historian, Spain owes her present possession of that province to this singular precaution, ¹² The soundness

---

8. The early part of the history of Sebastian must be gleaned from Idatius (*ap. Sirmond*, vol. ii.), and the conclusion chiefly from Prosper, (*ap. Canis. Antiq. Lect.* vol. i.)
9. Dion Cassius, *lib. xliii.* c. 50; Aurelius Victor De Caesaribus, c. 39
10. This tributeis mentioned by Procopius, and the division of territory by Prosper.
11. In his Vandal history (lib. i. c. 5,) Procopius states that the fortifications of all the cities in Africa, except Carthage, were demolished; and he is followed by Gibbon and other modern historians. They have not observed that Hippo Regius is afterwards termed εχυρα (*lib. ii.* c. 4 ;) and that Procopius in his history of Edifieea, explains that some other cities besides Carthage were exempted (*lib. vi,* c. 5.)
12. Robertson's *History of Charles V.* (vol. ii. ed. 1769.) See also the remarks of General Foy, (*Guerre de la Péninsule*, vol. iii.)

of this policy was allowed and admired by Genseric's contemporaries, but in a succeeding age the rapid progress of Belisarius was thought to be assisted by the want of fortresses to harass and delay his troops. But the prince, who then filled the African throne, was of a very different character from Genseric, and the resources most precious in the hands of an able sovereign, become elements of overthrow and ruin to a weak one.

The internal regulation of his kingdom was insufficient to employ the active mind of Genseric, and he determined to extend his power by the creation of a naval fierce. With him, project and performance were never far asunder. His ships soon rode in the Mediterranean, and carried terror and destruction in their train. He annexed to his kingdom the Balearic islands, Corsica and Sardinia, the last of which was afterwards allotted by the Vandals as a place of exile or imprisonment for captive Moors, and during many years the ports of Africa were what they have again become at present, the abode of fierce and unpunished pirates. With every returning spring the fleet of Genseric ravaged the coasts of Italy and Sicily, or even of Greece and Illyria, sometimes bearing off the inhabitants to slavery, and sometimes levelling their cities to the ground.

Emboldened by long impunity he attacked every government alike. On one occasion, when sailing from Carthage, he was asked by the pilot of his vessel to what coast he desired to steer. " Leave the guidance to God," exclaimed the stern barbarian, God will doubtless lead us against the "guilty objects of his anger!"[13] But the most memorable achievement of Genseric was his sack of Rome, (a.d. 455), to which he was invited by domestic discontent. Eudoxia, a descendant of Theodosius the Great, and widow of the late Emperor Valentinian, had become the reluctant bride of Maximus, who had murdered and succeeded him, and she fixed upon the King of Africa as her ally and avenger. The character of that reckless Vandal must have been altogether unknown to her, if she expected to move him by her arguments on the impiety of suffering an imperial murder to remain unpunished; but the anticipated wealth of Rome held out to him sufficient motives for compliance.[14]

Sailing to Italy at the head of a formidable fleet, he met with no

---

13. Procop. *Vandal, lib. ii.* c. 13.
14. Victor Tunnunensis, (ap. Canis. *Antiq. Lect.* vol. i. Jornandes, (*De Reb. Getic.* c. 45,) and Procopius, (*Vandal. lib. i* c. 4.) Consult the critical narrative of Muratori, (*Annal d'Ital.* vol. iii.)

resistance to his enterprise, and the usurper was torn to pieces by the fickle fury of the mob. But Eudoxia, though thus freed from her hated husband, was betrayed by her ungenerous champion, and carried captive to Carthage. She was afterwards restored to liberty at the intercession of the Byzantine court, but one of her daughters was compelled by Genseric to accept his son in marriage. During his stay (a fortnight) at Rome, he did not neglect to load his vessels with its spoils. From the Capitoline temple of Jupiter, he removed one-half of its roof, composed of the finest bronze, and covered with a profusion of gold, [15] and the preservation of such costly materials, is alone sufficient to disprove the loud but vague complaints of the extreme rapacity of Alaric. The same inference may also be drawn from the amount of booty at this time. It does not appear that Genseric, except in this instance, extended his depredation to any object beyond statues, furniture and plate, or inflicted the slightest injury on public or private buildings.

From the greater number of the successive western emperors all equally degenerate, Genseric had no retribution for his hostilities to fear; but the accession of Majorian suddenly raised up against him an enemy worthy of his talents and his power. This brave and accomplished prince determined to equip and lead in person an armament against the Vandals, Desirous of previously observing their resources, we are told that having tinged with black his yellow hair, he ventured to assume the character of his own ambassador, and as such to visit Carthage. The very strangeness of this story, when joined to the general accuracy and discernment of Procopius by whom it is recorded, is a proof of its truth, and I find two centuries later, the same disguise successfully practised by a King of the Lombards.[16]

The early death of Majorian, (a.d. 461), in a mutiny of his soldiers, soon afterwards freed Genseric from danger, and enabled him to renew his piracy. Such repeated outrages at length aroused the tardy resentment of the court of Constantinople, and its expedition deserves our peculiar attention as a contrast to that of Belisarius. Leo the First was then nominal emperor, under the guidance of Aspar, a too powerful subject, who from his attachment to the Arian doctrines, found it easier to bestow than to assume the purple. For the reduction of the Vandals, Aspar mustered an army amounting to nearly one hundred thousand men, and a fleet which flattery might declare the most formidable ever launched by the Romans, (a.d. 468).

---

15. See Donatus *Roma Antiqua, lib. ii.* c. 6; and *Nardini, lib. v.* c. 15.
16. Paul Warnefrid, *lib. iii.* c. 30.

The imperial resources were not spared in the equipment, and by the most lavish liberality, it was hoped to animate the future courage of the combatants. Procopius says:

> But as it had been destined that this mighty armament should fail, the command of it was entrusted to the worthless Basiliscus.

The choice of such a general might indeed account for the greatest reverses. His only merit consisted in his fraternal relation to the empress, and his conduct is this enterprise has been variously ascribed to treachery or weakness. His fleet after a prosperous voyage anchored at the ancient promontory of Mercury, the modern Cape Bonn, distant no more than forty miles from Carthage. Had he at once disembarked his troops and marched upon the capital, the Vandals thus suddenly surprised could have made no effectual stand, but this precious opportunity was lost by his fatal hesitation, and by the prudent policy of Genseric. Professing the utmost deference for the imperial pleasure, the Vandal monarch proposed and obtained a truce of five days to settle the terms of his submission, and availed himself of this seasonable respite to collect and prepare his forces.

At length a breeze favourable to his designs having arisen in the night, he silently manned his galleys with his bravest troops, approached the Roman fleet, and impelled many smaller vessels filled with combustibles into the midst of it. A conflagration speedily ensued, and the Romans starting from their slumbers, found themselves encompassed by fire and the Vandals.

The wild shrieks of the perishing multitude, mingled with the crackling of the flames and the roaring of the wind, and the enemy proved as unrelenting as the elements. The greater part of the fleet was destroyed in this memorable night, and Basiliscus, who led back to Constantinople a handful of survivors and a few shattered ships, only escaped the punishment he deserved by taking refuge at the sanctuary of St. Sophia. The powerful resources displayed in this armament induced the Vandals, and its failure the Romans, to desire peace, which was accordingly concluded a few years afterwards in the reign of Zeno, and which continued uninterrupted—till that of Justinian.

Genseric did not long survive this final ratification of his conquests, and dying in the fullness of years, (*a.d* 477), left behind him a new law for the succession to his crown. The most common source of decay and downfall to newly-founded monarchies has always been their partition after the decease of their founder, and to provide against this evil, as well as against that of long minorities, Genseric enjoined that amongst his descendants the eldest surviving male should, in every case, be the sole rightful heir, so that the son of an elder brother should yield to his uncle. Hunneric, son of the late king, was his first successor, and displayed all his cruelty without any of his talents. The savage Moors, who had refused to own the allegiance, but had been awed by the valour and renown of Genseric, now commenced a destructive, though desultory, warfare on the inland frontiers. The perfidy of this people seems to have been as proverbial as the ancient Punic fait, and they made as little account of their hostages as of their promises.[17]

None amongst them (except the tribes of Tripoli, in the reign of Justinian) were ever converted to Christianity, but persevered in their primitive worship till the conquest of the Saracens. Securely nestled in the fastnesses of Mount Atlas, or roving over the trackless desert they seldom suffered, and were always ready to inflict invasion, and gradually encroached on the limits of the ancient Roman province. During this reign, the peace of Africa was still more cruelly disturbed by the persecution which the Arian monarch decreed against his Catholic subjects. Many amongst them, rather than forswear their tenets, heroically bore a painful and ignominious death, and the courage of the remainder was upheld by real piety and doubtful miracles.

After the death of Hunneric, his nephew and successor, Gundamund, pursued the same mistaken policy for twelve years, (a.d. 484-496). Thrasimund, brother of Gundamund, then ascended the throne. He judiciously formed an alliance with the great Theodoric, King of Italy, which he cemented by his marriage with Amalafrida, sister of that monarch. As her dower, he obtained the district of Cape Lilybaeum, in Sicily, and the aid of six thousand warlike Goths, who attended the queen to Africa. The aversion of Thrasimund to the adherents of the Trinity was not less strong than that of his predecessors, but he employed more mild and effectual measures for conversion. He held out to the Catholics not the terrors of persecution, but the allurements of rewards and dignities; and if any amongst them became guilty of an offence, his pardon might always be gained by his apostasy.

After Thrasimund, who reigned twenty-seven years, Hilderic, son of Hunneric, was proclaimed King, (a.d. 523), as the eldest of the royal

---

17. Procop. *Vandal. lib. ii.* c 8 and 17. The base and character of the wandering Moors is admitted by their countryman Leo Africanus, with many apologies for his frankness. (*lib. i.* ed. 1556.)

race. Born of an orthodox mother, (he was grandson of the Empress Eudoxia), he showed great indulgence to the Catholics, but his advanced age and yielding disposition rendered him wholly unfit for business, and especially for war. Yet, since distrust and cruelty are the common results of weakness, we read without surprise of the close imprisonment and mysterious death of Queen Amalafrida, together with a general massacre of her Gothic guards, on the vague and improbable charge of having conspired against the reigning sovereign.[18] Had Theodoric the Great still lived he would doubtless have exacted a bloody retribution, and though the minority of his successor saved the Vandals from hostilities, they must have bitterly deplored their folly when they found themselves on the invasion of Belisarius, unprotected by so useful an alliance.

From the incapacity and infirmities of Hilderic much of his power devolved on Gelimer, his nearest kinsman and destined heir, who was renowned for martial prowess but fierce in disposition, impatient of control and thirsting for supreme authority. The sceptre, which from the age of Hilderic he must very shortly have received by right, he chose rather to seize by usurpation. To the bravest of the Vandals he spoke of the timid and unwarlike temper of their king; to the most cautious he represented the independence of the African crown as endangered by a late alliance of Hilderic with the Emperor Justin. Strongly moved by these insinuations, and emboldened by the fears of their king, the Vandals rose in arms and hailed Gelimer as sovereign, while Hilderic and his chief partisans were cast into a dungeon.

Meanwhile Justinian had ascended the imperial throne, and whether really pitying the fate of his ally, or whether, as was more probably the case, seeking a pretext to attack this mighty monarchy while weakened by internal factions, he dispatched ambassadors to Carthage, soliciting the restoration of Hilderic. There had been a remarkable similarity between the cases of Justinian and of Gelimer, each heir to an imbecile old man, and each controlling and directing the measures of government in his place: but Justinian, unlike the Vandal prince, had been satisfied with the reality without the trappings of sovereign power, and patiently awaited the death or resignation of his kinsman. He wrote to Gelimer:

> Do not incur the name of tyrant by too hastily assuming the title of king, and suffer Hilderic at least to enjoy the honours, if

---

18. Compare Cassiodorius (*Var. lib. ix.* ep. 1,) with Procopius, (*Vandal. lib. i.* c 9.)

not to exercise the rights, of royalty.

The only effect of this letter on the haughty and suspicious Vandal was an order for the still closer imprisonment of Hilderic, on the plea of an intended escape. The emperor then requested, that if Gelimer had determined to retain the crown, he would at least grant freedom to his captive, and allow him to spend the remainder of his life in a peaceful retreat at Constantinople. This proposal, also, was refused.

Having thus acquired a sufficient ground for hostilities, and being enabled, by his recent peace with Persia, to employ his forces elsewhere, Justinian undertook an expedition against Carthage. He was urged to this design by a considerable number of the Vandal partisans of Hilderic, who had hastened to the Byzantine court in search of refuge and revenge.[19] The announcement of his project was, however, received with dismay by everyone who contemplated either its expenses or its dangers, and was heard with pleasure only by the thoughtless rabble, which always rejoices in remaining a safe spectator of the perils which others undergo. The failure of the great armament in the reign of Leo had left a deep impression, and the losses it had occasioned, both in men and money, were computed with fearful forebodings. The soldiers complained that, scarcely returned from a long and laborious war, and not having for one moment enjoyed the happiness of home, they should again be summoned to arms, engaged in naval enterprises, the very name of which was previously almost unknown to them, and transported from the most distant oriental regions to the utmost limits of the west, in order forthwith to begin a doubtful contest against the Vandals and the Moors.

With the exception of Belisarius, the Roman generals shared so strongly in the public terror, that even their ambition yielded to alarm, and that, far from eagerly courting, they dreaded the responsibility, and shrunk from the command of the intended expedition.[20] On the other hand, the financiers, foreseeing the new demands upon the treasury, and the inquiries into their own fraudulent profits which so costly undertaking must bring on, concealed their fears detection and impoverishment under the convenient mask of national economy. The chief of this party John of Cappadocia, ventured in full council to dissuade the emperor from his project, on the plea of its uncertainty and danger; and his arguments would have prevailed, had they not

---

19. This appears from a subsequent passage in Procopius, (*Vandal. lib. ii.* c. 5.)
20. Compare Procopius *De Ædif. lib. vi.* c. 3; and *Vandal lib. i.* c. 1

been met by supernatural grounds. Justinian was on the point of yielding, when a bishop from the East requesedt admission to his presence, exhorted him to stand forth as the champion of the Catholic Church, and announced a seasonable vision. These, said the *prelate*, were the very words of the Lord:

> I will march before him in his battles, and make him sovereign of Africa.

It is rarely that men reject any tale, however fantastic or improbable, provided it tends to show that their own sect or country is the peculiar favourite of heaven. All the doubts of Justinian were removed; he commanded a fleet and army to be forthwith equipped for this sacred enterprise, and endeavoured still further to insure its success by his austerity in fasts and vigils.[21] Belisarius was named supreme commander, still retaining his high titular station as General of the East.[22]

Besides the alleged promise of divine aid, Justinian, at this important juncture, obtained a more solid advantage by the revolt of Tripoli and Sardinia from the Vandals. It is remarkable, that the loss of these very provinces should, in like manner, have preceded the expedition of Basiliscus. Pudentius, a stirring and popular citizen of Tripoli, having set on foot an insurrection, a small detachment of troops was, at his request, dispatched to his assistance. By his exertions, the town and territory of Tripoli acknowledged the imperial sway; a circumstance which might have served to show, at the outset, how little the rights of Hilderic were likely to be respected in a war professedly undertaken to defend them. Sardinia, perhaps the only portion of the ancient world which has never, at any recorded period, enjoyed the blessings either of freedom or civilisation, had been entrusted by Gelimer to the government of Godas, whose presumptuous ambition urged him to forswear his allegiance, and assume the ensigns of royalty; but whose prudent sense of weakness besought, and not in vain, some succour from Justinian.

Meantime, Belisarius was actively employed in collecting and mustering his forces at Constantinople. The army amounted to less than one-sixth of that which Basiliscus had formerly led so unsuccessfully to the same undertaking, since it did not exceed five thousand cav-

---

21. In one of his laws (*Novell.* 30,) Justinian himself boasts of having promoted the African war: and Cardinal Baronius does not fail to ascribe the prosperous result to these practices. (*Annal. Eccles. a.d.* 533, No. 43.)

22. The letter of Justinian to Belisarius, in the April following, is addressed *Magistro Militum per Orientem.* (*Cod. Justinian, lib. i. tit.* 27.)

alry, and ten thousand foot soldiers.[23] Nor were all these regular and well combined: a share of them consisted of barbarian confederates, more especially of Huns and Heruli. On Belisarius himself, Justinian bestowed the amplest authority by a written patent or commission; he left him at full liberty to pursue his own plans without restraint, and invested all his future commands with the same sacred character as though they had emanated directly from the sovereign. The fleet was manned by twenty thousand sailors, from Egypt and Asia Minor, and composed of five hundred transports, whose size might vary from thirty to five hundred tons.[24] To provide against any maritime engagement, the transports were escorted by ninety-two galleys, not remarkable, indeed, for their strength, since each contained but twenty mariners, and a single rank of oars, which was carefully protected from the darts of an enemy by a covering along the rowers.

A slight but characteristic incident, which took place shortly before the sailing of the fleet, will set forth in natural colours the superstitious spirit of this age. It had been resolved to dispatch, in advance of the principal forces, a detachment headed by two inferior officers, named Martin and Valerian, to await in the Peloponnesus the arrival of the rest. They had already embarked for this purpose, when Justinian, suddenly remembering some further directions which he had hitherto neglected to give them, sent a messenger, summoning them once more to his presence. On reflection, however, it occurred to him that to delay their departure would form an inauspicious augury; and preferring the avoidance of the omen to the execution of his orders, he hastily, through a second envoy, commanded Martin and Valerian to remain on board. Yet, by this prudent afterthought, he fell into the very evil which he endeavoured to shun.

It was universally considered by the people, that no augury could be more unfavourable than for a sovereign to withhold his subjects from landing; and everyone felt fully assured that neither of these ill-fated officers would ever again return to Constantinople. When, to the great surprise of the citizens, both Martin and Valerian were, many months afterwards, actually seen to disembark after the African war,

---

23. Montesquieu (*Grand. et Decad. des Rom.* c 20) mistakes the five thousand cavalry for the total numbers of the army; an error I should not have expected from this excellent writer. He has blindly followed a false translation by Cousin in another passage. (*Vandal. lib. ii.* c. 7.)

24. I follow Gibbon in this computation of the tonnage. Cousin, always careless, makes the number of ships fifty; and Montesquieu proves his dependence on the translation by falling into the snare. (*Grand, et Decad. des Rom.* c. 20.)

the presage even then continued to be trusted and believed, and was ingeniously applied to Stoza, one of the subalterns, who had risen in rebellion, and therefore staid abroad. How easy must the office of soothsayer have been amongst a people who thus, as it were, conspired with his predictions, and were determined, at all events, to find or to make a miraculous accomplishment to them!

In the month of June, and the seventh year of the reign of Justinian, (a.d. 533), the last armament of Rome against her ancient rival became ready for departure.

The general embarked, attended on this occasion by Antonina, and by his secretary, the historian Procopius, who at first had shared in the popular fear and distaste of this enterprise, but had afterwards been induced to join it by a hopeful dream. The galley of Belisarius was moored near the shore, in front of the imperial palace,[25] where it received a last visit from Justinian, and a solemn blessing from the patriarch of the city. A soldier recently baptised was placed on board, to secure its prosperous voyage; its sails were then unfurled, and, with the other ships in its train it glided down the straights of the Bosphorus, and gradually disappeared from the lingering gaze of the assembled multitude.

The first place where Belisarius anchored was Heraclea, the ancient Perinthus, a city which might boast of having, at one period, held Constantinople beneath its jurisdiction,[26] Here the fleet remained five days, awaiting a large supply of horses, with which the emperor had promised to furnish the cavalry from Thrace. It then proceeded to Abydos, where it was again delayed by a calm during four days, an interval which became remarkable from the firmness of Belisarius in upholding military order. Two of the Hunnish confederates had killed a comrade in one of those drunken brawls to which their nation was particularly prone, and by the prompt justice of the general they were executed on the hill above Abydos, Their punishment, which might appear harsh to barbarians, since murder with them is commonly a venial crime,[27] aroused the pity and indignation of their countrymen;

25. This palace was on the Propontis, between the cathedral of St Sophia and the Hippodrome. See Ducange (*Const Christ lib. ii.*) and Gibbon (vol. iii.)
26. *Dion Cassius, lib. lxxiv.* c14. At present, the harbour of Heraclea is almost choked up with the fragments of ancient edifices. (Grélot, *Voyage*.)
27. In almost every barbarous state of society, we find that the murder of a citizen might be atoned for by a fine to his nearest kinsmen. That this was the case with the ancient Germans, appears from Tacitus (*Germ.* c. 12); and his testimony is confirmed and illustrated by the provisions in the Codes of the, (continued next page),

and even the Byzantine soldiers unwillingly foresaw, from this example, an approaching check to their own license and irregularity. The assertion of savage freedom in the confederates, or the impatience of unusual discipline in the Romans, might have grown to a formidable mutiny, had not Belisarius repressed it in a public harangue, he said:

> Those who allow a murder to remain unpunished, become accomplices to its guilt, and partners in its infamy.

He urged that the drunkenness of the criminals was, in fact, an aggravation of their crime; since intemperance, even when harmless, outruns the bounds of military discipline; and he declared that he would acknowledge no soldier for his comrade, who could not march with pure and unpolluted hands against the enemy. After this wholesome exhortation, he availed himself of a favourable breeze to pursue the voyage. Apprehensive that so many ships might easily be scattered by a storm, and that the pilots would find it difficult in its darkness to recognise and follow his leading galley, he devised several judicious precautions for their guidance. His own and two other chief galleys were distinguished during the day by red streaks on the sails, and at night by lamps from the stern; and the moment of departure from a harbour was clearly announced to the most distant vessels by the signal of a trumpet. From Abydos, a fair wind wafted the fleet to Cape Malea; and the doubling of that stormy headland, which the multitude of the ships might have rendered dangerous, was accomplished during a fortunate calm.

On reaching Methone, now called Modon, in the Peloponnesus, the general found Martin and Valerian awaiting his arrival, and allowed a few days of repose to his soldiers, whom the unwonted fatigue of a voyage had already exhausted. They were here exposed to a peril which they had never contemplated, from the unfeeling avarice of John of Cappadocia, who, as minister of the finances, had furnished at Constantinople the provisions of the fleet. It was usual to harden the bread intended for naval or military expeditions, by a two-fold preparation in the oven;[28] a practice which continued till a recent period,

---

Visigoths, Franks, &c. According to the Salic law, a Frank who killed a Frank paid "*deux cent sous*," only one hundred when he killed a Roman proprietor, and only forty-five when a Roman vassal. (*Esprit des Loix*, lib. xxviii. c. 3.) This fine was independent of the *fredum* to the Lord of the soil, which usually amounted to one-third of the former. (*lib. xxx.* c. 20.)

28. For an account of this bread or biscuit, see Pliny (*Hist. Nat. lib.* xxii. c. 25,) where he calls it *nauticus panis*. Of the *panis militaria*, he says that it was heavier by one-third than the grain from which it was made. (*lib. xviii.* c. 7.)

and of which the word biscuit in its derivation still exhibits the trace. On account of the loss of weight which the bread must undergo from this process, a deduction of one-fourth was allowed amongst the Romans; and with the view of retaining for his private profit not merely this stipulated portion, but also the fuel which the treasury defrayed, John had given orders that the bread might only be slightly baked at the fires of the public baths.

No consideration for the health or life of the soldiers appears to have disturbed his projects of emolument; and he probably trusted to the politic silence of the general for concealing, or to his own influence with the emperor for overcoming, any complaints that might arise. When the sacks of bread were opened at Methone, their contents had sunk into a mouldering and offensive paste; so that greater evils could hardly have resulted from a scarcity of provisions, than their abundance now brought on. The sultriness of summer conspired with this unwholesome food: five hundred soldiers were swept away by a rapid disease; and its ravages might have extended still further, had not the activity of Belisarius procured a supply of fresh bread at Methone. Undismayed by the expected enmity of a powerful and vindictive minister, he made known to Justinian the whole of this shameless fraud; but though the emperor was sufficiently candid to praise the honest zeal of his general, he wanted firmness to punish the rapine of his favourite.

From Methone, the pilots, before undertaking to cross the Adriatic, thought it prudent to shorten the distance, by steering to the island of Zante, from whence they proceeded on what, in those days, might appear a difficult and dangerous voyage. Another calm (it was now midsummer) delayed the ships for sixteen days, in their passage between Zante and Sicily; and amongst the chief hardships of this tedious navigation, was the tainting effect of the heat on the casks of fresh water. Antonina alone, who had placed glass bottles in a deep recess of the hold, and covered them thickly with sand, still preserved a pure beverage for the table of her husband, and of his principal officers.

We may applaud the skill of Antonina in contriving, rather than the readiness of Belisarius in accepting this supply; since nothing tends more strongly to the encouragement of an army or to the glory of its leader, than to see him in trying circumstances share the privations as well as the perils of his soldiers. The conduct of Belisarius on this occasion might be disadvantageously contrasted with that of Cato and Charles the Twelfth, or with the heroic forbearance of our own great countryman, Sir Philip Sydney.[29]

The Roman Army landed in Sicily, on one of the rocky ridges of lava, extending from the base of Mount Etna to the sea. This spot was desolate and barren as it still remains, and seemed little in accordance with the proverbial fruitfulness of the island. At this station Belisarius determined to avail himself of a compact lately formed with Queen Amalasontha, Regent of the Gothic kingdom, who was desirous of maintaining and strengthening her alliance with the Byzantine empire, by every good office in her power, and had accordingly agreed to permit a free purchase of provisions and horses in Sicily to the armament of Belisarius.[30] Little did she then foresee how shortly the same forces commanded by the same general, would direct against her own countrymen a confidence augmented, and a valour disciplined by the very successes in Africa to which she thus imprudently contributed! To claim these promised supplies, but above all to obtain authentic tidings for the determination of his farther plans, Belisarius now dispatched his secretary on a mission to Syracuse. He was justly alarmed at the apprehensions of his soldiers, whom he had overheard, on the voyage, avowing to each other, that on land, indeed, they would encounter the enemy with boldness, but that if assailed by sea, they must betake themselves to flight, as unable to contend at once with the Vandals and the waves.

The doubts of the general as to the fittest place for landing in Africa, his uncertainty as to the designs of the barbarians, and the chance of their having prepared some hidden ambush to surprise his force in this island, combined with the naval terrors of his army to embarrass and disturb him. It was therefore his order, that Procopius should collect information on these points, and rejoin him as speedily as possible at Catania, a few miles below his actual station. See note following). The future historian accordingly embarked, and on his arrival at Syracuse, had the good fortune of finding in a merchant of the city, one of oldest and most trusty friends, A servant of this tradesman had returned but three days before from Carthage, and in answer to the inquiries of Procopius, assured him of the careless and confident

---

29. Lucan relates (*Pharsal. ix.* 500,) how Cato, during a sultry march in Africa, reproved a soldier for bringing him a helmet full of water, and dashed it to the ground. For the conduct of the Swedish monarch, on his progress to Pultowa, see Voltaire. (*Hist. lib.* 4.) The anecdote of Sir Philip Sydney, after the Battle of Zutphen, is, as it deserves, too well known to need a reference.

30. The provisions appear from Procopius (*Vandal. lib. i.* c. 14,) and the horses from another passage. (*Goth. lib. i.* c. 3.)

security of the Vandals.

******

Note:—The text of Procopius in this place, mentions Caucana a harbour on the southern coast of Sicily, and he is followed by all the modern writers. But the names in his history are so frequently corrupted by copyists, or editors, that very little dependence can be placed upon them. I am convinced, that in this place the real reading is not Caucana, but Catana, the ancient name of Catania. In the first place, Procopius states, that the spot is distant from Syracuse two hundred *stadia*, or less than thirty miles, which agrees very nearly with the distance from Catania to the ancient outer wall of Tyche, it being little more than thirty-one miles though the modern road is about seven longer from its making a circuit through Lentini.

Now Caucana is at least three hundred and fifty or four hundred *stadia* from Syracuse (*Cluver. Sicil. Antiq.* ap. Gibbon), and even further if I may venture to allege my own local knowledge, and Procopius having travelled the distance could not possibly be so much mistaken. Secondly, it is to be remembered, that Belisarius was fearful of some ambush or surprise in Sicily from the Vandals, and it was partly to clear up this fact that Procopius was sent to Syracuse. Now if Belisarius had, in the meanwhile, sailed along the eastern and southern coasts to Caucana, he would have been exposing himself to the very danger he apprehended, before he had ascertained whether or not it really existed. Thirdly, if Belisarius had any idea of proceeding to Malta, as he afterwards actually did, he must have foreseen that by his voyage to Caucana he made an unnecessary circuit.

******

Far from having planned any sudden attack upon the Roman armament in Sicily, Gelimer did not as yet expect its approach, and had in the meantime indulged his vengeance against Godas for the revolt of Sardinia, by dispatching to that island his brother Zazo, at the head of five thousand of his bravest soldiers. Unsuspicious of the coming storm, and by no means ready withstand it, he had left Carthage to spend the summer at the inland city of Hermione. On hearing these welcome tidings, Procopius wished to confirm them to his patron by the same authentic testimony from which he himself had received them, and hurrying the domestic along to his bark which was moored near the fountain of Arethusa,[31] and scarcely taking time to explain to the astonished merchant die motive of this arbitrary seizure, he forthwith steered again towards Catania.

No sooner had Belisarius been informed of the absence of Gelimer from Carthage, than he resolved to turn it to his purpose, and availed himself of an eastern breeze which wafted his fleet to Malta, and from thence to the African coasty three months after his departure from Constantinople. The ships drew near the shore at Caput Vada, whose name has been corrupted to Capoudia in modern times. It consists of a level and narrow strip of land jutting out very far into the sea, and was chosen in the latter years of Justinian for the foundation of a city, some remains of which are still to be discerned.[32] Its distance from Carthage does not exceed one hundred and fifty miles. Here a council of war was convened by Belisarius, to determine the question of landing; and Procopius, who was undoubtedly present, has recorded the principal speeches then delivered. The stake seemed full of hazard, the Vandals, it is true, were scattered and unprepared, but they had the advantage of a known and subject country and the forces which they could bring into the field exceeded in a five-fold proportion the numbers of the Roman Army. The Patrician Archelaus, who had filled important offices, both in Illyria and at Constantinople, and was now, as treasurer, second in command, thus opened the discussion.

> I cannot, my brother officers, but admire the moderation of the general, who surpassing us all so greatly both in talent and experience, and invested with unlimited power, yet refers to our common deliberations what his single wisdom might determine, and his supreme authority command. How comes it then, that you do not eagerly avail yourselves of his generous permission to dissuade him from the perilous project of disembarking at this place? It is true, that the office of adviser, in times of difficulty, is barren and unprofitable, since men too commonly attribute their success to the judgment they exerted, and their failures, only to the counsel they received.

---

31. This classic fountain has retained its ancient name, and with the exception of the fishes, seemed to me, in 1825, still to correspond exactly with Cicero's description. (*In Verr. iv.* c. 53) It is remarkable, that in the middle ages the ancient fable of the Alpheus survived at Syracuse, in the altered shape of a pious legend. It was asserted that the fountain had a submarine and miraculous communication with the River Jordan. See Marifiotti, (ap. Wilkinson's *Magna Greacia*.)

32. Procup. *De .Ædif. lib.* vi. c. 6. Shaw's *Travels* ed. 1738.

Yet this selfish consideration shall not check my zeal, at a juncture so momentous as the present. Tell me, chieftains—tell me, if you desire to land, by what harbour can you shelter your fleet, by what fortress your soldiers? Are you not aware that the coast, for nine days journey from Carthage, hardly affords a single harbour, and is open to every gale,[33] while on the other hand, Genseric has stripped every African city of its walls? If any disaster should befall us, to which from our human condition, and the uncertainty of fortune, we must naturally be exposed, on what resources could we then rely? Should a storm arise the fleet must either be driven to a distance, or dashed to pieces on the shore.

What distress meanwhile may we not undergo by land, from the want of provisions, or of fresh water, with which this region is said to be so scantily supplied! In such trying circumstances, let no one look to me as to the purveyor for assistance, since a public officer, when bereaved of all means for the fulfilment of his duties, becomes again levelled and degraded to the common rank. Where could I place in safety your magazines of arms and equipments, or where could you find refuge from the pursuing barbarians? But let me rather turn my thoughts from such ill-omened forebodings. I propose that we should sail directly towards Carthage, at the distance of only six miles from which there is a spacious haven, unguarded by the Vandals, and well adapted for the reception of so large a fleet as ours.[34] From this convenient station we could assault the capital, and as surely as the loss of the head is followed by the downfall of the limbs, so Carthage in all likelihood would yield to our very first onset, while thus forsaken by its sovereign. Consider fully these projects, I entreat you, and adopt the one which you may deem the wisest and the best.

---

33. The want of harbours on this coast, was one of the chief objections urged by Fabius against the proposed expedition of Scipio. (*Liv. lib. xxx.* c. 42.)

34. It will be seen from this circumstantial detail of the proposal of Archelaus, that Gibbon (vol. vii.) is wrong in representing it as a scheme to sail at once into the port of Carthage. The place meant by Archelaus is the present lake of Tunis, See Polybius, lib. i. c. 73, We learn from Dr. Shaw, that this ancient harbour has now become little more than a morass, with only six or seven feet of water in the deepest parts, being almost choked up by receiving the common sewers of Tunis. (Travels in Barbary). Dr. Shaw then proceeds to extol the size and sweetness of its mullets.

Several other officers having likewise spoken, Belisarius replied to them as follows:

My comrades, I trust that you will not, on this occasion, look upon my words as those of a master, nor fancy that I have delayed them to the last in order to close the discussion and compel your acquiescence. I have now heard your opinions, I will unfold my own, and then submit it with the others to our common judgment. In the first place, it seems to me important to remember how lately the soldiers expressed before us their terrors of a naval battle, and their intention, should they be encountered by the hostile fleet, of seeking security in flight. All our thoughts, all our prayers at that time were limited to the single wish of finding a safe and unmolested opportunity to land in Africa, and now that God has vouchsafed to us the fulfilment of this anxious wish, would it be wise to neglect and spurn the very favour which before it was bestowed we so eagerly desired to obtain?

Should we, as it has been proposed, sail at once towards Carthage, the fleet of the Vandals might meet ns on our way, and we then could not justly complain of the cowardly reluctance of our soldiers, since their formal avowal should have taught us to beware. Even the success which, notwithstanding their want of spirit, might by accident be gained, could not clear us from the disgrace of having unnecessarily exposed them to the dangers of their own timidity. Amongst all the arguments that should urge us to disembark, none appears to me stronger than the one employed to dissuade us, I mean the possibility of storms, by which, as it has been truly stated, our fleet must be either scattered or destroyed.

Which then is best, that our ships should perish alone, or that our army also should be submerged with them? Consider that by landing now, we shall find unprepared and unsuspecting enemies, and shall therefore probably defeat them, since success is always mainly promoted by surprise. On the other hand, even a short delay, such as a calm at sea might occasion, would enable the Vandals to take measures for active defence, and to collect and marshal all their forces against us. We might then, perhaps, have to fight for a landing, and seek in vain that favourable opportunity which we now possess, but which its very facility induces us to undervalue.

My opinion is, therefore, that we ought to disembark forthwith. We will surround our camp with entrenchments, which in case of disaster would afford us nearly the same shelter and protection as we could have derived from the ramparts of a fortress, nor need we doubt of supplies so long as we exhibit valour. Our security from danger, and our dependence for food, are both equally placed in our own right hands.

These arguments prevailed in the council, the troops were landed that very day, (September, *a.d.* 533), and a suitable position having been chosen by the general, the fortification of the camp was begun with alacrity. Great distress was felt for want of water, but in the digging of the ditch and rampart the discovery of a plentiful spring served both to quench the thirst of the soldiers, and to cheer them by its favourable augury.[35] According to the superstitious tendency of this age, or perhaps of human nature, they appear to have prized the omen still more than the relief. In each ship Belisarius left a guard of five soldiers, and appointed the galleys to the outward of the fleet, so as to shield it against any unforeseen attack.

Meanwhile some private soldiers, exulting in their deliverance from shipboard, had wandered from the camp to gather fruits from the neighbouring fields, and the general, as at Abydos, seized the opportunity of enforcing military discipline. The marauders were severely scourged, and Belisarius in a public harangue, besought his soldiers to be warned by this example. He pointed out to them the importance of soothing and conciliating the native Africans, and of detaching them from the Vandal cause, to which from religious differences they were already disaffected. He urged that rapine would raise up as enemies against them, not merely the Africans and Vandals, but even God himself, since none who disobey his precepts can venture to expect his protection, while on the other hand justice and forbearance would render the Deity propitious, the Africans friendly, and the Vandals forsaken.

The Roman general now commenced his march upon Carthage. He sent a detachment before him to seize the town of Sullecte, at one day's journey from the camp; and, in pursuance of his orders these soldiers silently entered the place (it was unwalled) before daybreak, without any resistance from the sleeping inhabitants. A meeting was

---

35. Compare Procopius *Vandal lib. i.* c. 15. *De Ædif. lib. vi.* c. 6.

then convened, of the bishop and principal citizens, who, wisely professing to do from inclination what necessity compelled, dispatched to Belisarius the keys oft town which his troops already occupied. All the horses of the public posts were likewise placed at his disposal, and one of the royal messengers was intercepted, whom his liberality induced to convey several copies of a circular letter from Justinian to the local authorities in Africa. In this document, which Procopius has preserved, it is remarkable that the emperor puts forth no claim of hereditary right, nor views of personal ambition, and represents his armament as undertaken solely with the object of checking usurpation and restoring the lawful king. He expresses his desire for the peace and happiness of the Vandals, and devoutly calls God to witness for the sincerity of his intentions.

From Sullecte, the Roman general advanced along the shore, through Leptis and Adrumetum, proceeding at the rate of about twelve miles each day, and never failing to fortify, or at least to guard, his encampments at night. During the march, he appointed to the van, three miles from the main body, a detachment of three hundred horsemen, who might apprize him of the approach of any danger, and whose command was entrusted to John, surnamed, from his country, the Armenian. A double number of Hunnish cavalry, at an equal distance, covered the left wing, and the right was protected by the sea. The rear was led by Belisarius in person, who supposed that Gelimer, hastening from the inland provinces, would probably follow and assail him in this quarter; and the result afterwards confirmed the truth of his conjecture. The fleet, by his directions, regulated its movements according to those of the troops, so as always to keep them in sight; and for this purpose the mariners, during calms or slight breezes, plied their oars to quicken their progress, while, during boisterous gales, they employed smaller sails than usual to retard it. Advancing in this manner, without meeting any opposition, the Romans arrived at Grasse, no more than fifty miles from Carthage, where they admired the country palace and delicious *paradise* [36] or garden of the Vandal kings.

Procopius declares that the latter exceeded any other he had ever seen; he extols its sparkling fountains and shady groves, and tells us that though the Roman Army plucked a plentiful supply of its various fruits, yet so great was their abundance, that the diminution thus oc-

---

36. In the middle ages the word Paradise was frequently used in its Persian sense of Garden, and sometimes signified a portico before a church. See Paul Warnefrid, *lib. v.* c. 31; and Ducange, *Gloss. Med. Lat* vol. iii.

casioned could hardly be discerned. The domain of Gelimer was freely surrendered to the troops by Belisarius; but with regard to private citizens, the strictest discipline had been established by his salutary rigour; and the moderation of his army, joined to his own courteous and friendly manners, entirely gained him the confidence and goodwill of the Africans. Far from shunning the presence of the Romans, and concealing or removing property, they crowded to the camp; they brought ample provisions for sale, and the reception they gave has been compared by a spectator to that which an army might meet with in its native country.[37]

When the intelligence of the lauding and progress of the Romans reached Gelimer at Hermione,[38] his first impulse was revenge. Orders were dispatched to his brother Ammatas, at Carthage, for the instant execution of the captive Hilderic and his chief adherents, and the effects of this barbarous decree afterwards manifested how much less it had proceeded from policy than from passion. The death of the rightful sovereign, whose claims had hitherto been the pretext rather than the motive of the war, inflamed with redoubled animosity his Vandal partisans, and freed the Roman invaders from an unwelcome and perplexing obligation. In the next harangue of Belisarius to his soldiers, we may discern his altered tone, and remark that the object of the contest is represented no longer as the maintenance of a regular succession in the reigning dynasty, but as the restoration of a former province to the empire.

Yet Gelimer, though in his first transports of rage he had commanded a crime of which the consequences so speedily recoiled upon himself, appears in the remainder of his conduct to have acted with the soundest judgment, and upheld his reputation for consummate military skill. His forces very far exceeded those of Belisarius, since the Vandals, during the century of their dominion in Africa, had increased from fifty to eighty thousand fighting men.[39] Of these imposing numbers, however, many were disaffected to Gelimer, and all unprepared for so sudden an attack; a large share was dispersed along the kingdom,

---

37. Procop. *Vandal, lib. i. c.* 17.
38. Hermione is not mentioned by D'Anville. but may be found in Ruinart (*Hist. Pers.*)
39. (*Hist. Arcan.* c. 18.) Alemanni has inadvertently translated this by one hundred and sixty thousand. Cousin, as usual, follows the Latin version; and Gibbon, by his dependence on the one or on the other, has fallen into the same serious error, (vol. vii.) In the time of Victor Vitensis (a.d. 488) the Vandal forces did not as yet amount to eighty thousand. (*De Persec lib. i.* c. l.)

from Tangier to Tripoli, and the flower of the forces was engaged in the useless conquest of Sardinia. Still Gelimer trusted, by rapidity and vigour, to counterbalance these disadvantageous circumstances, and overwhelm the scanty battalions of the enemy before they could reach his capital.

For this purpose, he formed plan with such ability, that even the Roman historian [40] owns that it only failed from the imperfect execution of his orders, and the excellent line march which Belisarius had established. As place of battle, the king fixed on Decimus, a village whose name indicates the tenth milestone from Carthage, and which lay directly on the route of Belisarius. The narrow defile of its position seemed well fitted to conceal and assist the designs of Gelimer, who hoped that the Roman Army might here be surrounded and hemmed in. He had the fore instructed Ammatas to lead forth the garrison of Carthage, and encounter the vanguard of the enemy at Decimus; while his nephew Gibamund proceeding from the same city in a different direction, was, with a chosen squadron, to attack the left wing of the invaders. On his part, collecting round Hermione an army as numerous as the urgent haste of the occasion would admit, the king followed the course of the Romans, in order to close upon and charge them in the rear, at the same time that the outposts were engaging with the other Vandal forces.

His approach from behind was unknown to the Romans till they arrived at Grasse, where some stragglers discovered the important secret; but their report did not arrest the march of Belisarius, who continued advancing towards Carthage. At Grasse, however, he was compelled to separate from his fleet, which had to double the projecting mountains of Cape Bonn, He entrusted its command to Archelaus, and from the uncertainty of the event directed him not to approach the shore within thirty miles of Carthage, unless he should receive good tidings of the army.

After a march of four days from Grasse the Romans reached the village intended for their encounter, and which might probably have been marked by their defeat had not the headlong rashness of Ammatas disconcerted the projects of his brother. He imprudently ventured forth with only a small share of his troops, (Sept. 14 a.d. 533), leaving orders for the rest to follow him as speedily as possible, and with this handful of men he attacked the Roman vanguard of three hundred cavalry. The personal valour he displayed was great but unavailing, and

---

40. Procop. *Vandal.lib. i.* c. 18

after the death, it is said, of twelve antagonists by his single prowess he himself was numbered with the slain. The soldiers, who had been cheered by the courage, were disheartened by the fall of their gallant leader, and retreating in confusion from the field carried along in their flight the scattered reinforcements from Carthage, which were advancing at intervals to join them.

They were pursued by John the Armenian to the very gates of Carthage, and their great loss in dead and wounded seemed strangely disproportioned to the numbers of the combatants. Meanwhile the attack of Gibamund on the left was equally ill-timed and equally unsuccessful. His troops exceeded two thousand men; the Roman wing consisted of only six hundred Hunnish confederate, but these were amongst the best of the imperial army, and their leader, with chivalrous daring; claimed the hereditary privilege of beginning the conflict by a personal encounter. On this occasion, the courage of the North prevailed, as usual over Southern degeneracy. The Vandals were put to flight, and the desolate plain in which they had fought (it was called the Field of Salt) became thickly strewed with their slain.

These two skirmishes, however successful, could only be considered as slight preludes to a battle, since but a small number of the Vandals, and less than one thousand Romans had engaged in them. The rugged hills which interposed shut them from the sight of Belisarius, who was still with the main forces in the rear, about five miles from Decimus. Yet before any tidings had reached him he had discovered the intention of the Vandals to assail him, and under these circumstances adopted a decisive measure. He determined to anticipate their project of surprise, and to retort it upon them, by sallying forth at the head of his horsemen, leaving his infantry and baggage in his camp. Previously, however, he strengthened the retrenchments of the soldiers whom he designed to quit, and aroused the spirit of the others by a public address. He reminded them of their Persian campaigns, he urged them to re-conquer an ancient province of the empire, and derived some advantage even from the want of any fortress in his rear, by showing them how entirely they must depend on their own courage for security.

On issuing from the camp, Belisarius again subdivided his forces, sending the confederates in front and following with the Roman cavalry, and especially his guards. The confederates soon reached the field where Ammatas had fallen, only one or two hours before, and they obtained from the neighbouring peasantry the first news of the recent skirmish. While still engaged in contemplating the bloody relics of the fight a cloud of dust suddenly appeared to the southward, which by degrees disclosed to their anxious gaze a large body of horse, the van of Gelimer's army. The number and intricacy of the hills had misled him in his march, and hidden from his view both the encampment and the sally of the Roman general. Messengers were instantly dispatched from the confederates to Belisarius, informing him of the presence of the enemy and entreating speedy succour. In the mean time their officers, computing the formidable forces which approached, were divided in opinion, some extolling the honour of a brave resistance, and others of a regular retreat, whilst the delay of this discussion alike precluded either.

Yet a trial of speed was attempted by the Romans in rushing to take possession of the highest adjacent hill before the troops of Gelimer could reach it; but disappointed in this enterprise, and already wavering, a single charge from the Vandals was sufficient to disperse them. They hastily fled to meet the squadron of Belisarius, and had Gelimer at this decisive instant either closely pursued them, or fallen unexpectedly on the Roman outposts, which after the defeat of Ammatas had tumultuously followed to the gates of Carthage, it is admitted by his adversaries that he would yet have retrieved the fortune of the day. But on beholding the lifeless body of his brother, the first and only announcement of his death, Gelimer gave way to fraternal fondness, and indulged it by an unseasonable performance of sepulchral rites.

He thus lost an opportunity which he was destined never to regain. These precious moments were actively employed by Belisarius in advancing with his guards, and collecting the scattered or rallying the fugitive soldiers, and with all these forces united he charged the army of the African monarch. The general battle which ensued was not long contested, the Vandals were totally defeated, and night alone put a period to the slaughter. Gelimer fled from the field with a few faithful surviving adherents, and being aware that the ruinous walls of Carthage were incapable of sustaining a siege, he unwillingly averted his course from his capital, and turned towards the deserts of Numidia.

On the same evening, the Roman general was rejoined by the two detachments victorious over Gibamund and Ammatas, and on the ensuing day by the infantry and baggage from the camp. The Battle of Decimus, however complicated in its plan, and disorderly in its operations, was decisive of the fate of Carthage. All idea of resistance was abandoned. The gates were thrown open, and the chains across the entrance of the port removed. The Vandals in the city sought the sanctuary of churches, while the loyal Africans testified their joy by the blaze of innumerable lights. It was the eve of St. Cyprian's festival, which was celebrated each year with extraordinary splendour, and this coincidence was considered by the exulting Catholics as evidently showing his approval of their doctrines. Several dreams were remembered, in which during their persecutions he had assured them of speedy rescue and revenge, and the miraculous fulfilment of this promise was loudly asserted.[41]

Every preparation had been made for solemnising his anniversary in a stately church upon the shore dedicated to his worship, but at the tidings of the Battle of Decimus the Arian priests escaped, and the Catholics joyfully taking their place substituted their own ritual to that of their vanquished antagonists.[42] Yet Belisarius, in spite of the favourable disposition thus manifested towards him, resolved not to enter the city that evening, partly from a suspicion of Vandal stratagem, but principally from a well-founded apprehension lest the convenient darkness of night should tempt his soldiers to pillage and disorder. Whilst thus encamped near the walls of the city he was gladdened by the arrival of his fleet.

The naval officers had received intelligence at the town of Hermaeum of the good fortune which had attended the arms of their general, and a north-east wind opportunely springing up enabled them within a few hours to anchor safely in the lake of Tunis. They had determined not to steer at once into the harbour of the capital, from a doubt not only whether the iron chains which guarded its entrance had been yet removed, but also whether it was sufficiently ample for the reception of so large an armament. Yet the ships could be discerned from Carthage, and the jailor of some imprisoned merchants of Constantinople, foreseeing the approaching liberation of his captives, first exacted from their ignorance of the late events a solemn oath of protection in reward for their freedom, and then throwing

---

41. A prophecy, according to Procopius, was also remembered as formerly current, and as then accomplished. It imported that G. should expel B., and afterwards B. expel G. This was applied to Genseric and Boniface, and to Belisarius and Gelimer.
42. The Arians, says Procopius (*Vandal. lib. i. c.* 21), had prepared the sacred candles, but the Catholics lighted them. We may gather from thence that this rite of the Roman Catholic Church was then already in common use. Mosheim complains of the "enormous burthen of ceremonies" in this century. (*Eccles. Hist.* vol. ii.).

open the casement of the dungeon displayed to them the advancing galleys of the Romans in full sail.[43]

Belisarius now commanded the greater part of the sailors to disembark and join his troops, resolving at the head of these seemingly formidable numbers to make a solemn entry into Carthage on the morrow, St. Cyprian's day, which, by a reference to the Roman Catholic calendar, I find to be the sixteenth of September.[44] His soldiers were adorned as for a triumph, to add to the splendour of the scene, and armed as for a battle, to guard against surprise. Anxious to uphold their discipline, he recapitulated to them the advantages which they had already drawn from it in Africa, and stated that its necessity was still more urgent at Carthage than elsewhere. He desired them to recollect that the Africans had formerly been, like them, subjects and citizens of Rome, and that their allegiance was transferred to the Vandals, not through any voluntary rebellion, but through a foreign conquest, fix)m which none had suffered so severely as themselves.

It was, added Belisarius, the knowledge of these sufferings which impelled the emperor to send forth this expedition, and it would be as absurd as criminal for the Roman soldiers to treat with outrage or oppression the very people for whose deliverance they were dispatched. These remonstrances, enforced by the memory of the rigorous examples which the general had lately made, produced in entering the African capital a degree of order and of discipline, wholly new in that degenerate age, and to which even the Roman Republic could hardly afford a parallel. The soldiers marched peaceably to the quarters which had been assigned them, all the shops continued open, and, in spite of the change of sovereign, public business was not for one moment interrupted.

The suppliant Vandals in the churches were assured of protection and security. Not a single instance of tumult or rapacity occurred, with the exception of a captain of the fleet, who, on the foregoing night, had, contrary to the injunctions of Belisarius and to the example of his colleagues, steered into the harbour of Carthage, and plundered some

---

43. This anecdote might form the subject of a very striking picture, and would probably have been long ago selected for that purpose had it occurred in a more classic age.

44. It may be observed that this day is considered by the modern Africans as the autumnal equinox. See Leo *Africanus* (*lib. i.* ed. 1556). This St Cyprian, of Carthage, must not be confounded with another of the same name, whose festival is celebrated on the twenty-sixth of the same month, and who, from a Pagan magician, became a martyr under Diocletian. See his curious adventures in Blemur (*Vies des Saints*, vol iii.).

of its inhabitants. He was sternly commanded to restore the spoil, and this was the first public act of Belisarius on proceeding to the royal palace, and seating himself upon the throne of Gelimer.

In the evening a sumptuous banquet was served to himself and to his principal officers, in the same apartment, and with the same household attendants so lately employed by the Vandal monarch; and in admiring on this occasion the strange vicissitudes of fortune the grateful Carthaginians must have acknowledged, that while Belisarius almost rivalled Scipio the Younger in the glory of his conquest, he far surpassed him in clemency and consideration to the vanquished.

After the few first hours of his arrival, Belisarius, with his usual activity, applied himself to repair the ruinous fortifications of the city. The ditch was deepened, the breaches were filled, and the ramparts strengthened, and the number of workmen combined with the largess of the general to hasten the completion of the work. It was finished in so short a time as to strike the Vandals with astonishment, and to make Gelimer himself confess that his own previous negligence had been the real cause of his disasters. Envoys from many tributary Moorish chieftains soon arrived at Carthage, disclaiming all allegiance to Gelimer, and as a mark of their submission to the authority of Belisarius, requesting him to bestow upon them the ensigns of their dignity.[45] It was an ancient custom, founded on the former majesty of the Romans, that no Moorish prince, even if disaffected to them, ventured to assume the title till he had received from the emperor the trappings of sovereign power.

Belisarius gladly yielded to their welcome entreaties, and added large presents in money, to attach them more strongly to his interest. Yet these Moors, still doubtful of the final issue of the war, did not proceed further in his favour than by observing a strict neutrality, and, according to a common course of policy, deferred any offer of assistance till the victories of either party should render it superfluous. At this time, also, the rapidity with which Belisarius had succeeded in subduing Carthage, betrayed into his power several of its citizens returning homewards, and wholly unsuspicious of this sudden change of masters. Before the landing of the Roman army, Ge-

---

45. These ensigns consisted of a sceptre of gilt silver, a small silver cap with some resemblance to a crown, a white cloak fastened by a gold clasp over the right shoulder, a white tunic adorned with embroidery, and gilt sandals (Procopius *Vandal. lib. i.* c. 25,) Compare these with the ensigns of the Lasic kings in Agathias, lib. iii. and John Malala, vol. ii.

limer had dispatched an embassy to Theudes, King of the Visigoths, in Spain,[46] proposing an alliance which might then have been contracted on equal terms. But some merchants who had quitted Carthage at a later period, and travelled with unusual expedition, secretly conveyed to Theudes the important intelligence that they had left that city in possession of the Romans.

It will be readily believed that Theudes, after these tidings, showed but little inclination to attach himself to a state already almost overthrown; and, in answer to the solicitations of the envoys, he merely desired them to sail back to Africa, and learn the real state of their affairs. The disappointed Vandals accordingly embarked for Carthage, entered in full security the port of their ancient capital, and, to their inexpressible surprise, found themselves, on landing, captives of the Romans. A similar incident occurred in the arrest of a messenger dispatched to Carthage by Zazo, to inform his brother of his proceedings in Sardinia. He had defeated and killed the rebel Godas; he had taken Calaris or Cagliari, his capital, and his letters expressed a confident expectation that the Roman Army, of whose invasion he had just been apprised, had already undergone a similar fate from the victorious arms of Gelimer.[47]

During this time the Vandal monarch was assembling a fresh army in the plains of Bulla, near the confines of Numidia, and at the distance of four days' journey from Carthage. Desirous of raising the African peasantry against the invaders, he set a price on the head of every Byzantine soldier; but this ferocious and desperate offer merely occasioned the death of socio scattered stragglers and marauders, and therefore supplied the Romans with further grounds for persevering in their newly-acquired discipline. Thus, as in the murder of Hilderic, the cruelty of the tyrant proved advantageous to his enemies, and hurtful chiefly to himself. It was with greater judgment that he dispatched a messenger to Zazo in Sardinia, commanding his immediate return. Gelimer wrote:

> It would seem as if your expedition had tended less to the conquest of Sardinia than to our overthrow in Africa. The Vandals have lost their courage, and with their courage their prosperity; our magazines, our arms, our horses, nay, even our capital itself,

---

46. For the reign and character of Theudes see Mariana (*Hist. Hisp. lib. v.* c. 8).
47. By a strange oversight, Gibbon talks of Gelimer reading and answering this letter, as if it had not been intercepted (vol. vii).

all are in possession of the Romans! Nothing now is left us but the field of Bulla and the hope which your valour still inspires. Resign, then, all thoughts of Sardinia, and join me, where, with united forces, we may either restore our empire, or at least not be separated in adversity.

The receipt of this letter filled Zazo and his officers with consternation, but showed them the necessity of instant exertion. Concealing this event from the people of Sardinia, in order not to shake their recent and suspicious fidelity, Zazo hastily embarked with his troops at Cagliari, and in three days reached the African coast at the limits between Mauritania and Numidia, from whence by forced marches he proceeded to the camp of Gelimer. The first meeting of these armies such, says the historian,[48] as might have raised compassion even of an enemy. The two brothers clung to each other in a long and mute embrace, tears alone declared the feelings which they wanted fortitude to speak. Similar silence pervaded both armies. The troops of Gelimer asked no details of a conquest of which they felt the inutility, those of Zazo required nothing beyond the scene before them to show the full extent of their misfortunes; and the absence of their wives and children too clearly announced their captivity or death.

Yet these mournful feelings soon yielded to the hopes of victory and vengeance. The Vandals had obeyed the summons of Gelimer, several Moorish tribes had gathered round his banners, and his forces, when augmented by those of Zazo, exceeded one hundred thousand men.[49] But the result of the last battle had shown Gelimer that with Belisarius for an enemy, he could not trust implicitly to numbers. He therefore had recourse to the additional aid of treachery, by working upon the Arians and Vandals at Carthage, and tempting the fidelity of the Hunnish confederates in the Roman Army. These barbarians lamented their distance from their homes, whence they had been allured to assist an enterprise foreign and indifferent to them, and of which they avowed that they dreaded the success far more than the failure, since they might afterwards be detained for many years in Africa, to guard the country they had conquered. They therefore lent

---

48. Procop. *Vandal, lib. i. c.* 26.
49. Gelimer himself boasted that his army outnumbered the Romans in a tenfold proportion; but this statement should of course be received with some latitude. Now the army of Belisarius, deducting on the one hand his loss in the Battle of Decimus and at Methone, and adding on the other the soldiers whom he had left in his ships, but who were now again at his disposal, must have been at least 13,000 men.

a ready ear to the secret offers of Gelimer, and promised, in the approaching battle, to join his forces and turn their arms against their Roman comrades.

But these designs could not escape the vigilant attention of the general. To provide against any treachery in the Carthaginians, he determined not to march with his troops from their city till its fortifications were completed; while on the other hand he terrified and checked the Arian conspirators by the dreadful severity of impaling[50] one of their number, named Laurus, on a hill before the gates. The necessity of punishing citizens whose only crime is attachment to their lawful sovereign and to their national religion, and whose example every brave man would wish his own countrymen to imitate, is one of the most painful obligations imposed by war. With the Huns Belisarius pursued an opposite course, being well aware that rigour will restore and maintain the discipline, but not the loyalty of soldiers. By frequent gifts and unvaried kindness, by the ascendant which a strong mind always possesses over the ordinary race of men, he induced them to avow their perfidious designs, he forgave, in order that they might never accomplish their guilty and he promised them a speedy return to their native country, and a full participation in the booty of the Romans.

Having thus in some degree secured their wavering allegiance, and repaired the ramparts of Carthage, Belisarius resolved to march against Gelimer, without further delay. He said to his soldiers:

> Let no one dishearten you by an overcharged and fearful computation of the Vandal forces; Romans should disdain to count their antagonists. We have now still greater interests at stake than in the former battle, Carthage and Africa are already ours, and to lose possessions is far more intolerable than to fail in conquest.

Thus, in three months from the taking of Carthage, Belisarius led forth his army from its walls, leaving only five hundred men for its garrison. He could place but little reliance on the fidelity of the Huns, who had, indeed, been persuaded to give up their first project of desertion, but who had privately determined to keep aloof from battle,

---

50. This cruel punishment was not uncommon in this age, and appears to have been borrowed from the barbarian tribes. I find it practised by the Sclavonians, (Procop. *Goth. lib. iii. c.* 38); by the Franks (Greg. *Turon. lib.* v. c. 40); by the Lombards, (Paul Warnefrid, *lib. iv.* c. 38); and by the Huns, (*Prisc. Excerpt. Legat.*)

and afterwards side with the victorious. The command of some chosen cavalry was entrusted by Belisarius to John the Armenian, who was directed to avail himself of any favourable opportunity for skirmishes. During the first night of their encampment, the soldiers beheld with consternation some flashes of fire play around their lances. They looked on this phenomenon as a sure omen of defeat; but the result of the campaign altered their opinion of the presage, and, some years afterwards, they hailed its reappearance in Italy with transport.

On the other part, the Vandals, headed by Gelimer and Zazo, had advanced within twenty miles of the capital, and were encamped at the village of Tricamaron, from which the ensuing battle has derived its name. Their neighbourhood to Carthage had been felt by the cessation of all intercourse with the provinces, and by the cutting of the aqueduct [51] which supplied that city with water; but Gelimer carefully prevented all pillage or devastation of the open country, partly from the politic dread of provoking the inhabitants, and partly from the natural wish to spare a country which he still considered as his own. As soon as the Romans had sallied forth from Carthage, he began his dispositions for battle. He confined to his camp all the women and children who had followed in the train of his army, and addressed his soldiers in public, according to the custom of this age. While he bid his followers recollect the danger of their families and the glory of Genseric, the troops from Sardinia were exhorted by his brother Zazo, to renew their late achievements, and outvie their comrades in valour.

The king then marched against the Romans, (Dec. 16 *a.d.* 533), whom he found preparing for their mid-day meal, but who, by the diligence of Belisarius, were quickly marshalled along the banks of a small and nameless rivulet, a confluent, as it would seem, of the Mejerda.[52] On the left were placed the confederates, on the right the cavalry, the guards of Belisarius occupied the front of the centre, while the infantry was drawn out in the rear. The Huns, according to their previous resolution, maintained a separate station, awaiting the event, and ready to declare against the vanquished. The centre of the Vandals

---

51. The beauty of this aqueduct is praised by Procopius, but not, I think, by any other ancient writer. It is now almost the only remaining relic of Carthage. Several of its arches are still entire, and attract the admiration of Europeans. See Shaw's *Travels*; and Lady Mary Montague's *Delightful Letters from the East* (vol. ii. ed. 1820.)

52. The Mejerda is the ancient Bagradas, on whose banks was killed the extraordinary serpent which is said to have delayed the march of Regulus. (Plin. *Hist. Nat. lib. viii.* c. 14.) See an account of this river in Marmol, (vol. i. ed. 1667,) and Shaw, "It is," said this learned Oxonian, "of the bigness of the Isis, united to the Cherwell."

was commanded by Zazo, and each wing by *chiliarchs*; behind these stood the Moorish auxiliaries; and Gelimer, without confining himself to one particular post, could rush towards any quarter of the field which required hit presence.

The plan of Belisarius was to direct all his endeavours against the Vandal centre, since, if this could once be pierced, the wings would be disunited, and taken in the flank. Accordingly the battle began by a charge from some squadrons of the general's guards, commanded by John the Armenian. He was repulsed by the barbarians, to whom the king had enjoined to cast away their spears and javelins in close combat, and employ their swords alone.

A second onsets though with more numerous forces, proved equally unsuccessful; but, in the third, all the guards passed the rivulet with loud shouts, and the standard of Belisarius was unfurled. After an obstinate resistance the enemy's ranks were broken, Zazo himself was slain, and the consternation at his death, together with the advance of the Roman infantry, completed the rout of the Vandals. The wings, which might have closed around the scanty numbers of the assailants, and retrieved the fortune of the centre, followed its example, and the Huns, now no longer doubtful, turned against them. The Vandals fled to their camp with such headlong speed that their loss amounted only to eight hundred men, and that of the Romans is said not to have exceeded fifty.

But Belisarius unsatisfied with their flight, determined to render their defeat decisive, and marched with all his forces to storm their last retreat. They might still, by their numbers, have hoped to overwhelm the victorious valour of the Romans, had not Gelimer, in a sudden panic, (cowardice is often attendant on cruelty,) betaken himself to that flight from which he had dissuaded his army.[53] His absence was soon perceived, and his conduct imitated. The Vandals abandoned all thoughts but those of personal safety, and dispersed on every side at the first onset of their enemies.[54] Even the approach of night could not shield them from pursuit and slaughter, and their camp, with their goods and families, fell into the hands of the Romans.

As the first prize of victory, Belisarius seized for his sovereign the

---

53. Aimoin asserts that only twelve Vandal soldiers escaped with Gelimer, but this ignorant monk is undeserving of the slightest credit. His whole account of this war is a series of ludicrous blunders. (*De Gest. Franc, lib. ii.* c. 6.) Elsewhere he makes Theodora and Antonina sisters, of the tribe of Amazons, &c.

54. This scene is described with spirit by Procopius, (*Vandal. lib. ii.* c. 3.)

royal treasure, more ample, according to Procopius, than any which had ever been amassed before; nor will this appear unlikely, if indeed it contained, as he tells us, a large share of the hoarded tribute of Africa for one hundred years, and all the piratical spoils of Genseric. Yet the prudent general viewed with regret the vast amount of private booty, which engrossed the attention and suspended the discipline of his army. No commands of their officers, no thoughts even of their own security, could withhold the licentious soldiers, when they beheld the beauty of the women and the richness of the spoil, and they found the nocturnal darkness equally favourable to their designs of pleasure or of pillage. Had but a single squadron of the Vandals kept to its ranks, it might have changed the fate of Africa by falling unexpectedly on these careless freebooters; and Belisarius, after a vain attempt at restoring discipline, passed the night of his victory with all the anxiety and alarm of a defeat.

At daybreak next morning, the general climbed a conspicuous hill, reassembled his scattered guards, and restrained, by merited upbraidings, those base spirits who wished to secure their booty by bearing it away from the scene of active service. He dispatched John the Armenian with two hundred horsemen in pursuit of Gelimer, and transmitted to safe custody at Carthage the Vandal treasures and captives. He took care, however, that these last should be previously disarmed, and sent off in small and separate detachments, lest any sudden act of violence should arise from their united and superior numbers. Traversing the adjacent country, he assured of protection the Vandals who had sought sanctuary in churches, (none were to be seen elsewhere,) and he rallied from all sides the returning soldiers to his standard. When, after some unavoidable delay, the Byzantine Army had been restored to order, it was led by Belisarius with forced marches, to extinguish the last hopes, and, if possible, to seize the person of the Vandal monarch.

John the Armenian had continued in his pursuit during five days, and was on the point of overtaking him, when he himself was slain by a random blow from one of his own soldiers. Belisarius, who was attached to him by the closest ties of friendship, shed tears at the tidings of his death, and assigned a yearly payment for the maintenance and repairs of his tomb. Yet he forgave the involuntary murderer, not only since he had taken shelter at a shrine, but because the dying words of John had avouched his innocence, and with a solemn oath adjured his comrades to refrain from his punishment. The loss of this generous officer had suspended the progress of the cavalry under his command, had favoured the escape of Gelimer.

The Roman general followed the course of the royal fugitive so far as Hippo Regius, where he learnt that Gelimer had entrenched himself on the neighbouring mountain of Papua,[55] inhabited by a savage but friendly tribe of Moors. Its steep and craggy sides presented an insurmountable barrier to assailants, and the small town of Medenus on its summit had afforded refuge to the king. In the hope that, though force was useless, famine would prevail, Belisarius resolved to blockade the monarch in his last retreat. Unwilling, however, to expose his whole army to the hardships of a winter campaign, or to continue absent from Carthage, where his active exertions were required to extend and consolidate his conquests, he entrusted to the command of Pharas, one of the Herulian confederates, a squadron sufficient to invest the mountain, and to prevent either the escape of Gelimer, or the arrival of supplies.

At Hippo the clemency of Belisarius was again extended to the suppliant Vandals, who were by his orders saved from slaughter. but disarmed and sent to Carthage to increase the train of prisoners. At this place also he became possessed of the private royal treasure, which had been confided by Gelimer to one of his officers, named Boniface, with directions to sail with it from Hippo, if he should learn that the result of the final battle had been adverse to his countrymen. It was expected by means of so powerful an auxiliary as gold, to secure the intended retreat of Gelimer to Spain, and perhaps to purchase the alliance of its Visigoth king. After the defeat of Tricamaron, Boniface accordingly embarked, but a storm threw him back upon his native shores. This event, which in the month of December it needed no miracle to explain, was thought by the superstitious officer to prove that the will of Heaven opposed his undertaking.

He entered into treaty with the Roman general, and offered to surrender his charge, provided his own fortune were left untouched. Such terms were readily granted, but this zealous assertor of the ways of Providence carried off, under the name of private property, no in-

---

55. D'Anville (*Géograph. Anc.* vol. iii.) places Mount Papua near Hippo Regius and the sea; but his opinion is controverted by Gibbon (vol. vii.) on two grounds, the long pursuit beyond Hippo" and the words of Procopius (Vandal lib. ii. c. 4). With regard to the long pursuit beyond Hippo, I find no trace of it in the original authorities. As to "the extremity of Numidia," I do not see why this phrase should not apply to the eastern as well as to the southern limits of the province. I, therefore, adhere to the judgment of D'Anville.

considerable share of the royal wealth.

On returning to Carthage, Belisarius sent forth several expeditions at once, and rapidly subdued the most distant portions of the Vandal kingdom. One detachment was dispatched to defend Tripoli against the Moors, and another to seize the fortress of Septem,[56] or Ceuta, in the straights of Gibraltar. The Balearic islands were reduced by Apollinarius, a Vandal deserter in the Roman service, and both Corsica and Sardinia surrendered as soon as the severed head of Zazo, which had been sent to them, attested the death of their former conqueror. Belisarius next resolved to claim the castle and promontory of Lilybaeum, which, it will be recollected, had been given by Theodoric the Great as a dowry to his sister, on her marriage with King Thrasimund. From that period it had continued annexed to the dominions of the Vandals, till their defeat by Belisarius, when it was resumed by the Gothic chief in Sicily, who justly thought that such a footing in the island could not safely be conceded to the conqueror of Africa.

But their usurpation was not tamely permitted, and, on their refusal to restore the disputed territory, they were sternly admonished by a letter [57] from Belisarius. His haughty mandate was communicated by the Goths in Sicily to Queen Amalasontha, and the answer sent, according to her orders, appears dictated rather by the weakness of her sex, than the lofty spirit of her ancestors, or the resources of her kingdom. Her style was humble and conciliatory; she reminded the Roman general, that, while enemies decided their contests by battle, those of friends might be adjusted in a conference, and though she did not directly yield the point in dispute, she offered to submit it to the arbitration of Justinian. To him the affair was accordingly referred, and we shall hereafter find that, in his experienced hands, it became one of the pretexts of a memorable war.

Immediately after the taking of Carthage, Belisarius had dispatched one of his principal officers, the eunuch Solomon, to inform Justinian of this prosperous event, and he now determined that the Vandal captives should shortly proceed to Constantinople, as the heralds and pledges of their own defeat. The joyful intelligence arrived at the very period when the emperor had completed his far-famed Pandects, and it is remarkable

---

56. This city derived its ancient name from seven small hills, which may still be observed, behind it. (Laborde, *Itinéraire de L'Espagne*, vol. iv.) This part of Africa was annexed by Otho to Spanish jurisdiction. (Tacit. *Hist. lib. i.* c. 78; and Mariana, *Hist. Hisp. lib. iv.* c. 3.)

57. See this letter and the answer in Procopius, (*Vandal. lib. ii.* c. 5.) I am surprised not to find this answer in Cassiodorius.

that they were published on the same day that the African Army was gaining the Battle of Tricamaron, (Dec. 16, *a.d.* 533).[58] The exultation of the monarch was conspicuous, in the proud titles which he assumed in the preamble of his laws. All mention of the general, by whom these conquests had really been achieved, was judiciously suppressed, while the unmerited epithets of Alamannic, Gothic, Francic, Germanic, Antic, Alanic, Vandalic, African, Pious, Happy and Illustrious, Victorious and Triumphant, were blazoned after the name of Justinian. In his *Institutes*, we find him boasting of the warlike fatigues he had borne, and we can hardly suppress a smile, on recollecting that this prince, so weary with laborious campaigns, had never quitted his palace at Constantinople, unless for the villas in its neighbourhood. By his directions, Belisarius now exchanged the duties of a soldier for those of a statesman. A letter from Justinian which is still preserved, assigned certain general rules for the settlement of Africa, leaving, however, most of the details to the discretion of his victorious officer.[59]

Some novels afterwards published, (April, *a.d.* 534) completed the political and religions regulation of the province. In memorial of his conquest, the emperor enjoined that Carthage should henceforth be called Justiniana, but this innovation, though adopted in public edicts, or by flattering courtiers during the remainder of his reign, very speedily yielded to the former Punic appellation.[60] It may be observed, that from the attachment of mankind to ancient sounds, and their desire of detracting from contemporary reputation, it is a very difficult task to make a lasting change in the name of any city. Even Constantine the Great, in spite of his brilliant renown, and the peculiar claim which he drew from his second foundations and stately buildings, did not succeed at once in altering the ancient denomination of Byzantium, and the new one has very slowly and gradually prevailed.[61] In the course of his long reign, Justinian appears to have imposed his name on no less than nineteen cities,[62] and of these not a single one has served to prolong his memory.

The emperor trusted that the arms of his general would soon restore the African province to its former limits before the encroach-

---

58. See Ludewig, *Vit. Justinian.*
59. Cod. *Justinian, lib. i.* tit 27.
60. See Novell 131, and Procopius *De Ædif. lib. vi.* c 5.
61. Thus for instance, I do not recollect that in all the fifteen books of Procopius, the name of Constantinople appears a single time in the Greek text.
62. See the enumeration in Alemanni (*Not. Hist.*) The name of Theodora was given to eight more.

ments of the Moors, and he judiciously provided for its security in future. Belisarius was instructed to repair the frontier fortresses, and at the same time, whenever he might judge it necessary, to diminish their extent, so as to render them defensible by a smaller number of men. A system was also pointed out to him, of allotting lands at the extremities of the province to veteran soldiers, who could thus prevent any petty inroad by their reputation, or repel it by their valour, and who might naturally be expected to defend their own property and families with greater zeal than they displayed when enlisted for some foreign and distant object.

The wild mountains of Sardinia were infested by the Moorish exiles, who had endeavoured on another scene, to renew their predatory habits and savage independence, and it appeared requisite to protect the more peaceful inhabitants from their depredations by some further forces.[63] A *tribune*, a squadron of soldiers, and some galleys, were to be stationed at Ceuta, not merely to guard the passage of the Straights, but to watch the proceedings in Spain, and Ceuta itself was rendered altogether impregnable at least in the opinion of the Byzantine court, by strong ramparts and a consecration to the Holy Virgin.[64]

Such was the military distribution which Belisarius was enjoined to follow; and with regard to the civil settlement of the province, the emperor made it subject to the same laws as the rest of his dominions, and ordained that the native Africans might claim within five years, and till the third degree, any houses or lands of which their Vandal conquerors had dispossessed them. But the darling object of Justinian was the re-establishment and exaltation of the orthodox church. By his favour the African priesthood became richly endowed, the right of sanctuary was granted for any crimes except rape and murder; and all gifts or legacies which they might receive in future, either from imperial or private piety were legally secured to them. To resume the clerical property or privileges which had been usurped by the Arians, was undoubtedly just and reasonable; but the Catholics by too common a change passed at once from suffering to infliction, without pausing for one moment on the intermediate line of toleration.

The heretics were excluded from holding any office in the state, no place of public or private worship was allowed them, and they were

---

63. Compare Procop. *Vandal, lib. ii.* c. 13, with Cod. *Justinian, lib. i. tit.* 27. These Moors are probably the same as the Barbaricini whom Pope Gregory the Great attempted to convert. *Epist. lib. iii. e.* 23, 24, 25.
64. Procop. *De Ædif. lib. vi.* c 7.

even debarred the rites of baptism for their children, unless from the hands of their religious opponents. [65] All the ancient penal laws against the Donatists were re-enacted, and thus instead of striving to blend opposite parties, and to heal the necessary evils attendant upon conquest, the pen of the theologian rendered envenomed and incurable the wounds inflicted by the sword of the soldier.

While the Roman general was in this manner actively employed at Carthage, Pharas was proceeding in the siege of Papua. After one headlong assault, of which the rashness was proved, and punished by considerable loss of men, he restrained himself to the safer task of a strict blockade. The sufferings undergone by Gelimer from the want of supplies, and from the savage habits of his Moorish hosts, were embittered by the recollection of the soft and luxurious life to which he had till lately been accustomed. During their hundred years of dominion in Africa, the Vandals had declined from their former hardihood, and yielded to the enervating influence of climate and success; their arms were laid aside, gold embroidery shone upon their silken robes, and every dainty from sea and land united in their rich repasts. Reclining in the shade of delicious gardens, their careless hours were amused by dancers and musicians, and no exertion beyond the chase interrupted their voluptuous repose.

The Moors of Papua, on the contrary, dwelt in narrow huts,[66] sultry in the summer, or pervious to the snow; they most frequently slept upon the bare ground, and a sheep-skin for a couch was thought a scarce refinement. The same dress (a coarse cloth and tunic) [67] clothed them in every season of the year, and they were strangers to the use both of bread and wine. Their grain was either devoured in its crude and natural state, or at best was coarsely pounded and baked with little skill, into an unleavened paste. [68]

---

65. Novell. 37. Compare Baronius, *Annal. Eccles. a.d.* 535. No. 21, and Ludewig, *Vit. Justinian.*

66. See an account of these huts, the Mapalia, in Sallust (*Bell. Jugurth.* c. 21), and Livy (*lib. xxx.* c. 3). In the wilder parts of Barbary the huts are still constructed, (1829), in their ancient figure of inverted ships, as described by Sallust (Shaw's *Travels* ed. 1738).

67. This dress is still, (1829), fashionable in Barbary, the men of almost every clan are shrouded in their *haick*, whose white colour and graceful folds produce, as it seemed to me, when travelling in that country, a very striking effect These are the *"grans pelices"* mentioned by Joinville (ed. 1663).

68. In many parts of Barbary, the food of the inhabitants continues the same, (1829). Near Tetuan the Bereberes subsist chiefly on crude barley (Marmol, vol. ii. ed. 1667). A sort of unleavened barley bread is made in other places (Leo *Africanus, lib, i.* ed. 1556, and Shaw)

Compelled to share this savage mode of life, Gelimer and his attendants began to consider captivity or even death, as better than the daily hardships they endured. To avail himself of this favourable disposition, Pharas, in a friendly letter, proposed a capitulation, and assured Gelimer of generous treatment from Belisarius and Justinian. The spirit of the Vandal prince however was still not wholly broken, and he refused the offers while acknowledging the kindness of his enemy. In his answer, he entreated the gifts of a lyre, a loaf of bread, and a sponge; and his messenger explained the grounds of this singular petition. At Papua he had never tasted the food of civilised nations, he wished to sing to music an ode on his misfortunes, written by himself, and a swelling on his eyes needed a sponge for its cure. The brave Herulian, touched with pity that such wants should be felt by the grandson and successor of Genseric, forthwith sent these presents up the mountain, but by no means abated the watchfulness of his blockade.

The siege had already continued for upwards of three months, several Vandals had sunk beneath its hardships, but Gelimer still displayed the stubborn inflexibility usual to despotic rulers[69] when the sight of a domestic affliction suddenly induced him to yield. In the hovel where he sat gloomily brooding over his hopeless fortunes, a Moorish woman was preparing at the fire a coarse dough, according to the barbaric fashion which has already been described. Two children, her son and the nephew of Gelimer, were watching her progress, with the eager anxiety of famine. The young Vandal was the first to seize the precious morsel, still glowing with heat and blackened with ashes, when the Moor, by blows and violence, forced it from his mouth. So fierce a struggle for food at such an age, overcame the stern resolution of Gelimer. He agreed to surrender on the same terms lately held out to him, and the promises of Pharas were confirmed by the Roman general, who sent Cyprian as his envoy to Papua.

April, a.d. 534, the late sovereign of Africa re-entered his capital as a suppliant and a prisoner, and at the suburb of Aclas beheld his conqueror for the first time. His demeanour at this interview was unexpected; he burst into a fit of laughter, which his enemies represented as wandering of mind, but which, by his partisans, was more justly ascribed to his reflections on the vanity of human grandeur. If Gelimer, at this time, could really divest himself of useless sorrow for his throne, he far surpassed in wisdom and in happiness the greater number of mankind, who seldom enjoy any object during iti possession, and only

---

69. Mariana, *Hist. Hisp. lib. vi.* c. 21.

become alive to its value from the moment they have lost it.

With the capitulation of Gelimer, the Vandal war was at an end. There now remained for Belisarius, the grateful and important task to render the country he had conquered, permanently useful to the Romans. He might have succeeded in extending his dominion over the restless tribes of Moors, and raising Africa into one of the strongest bulwarks and richest resources of the empire, but the pre-eminence of his glory provoked the envy, as his strict discipline displeased the licentiousness of several subaltern officers. By them it was secretly intimated to the emperor that the conqueror of the Vandals aspired to the independent throne of Africa, and suspicions were thus excited, which Justinian wanted firmness either to despise or to avow.

Like all weak men in doubtful circumstances, he adopted a middle course, and sent back to Carthage the eunuch Solomon, to propose to Belisarius an apparent alternative, either of retaining his command in Africa, or of accompanying Gelimer and the other captives to Constantinople. Secure in his upright intentions, Belisarius might not have discerned the jealousy lurking in the specious offer of Justinian, had not the very caution of his enemies at Carthage served to reveal their perfidious machinations. They had dispatched two emissaries with duplicate letters to Justinian; the one reached his destination and delivered his charge without accident, but the other, having excited distrust by his mysterious demeanour, was arrested in the port of Carthage.

Thus becoming acquainted with the private intrigues against himself, Belisarius now perceived, that the only alternative really in his choice, was to return from Africa, or to raise the standard of rebellion. Had he, in fact, been animated by the unprincipled ambition so falsely imputed to him by his accusers, he would, in all likelihood, have found but little difficulty in supplanting his master on the imperial throne. The sedition of Nika had proved that even the personal guards of Justinian were disaffected to him, and the recent rise of his family precluded any hereditary tenure on the affections of the people; his rapacity had made him hateful, and his marriage ridiculous. His bounty had only enriched a few worthless favourites, and the soldiers despised the unwarlike monarch who disdained to share the labours, though he claimed the glory, of their exploits.

What obstacles had then Belisarius to fear, if, in imitation of so many Roman generals since the times of the republic, he had suffered his army to invest him with the purple? Of all the emperors since the time of Augustus, nearly one half had only derived their dignity from the tumultuous proclamation of the soldiers. But these inducements, which might have persuaded so many inferior spirits to revolt, do not appear to have even tempted that of Belisarius. He knew that loyalty to a sovereign is a real and sacred obligation, not to be shaken off and discarded from motives of expediency, and he resolved not merely to preserve his allegiance, but to manifest a cheerful and immediate compliance with the secret wishes of Justinian. He appointed the eunuch Solomon to the government of Africa,[70] left with him his secretary Procopius, a large share of his troops, and even of his personal guards, and then embarked with the spoil, the captives, and the remaining soldiers, for Constantinople.

Such ready obedience must have satisfied the most suspicious temper, and disarmed the most determined envy. The truth could no longer be doubted by Justinian. The reparation he made for his unfounded jealousy was prompt and ample, and had his relations with Belisarius terminated here, posterity would have to applaud his gratitude and generosity. Medals were struck by his orders, bearing on one side the effigy of the emperor, and on the other that of his victorious general, in full armour, surrounded by the appropriate inscription, *Belisarius, the Glory of the Romans*.[71] It is to be regretted that none of these coins should have been discovered or preserved in modern times, as they would afford the only certain representation now existing of the features of the hero.

Not satisfied with the great and almost singular honour of joining the emblem of a subject with his own,[72] Justinian decreed to Belisarius the honours of a triumph, a ceremony to which Rome had long been a stranger, and which had never been witnessed by the eastern capital. The liberality of Justinian may be justly praised on this occasion, for disregarding the example of his predecessors, who, since the

---

70. In the reign of Justinian, we may observe three eunuchs appointed to the command of armies, Solomon, Narses, and Scholasticus. (Procop. *Goth. lib. iii.* c. 40.) This practice was often renewed in the Byzantine empire. Observe the indignation of Luitprand, in the tenth century, at finding an eunuch a general at Constantinople; (*Leg. ad Niceph. ap. Murat Script. Italic* vol. ii.) The Byzantine laws provided, however, that no could become emperor. (Evagrius, *Hist. Eccles. lib. ii.* c 2.)
71. (Cedrenus, vol. i.) As the inscriptions were in Latin, the real words were *Gloria Romanorum*, which appear on another medal of Justinian, as applied to himself. (Ducange *Fam. Aug. Byz.*)
72. The only other instance on record is that of Count Boniface, the same who invited the Vandals to Africa. From overlooking the passage in Cedrenus, Gibbon has imagined that the example of Boniface is without a parallel (vol. vi. p. 25.)

days of Tiberius, had reserved this pageant exclusively for themselves, and sometimes assumed it on the most frivolous occasions. This imperial monopoly of honours appears to have proceeded partly from the despotic fear of exalting a subject, and partly from an ancient principle of the republic, by which the victories of a lieutenant were always ascribed to his general. [73]

In the solemn ceremony now renewed by order of Justinian, the people might admire a rich procession of the Vandal treasures, many thousand talents of silver, copies of the Gospel embossed with jewels,[74] golden vases, chariots and thrones, the refinements of luxurious opulence, or the accumulated resources against danger. This splendid array, however it might dazzle the eyes of a spectator, could claim but little interest in those of posterity, had it not included some of the most striking memorials of religion. The golden instruments of the Jewish worship, especially the holy table, and the candlestick with six branches,[75] had rewarded the victory and graced the triumph of Titus, and their emblems may yet be discerned upon the arch erected to his honour.

These sacred spoils, which had been deposited in the Temple of Peace,[76] received a double value, after the conversion of the empire to Christianity, and long continued undisturbed, amidst all the troubles of the times.

But when Rome was pillaged by the Vandals, they could not escape the prying avarice of Genseric, they were borne away to Africa, and remained at Carthage for nearly fourscore years, until the conquests of Belisarius restored them to orthodox hands, and brought them to form, for the second time, the ornaments of a Roman triumph. It was intended by Justinian to keep these precious relics in his palace, but a zealous Jew expressed his doubts whether they would ever rest in any spot besides their original station. It was, he said, in just punishment for their detention, that Rome had been taken by Genseric and Carthage by Belisarius. The emperor yielded to the force of these arguments, and after so many vicissitudes and wanderings, the spoils

---

73. Middleton's *Life of Cicero*, vol. ii. ed. 1741.
74. Zonaras, *Annal.* vol. ii. We find some of these spoils many years afterwards, commemorated amongst the crown jewels of Justin the Second.
75. See Exodus, xxv. 23—10, and an accurate representation in Relandus. (*De Spoliis Templi Hierosol.*)
76. Baronius *Annal. Eccles.* a.d. 73, No. 3. The Temple of Peace was burnt in the reign of Commodus, and it is not known in what building these spoils were afterwards preserved. (*Relandus de Spoliis Templi Hierosol.*)

of the Temple of Solomon were again conveyed to Jerusalem, and placed in the Christian cathedral of that city. Their future fate is not recorded in history, but they were exposed in the ensuing century to the double danger of Persian and of Saracen invasions, and the value of the material would certainly prove fatal to the permanent preservation of the object.

The triumphal procession moved onwards from the house of Belisarius to the Hippodrome, which was filled with exulting crowds, and where Justinian and Theodora sat enthroned. No chariot drawn by elephants or horses was, according to ancient usage, allotted to the conqueror, who marched on foot at the head of the companions of his exploits. Immediately after the Vandal spoils appeared the Vandal captives, and among them Gelimer was still distinguished by the of a sovereign. His demeanour was not disgraced by womanish tears or wailings; but he frequently repeated the words of Solomon, of which his mind must have acknowledged the melancholy truth: "*Vanity of vanities! all is vanity!*"

On reaching the Hippodrome he was commanded to cast aside the ensigns of royalty, and to prostrate himself before the imperial throne, and the haste of Belisarius in performing the same ceremony, was designed to show him that he had undergone no peculiar degradation or insult as a prisoner, and had merely yielded the customary homage of a subject.[77] We may pause for a moment to reflect on the strange caprice of fortune, which had raised a comedian from the theatre, to see prostrate, as slaves, before her footstool, the successors of Genseric and Scipio.

Both the conqueror and the captive experienced the effects of imperial generosity. The former appears to have received, as usual in this age, no inconsiderable portion of the spoil for his reward, and was named sole consul for the ensuing year. This title, which had long degenerated into an empty name, had only been preserved from imperial jealousy and abolition by its utter insignificance, yet there was still something dear and venerable in its sound; it was cherished by the Roman people as the proudest recollection, and solicited by foreign monarchs as the highest honour.

Belisarius was almost the last subject ever invested with this dignity, which, soon after this time, was silently suppressed, after a duration of above a thousand years. The ceremony of his inauguration in the consulship, (Jan. 1, *a.d.* 535), appears a second triumph from its splen-

---

77. Zonaras, *Annal.* vol. ii.

dour. Borne in his *curule* chair,[78] on the shoulders of captive Vandals, he lavishly showered on the multitude silver cups, gold girdles, and other precious spoils.

On the other hand, the liberal promises he had made to Gelimer were ratified and performed by Justinian, an extensive estate in Galatia was assigned to the Vandal monarch, and his adherence to the Arian doctrines alone prevented his obtaining the honours of Patrician. He retired to his peaceful and obscure retreat, and history makes no further mention of his name. It is difficult to understand with clearness, or define with accuracy, a character of which such various and discordant features are portrayed. We find him in early life a courageous soldier, at Tricamaron a dastardly fugitive, ambitious of power, yet full of resignation in defeat, melting into tears at the sound of a lute, and sternly commanding the murder of his royal kinsman.

Like Sylla he seemed alternately under the dominion of two separate and conflicting dispositions, which rendered him equally capable of the bravest or the basest actions. With regard to the other captives, they were treated with the policy of which Hannibal had given the earliest example, and which was afterwards so successfully adopted by the Romans.[79] The Vandal youth, divided into five squadrons of cavalry, and called by the name of Justinian, were appointed to several cities of the east. At this distant station, without hope of flight or fellow-feeling with the enemy, their services were often experienced against the Persians, and it appears that Belisarius, in his latter Oriental campaigns, directed the valour of the enemies he had formerly encountered.

On viewing the conquest of Africa with that calmness and knowledge of results to which a contemporary writer cannot aspire, but which, at this distance of time, it is so easy to display, we shall find reason, both on political and religious grounds, to deplore the success of Belisarius. Had the Vandals remained in possession of this country, and had their valour been roused and their discipline restored by an-

---

78. Besides the *curule* chair, we find in this age a staff, the ensign of the consulship (John Malala, vol. ii.). It was still usual to mark the date by the names of the consuls. The first introduction of an era from the birth of Christ was a.d. 533, by Dionysius Exiguus, but it did not prevail till long afterwards. See Jortin's *Remarks on Ecclesiastical History*, vol. iv.

79. Hannibal sent the Spanish troops to Africa, and the African to Spain, by which means he secured the allegiance of both (*Polyb.* lib. iii. c. 33). In the first century of our era the Roman policy was truly described by Claudius Civilis, the Batavian chief, (Tacit. *Hist. lib. iv.* c. 17).

other Genseric, a formidable and perhaps effectual barrier would have interposed, before the tide of Mahometan invasion. Those hordes of Saracens who founded a monarchy in Spain, and carried their victorious arms to the Tiber and the Loire, might, at least in this direction, have been restrained to their native deserts: and Africa, in common with other ancient provinces of Rome, might now enjoy the benefits of civilisation and of Christianity. But the distracted and persecuting government of the Greeks in that country could only subsist by the weakness of its foes, and was subverted with little difficulty by the daring fanaticism of Hassan and Abdallah, (*a.d.* 648-698).

CHAPTER 4

Reign of Theodoric

The conquest of Italy by the Great was not less glorious to his valour and military skill, than its government to his wisdom and his virtue. History can record but few similar instances of a successful soldier so readily and so ably exchanging his warlike undertakings for the duties of civil administration, uniting the conquered and the conquerors in one firm bond of allegiance, and never again impelled into the field by a mere thirst of personal renown. During a reign of three-and-thirty-years, Theodoric fully justified the surname of the second Trajan, which the grateful affection of his Italian subjects had bestowed upon him;[1] and it is scarcely an exaggeration in one of his successors to assert, that all monarchs may be judged by this model, and be respected and admired in proportion as they have approached it.[2] Upright and active in his conduct, he enforced amongst his soldiers that discipline of which he gave the first example, and knew how to temper his general kindness by occasional acts of salutarj' rigour. He was loved as if indulgent, yet obeyed as if severe.

He earnestly applied himself to the revival of trade and manufactures, and still more to the support of agriculture, the only solid base of national prosperity. By a liberal system of economy he was enabled, while giving up a share of the public burthens, to repair and ornament the principal cities, to display a royal state, to maintain a formidable army, and to reward or encourage merit. But the quality for which Theodoric deserves the greatest admiration, in that dark age, was toleration. Though a zealous Arian, he confirmed to the Catholics every right and privilege which they had heretofore enjoyed, except that of

---

1. Anonym. *Vales*. Trajan was proverbially the best of the Roman emperors (*Eutrop. lib. viii.* c 5).
2. See Cassiodorius (*Var. lib. x. ep.* 31).

persecution, and freely admitted them to his confidence and counsels. If shortly before his death he departed from his usual maxims, and assumed the character of tyrant, it must not be forgotten by what strong provocations he was urged, and the virtues of his long and glorious life may well atone for the errors of its close.

At the decease of this high-minded monarch, (a.d. 526), a few months before that of the Emperor Justin, his grandson Athalaric became King of the Ostrogoths. The minority of Athalaric (he was then only ten years of age [3]) was protected by the spirit and talent of Amalasontha, his widowed mother. His dominions, which on one side were bounded from the Franks and Visigoths by the Rhone, extended on the other to the Danube, and comprised Noricum, Pannonia, and Dalmatia. The Gothic capital, as that of the last western emperors, was Ravenna, although Rome, Pavia, and Verona, might boast of frequent visits from their sovereign; and these, with Milan, Auximum, and Naples, were his strongest and most flourishing cities at this time. An iron mine in Dalmatia,[4] a gold one in the peninsula of Reggio,[5] supplied the two chief requisites of war, and the proverbial fruitfulness of Sicily yielded a large yearly tribute of corn.[6]

Unlike the Vandals, the valour of the Goths had never since their conquest been suffered to languish and decay; their military force consisted of no less than two hundred thousand soldiers, and it was shown by the event that an army, amounting to three-fourths of that number, might be mustered at Ravenna in less than four months.[7] Of the naval strength of the Goths, we do not possess any such positive account; but it appears that, on a sudden emergency, Theodoric was able to protect the coasts of Italy by one thousand small vessels.[8] In this government, the king's prerogative was in fact unlimited; no more than empty honours were allowed the Roman senate, which Theodoric had artfully converted into a seeming barrier, but a real bulwark to his power. He had always addressed the senators with the most flattering respect, he had affected to refer important matters to their deliberation, and had interposed their venerable name between him and his subjects, but he never allowed them the slightest efficient

---

3. *Jornandes de Reb. Getic.* c. 59.
4. Cassiod. *Var. lib. iii. ep.* 25.
5. *Ibid. lib. ix. ep.* 3. The sentiments of Theodoric or Cassiodorius, in giving directions to work this mine.
6. Procop. *Goth. lib. iii.* c. 16.
7. *Ibid. lib. iii.* c. 4. *lib. i.* c. 16.
8. Cassiod. *Var. lib. v.* ep. 16..

control upon his actions.

It required, however, the most skilful hand to poise this delicate machine, so as to render it neither despised by the people, nor dangerous to the sovereign. Such was the state of the kingdom to which Athalaric succeeded. His claim to obedience was enforced by the recent recollection of his grandsire, and by his own illustrious birth, the sixteenth in lineal descent of the royal race of the Amali.[9] Yet all these advantages were counterbalanced and impaired by the unfortunate difference of creed between the Goths and the Italians, which always left them, if not hostile, at least foreign, to each other, and which needed only a slight spark to be blown into a flame. It will be seen, in the sequel, how greatly the religious zeal of the Catholics contributed to aid and forward the enterprise of Belisarius.

The first act of Amalasontha, on assuming the regency, was to apprise Justinian of her son's accession, and request the continuance of the treaties and good understanding between him and the Goths.[10] His alliance was readily granted her, so long as her influence and power seemed unshaken, but began to waver as her fortune declined. These haughty barbarians, whose ancestors had cheerfully submitted to queens, and had thereby, according to the harsh prejudice of Tacitus, sunk below slavery itself,[11] now bore with impatience the dominion of a woman. His youth and beauty of Amalasontha appeared better fitted to adorn than to support a throne; and her lofty courage and superior talents were stained by the female frailties of capriciousness, cunning, and revenge. By her secret orders, three of the most powerful nobles, whose rivalry she feared, were treacherously seized, and executed without trial; their partisans were justly irritated by their fate, and so nearly was she overcome by domestic faction, that, on several occasions, she meditated flight to Constantinople, and had once already dispatched a vessel, laden with her treasures, to the coast of Epirus.

Her genius, however, succeeded in surmounting all these difficulties, but they could not fail to excite hopes of conquest in Justinian, who had probably intended to vindicate her cause, for his own advantage, had she taken shelter at his court, and who afterwards eagerly availed

---

9. *Jornandes de Reb. Getic.* c 14. Cassiodorius reckons one generation more. (*Var. lib. ix. ep.* 25).
10. Cassiod. *Var. lib. iii. ep.* 1.
11. (*Germ.* c. 45.) Perhaps, however, the Sitones should be regarded as the neighbours rather than as the ancestors of the Goths.

himself against her of the pretext which the seizure of Lilybaeum, afforded. This claim, which, as we have seen, had first been urged by Belisarius at Carthage, was prosecuted with vigour at Constantinople; nor was the emperor sparing in threats, or warlike preparations, until a sudden change of circumstances induced him to alter his tone, and to perceive that his object would be most effectually attained under the mask of friendship for the Gothic queen. This singular revolution will require some detail.

In the education of her son, Amalasontha had been desirous to enlarge his mind by liberal studies; but the loud clamours of the principal Goths, their opinion that learning was incompatible with valour, and their appeals to the ignorance of their ancestors, at last compelled her to abandon any idea of instruction, and to leave the royal stripling almost without control. The consequences may be easily foreseen, Athalaric launched forth in pursuit of pleasure, with all the passionate ardour of early youth; his health sunk beneath his intemperance, and he expired after a nominal reign of eight years, and at the age of eighteen, (*a.d.* 534). It was the object of his mother to prolong her authority after his death, but as the laws now excluded females from the throne, she could only hope to govern under the protection of some other name. For this purpose, she cast her eyes on Theodatus, the nephew of the great Theodoric, and offered to proclaim herself and him joint sovereigns of Italy, provided he would bind himself by a solemn oath, to content himself with the honours of royalty, without aspiring to its power and prerogatives.

His advanced age, his secluded studies, his want of resolution, and his unpopularity with the Italians, were amongst his chief recommendations to her favour, for these qualities seemed auspicious to her views. She had lately, it is true, deeply wounded both his interest and his pride, by a sentence against him for some acts of oppression in his Tuscan domains; but she trusted that the preference which she showed, and the rank to which she raised him, would change his resentment into gratitude. She was not aware that, with most minds, there can be no greater aggravation to an injury, than a subsequent benefit. Theodatus subscribed to every condition, swore every oath which she required, and, having concerted his measures during a few months of seeming deference and respect, suddenly massacred her most faithful attendants, and confined her a close prisoner to an island of the lake of Bolsena. His attentive consideration spared her, at least, the pangs of suspense and uncertainty; within a few days from her arrival, she was stifled in the bath, (April, *a.d.* 535), by order of her thankless colleague.[12]

A crime so atrocious supplied the emperor with a far more plausible and popular ground for hostilities, than his claim to the barren rock of Lilybaeum, to ten Hunnish deserters, or to compensation for the plunder of a small Illyrian town; complaints which he had hitherto, for the want of better, been reduced to urge. It was natural for him to seize this favourable opportunity of entering the field as the champion and avenger of his murdered ally, and, even exclusive of any schemes of conquest, no legitimate sovereign could view so shameless an usurpation with indifference. Till, however, his warlike preparations were completed, Justinian condescended to dissemble, and flattered Theodatus with the hopes of his friendship, whilst secretly deliberating on the most effectual measures for his overthrow.[13]

The emperor determined to invade the Gothic kingdom in two different quarters, through a naval armament under the command of Belisarius, and through an inroad into Dalmatia by Mundus, governor of the Illyrian provinces. The army entrusted to the former for the conquest of Italy, was by no means answerable in its numbers to the greatness of its object. It consisted only of four thousand confederates, and three thousand Isaurian mountaineers, besides detachments of Hunnish and Moorish cavalry, and a large and valiant guard of horsemen, attached to the person of the general. The whole amount of the forces cannot be thought to have exceeded twelve thousand men, but they were directed by the genius, and animated by the fame, of the conqueror of Africa. During this new expedition, he was again accompanied by Antonina, whose active and daring spirit was, as will be seen, not useless to him in the prosecution of the war; but whose mischievous counsels, and ungovernable passions, have cast a shade upon his glory.

Photius also, her son by her first marriage, scarcely yet grown to manhood, but of prudence and judgment, says Procopius, far beyond his years, had determined to indulge his youthful courage, and partake in the future exploits of his kinsman. The armament sailed in the au-

---

12. The authentic account of the death of Amalasontha is to be found in Procopius (Goth, lib. i. c. 4.) and Jornandes (*De Reb. Getic.* c. 59.) I follow Muratori in rejecting on this point the suspicious testimony of the secret historian, who represents the Empress Theodora as instigating the murder of Amalasontha, from jealousy of her charms. (*Hist. Arcan.* c. 16. and *Annal. d'Ital.* vol. iii.)

13. This artifice is not avowed by Procopius, but may be traced from the authentic documents of Cassiodorius. (*Var. lib. x. ep.* 23-26.)

tumn, with the avowed object of reinforcing the troops of Africa, by which pretext it was expected to reach Sicily, before the Gothic troops in that island could be aware of its real purpose, or ready for defence. Should they, however, seem prepared for hostilities, Justinian had commanded Belisarius to proceed in fact to Carthage, without attempting to accomplish his secret designs against them. This artifice, concerted by the subtle policy of the emperor, was attended with full success; Belisarius landed, as before, at Catania, surprised the Goths by his unforeseen attack, and found but little difficulty in the reduction of the island. Panormus, almost alone, ventured to withstand him. This city, which, since the decay of Syracuse, has, under the name of Palermo, become the capital, is placed on a beautiful plain, bounded on the one side by the sea, and on the other, at various distances, by craggy and romantic mountains, which seem to enclose chap. and conceal this favoured spot from the remainder of the world.

Such a level situation was ill fitted for defence, but the inhabitants, confiding in their fortifications and Gothic garrison, rejected all terms of surrender, and determined to stand a siege. They even sent to Belisarius an arrogant mandate to retire from their waits; but a few days proved sufficient to subdue their haughty presumption. The Roman general, to avoid the difficulty and delay of a regular investment, devised an ingenious stratagem in its place. He ordered his ships to sail into the harbour, which was open and undefended, and having brought them as close as possible to the shore, he hoisted their boats to the mastheads, which far overtopped the adjacent ramparts of Palermo. The boats were then filled with soldiers, who, from this commanding station, poured so constant and well-directed a shower of missiles into the city, that the garrison, struck with terror, forthwith solicited and obtained a capitulation. From Palermo the conqueror proceeded to Syracuse, where Sinderic, the Gothic governor, had yielded almost to the first summons of surrender.[14] On the very day, (Dec. 31, *a.d.* 535), when his consulship ceased, Belisarius entered this city in triumph at the head of his army, and celebrated the twofold solemnity, by scattering, with a lavish hand, gold coins and medals amongst the applauding multitude.

At Syracuse Belisarius fixed his headquarters, until the return of spring might enable him to carry the war into the heart of Italy, or until the negotiations between Theodatus and Justinian should have led to some result. The rapid and easy conquest of Sicily may princi-

---

14. Jornandes, *de Reb. Getic.* c. 60.

pally be ascribed to the goodwill and cheerful assistance of the people. The Gothic sovereigns had always treated this province of their kingdom with peculiar friendliness and favour, and so far depended on the sentiments of loyalty which such rulers should inspire, as to diminish the force of the barbarian garrisons, and in great measure entrust the defence of the island to its native inhabitants.[15]

But the whole course of history, and, above all, the treatment of most great men in republican governments, sufficiently shows how little dependence should be placed on national gratitude. The Sicilians eagerly welcomed the arms of the invaders, and must probably very soon have repented of their treachery, when exposed to the subtle financiers and exorbitant taxes of Justinian. This fruitful province had yielded a tithe [16] of its grain as a tribute to its native princes, and the Romans, on their first conquest, continued to receive the same proportion. During the dominion of the Goths, the city of Rome was constantly supplied with corn, and moreover derived a yearly income in money from her ancient granary. Annexed once more to the empire by the arms of Belisarius, the island remained under Greek dominion for above three hundred years, till the conquest of the Saracens; but, according to the common and just retribution of tyranny, the vices of its government appear to have recoiled upon its rulers. The excessive weight of tributes depressed and overwhelmed its industry; the complaints of such distant subjects were unheeded at Constantinople, and it gradually sunk from one of the most active principles of public wealth, into a lifeless and burdensome appendage.[17]

While the eyes of Belisarius were anxiously directed to the Gothic kingdom, events were occurring in another quarter which needed his immediate interference. His hasty return from Africa, had left that newly-conquered province exposed to the double danger of turbulent

15. For the favours conferred by the Goths on Sicily, see Cassiodorius (*Var. lib. ix. ep.* 10, 11, and 14), and, for its ingratitude, Procopius, (Goth. lib. iii. c. 16). Theodoric (*Var.lib. i.* c. 72.)

6. For an account of these tithes, see Middleton's *Life of Cicero*, vol. i. ed. 1741. It is probable that the Carthaginians, during their possession of the island, obtained a higher tribute, since in Africa, during the first Punic war, we find them levying one half the produce of the country. (*Polyb. lib. i.* c. 72.) In the seventh century, a third portion of the produce of Italy was exacted by its Lombard kings. (*Paul Warnefrid, lib. ii.* c. 32.)

17. In the middle ages, Sicily is said to have been rugged and overgrown with trees, which implied a total decay of agriculture. (*Leo Diaconus, lib. iv.*) We are indebted for this author to the industry of M. Hase in 1819. Some fragments had already been published by Pagi. (*Critic*, vol. iv.)

neighbours, and of a government weak, because oppressive. No apprehension, it is true, was caused by the remaining Vandals, who had finally yielded their power, and even merged their national name under the supremacy of Rome, whilst a more warlike band is supposed to have fled to the shores of the Atlantic in search of solitary freedom.[18] But the Moors had instantly availed themselves of the absence of Belisarius. His terror of his name had restrained their lawless spirit, although, according to the frequent effect of trivial causes on an ignorant and superstitious people, they had been strongly tempted to hostilities by his ample beard. Like the ancient Germans and Egyptians, they entertained for women some degree of religious veneration,[19] and it had lately been foretold to them by their female prophets, that they could only be defeated by a beardless adversary.

During the command of Belisarius, and before the eunuch Solomon had returned from Constantinople, secret emissaries were accordingly commissioned by the Moors, to observe the chins of all the Roman generals, and their favourable account filled their countrymen with a presumptuous confidence, which their discipline was but ill adapted to support. Their savage mode of life has already been described, and in war against the civilised provincials they possessed no advantages beyond swiftness of movement and superiority of numbers. Almost naked and provided only with weak and narrow shields, their limbs were freely exposed to hostile darts, and their principal weapons consisted of two javelins, which they successively hurled against the enemy. If these were withstood, they seldom attempted any further contest, and speedily betook themselves to flight.[20]

The departure of Belisarius was now the signal for hostilities, which the barbarians commenced by predatory inroads through the peaceful provinces, and by surprising and cutting to pieces a detachment of

18. See Pagi (*Critic*, vol. ii. p. 551.) A great number of the remaining Vandals were afterwards banished by Solomon, and probably rejoined the voluntary exiles on the Atlantic coast. (Procop. *Vandal. lib. ii* c 19,) Yet many Vandal chiefs are afterwards mentioned at a festival of the usurper Gonthar. (*lib. ii.* c 28.)
19. This very curious coincidence, which has not been sufficiently observed may be traced for the Germans (Tacit. *Hist. lib. it.* c. 61. and *Germ.* c. 8), for the Egyptians (Diodor. *Sicul.* lib. i c. 27), and for the Moors (Procop. *Vandal, lib. ii.* c. 8). Yet these nations were distant and unconnected with each other. Should we attribute their similarity on this point to their common descent, or to the operation of natural causes?
20. Their swiftness is praised by Procopius. (*Goth. lib. i.* c. 25.) For discipline, and perhaps courage, they were much less distinguished. See in Hertius how thirty Gallic horsemen succeeded in routing two thousand Moorish cavalry. (Bell. *African*, c. 6.)

the Roman army. The *exarch* or Governor Solomon marched against them at the head of all his forces, and though in the first onset his cavalry was thrown into some confusion by the aspect of their camels,[21] his skill and their superstitious terrors combined to the fulfilment of the prophecy, and the Moors were completely routed. A second, and still more bloody battle was fought on Mount Burgaon, where the Moors had entrenched themselves, and it is more easy to believe that fifty thousand of the barbarians perished, than that not a single Roman soldier was either killed or wounded.[22] So considerable was the number of prisoners, that a Moorish boy, or an African sheep, might be purchased for equal prices at Carthage.[23]

Yet this double overthrow served rather to irritate than subdue the ferocious tribes of the desert, and they continued to desolate the Roman province by frequent incursions, which the seditions spirit of his army hindered Solomon from either repelling or avenging. Any soldier (and there were many) who had married a widow or daughter of the Vandals, claimed their forfeited estates as the inheritance of his wife, and the reward of his valour. It was in vain that Solomon, desirous of annexing these lands to the imperial domain, represented to the army that such public resources were necessary to supply its own pay and provisions, and that its victory had already obtained a sufficient recompense in slaves, furniture, and money. This fruitful cause of disaffection was artfully fomented by the Arian troops, who amounted only to one thousand men, but whose ardent zeal appeared to multiply their numbers.

They bore, with scarcely suppressed resentment, the harsh edicts of Justinian against their paternal faith, and especially the denial of the rites of baptism to their children, a prohibition which appears not merely unpopular, but useless; whilst the compulsory instruction of the youthful Arians in orthodox schools, would have been equally

---

21. The ancients all concur in affirming this natural aversion. Their testimonies are collected by Gibbon (vol. vii.), and he might have added that of Herodotus, (*lib. i.* c. 80.) I am inclined to place reliance on their unanimous and unbiased judgments. It is true, that horses and camels travel quietly together in the eastern caravans; but does this prove, that they may not have a natural antipathy to each other, afterwards surmounted by habit and education? In the passage already quoted. Gibbon asserts, that this opinion is "disproved by daily experience," yet elsewhere (vol. x.) he speaks of it as of a certain fact.
22. Procop. *Vandal. lib. ii.* c. 12.
23. The African sheep are praised by Homer, (*Odyss. lib. iv. v.* 85.) In his time we find a young female slave, sold for the price of twenty oxen. (*lib. i. v.* 431.)

unjust, but more effectual. As a further excitement to mutiny, four hundred captive Vandals, who had been embarked, like the rest of their comrades, at Constantinople, for their destined station in the east, had no sooner put to sea than they rose in revolt, overpowered the sailors, and compelled the pilot to steer again to Africa. Landing on a desert district of the coast, they secretly joined the Roman troops on Mount Auras, and united with their recent antagonists to raise the standard of rebellion. Meanwhile a conspiracy was impending at Carthage against the life of Solomon; the fanatic Arians having impiously selected the approaching festival of Easter as the most appropriate time, and the cathedral of Carthage as the fittest place, to murder their religious enemy. Some feelings of fear, which they probably mistook for scruples, restrained the execution of their project at the time assigned, but the disappointed fury of the soldiers broke out five days afterwards, (March 28, *a.d.* 536), in the shape of an open mutiny.

On receiving intelligence of the rebellion at Mount Auras, which afforded them both example and encouragement, they assembled in the public circus, from complaints proceeded to bloodshed, and loudly forswore their allegiance to the *exarch*. Rushing through the streets of Carthage, they first gratified their animosity by an indiscriminate massacre, and then their avarice by forcing open and despoiling the houses of wealthy and peaceful citizens. Solomon passed a fearful day, concealed in the chapel of the palace. At night, when the tumult had somewhat abated, and the mutineers were oppressed with sleep and wine, the general silently stole from his retreat, and with only seven attendants, among whom s the secretary Procopius, directed his steps to the harbour and seized an open boat. In this frail conveyance they steered towards Sicily, where Solomon tended to represent his forlorn situation, and beseech the aid of Belisarius.

Next day, (March 29, *a.d.* 536), the insurgents, sated with the plunder of Carthage, marched to the plains of Bulla, for the purpose of meeting and confederating with their comrades from Mount Auras. Their united forces amounted to above eight thousand men, and the inborn ascendancy of genius impelled than to elect, as their chief, a private soldier of the name of Stoza,[24] whose talents were worthy of employment and distinction in a better cause. They then returned towards the capital, expecting to find it open and defenceless as before,

---

24. See Jornandes (*De Regn. Success.* ed. Lindenbrogii.), also Victor Tunnunensis. (*Chron.* ed. Canis. 1725. vol. i.)

when their hopes were suddenly blasted by the news that Belisarius had landed.

The account of Solomon had shown to the general the necessity of active and vigorous exertions, and he felt how much the danger might be aggravated by a single moment of delay. Although at that time there was only one small vessel at Syracuse ready for immediate sailing, he had fearlessly embarked with one hundred of his guards, [25] (there was no room on board for more,) and had reached Carthage on the very evening before the rebels had trusted to re-enter its walls. The magic of a name was never more strongly apparent, than in the consternation which the tidings of his arrival spread amongst the troops of Stoza. Far from venturing to attack the city which contained him, they would not even await his onset, and hastily retreated towards the interior of the country. They were pursued by Belisarius at the head of his guards, and of two thousand soldiers whom he collected at Carthage, and whose fidelity he rewarded or secured by a lavish donative.

The whole force, however, hardly exceeded one-fourth of the numbers of the enemy. At the city of Membresa, [26] distant about fifty miles from Carthage, the Roman general came up with the insurgents, who, finding escape denied them, prepared for a brave resistance. No protection could be derived from Membresa, which was destitute of walls, and they therefore entrenched themselves on a steep and lofty hill, while Belisarius encamped on the banks of the Bagradas. On the ensuing day, both parties sallied forth for battle: the rebels, confident in their superior numbers, and the Romans despising their antagonists as mutineers and outlaws. To confirm this favourable disposition, Belisarius addressed his troops in a public harangue:

> Soldiers, in marching to battle this day, we cannot but bewail the sad necessity which impels us against our brother Romans, and even the joy of a victory will not be pure nor unmingled with tears. We possess, however, one great source of consolation, we have not merited nor provoked this war, but come here in self-defence, to withstand a lawless aggression. That our present antagonists are enemies, barbarians, or whatever harsher term

---

25. Procop. *Vandal lib. ii.* c. 15. The number is rightly translated by Maltret, but Cousin, who is not always faithful even to the Latin version, has increased it to one thousand, and Gibbon, depending on the French translator, whose inaccuracy he so often condemns, has committed the same mistake. (vol. vii.)

26. See on this city Dom. Ruinart. (*Hist. Persec. Vandal*) and a note of Wesseling, (*Itiner.*)

may yet exist is attested by Africa, which they have sacked and plundered, by those of its inhabitants whom they have wantonly slaughtered, and, more than all, by our murdered comrades, who have suffered for no other crime than their fidelity and attachment to the state. It is as their avengers that we now appear; it is in their cause that we are, and ought to be, the bitterest foes of those whom we formerly cherished and esteemed. As to the force of these perfidious rebels, it must be utterly contemptible. How should base mutineers, bound together by no rightful obligation, and united only by thirst for pillage and community of crime, display the intrepidity or obtain the success of honourable soldiers? Courage can never exist with the consciousness of guilt, and speedily forsakes the man who has forsaken his duty.

The ranks of the insurgents will be tumultuous and irregular, and the orders of Stoza despised and disobeyed. His new and unwonted dominion can inspire confidence neither in his soldiers nor himself; he cannot prevail by affection, since a sudden rise is always hateful; nor by terror, when he himself is trembling at his own inexperience. Thus the rebels, devoid both of courage and of counsel, will become an easy and almost unresisting prey. March, then, with generous contempt, against these unworthy adversaries, and convince yourselves that superiority in numbers is altogether unavailing, when supported neither by skilful combination in the general nor by noble spirit in the soldiers.

On the other part, Stoza did not fail to animate his troops by setting forth the heavy and inevitable punishment which must await them from their former masters, and exhorted them to prove their rebellion meritorious by the certain touchstone of success. The two armies were approaching each other in battle array, (April, *a.d.* 536), when a sudden wind arose, blowing straight upon the troops of Stoza. Apprehensive lest the speed of their darts and arrows should be retarded by the adverse gale, the rebel chief issued orders for his squadrons to wheel round and occupy a position in flank. Such a movement could not be effected without some disorder. This decisive instant was seized by Belisarius, who commanded a charge on the enemy whilst quitting their ranks, and by this seasonable and unexpected onset found them off their guard. His skill improved their first confusion into a general rout; their resistance was slight and ineffectual, and they were driven in every direction from the field.

Nearly all their slain consisted of Vandals, and a greater loss of men was prevented, partly by the humanity of Belisarius, who, as soon as the victory seemed certain, had enjoined his soldiers to spare their fellow-countrymen,[27] and partly by the headlong flight of the rebels to the distant deserts of Numidia. To have pursued them so far would have been a long and difficult undertaking, but orders were dispatched to the Roman garrisons in that quarter to intercept the fugitives, and complete their overthrow. Their camp was given up by Belisarius to the pillage of his soldiers; it contained considerable treasure, and many of those women whose claims had formed one of the principal grounds of the rebellion. From thence the conqueror led back his triumphant bands to Carthage. Scarcely, however, had he entered its gates, before he found himself compelled to relinquish the fruits of the Battle of Membresa, by a messenger from Sicily announcing that a formidable mutiny had broken forth in his army, which it required his immediate presence to allay.

Belisarius according embarked with Procopius and his hundred guards, leaving the temporary government of the province in the hands of Hildiger and Theodore. This was the last occasion when the Africans beheld him, and the hopes of tranquillity, which his appearance had raised, were disappointed by the shortness of his stay. Under the languid administration of his successors, Stoza, instead of being cut off by the Roman Army in Numidia, induced it to betray its allegiance, and to join his standards. Other vicissitudes afterwards compelled him to league with the Moors against his countrymen, and he finally fell in single combat; but the evils he had inflicted on the Romans did not terminate with him. The Moors continually renewed their inroads and encroachments on the unhappy province, (a.d. 542-545), and Solomon, when once more appointed to its government, was defeated and killed in battle by their undisciplined numbers.

The whole country, in fact, was quickly verging to that state of depopulation and ruin from which it never has recovered to this hour. While the barbarians of Numidia assailed it on one side, it was drained on the other by the rapine of the *exarchs* or the emperor. Justinian had laid upon the province some new and intolerable taxes,[28] which appeared to be augmented in proportion to its poverty, and which it

---

27. Theophan. *Chronograph.*
28. Procopius, in his public history. (*Vandal lib. ii. c. 8.*)

became every year less able to support, nor did the governors neglect to promote their private interest by further claims. They wanted large sums to purchase the preservation of their office at Constantinople, and the corruption of the ministers rendered necessary the plunder of the people. On their part, the Moors in their ferocious massacres spared neither sex nor age, and the affrighted survivors either entrenched themselves in cities, or fled to Sicily and the neighbouring islands for refuge. It is asserted by Procopius, that not less than five millions of Africans perished in these distracted times, and that a traveller in this province might proceed for several days upon his journey without meeting a single inhabitant.[29]

From the affairs of Africa we must now return with Belisarius to the prosecution of the Gothic war. His rapid conquest of Sicily had struck with terror the mind of King Theodatus, which was weak by nature, and depressed with age. The maxims of his favourite Plato were familiar to his ears, but had never sunk deeper;[30] nor steeled his breast with fortitude and courage; and he could not, says Procopius, have displayed greater consternation, had he been already, like Gelimer, a helpless captive in the hands of the Romans. These feelings, unworthy of his royal rank and valiant subjects, were to skilfully improved by Peter, the ambassador of Justinian,[31] that he was induced to subscribe a treaty far too ignominious to be permanent. The cession of Sicily, the yearly tribute of a golden crown three hundred pounds in weight, and the promised aid of three thousand Gothic auxiliaries at the requisition of Justinian, were amongst its smallest stipulations.

It was further agreed that no Italian senator or Catholic priest should be punishable by his sovereign, without a special permission from the emperor, nor any promotion to the patrician or senatorial dignities be made till his pleasure should be known. Theodatus promised that no statue should be raised in his honour without another of Justinian at his right hand; and that the imperial name should always precede his own in the acclamations of the people at public games and festivals, as if the shouts of the rabble were matter for a treaty. We may easily trace the characteristic vanity of Justinian in these latter stipulations, A more judicious policy would surely have hesitated to propose

---

29. *Hist. Arcan.* c. 18. Observe the reverse of the picture, in *Goth. lib. iv.* c. 17. Subsequent rebellions and wars may be traced in Theophylact *Simocatta, lib. vii* c. 6. &c.
30. I have ventured to copy from Tacitus; (*Annal. lib. xv.* c. 45.)
31. This Peter united the characters of a lawyer and soldier, and was afterwards employed in negotiations with Persia. (Menander *Excerpt. Legat.* Alemanni *Not. Hist.*)

such humiliating terms as could only serve to irritate the vanquished without adding anything to the power or real glory of the victors.

Yet even the remembrance of these ample concessions could not quiet the alarms of Theodatus, and the Byzantine ambassador, who had already reached the Alban hill on his return towards Constantinople, was recalled by a messenger from the wavering monarch.

" Do you think," asked Theodatus, "that the emperor will be satisfied with these terms, and if no, what result will ensue?"

"The emperor probably will," answered Peter; "if not, you must prepare for war."

"Would such a war be just?" said the Gothic King.

"It would," replied the Roman, "for ought not actions to be consistent with principles? You are attached to philosophical studies; Justinian is resolved to assert the majesty of the Roman crown. According to the precepts of Plato, you cannot rightfully take the life of any one man,[32] and still less of so many thousands as must perish in a war, hut there is no reason why Justinian should not strive to reconquer an ancient province of the empire."

Such arguments, even allowing them the utmost weight, might have persuaded Theodatus to resign his crown to some less Platonic Goth, but not to betray his country to the Romans. Yet the feeble monarch was induced to pledge himself, and his Queen Gudelina, by an oath to surrender their dominions to Justinian, in case the original treaty should not be accepted. On his part, Theodatus bound the ambassador, by the same sacred rite, not to bring forward the latter proposal unless the emperor should decidedly reject the first, and together with Peter he dispatched Pope Agapetus to the Court of Constantinople.[33] It appears that the emperor would not ratify the former compact, and the refusal of such advantageous terms, which had probably been dictated by himself, must, in all likelihood, have proceeded from the perjury of his own, or the treason of the Gothic ambassador. The following letter from Theodatus was then put into his hands:

My experience in the council or the field has been limited

---

32. I do not think that this opinion was ever held by Plato. See his remark on the homicides caused by war. (*De Legibu, lib. ix.* vol. ii. ed. 1578)

33. On this point, the authority of Procopius, (*Goth. lib. i.* c. 6) who gives to the Gothic envoy the name of Rusticus, and represents him merely as a priest, must yield to that of Liberatus and Marcellinus. See Muratori, *Annal. d'Ital.* vol. iii. Cardinal Baronius endeavours to reconcile the two, by supposing Rusticus to have been another name of Agapetus. (*Annal. Eccles. a. d.* 536, No. 4.)

by my long and laborious studies. I am weary of reigning and averse to war. I prefer the tranquil enjoyment of philosophical repose to the fatigues of royalty, and would willingly give over my dominions to your imperial sway, were I assured of an estate producing a yearly income of at least twelve hundred pounds weight of gold.

Such easy terms were granted. An answer, full of promises and professions, was composed by Justinian; Peter and some other statesmen were again dispatched to the King of Italy, and Belisarius received orders to hold himself in readiness to embark for Rome as soon as the treaty should be finally concluded, and to take peaceable possession of the Gothic kingdom.

An unforeseen occurrence disconcerted this project on the very point of its execution. While Belisarius was engaged in the conquest of Sicily, Mundus, governor of Illyria, had, according to his instructions, the frontier, defeated the Goths, and obtained possession of Salona. Some Gothic reinforcements, however, soon changed the aspect of affairs, they overthrew and killed Maurice, son of Mundus, in a second battle, and in a third, of which the result was undecided,[34] Mundus himself was slain. After such reverses the Romans prudently retired to their ancient quarters in Illyria.[35]

These skirmishes broke through, as it were, the magic charm of Roman power, which the conquest of Africa and Sicily had cast over the mind of the Gothic monarch, and his presumptuous arrogance at the slight advantage of his arms, equalled his despairing terrors in adversity. Not satisfied with the violation of his oath in refusing to surrender his dominions, Theodatus likewise set at naught the laws of nations and of hospitality by the close imprisonment of the Byzantine ambassadors. On being informed of this insult, the emperor announced to Belisarius that all hopes of negotiation had vanished, that he might forthwith renew hostilities, and depend only on his own victories for peace.

Accordingly, the Roman general, having left sufficient garrisons in Syracuse and Palermo, concentrated his forces at Messina. The opposite coast was guarded by a body of Gothic troops, whose com-

---

34. Procopius says that the Romans were successful, but that it was a "victory of Cadmus." (*Goth. lib. i. c.* 7.) He probably copied this proverbial expression from Herodotus, (*lib. i. c.* 166.)
35. An oracle of the Sybil was then remembered and applied, which, from the double sense of Mundus, had been thought to denote the destruction of the world.

mand had been entrusted by Theodatus to Ebrimur, the husband of his daughter.[36] This prince, whose name and whose fickle allegiance both appear to denote a foreign birth,[37] either shared the timidity or hated the person of his kinsman. He embraced the secret offers of Belisarius, fled to Sicily, accompanied by a few personal adherents, and proceeded from thence to Constantinople, where he was invested with the Patrician dignity, and spent the remainder of his days loaded with honours and contempt His troops, downcast and dismayed at the desertion of their leader, scattered in every quarter, and Southern Italy was thus left utterly defenceless. Belisarius immediately crossed over with his army to Reggio, where Procopius looked in vain for the imaginary monsters of Scylla and Charybdis.[38]

In his further operations the Roman general followed the same system as in Africa; his army marched along the shore, and the fleet was directed to keep in sight as much as possible, and accommodate its progress to the movements of the troops. While advancing through Bruttium[39] and Lucania, the people cheerfully acknowledged his authority, and gathered round his standards, partly from the impossibility of sustaining sieges in their open towns, and partly from aversion to an Arian government, and, according to the event of the war, either motive might be urged. No opposition was encountered by the Romans till they reached the walls of Naples.

This city was strongly fortified both by art and nature; it contained a large Gothic garrison, and could not be reduced without a regular siege. Belisarius accordingly invested it both by sea and land; and obtained, by capitulation, a castle serving as an outwork to the suburbs. Meanwhile a deputation from the Neapolitans endeavoured to dissuade him from his enterprise. Their spokesman, whose name was Stephen, represented that the native inhabitants were withheld by the Gothic soldiers from displaying their feelings in his favour, and that these soldiers, having left behind them, at the mercy of Theodatus, their wives, their children, and their property, could not surrender the city without incurring the certain vengeance of the tyrant. He added:

---

36. Jornandes, *De Reb. Getic.* c. 60, and *De Regn. Success.* ed. Lindenbrogii
37. According to Grotius, Ebrimur signifies "beyond sea." (*Hist. Goth.*) It corresponds to the French surname of Outremer, applied to Louis the Fourth.
38. Compare *Goth. lib. i.* c. 8, and *lib. iii.* c. 27. An interesting Reggio at this time is given by Cassiodorius, (*Var. lib. xii.* e, 14). The country produced little corn, but was fruitful in wine and oil.
39. With inconceivable carelessness, or ignorance, Cousin here transforms Bruttium into Beotia. One might suspect him of having been born in the latter.

And what benefit could ensue to the imperial army from our forcible subjection? Should you succeed in your subsequent attempts upon the capital, the possession of Naples will naturally, and without effort, follow that of Rome; should you on the contrary, as is not improbable, be worsted, your conquest of this city would be useless, and its preservation impossible.

The Roman general replied:

> Whether or not the siege I have undertaken be expedient, is not for the citizens of the invested city to determine; but it is on the situation of your own affairs, and the alternatives now offered to you, that I desire your deliberation. Do not close your gates against an expedition aiming to vindicate Italian freedom, and your own amongst the rest, nor prefer a barbarian bondage to the laws and liberties of Rome.[40] With regard to the Gothic soldiers, I offer them their choice, either of enlisting under my command, and sharing the exploits and rewards of the imperial army, or else of a safe and unmolested return to their homes. Should you accede to these conditions, I will secure your property and persons by the same solemn promise which I pledged to the Sicilians, and of which not one amongst them can deny the entire fulfilment.

The public admonition of Belisarius was enforced by his secret largesses to Stephen, who hereupon zealously espoused the Roman interest, and earnestly exhorted his fellow citizens to yield. On the other side, resistance was pressed upon the Neapolitans by Pastor and Asclepiodotus, two rhetoricians, entirely devoted to the Gothic cause. Not venturing at first to oppose directly the evident inclinations of the people, they brought forward a great number of vexatious conditions, in hopes that the refusal of Belisarius might supply them with a plausible pretext for withstanding the capitulation. This expectation was disappointed by the ready acquiescence of the Byzantine general, who preferred the burthen of any stipulations to the dangers of delay, and the Neapolitans were already rushing to unbar the gates of the

---

40. It most be observed that the later Romans, even under their most despotic tyrants, always boasted of their freedom as compared to the barbarians. Thus, for instance, Victor Vitensis mentions the subjection of Carthage to the Greek emperors as *libertas*, to the resident Vandal kings as *servitudo*. (*Hist. Persec. lib. i.* c. 4.) Thus, also, in the life of the Empress St Adelheid, (c. 7) the phrase *sub libertate Romanâ* is used for the Byzantine dominions. I am indebted to Ducange for this last quotation.

city, (the garrison being insufficient to restrain them,) when they were arrested by the eloquence of Pastor and his colleague. It was urged in their harangue, that the promises of Belisarius might indeed be advantageous, should he be successful, but could not shelter and protect the city in case of his defeat. The artful orators said:

> We should then, remain exposed as rebels to the merited resentment of the Goths. But if even Belisarius should, after our surrender, prove victorious at Rome, he will then despise us for the very perfidy which he now solicits, and the emperor will think it necessary to secure our future allegiance by a numerous and arrogant garrison. Treachery is only rewarded till the triumph to which it contributes is attained. By a brave resistance to the Roman arms, we shall, if the Goths prevail, receive a recompense from their gratitude, if Belisarius, a pardon from his generosity. And why should you so greatly dread a siege? Are your walls less strong, your soldiers less courageous, or your provisions less abundant than they used to be? Think you that Belisarius would have proffered such advantageous terms had he entertained any reasonable hope of subduing you by force?

These remonstrances were assisted by the report of some Jewish purveyors, affirming that plenty prevailed in the public magazines, and by the Gothic soldiers, who pledged themselves to activity and valour in a siege. Thus emboldened, the Neapolitans decided against surrender, and, in a haughty message, commanded the Romans to withdraw from their walls. Belisarius, on the contrary, pressed the siege with an ardour proportioned to the value of his time at that period. A fortress of such importance could not safely be left behind him in power of the enemy, and his troops were not sufficiently numerous to allow of his stationing a detachment before Naples, whilst leading the rest against Rome. He was harassed by difficulties no less than by delay, the ramparts were guarded by the sea on one side, and by the steepness of the ground on the other, and in several unsuccessful assaults the Romans sustained considerable loss.

As a last expedient Belisarius intercepted the aqueduct of Naples, but the number of wells within the city rendered this privation harmless. It may be observed, that the cutting of aqueducts was a measure to which besiegers in this century seldom failed to have recourse,[41] and

---

41. Besides Naples, we find the aqueducts cut at Rome, (Procop. *Goth. lib. i.* c. 19,) at Petra, (*lib. iv.* c. 12,) at Constantinople, (John Malala, vol. ii.).

that from the dread of another approaching investment, or from the sufficiency of natural fountains, these fabrics were often left in ruins by the citizens, especially as in most cases the munificence of their forefathers had provided a far greater supply of water than their less luxurious habits and diminished numbers could require. The interrupted stream, oozing out from its channel of stone over the adjacent country, assisted the ravages of war, gradually reduced the most fertile plains to stagnant morasses, and greatly contributed to those deadly vapours which taint the air of modern Italy.[42]

Although the usual cowardice of Theodatus had withheld all succours or supplies from the Neapolitans, in spite of their solicitations, yet Belisarius found himself no nearer to his object. His proposals had been scorned, his attacks repulsed, and he perceived with sorrow that, after having wasted many precious autumnal days in this unsuccessful undertaking, he should have, in his following march against Theodatus, to encounter the hardships of a winter campaign. Already had he, with grief and reluctance, issued orders for raising the siege, when a fortunate discovery suddenly revived his hopes. An Isaurian soldier, admiring the structure of the aqueduct, to which these rude mountaineers were but little, accustomed, was led by curiosity to explore the inward recesses of this mighty fabric. Creeping along the empty channel of the intercepted portion towards the city, he reached the ramparts, where, he found his further advance impeded by a natural rock, which the architect had pierced with a passage sufficiently Urge for the water to flow, but not for a man to pass. No sooner had this observation been made known to Belisarius, than he resolved, by widening the channel through the rock, to introduce his troops into the city.

Some Isaurians were, therefore, secretly posted within the aqueduct, but directed to use no pickaxes nor hatchets, lest the sound should apprise Naples of its danger. The slow but noiseless progress of smaller instruments at length enlarged the passage, enough for the easy admission of a soldier in full armour, and from this unsuspected mine the city might be considered as already in the hands of Belisarius. Yet with a degree of humanity and forbearance to the vanquished, which

---

42. The malaria, near Rome, has been much increased, but was not produced by this cause. We find Roman soldiers complaining so early as the year 340 before Christ: (*Liv. lib. vii.* c. 38.) See another remarkable passage in Livy, (*lib. vi* c. 12,) and one in Pliny, (*Hist. Nat lib. iii.* e. 9,) as to the depopulation of some neighbouring districts. In the time of Procopius, the country between Rome and Ostia was overgrown with wood. (*Goth. lib. i.* c. 26.)

few other generals have shown, he hazarded the disclosure of his secret for the preservation of his enemies, and once more summoned Stephen from Naples to his presence. He said:

> I have often seen cities taken by storm, and know too well, from experience, the sad results which commonly ensue. In the memory of these I view, as in a mirror, the future fate of Naples, and my compassion is strongly moved at its impending ruin. I frankly tell you that I have prepared an expedient for entering your walls, of which the success is altogether certain. It would fill me with grief were so ancient a city, inhabited by brother Christians and Romans, to undergo the havoc of war, and especially from an army under my command.
> My authority would be insufficient to restrain the victorious troops from pillage and bloodshed; they partly consist of barbarians, who claim no kindred with you, and would view your downfall without pain, whilst the resentment of the rest is kindled by the loss of so many comrades before your walls. During the short respite that is yet allowed you, while it is still in your power to deliberate and choose, prefer, I beseech you, your own safety, and shun the destruction already hovering above you. Should you still persevere in rejecting my proposals, impute not, hereafter, your sufferings to the harshness of fortune, but rather to your own stubborn determination.

This message proved unavailing. It was delivered by Stephen with great earnestness and show of patriotic zeal (he was mindful of the money given him); but the Neapolitans continued steadfastly bent on resistance, and Belisarius could no longer avert from them the calamities of a captured city. The important secret of the aqueduct had hitherto been prudently confined to himself and a few faithful Isaurians, nor did he entrust his officers with it till the very moment he had chosen for the execution of his scheme. He had merely given them general orders to remain watchful, and prepare for an engagement in the ensuing night, the twentieth since the beginning of the siege. As soon as twilight had closed, he summoned a tribune named Magnus, and, confiding to his command four hundred soldiers in full armour, pointed out to them the aqueduct, and encouraged them to surprise the city by its aid. He provided them with lanterns, to dispel the double darkness of the night and of the covered channel in which they were to march, and appointed two trumpeters to accompany them, in order that a loud flourish, when they emerged into the city, might apprise him of their safe arrival, and strike the enemy with terror. For himself, Belisarius had prepared a great number of ladders; intending, with Bessas, one of his best officers, and some chosen troops, to assail the walls whenever the signal should be heard from within.

This well-concerted scheme was nearly disappointed, by the cowardice of some of the soldiers. Not less than half the detachment in the aqueduct shrank from the enterprise assigned them, and were brought back by their indignant leader to the presence of the general. They were received by Belisarius with deserved upbraidings; but the degeneracy of the age no longer admitted of the rigorous punishment which ancient Roman discipline would have enjoined.[43] Declaring them unworthy of the honour he had intended for them, he selected two hundred other soldiers to supply their place. Photius, thirsting for fame, hoped to obtain the command of this battalion, and had already put himself at its head; but the general refused to entrust his youthful courage with so momentous a commission.

At the same time, the fugitives from the aqueduct, stung by the reproofs of Belisarius and by the readiness of their comrades, earnestly entreated and obtained permission not to be excluded from the very danger which they so lately had dreaded to share. Such is the effect of example on the vulgar! When these six hundred soldiers began their march along the secret passage, Belisarius was not free from alarm, lest the Gothic sentinels on the battlement nearest to the aqueduct might observe an unusual sound, and suspect the stratagem. He therefore ordered Bessas to advance towards the foot of the rampart, and, in the Gothic language, to make a feigned attempt on the allegiance of the garrison. The besieged, as was expected, replied to the offers of Bessas with angry clamour and loud scoffs against himself, Belisarius, and the emperor. Little did they know, that by these insults and revilings they were drowning the noise of the footsteps which advanced to their destruction, and rendering the most essential service to the enemy.

Meanwhile, the troops of Magnus passed the walls unheard, and continued their subterranean progress, not without uneasiness from their ignorance of their exact position, and their doubts where the aqueduct might lead. At length, the first ranks had a glimpse of the sky, and soon found themselves at the extremity of the passage, situated in the court of a ruinous and deserted dwelling, and overshadowed by

---

43. That punishment was death. See *Polybius, lib. i. c.* 17.

an olive tree, which had twined its roots among the stones. Whether or not this spot were wholly uninhabited, appeared uncertain; and the steep sides were not easy to climb, especially for men encumbered with armour; but the necessity of dispatch, and the advancing troops who pressed upon the foremost from behind, left but little leisure for deliberation.

A soldier laid aside his coat of mail and offensive weapons, and, thus lightened, clung to the wall with his feet and hands, and succeeded in ascending. He found the house above tenanted only by an old and indigent matron, whom his threat of instant death, should she give the alarm, maintained in terrified silence. Flinging a rope to his comrades below, which he fastened to a branch of the olive tree, he enabled all the soldiers to free themselves from their confinement. They now had reached the centre of Naples, and a fourth part of the night still remained to profit by their situation. They hastened to the walls of the city, on the northern side, where Belisarius was expecting their signal, cut down the sentinels on the ramparts, and, by the appointed clangour of trumpets, summoned the assistance of their countrymen.

Their call was quickly answered by the Roman general, but some delay ensued from the shortness of the ladders, which were far from reaching the summit of the battlements. This defect, however, was repaired, by binding two of them together, and the walls were immediately scaled by the Roman forces. Roused from their slumbers, and rushing to the ramparts, the Goths were overwhelmed with little difficulty; but the Jews, despairing of forgiveness from their own exertions in the siege, and from the intolerant edicts of Justinian,[44] fought, to the last, with their customary national enthusiasm. Dreadful slaughter followed the final triumph of the Romans, and those, above all, who had lost a friend or relative by the darts of the garrison, now revelled in the pleasures of revenge. Peculiar fierceness was shown by the Hunnish confederates; and while the rest, even in their wildest excesses, never forgot their veneration for the church, these heathen stripped the altars, and murdered the priests without remorse.[45]

Such outrages, however, were not of long continuance: they were checked and suppressed by the authority of Belisarius, who had no

---

44. See the forty-fifth Novel of Justinian, the *Historic Arcana* of Procopius (c. 28.), and a note of Alemanni. The emperor gives a very satisfactory reason for his persecution.
45. Consult Anastasius *De Vit Pontif.* c. 59, and *Hist. Miscell. lib.* 16. ap. Murat. *Script Ital.* Vol. i.

sooner secured the fortune than he strove to restrain the bloodshed of the day. He hastened from side to side, everywhere recalling the soldiers from pillage, and exhorting them to moderation. He said:

> Let the Neapolitans feel, by your generous forbearance, the full shame and sorrow of their obstinate refusal to acquire such friendship as yours.

By dint of entreaties and upbraidings, Belisarius at length prevailed on his soldiers; withdrew from their reluctant hands the women and children seized as captives, and restored them in full security and honour to their kinsmen. The surviving Gothic soldiers, to the number of eight hundred, were preserved by his care, and induced, from his generous treatment, to enlist beneath his standards, nor does it appear that they ever proved unfaithful to their new allegiance. The citizens were assured of protection and tranquillity, and, besides the restoration of their families, were consoled by the possession of secret hoards which had escaped the prying avarice of the Romans in their dwellings.

No sooner were their fears allayed, than their rage burst forth against the former partisans of the Goths; and the orator Asclepiodotus was, above all, the object of their resentment, as if the calamities of Naples were not rather to be imputed to their own concurrence with his views, or as if the ill result of his advice proved it, of course, to be criminal. But, with common minds, there is no other measure of merit than success. Asclepiodotus was torn to pieces by the furious populace; and his colleague, Pastor, only escaped the same fate by a seasonable death from disease. It may be worthy of remark, as a singular coincidence, and as showing the uselessness of national experience, that, nine hundred years from this time, the same aqueduct and the same stratagem brought Naples into the power of Alphonso, King of Arragon.[46]

The advantage which the Romans had obtained by the taking of Naples was balanced, immediately afterwards, by the dethronement of Theodatus, whose weakness they must have considered as their best ally. His warlike subjects had already viewed with indignation his delay in marching to encounter the approaching enemy, and variously attributed his conduct to a private treaty with Justinian, or to natural cowardice of temper. Such were the bitter feelings of the Gothic nation, and the intelligence of the loss of Naples was the last drop, which made them overflow. The few troops at hand were quartered

---

46. Muratori *Annal. d'Ital.* vol. i.

about forty miles from Rome, so as to cover the capital on the side of Campania; and their command had been entrusted, by Theodatus, to an officer of humble birth, who had distinguished himself under the great Theodoric in the Pannonian war. His real name was Wittich, which the Greeks, with their usual dislike to the harshness of barbaric sounds, have softened into Vitiges.[47]

The soldiers now convened at a spot which Procopius calls Regeta, but which is perhaps no other than Lake Regillus, celebrated for the defeat of the Latins,[48] At this time, it was remarkable for the fertility of its pastures, and therefore well adapted to an encampment of cavalry. Here a sentence of deposition was tumultuously passed on the degenerate possessor of the throne, and Vitiges, raised on shields according to national custom,[49] was hailed as the worthy successor of Theodoric. They could not have made a better choice: Vitiges was a man of experience, energy, and courage. The first act of his new authority was a prudent attempt to forestall a civil war, by forthwith crushing the pretensions of Theodatus, who, on the first news of a revolt, had quitted Rome, and was escaping towards Ravenna. A Goth named Optaris was commanded by Vitiges to pursue the royal fugitive, and to bring him back, dead or alive. This messenger obeyed with alacrity; he thirsted for revenge against Theodatus, who had formerly deprived him of a rich and beautiful bride, the king having been induced, by a liberal present, to bestow her on one of his rivals.

Delighted at this opportunity for full retribution, Optaris closely followed on the traces of Theodatus, without intermission either by night or by day; and having at length succeeded in overtaking him, at the fifth milestone from Ravenna,[50] threw him prostrate on the ground before him, and sacrificed him, says Procopius, like a victim at the shrine. Such, in the third year of his reign, was the fate of Theodatus, a prince who mistook learning for wisdom; and because he found himself incapable of business, thought himself fitted for study. His son Theodegisel also fell into the hands of Vitiges, and was by his orders

---

47. See the *Nibelungen Lied, lib. xxriii.* v. 6809, with the remark of Zeune.
48. *Liv. lib.ii* c. 19,20.
49. This custom, which was very ancient and universal amongst the barbarian tribes, (Tacit *Hist. lib. iv.* c. 15, Gregory of Tours, &c.) was afterwards adopted by the Byzantine emperors. (Theophylact Simocatta, *lib. viii.* c. 7.)
50. Marcellin *Chron. ap. Sirmond, Op.* vol. ii. The date of this event is fixed by Sigonius in August, which appears irreconcilable the entrance of Belisarius into Rome, so late as December. Now the latter date being certain, we may suspect the former. (*De Occident. Imp.* vol. i.)

held in close captivity.

The election at Regeta was gladly confirmed at Rome, by the senators, the nobles, and the Catholic clergy; all of whom Theodatus had threatened (for cowards always love to threaten) and insulted, from their supposed correspondence with Constantinople.[51] Thus freed from any fear of internal opposition, the new monarch turned his whole powerful mind to the means of repelling the attack of Belisarius, and securing the kingdom which he had just acquired. The resolution which he formed was singular, but judicious and decisive. No effectual preparations had been made by Theodatus for resistance; the greater part of the Gothic forces was scattered through Liguria and Venetia, and but few could then be mustered at Rome. No stores were in readiness for a campaign, no line had been chosen for defence. Had Vitiges, in spite of all these disadvantages, dared to try the fortune of a battle, and met with a defeat, the consequent loss of Rome would certainly have been imputed to himself, whilst its immediate abandonment might be fairly thrown upon the fault of his predecessor. He might have been pursued, by the victorious Greeks, to the very walls of Ravenna, and, arriving as a helpless runaway, would probably not have been acknowledged as king by the Gothic Army in the northern provinces.

He therefore determined to retreat with his troops to Ravenna, to collect his forces, and establish his power; and he trusted that, returning against Belisarius in a few months, at the head of a formidable army, he should easily overwhelm the scanty numbers of the enemy. The chief difficulty attending this project, was to reconcile his haughty soldiers to the idea of a retreat; and we may admire the address of his harangue, which unfolded his unwelcome proposal by degrees, and rendered it alluring by the promise of future victory.[52] Persuaded by his eloquence, the Goths cheerfully prepared for departure. A garrison, commanded by Leuderis, was left at Rome, but it consisted only of four thousand soldiers. To secure the loyalty of the citizens, Vitiges removed to Ravenna, as hostages, the most distinguished senators, and forced the remainder, with Pope Silverius,[53] at their head, to take a solemn oath of allegiance.

---

51. For his treatment of the senators, see Liberatus, (*Breviar.* c. 2,) His conduct towards the orthodox clergy may be presumed from a remark of Anastasius, who attributes his dethronement to inspiration, "*nuto divino.*" (*De Vit Pontif.* c, 59.)

52. See his speech to the army, in Procopius (*Goth. lib. i.* c. 11) and his circular letter to the Goths, on his accession, in Cassiodorius, (*Var.lib. x. ep.* 31.)

53. Silverius was the successor of Agapetus, who had died on his embassy to Constantinople. (Muratori, *Annal. d'Ital.* vol. iii.)

On arriving at his Adriatic capital, he endeavoured to confirm the favour of the soldiers, which had called him to the throne, by the more lasting claims of hereditary right. Knowing that the name and kindred of the great Theodoric were still justly dear to the Goths, he compelled the reluctant Matasontha,[54] sister of Athalaric, to bestow on him her hand in marriage. His next step was to enter into negotiations with Childebert, Clotaire, and Theodebert, the three kings of the Franks, who had lately been summoned by Justinian, as brother Catholics, to share in the subversion and the spoils of the Arian monarchy in Italy. They had accordingly taken arms, but Vitiges, fearing to contend at once with invaders in the north and south, thought it requisite, and found it easy, to gain them over to his interest. The cession of the Gothic provinces between the Alps and the Rhone, together with the payment of two thousand pounds weight of gold, suddenly changed these antagonists into zealous friends. They could not indeed, after their engagements with the emperor, conclude a public alliance with Vitiges, and send him their own troops as auxiliaries, but they promised, by secret orders, to dispatch some powerful reinforcements to his aid, from amongst their tributaries and dependents.

Scarcely had Vitiges left Rome, before Pope Silverius broke through the oath of fidelity which he had been compelled to take; whether thinking that forced engagements are from their very nature null and void, or whether holding the convenient maxim, that *no faith need be kept with heretics*. Through his persuasion, and their own pious zeal, the citizens, in spite of their Gothic garrison, declared loudly in favour of the orthodox invaders, and a messenger was dispatched to the camp of Belisarius, to make known their friendly intentions. They were also strongly influenced by the dread of suffering calamities, like those which Naples had lately undergone. Even before receiving their deputation, Belisarius had prepared to march upon their city. He could spare no more than three hundred men for the garrison of Naples, and stationed a similar detachment at Cumae, the only other fortress in Campania, and one of the strongest in Italy.[55]

From thence he proceeded along the Latin way, leaving to his left the stately road of Appius, the Censor.[56] The latter was, however, at-

---

54. The two last syllables of her name, as of her mother's, Amalasontha, seem to be a corruption from *Schuente*, or beauty, in old German. See Grotius, *Hist. Goth.*
55. Agathias, *lib. i.*
56. *Liv. lib. ix.* c 29. Procopius makes Appius a Consul; a which may be forgiven in a Byzantine historian.

tentively surveyed by Procopius, who observed with astonishment, that, after nearly nine centuries of constant use, the hard and polished stones still maintained their junction, and presented the appearance of one unbroken mass. To this day, the traveller from Rome to Naples passes over some remains of this classic pavement, [57] which, however, are very far from still deserving their ancient praise of smoothness. On descending the long ridge of Albano, the Roman general beheld before him that venerable birthplace of empire which his countrymen had once hailed as their capital, and whence they still drew their national name. With so interesting an epoch in his life, this chapter shall conclude.

---

57. As at Fondi. See Forsyth's *Italy*, Geneva ed.

CHAPTER 5

Active Preparations

At the period when Belisarius approached the walls of the Eternal City, it had been for sixty years under the dominion of barbarians. During that time, it had fully enjoyed the blessings of peace and prosperity; it had been an object of peculiar care, attention, and munificence, and had received the respect and honours due to the ancient mistress of the world. The recollection of the grievous and distracted government of the Western Emperors, might have taught the citizens of Rome affection to their Gothic rulers, could one generation ever profit by the experience of the last. They did not perceive that the Kings of Italy might indeed be termed barbarian, but were national monarchs; while the Byzantine government, though nominally Roman, was in fact the oppressive bondage of a stranger. The public feelings, both in Africa and Italy, in favour of the imperial invasion, may serve as memorable examples to show how precarious is the authority of those princes who array themselves in sects opposed to the tenets of their subjects. The national altar and the national throne cannot be merely foreign and indifferent to each other; if not allied, they must be hostile. It was not from any love to the Byzantine empire, but from attachment to the Catholic religion, that the Vandal and Gothic rulers were forsaken on the first favourable opportunity, and, had they not been Arians, they would never have been regarded as tyrants.

Unable to withstand the evident inclinations of the Roman people, and to sustain a siege without their co-operation, the Gothic garrison marched out, through the Flaminian gate, as soon as they learnt that Belisarius was entering by the Asinarian.[1] Their commander, Leuderis,

---

1. Antiquarians are not entirely agreed which was the Asinarian gate. (Donatus, *Roma Antiqua, lib.* i. c. 21.) It is supposed to be a small gate, now closed, near that of San Giovanni, and Nardini adduces a passage in point from Anastasius: (*Roma Antica, lib.* i. c. 9.)

however, with noble stubbornness, refused to join in even a necessary flight, and continued firm, though forsaken, at his post. He was accordingly taken prisoner by the imperial troops, and sent by Belisarius to Justinian, with the keys of Rome, as trophies of success. It was on the tenth day of December that Belisarius entered the city.[2] The first care of the prudent conqueror, who foresaw the possibility of an impending siege from Vitiges, was directed to the walls, which, in spite of the partial repairs of Theodoric the Great, were ruinous in many places.[3] The ancient ramparts were strengthened; new battlements were constructed, with an angular point, and with lateral bastions; and the ditch, which appears to have been partly choked up with fallen fragments, was cleared, deepened, and extended.

The citizens beheld with surprise and admiration the strong bulwarks rising around them, and found with regret that their ready submission to the conqueror would not succeed in saving them from the havoc of a siege. With all the eloquence of cowardice, they attempted to dissuade Belisarius from his project of fortifying Rome, and represented, in glowing colours, the inadequate store of provisions for its maintenance, and the vast and untenable extent of its walls. They urged, that its inland position cut off all maritime supplies, and that its level site presented no natural advantage for defence. Such reasoning served only to apprise Belisarius how far he might rely in future on the zeal of his friends, but could not shake his deliberate determination. His repairs of the ramparts were continued with unabated activity; he drew from his fleet, and placed in the public granaries, a large supply of Sicilian corn, and compelled the reluctant Romans to bring in the harvests of the neighbouring country.

Nor did he neglect in the meanwhile to spread his conquests in southern Italy, where he found that the fame of his past successes, in some degree precluded the necessity for further exertions. The Gothic troops in Samnium submitted to his power, and many districts, which had no barbarian forces to withhold them, gladly acknowledged the orthodox conqueror. The central and important city of Benevento opened its gates to him. This city, founded by Diomede, was originally called Maleventum, from a violent eastern gale,[4] to which its situation

---

2. The date of this remarkable event is ascertained by the skill of Pagi. (*Critic*, vol. ii.)
3. For the repairs of the walls by Theodoric, see Cassiodorius. (*Var. lib. i.* ep. 25. *lib.* 2. ep. 34.)
4. Benevento is said by Procopius to be built upon a hill, and exposed to the gales from Dalmatia. His description may be compared with, (continued next page),

is exposed; but the name was afterwards altered by the Romans, from a dread of its evil augury.[5] Its inhabitants still displayed, in the time of Procopius, the tusks of the Calydonian boar, which the historian asserts to have extended twenty-seven inches in length; and I should be less unwilling to admit this extraordinary size, than to imagine that an animal of smaller proportions Could render it necessary for thirty chieftains to confederate against him.[6]

After the reduction of Benevento, the Roman general dispatched some light troops under Bessas to occupy the town of Narni, of which the strong situation might have retarded the capture, had it not been freely surrendered by the citizens.[7] This Bessas, who had already distinguished himself in the siege of Naples, was a Thracian by birth, and a Goth by nation; his abilities were great, but his avarice and cruelty still greater. Another detachment, headed by Constantine, was sent from Rome into Tuscany; and here also the favour of the Italians afforded them an easy entrance into Spoleto, and afterwards into Perugia, which was then considered as the capital of that province, and of which the wide circuit still attests the former importance. The neighbourhood of this city was the scene of the first encounter, in the open field, between the Romans and the Goths, (February, *a.d.* 537). Constantine was attacked by some barbarian forces under the command of Hunnilas, but his valour succeeded in repulsing their superior numbers with considerable loss.[8]

Roused by resentment at this check, Vitiges resolved to linger no more at his Adriatic capital, especially as the spring had now begun, and his warlike preparations were almost completed. It must be owned that his time at Ravenna had not been employed with less activity and effect, than that of his rival at Rome. Though he dispatched some strong reinforcements to Dalmatia, against the imperial troops

---

that of Mr. Keppel Craven. (*Tour in the Kingdom of Naples*). May not the wind in question be the same as the Atabulus of Horace? (*Serm.* 1. v. v. 78.)

5. A very similar change of name has taken place with regard to the district near Hybla in Sicily. It was first called Mel Passi, then Mal Passi, then Bel Passi, and at last Mal Passi again. (Brydone's *Travels*, vol. i. 1773.)

6. Procop. *Goth. lib. i.* c. 15. It is very rarely that the tusks of a wild boar exceed nine or ten inches in length. (Buffon, *Quadrupèdes*, vol. i. ed. 1786.) Ovid says vaguely, that these tusks were as large as those of an elephant. (*Met. lib. viii.* v. 288.)

7. Of the site of Narni, and the magnificent bridge built by Augustus, an interesting description is given by Procopius (*Goth. lib. i.* c. 1 7.), which may be compared with that of Labat in modern times. (*Voyages*, vol. vii.)

8. The text of Jornandes here is evidently corrupted. We probably to read seventy, or seven hundred, instead of seven (*De Regn. Success.*)

in that quarter, yet the army with which he now commenced his march against Belisarius, amounted to no less than one hundred and fifty thousand men. Of these the most formidable were his heavy cavalry, or *cuirassiers*, whose horses, like themselves, were protected by breastplates. On the other hand, the Roman Army, which never seems to have exceeded twelve thousand soldiers, had been much reduced by the bloody siege of Naples, and even by its own successes, since these imposed the necessity of leaving garrisons in the conquered towns. [9] No wonder, therefore, if Vitiges, not sufficiently considering how many thousand men the genius of one hero may outweigh, felt secure of an easy and rapid victory, and was even disposed to regret, as unnecessary caution, his former prudent retreat. He only expressed alarm lest Belisarius should not await his arrival, and might thus elude his intended vengeance; and, on his march, he is said to have inquired of a priest, whom he met arriving from Rome, whether the Greek general had not yet fled from that city.

As soon as the advance of Vitiges became known to Belisarius, he recalled the detachments of Bessas and Constantine to the capital, commanding them however to leave garrisons in Spoleto, Perugia, and Narni. In executing these instructions with regard to Narni, Bessas was so dilatory, that the vanguard of the Gothic army surprised him; but he retrieved his fault by a successful skirmish, and made good his retreat upon Rome. The chief object of Belisarius, in maintaining these cities, was to harass and delay the march of Vitiges, being himself in expectation of reinforcements from Constantinople, and desirous of protracting hostilities till their arrival. He knew that, were he to be encompassed in Rome, they could not, without much difficulty and many hazards, find it possible to join him, and he also wished for further time to complete his stores of provisions. These views were disappointed by the rapidity of Vitiges, who was hurried on by the fear lest Belisarius should escape him. He passed by without attack the strong battlements of the Tuscan cities, and the rocky height of Narni; and, probably stationing some detachments to watch and restrain the

---

9. So great a disproportion of forces between the Goths and Romans, may, perhaps, excite some doubts in the reader. (Muratori, *Annal. d'Ital.* vol iii.) Yet several similar examples are attested by history. At the siege of Rhodes, *a.d.* 1522, the Turkish forces amounted to one hundred and forty thousand soldiers, and sixty thousand pioneers, while the garrison could muster only five or six thousand men. See Vertot, *Histoire de Malte*, vol. ii. In the Battle of Tusculum, *a.d.* 1167, an army of thirty thousand Romans was defeated by little more than one thousand German cavalry. (Murat. *Annal. d'Ital.* vol .vi.)

garrisons, led the remainder of his vast armies to the Milvian bridge, within two miles of the Eternal City.

But at this place the skill of Belisarius had provided another obstacle to retard their progress. He had fortified the bridge by a massy tower and sufficient garrison, so as to command its passage, and he intended to sally forth with some light troops, to line the banks of the Tiber. He well knew that by collecting boats the Goths might easily cross the river, but he had reckoned that, on this occasion, the very number of his enemies would act in his favour, and that not less than twenty days must be consumed in transporting so many thousand soldiers. Should they, on the other hand, march round to some other bridge, the loss of time must be equally considerable. A scheme so judicious, and apparently so certain of success, was baffled by a circumstance against which no prudence could provide, the panic terror of the soldiers to whom the guard of the Milvian tower was entrusted. On beholding from their elevated station the innumerable battalions of the enemy darkening the horizon, and appearing to augment as they advanced, they were filled with dismay at such overwhelming strength, and availed themselves of the darkness of the ensuing night to escape, unperceived.

Dreading, however, the stern reproaches of the general, no less than the irresistible numbers of the Goths, they did not dare to re-enter Rome, but fled across the open country to Campania, so that Belisarius had not even the advantage to be apprised of the failure of his plans. Early the next morning, (Mar. 11, a.d. 537), the Goths, who till then had been perplexed and dismayed. at the unexpected barrier before them, finding it abandoned, forced its gates, and secured their passage with ease.[10]

On his part, Belisarius, wholly ignorant of their progress, was, according to his previous resolution, sallying forth with a thousand of his guards from the city, to encamp on the shore of the Tiber, and observe the movements of the enemy. Suddenly, to his utter surprise, he found himself encompassed by the Gothic vanguard of cavalry. In this emergency Belisarius displayed, as at the Battle of Callinicum, not merely the judgment of a general, but the personal intrepidity of a soldier. Distinguished by the charger whom he had often rode in bat-

---

10. It will be seen that this skirmish took place the day before the commencement of the siege. In his first Gothic book, (c. 24) Procopius merely states that the siege began in March, but I deduce for it the precise date of the 12th of that month, on grounds which I shall afterwards explain.

tle, a bay,[11] with a white face, he was seen in the foremost ranks. "That is Belisarius!" exclaimed some Roman deserters. "Aim at the bay," was forthwith the cry through all the Gothic squadrons, and re-echoed by thousands unacquainted with its real motive. A shower of darts and arrows was directed against this conspicuous mark.

It seemed, says Procopius, to be clearly felt both by the Romans and their enemies, that the fate of Italy depended on this single life. The boldest Goths rushed forward, eager to signalise their valour against so illustrious an antagonist, or to serve their cause by so important a captive. In these close combats Belisarius displayed great prowess; many amongst his assailants fell by his single arm, and his exploits are said to have outdone those of any other Roman on that day. His guards, on their part, manifested the utmost courage and devotion to his person; they crowded around him to the right and left, and raised their bucklers on both sides, to receive and ward off the innumerable missiles which flew.

Not less than one thousand of the enemy were slain, a number which equalled the whole force of the Romans, and though this advantage was purchased by the death of many of their bravest soldiers, yet Belisarius, against whom the attack had been chiefly pointed, by a singular favour of fortune remained without a wound. There being but a single bridge to convey the Goths across the Tiber, their passage was unavoidably slow, and often obstructed, and but few reinforcements could come up to the scene of action. Their foremost squadron at length, disheartened by the desperate resistance it encountered, fled back towards its camp, and the Romans were also hurried forwards by the thoughtless ardour of pursuit.

The advance of some Gothic infantry immediately checked the Romans; they retreated to a neighbouring hill for protection, but were quickly overtaken by some fresh barbarian cavalry, and a new conflict began. The Romans endeavoured to return into the city, and the Goths to intercept them. Amongst the many achievements on this memorable day, there was one act of generous self-sacrifice, to which history could hardly, perhaps, afford any other parallel than that of Winkelried, the martyr for his country at Sempach.[12] Valentine, one of the military attendants of Photius, perceiving the foremost of the

---

11. A bay horse was called φαλιος by the Greeks, and *balan* by the barbarians. (Procop. *Goth. lib. i.* c. 18.) The last is connected by Giphanius with the Gorman *ein fahl pferd.* (*Comment.*) See also the *Nibelungen Lied.* (v. 2307.)

12. Muller, *Geschichte der Schweitz*, vol. it. ed. 1006.

Goths pressing closely against his exhausted comrades in some narrow defile, threw himself upon their levelled spears, arrested their progress for some moments, and by his seasonable death afforded the Romans leisure for escape. Thus they succeeded in attaining the Flaminian gate, which, in memory of the exploits of the general on this occasion, was afterwards called the Belisarian. His merit was not unworthy of this honour, and I cannot but regret that both the first and second appellation should now have yielded to one derived only from some legendary miracles of the darkest ages.[13]

On reaching the Flaminian gate at sunset, the Romans naturally thought that they at last had overcome all the toils and dangers of this weary day. But the terrified soldiers on the ramparts, observing the close pursuit of the enemy, dreaded lest, in opening the gate, the barbarians might enter it, together with the Romans, and they remained deaf to the earnest solicitations of their comrades, and even to the loud commands and threats of Belisarius. The blood and dust with which his face was covered, and also the shades of twilight, hindered recognition of his person and obedience to his orders. A report of his death had also been spread in the city by some runaways from the battle, who had witnessed the vigour of the attack but had not remained to see the intrepidity of the resistance. During the parley the barbarians pressed still closer against the Romans, who had now been driven under the very wall beyond the ditch, and were every moment expecting a destructive and final assault.

The troops within the city, unknowing of the event, fearful for themselves and deprived of a commander, did not venture, by a sally, to assist their distressed companions. In this utmost need, the gallant band of Belisarius had no resource but their courage alone. Animating the soldiers around him to follow, Belisarius rushed forward in a last and desperate charge against the Gothic troops, who were then unsuspicious of attack, and dispersed from the confidence of victory. They could not imagine that so much energy was manifested by the faint and harassed soldiers, exhausted by the toils of the day; the dimness of the evening assisted the illusion, and a new army was supposed to have issued from the city.

---

13. The Flaminian gate at present, (1829), bears the name of Porta del Popolo, from the neighbouring church of St. Maria del Popolo, which was founded by Pope Paschal II., towards the year 1100, to relieve the people from the spectre of the Emperor Nero, which frequently alarmed them. The remedy has proved effectual, and Nero now leaves the Romans in quiet (*Donat. Rom. Antiq. lib. iv. c. 9.*)

The barbarians once more fled before the hero, and Belisarius, after a short pretended pursuit, suddenly turned round, and hastened back to the gates of Rome, which now were opened to receive him. New fatigues awaited him within the walls. He assembled the scattered troops and a great number of the citizens, and, for fear of a surprise in the midst of this confusion, commanded them to light fires on the ramparts, and to watch during the ensuing night. He made the circuit of the walls, and appointed an officer to the defence of each separate gate.

While thus employed, he received a messenger from Bessas, whom he had stationed in another quarter, to inform him that the Goths had just effected an entrance by the gate of St. Pancratius, on the Tuscan bank of the Tiber.[14] Struck with dismay at this intelligence, the attendants of the general besought him to provide for his personal security and theirs by escaping without delay through an opposite outlet, while Belisarius endeavoured to calm them by asserting it to be a false alarm. Such, in fact, it proved to be; but this instance of the tumult and disorder, growing out from unfounded rumours of defeat, suggested to Belisarius an useful direction for the future. He enjoined each officer on the ramparts not to leave his post on any consideration whatever, not even if he should believe the city to have been entered by the enemy elsewhere, but to think only of defending his own allotted station, and trust to the general for the safety of the whole.

Having thus provided for the immediate exigencies of the time till late at night, after many hours of continual abstinence and labour, Belisarius was at length persuaded by Antonina and his attendants to partake of some food and repose. The Roman citizens, unable to emulate, or even to comprehend his lofty spirit, could hardly suppress their sarcastic smiles of disbelief, when he assured them that they should ultimately triumph over the barbarians; and they considered such confidence as the height of presumption in a man just escaped with so much difficulty from their innumerable squadrons. The field on which the skirmish of this day was fought, is nearly the same on which the cause of the first Christian emperor prevailed, and it may not be wholly undeserving of mention, as a singular coincidence, that two of the most distinguished officers of Belisarius, on this occasion, were named Maxentius and Constantine.

---

14. This gate is supposed without any certain proof, to be the ancient Janiculensis. Contrast the doubts of the learned Nardini (*lib.* i. c. 9.) with the certainty of the superficial Vasi (*Itinéraire*.) Ignorance is always positive.

The morrow of this eventful day, (Mar. 12, *a.d.* 537), was the first of the siege of Rome, which continued for upwards of a year, and which, whether we consider the importance of the object, the number of the combatants, or the classic associations of the ground, may perhaps vie with any other recorded in history. The Goths appear to have been less delighted at their easy and unexpected passage of the Milvian bridge, than mortified by the inglorious though successful skirmish which ensued. They had to deplore the loss of many of their bravest soldiers, and above all of the standard bearer,[15] Visandus, who, after a close combat with Belisarius himself, fell from his horse, pierced with thirteen wounds, and was left for dead upon the field. Three days afterwards, however, on the interment of the corpses by the Goths, he was found still to breathe, and, by the care of his comrades, survived this conflict many years.

On the very evening of the skirmish, Vitiges indulged his angry feelings by dispatching Vaces,[16] one of his most distinguished officers, beneath the walls of Rome, to upbraid the citizens for their perfidy and treason to the Goths. The envoy said:

Why should you prefer the dominion of the Greeks to ours? Far from protecting you, the feeble forces of that empire are scarcely sufficient for its own defence, and from that quarter your great ancestors would never have acknowledged a master. They only knew the Greeks as pirates, players, and buffoons.

Next day the Goths had recourse to more effectual arguments than words. Expecting, from the vast extent and slender garrison of Rome, to find it an easy conquest, they did not think it requisite to surround the whole circumference of twelve miles, and, in fact, even their multitudes of soldiers appeared inadequate for its complete investment, without exposing themselves to the chance of a sudden and successful sally on some particular point. Yet their army seems to have amounted to full its original number, since any detachments which they may have left before the Tuscan cities, were compensated by the arrival of some fresh troops, which, according to the treaty with the Franks, had ceded the provinces between the Alps and the Rhone, and were thus

---

15. The penetration of Gibbon has discerned that in Procopius, (*Goth. lib. i.* c. 18.) it is not, as was formerly thought another name of Visandus, but a word of barbaric origin for standard bearer. See his note, vol. vii. And Ducange, *Gloss. Graec.*
16. This name is explained by Grotius as *Waack-hais, excubitoribus imperans* (*Hist Goth.*)

at liberty to act elsewhere.

On the scene of the late skirmish, and from the Pincian to the end of the Esquiline hill, the Goths formed six camps, which they fortified with deep ditches, pointed stakes, and entrenchments of earth. Apprehensive, also, that the enemy might destroy the Milvian bridge, and thus interrupt their communication with the other side of the Tiber, they commanded this important station by a seventh encampment in the plain of Nero.[17]

Thus, of the fourteen[18] principal gates of Rome, they only encompassed five on the southern and two on the northern bank, and though their light troops scoured the adjacent country, they did not altogether stop the intercourse between Rome and Campania. Their next measure was to cut through the aqueducts, which, like the gates, were fourteen in number, built of brick, and with each arch of sufficient height for the passage of a horseman beneath it. The greater part of these noble monuments has never been repaired, and their scattered ruins, extending at intervals along the dreary Campagna, are finely compared by Poggio to the outstretched and broken limbs of an expiring giant. On this occasion no immediate injury was suffered by the Romans; the public baths, indeed, were no longer supplied, but the turbid stream of the Tiber, and the wells in the remoter districts of the city, were adequate for every needful object. The city mills, which were placed on the Tuscan side, and turned by the fall of water from an aqueduct, were however stopped, nor could horses or oxen for working them be allowed, in prudence, to consume the limited forage of the garrison.

The active mind of Belisarius soon devised another expedient, which may appear more simple to the present times than it did to an age when the very use of aqueducts proves the ignorance of hydraulic principles. He perceived that the current of the river was most rapid below the bridge,[19] its channel being there contracted by the piers, and he therefore moored under the arches some small boats, containing mills, which the impulse of the stream proved sufficient to turn. No sooner had some deserters apprized the Goths of this contrivance than they attempted to defeat it by throwing into the river large

---

17. See Donat. *Rom. Antiq. lib. iii* c. 23.
18. Such is the number stated by Procopius. In the time of Poggio there were only thirteen. (Gibbon, vol. xii.)
19. It appears from this passage of Procopius, as also from another, (*Goth. lib. iii.* c. 17,) that only one bridge in Rome at this time remained entire. This was the ancient Ælian, opposite the castle of St. Angelo.

trunks of trees, and even the dead bodies of the Romans slain in the previous skirmish, which, floating down the stream, broke through the cords, and shattered or sunk the machines. But Belisarius found means to guard against such havoc in future. He fastened massy iron chains along the bridge on the outer side, which detained any solid substances borne along by the current until the neighbouring sentinels could draw them to the shore. By this protection the Roman mills continued to work without further intermission during the remainder of the siege, and a security was also thus obtained that the Goths might not, by secretly embarking in boats, and trusting themselves to the current at night, penetrate unperceived into the heart of the city.

It was on the front of the Pincian hill, the same spot at present occupied by the public walk of Rome, that the head-quarters of the Byzantine general were fixed. This station above all others needed the care of the commander, because the adjacent ramparts were the weakest and most easily accessible, and it was also well chosen as affording an extensive prospect over all the districts of the city and encampments of the Goths. Warned by his own success at Naples, and anxious to prevent a renewal of his former stratagem, Belisarius carefully walled up the passage of the aqueducts. He likewise closed and entrenched with large stones, the Flaminian gate, lest its nearness to one of the Gothic camps might aid some nightly surprise, yet all this prudence would have proved unavailing, unless Belisarius had devised some means for watching and defending the vast circumference of the walls. His own diminished band of veterans was wholly insufficient for this purpose, and the expected reinforcements from Constantinople had never yet arrived.

To supply this deficiency he availed himself of the public distress at Rome, where a considerable number of mechanics and workmen had since the siege been dismissed from their daily labours. It would have been dangerous as well as cruel to leave them thus inactive, since whenever an artisan is either too wretched to find, or too rich to require employment, his leisure is always filled up by disaffection to the state. These men were now enlisted and formed into squadrons; a stipulated pay, and rotation of service, was assigned to each, and some experienced soldiers were mingled amongst them, so that, in case of assault on any particular point, Belisarius was enabled to collect in that direction almost all his regular forces, without leaving the circuit of the walls unguarded. Thus, says Procopius, the general, provided by the same measure for the security of the city and the relief of the inhabitants.

Yet to insure the fidelity of these civic bands was a task of peculiar difficulty. Thrice every month Belisarius altered the keys of all the gates, and still more frequently transferred the station of each detachment. Different officers were commissioned every night to make the circuit of the ramparts, and to call from a muster-roll the names of the sentinels on duty; if one were found missing, another was forthwith appointed in his place, and the list of the defaulters was transmitted to Belisarius for their punishment or detection. Some soldiers, principally Moors, as least open from their savage manners and language to the seductions of the Goths, were posted by night without the walls accompanied by dogs, whose trusty baying might announce the coming of an enemy; and the watchfulness of these nightly patrols was still further secured by the animation of military music. The general endeavoured to conciliate the Italians, by avoiding rigorous punishments, even in cases of convicted treason; and his sentence of banishment against some senators may be favourably contrasted with the vengeful fury of Vitiges, who had dispatched orders to Ravenna for the instant massacre of all those Roman nobles formerly carried off as hostages.

Through his numerous precautions, Belisarius succeeded during the whole of the siege in forestalling or discovering the perfidy, but could not retain the attachment, of the Roman citizens. The close approach of warfare terrified their feeble minds, they bore with unwillingness the fatigue of vigils and the hardships of confinement, their fancy painted the probable devastation of their neighbouring fields, and they compared the luxurious plenty of peace with the spare and scanty rations of a siege. Their zeal for Belisarius had proceeded from his fortune, and ceased at the first appearance of adversity. Of his ultimately prevailing, they appear to have entertained no expectation, but they looked forward with eagerness to the terms of a capitulation, which they thought would be favourable to them in proportion to its speediness. Accordingly they assailed the general, sometimes with entreaties, but more frequently with angry clamour.

The senate was more disguised, and therefore more dangerous in its discontent. Within a few days from the commencement of the siege, Vitiges became informed of these feelings in the people, and in order to inflame them still further, and to throw upon the Byzantine invader the whole odium of the war, he dispatched some ambassadors with insidious proposals to Rome. They were received by Belisarius at a public audience, in presence of the senate and principal officers. They urged him to meet their countrymen fairly in the field, to pity the impending sufferings of Rome, and not to seek from its walls the protection which his arms should afford him. As terms of surrender,. they offered to his troops a free retreat, with all their private property. Belisarius said in reply:

> My system of warfare shall be guided, not by your judgment but by my own. Far from viewing my prospects at present with any gloomy forebodings, I tell you that the time will come, when, reduced to your last detachment, and driven from your furthest village, you shall seek and scarcely find a refuge in bushes and brambles. We are engaged in a national and rightful cause. If anyone amongst you thinks to enter Rome, without disputing every foot of ground, and meeting with the most determined resistance, he shall find himself grievously mistaken. So long as Belisarius shall survive expect no surrender.[20]

This answer was received by the ambassadors in silence, by Vitiges, with indignation. The Gothic monarch forthwith issued orders for a general assault, which he fixed for the eighteenth day from the commencement of the siege, having in the meanwhile made unwearied preparations for it. Square towers of wood had been built, equal in height to the battlements of Rome, and rolling on four wheels. Numerous ladders were at hand to scale the rampart, and in order to make a breach in it, four of the weighty engines called *aries* had been constructed. This, battering-ram of prodigious power, was likewise moved (Mar. 30, a.d. 537), on four wheels, and was wielded by no less 537. than fifty men, securely enclosed in a covered chamber at the base.[21] Nor had the Goths forgotten faggots of branches and reeds, with which it was intended to fill up the intervening ditch, and allow a close approach of these engines against the Roman walls.

On the other part, the multitude of precautions and cares which have already been set forth, had not distracted Belisarius from providing military machines for the protection of the city. The towers were lined with *onagri*, or large mechanical slings, and with *balistae*, power-

---

20. The literal version of these words (Procop *Goth. lib. i.* c. 20.) would be, "Belisarius will never surrender this city whilst he continues alive"—rather an Hibernian clause. Yet a similar message was once sent by General Muscar, governor of Dunkirk, in the French revolutionary war. See Edgeworth's *Essay on Irish Bulls*.

21. Compare Ammianus Marcellinus (*lib. xxiii.* c. 4), with Procopius (*Goth. lib.* i. c. 21)

ful crossbows which discharged an arrow only half as long, but four times as massy as the common ones, and of such force as to cleave without difficulty a tree or a stone. Over each gate was suspended a *lupus*, consisting of a beam perforated with holes, through which, on the approach of an enemy, thick iron spikes could be thrust forward, to transfix him.

Such were the preparations on both sides, when on the appointed day the Goths marched to the contest, having fixed on the Salarian gate,[22] as the principal object of attack. The success of Alaric, who had entered Rome in this quarter, might seem to them an auspicious augury, and they resolved to leave unattempted the Flaminian gate, since it had been closed and entrenched by Belisarius, and since there would have been also some obstacles to encounter from the steep or rugged nature of the ground.[23] The spot which appeared to offer the greatest advantages to an assailant, was near the small outlet on the slope of the Pincian hill. Here the city wall was full of crevices and fissures; it had greatly declined from the perpendicular and overhung the space in front of it, so that in all likelihood a single blow from a battering-ram would have been sufficient to demolish it. This defect in the ramparts had not escaped the eye of Belisarius, but his intention of repairing it was met by the earnest and repeated remonstrances of the Roman people.

They asserted, that as a reward for the peculiar fervour of their devotion to St. Peter, he had promised them to take this chasm under his apostolic guard. They therefore maintained, that the portion which, to mere human eyes, might seem the least secure, was in reality the strongest of the ramparts, and that it would be a tempting of Providence, and an impious disregard of revelation, to take means for its defence. These arguments prevailed with Belisarius, either from himself believing their superstitious tale, or from knowing that it was believed by the barbarians. Nor were his expectations disappointed. The Goths religiously abstained from attacking this consecrated spot, and the same bent in the wall has been suffered to continue till the present time.[24]

---

22. This gate in ancient times bore the name of Collina (Tacit. *Hist. lib. iii.* c. 82,) but the road was called Salaria, (Plin. *Hist. Nat. lib.* xxxi, c. 7.) By an easy transaction the name of the road was afterwards given to the gate
23. (Procop. *Goth. lib. i.* c. 23.) Donatus and Nardini feel themselves bound by this passage, to move the Flaminian gate to the summit of the neighbouring hill. But may not the words of Procopius merely imply inequalities and broken ground in the approach?
24. The devotion of the Goths, or at least of Theodoric to St Peter, is attested by Anastasius (*De Vit. Pontif.* 53,) and *Anonym. Vales.*

It was at daybreak that the Roman garrison, drawn out upon the ramparts and under the personal command of Belisarius, saw the innumerable squadrons of the enemy and their lofty engines drawn by teams of oxen, slowly advancing against the Salarian gate. At this formidable sight the new levies were struck with sudden terror, and it was with surprise that they beheld the smile of confidence which played upon the features of the general, and heard his orders to. refrain as yet from discharging their arrows. As the assailants came nearer he stepped forwards to the edge of the rampart, seized a bow, and with a deliberate aim transfixed the foremost Gothic chief. His shaft against a second was equally successful, and the Romans, regarding the prowess of their leader as a happy presage of victory, raised a loud shout of hope and exultation.

Belisarius now commanded the archers to let fly, taking aim at the oxen only. In a few moments these animals fell lifeless to the ground, and the military engines remained immovable at an useless distance from the walls. In this manner the laborious preparations of Vitiges were baffled, and he now considered it advisable to alter his original plan. Leaving a large share of his forces under experienced officers, to continue the assault on the Salarian gate, and thereby still engage Belisarius in that quarter; he resolved to attempt the city on two other points nearly opposite to each other, and thus weaken by extending the feeble line of the Roman garrison.

For this purpose he undertook the Praenestine gate for his personal station, and dispatched other troops to the Tuscan bank, to storm the ancient sepulchre of Hadrian, the modern castle of St. Angelo.[25] This structure, one of the most singular and striking which even Rome can display, and by turns a tomb, a fortress, or a prison, has undergone almost as various vicissitudes of fortune as the surrounding city. From the age of Belisarius to the present scarcely any domestic tumult at Rome appears to have occurred in which this castle has not born an important part, and it has often retarded, though rarely prevented, surrender to a public enemy.[26] In its present condition, the new forti-

---

25. Such are the two extreme appellations, but it also bore the intermediate names of Theodoric and of Crescentius, (*Donat. lib. iv* c. 7.) The description of Procopius in the sixth century may be compared with that of Liutprand in the tenth, (*Hist. lib. iii.* c. 12.) No reliance should be placed on the modern plans.

26. It saved Pope Gregory the Seventh when Rome was taken by the Germans, but in a similar case was of no avail to Clement the Seventh. (Murat *Annal. d'Ital.* vol. vi., and vol. x.) In 1814, the French captain, when summoned to give up the castle, nobly replied that the bronze angel on the summit should sheath his sword before his troops would theirs. He then surrendered.

fications at its base, the vast and rugged mass of peperine stone which rises from them, and the unwieldy angel of Flemish origin, by which the whole is surmounted, no longer bear the slightest resemblance to the fabric which Procopius has described.

At that time the base was square, and the circular mole above it was cased in large blocks of Parian marble, closely fitted into each other without the assistance of cement. Its breadth is expressed by the vague comparison of a stone's throw, and of its height we are only told that it overtopped the neighbouring ramparts. Its summit appeared peopled with statues of beautiful sculpture and colossal size, some of them equestrian, and all composed of the same white marble which adorned the rest of the building. This monument stood without the walls, but, as it appeared a convenient bulwark, it had formerly (probably in the time of Alaric) been connected with them by lateral ramparts. Its command on this day had been entrusted by Belisarius to Constantine, but this officer, apprehending an attack on some other point, had imprudently hastened thither, leaving the sepulchre of Hadrian defended merely by a handful of soldiers.

In the meanwhile the Gothic troops advanced against it beneath the arcades and porticoes of the neighbouring church of St. Peter, which held the same site as the present unrivalled *basilic*, but which, at that time, was not enclosed within the circuit of the walls. By its useful shade the barbarians were concealed till close at hand, when they were seen rushing forwards, provided with ladders to scale the ramparts, and with large shields to intercept the missiles of the Romans.

Their unexpected appearance struck the garrison with consternation. Their shields precluded the effect of arrows, their closeness the use of the *balista*. Already had they applied their ladders to the castle, and were ascending its walls; already were the besieged on the verge of despair and defeat, when the aspect of the statues around them suggested a new resource. They broke these precious monuments of art, now less important from their workmanship than from their materials, and each soldier raising a massy fragment with both hands hurled it on the heads of the assailants.[27] Overwhelmed with a sculptured quarry, the Goths gave way, the courage of the Romans revived, and their attempt, amidst loud shouts, to play their-military engines, completed the dismay of the barbarians. They fled with precipitation: Constan-

---

27. In the civil war between Vitellius and Vespasian, the statues of the Capitol were in like manner torn down by Flavius Sabinus to supply the place of a wall. (Tacit. *Hist. lib. iii.* c. 71.)

tine, just returned with his troops, made a vigorous sally, and Rome was rescued on the very point of capture. The citizens may, with a pardonable superstition, have regarded this triumph as a last benefit from their ancient heroes, whose very emblems appeared to arise as guardians and preservers of the city.

Meanwhile the Gothic monarch, in person, was attacking the Praenestine gate [28] with such vigour, that Bessas, who commanded in this station, found it necessary to solicit immediate aid from the general. On receiving this message, Belisarius redoubled his exertions at the Salarian gate, and having succeeded in driving back the barbarians was enabled to quit the post which his valour had secured. With the flower of all his forces he hastened to the relief of his lieutenant. On his arrival he found the soldiers much disheartened, and their situation very critical. The *Vivarium*, which the enemy were battering with their smaller engines, was an enclosure serving to confine wild animals for the public games, and consisting of an angle in the ramparts, across which the ancient Romans had built a low bulwark.[29]

Thus, therefore, the walls were double in this place, but they had been less strongly built than in any other quarter, and from some natural defect in the bricks were now full of fissures. Belisarius perceived that to defend the external wall any longer was impossible, but he devised a scheme to render its loss harmless and even advantageous. Withdrawing the troops from this outwork, he stationed them at the foot of the inner wall, and commanded them to cast aside all arms but their swords for close combat.

As soon as the Goths had broken through the feeble barrier, and rushed by tumultuous crowds into the confined space of the *Vivarium*, they found themselves unexpectedly encountered by a furious charge of the Romans. In such narrow limits their very multitude proved injurious to them, and rendered them equally incapable of resistance or of flight. Pent in like sheep for slaughter, and overwhelmed with missiles from above while closely pressed from below, the greater part were easily dispatched. Not satisfied with this success, Belisarius forthwith cast open the neighbouring gates, sounded the trumpets, and sallied forth with all the forces around him. The previous disaster of the Goths and their consequent confusion. The consternation of their flight was augmented by his firing the machinery with which they had

---

28. Praeneste is the modern Palestrina. The Praenestine gate is supposed to be the present, (1829), Porta Maggiore.
29. Procop. *Goth. lib. i. c.* 23. Nardini, *lib. iv. c.* 2.

expected to conquer Rome, and the flames rapidly spread through the wood-work of which it was composed. Another sally at this decisive moment was directed by Belisarius from the Salarian gate, the Goths in this quarter also were put to flight, and their engines reduced to ashes. Great numbers of the enemy fell in the battle, still more in the pursuit, and the relentless carnage was continued till the night. By the confession of their own officers (so at least says Procopius) thirty thousand Goths were slain in this memorable battle, and the amount of wounded was hardly less considerable.

But the Gothic forces were too large to be wholly broken by these heavy losses, and those of the Romans too scanty to follow up their victory. The Byzantine soldiers were now reduced to five thousand, a number which in the flourishing epoch of the empire was thought inadequate for the defence of a single camp.[30] In a letter to Justinian, written at this period and still extant, Belisarius strongly urges the necessity of ample reinforcements. He relates his past successes, which he modestly ascribes to his fortune rather than his merit, and observes that the numerical superiority of the barbarians may at last prevail.

He beseeches the emperor not to forsake and sacrifice the citizens of Rome, who had endangered their own security to show forth their attachment to his cause. He said, in conclusion:

> For my part, I know my duty, and am ready to lay down my life in defence of your empire. So long as I survive, fear no surrender of Rome. But it is for you to reflect how far my death in such a situation could forward or assist your service.

These representations had their effect at Constantinople, and orders in compliance with them were issued by Justinian. A squadron of Hunnish and Sclavonian cavalry had been embarked at the close of the last year, under Martin and Valerian, for the relief of Belisarius; but the damage or the apprehension of a storm induced them to suspend their voyage and winter quietly in Greece. They reached Rome in safety from the Campanian coast twenty-three days after the battle, (April 22, *a.d.* 537), but amounted to no more than sixteen hundred men. A little more diligence on their part would have saved the town and harbour of Porto, of which the great importance to the Romans will be clearly perceived by a reference to the nature of the ground. The Tiber, which at its mouth forms an island about two mites both in length and in breadth, was defended on its northern bank by a for-

---

30. Tacit. *Hist. lib, iv,* c. 22.

tress surnamed the Port of Rome, and on the southern by the town of Ostia.[31] The former, which now bears the name of Porto, had been fortified with the greatest care, and was connected with Rome by a stately ancient road, which followed the course of the Tiber, and was about eighteen miles in length.

As soon as merchandise and stores were disembarked at Porto, it was customary to load them in boats always ready for that purpose, and to tow them by the labour of oxen against the current of the river. Ostia had formerly been likewise a fortified city,[32] but it had then declined into an open village, and its road to Rome of sixteen miles, which passed far from the windings of the Tiber, afforded no assistance in the navigation of transports. Goods could not be conveyed to Rome from Ostia without great difficulty, besides which the want of walls and shallow harbour of this station rendered It almost useless. The fortress on the Tuscan bank was, therefore, of the utmost consequence to Belisarius for his communication with the sea, and, according to the opinion of Procopius, three hundred soldiers would have been fully sufficient for its maintenance, but even this handful of men could not be spared from the diminished garrison of Rome. On their part the Goths, disappointed in their hopes of carrying the city by assault, had resolved to make famine their auxiliary, and seized Porto on the third day from their defeat.

All maritime convoys of provisions were now at an end; nor were the granaries of the city sufficiently well stored to render this cessation indifferent. The cowardly desertion of the Milvian bridge, which hastened the investment of Rome by twenty days, had baffled the projects of Belisarius for completing his supplies. Foreseeing that in his circumstances Porto could not be maintained, he also perceived the necessity of vigorous measures to anticipate the impending distress. On the last day of March he commanded the immediate departure of a great number of the women and children, for whose reception a secure retreat was prepared in Campania. A long procession of melancholy exiles crowded the Appian way, and the consternation of Vitiges at his late defeat allowed diem a safe and unmolested passage. This banishment may appear a harsh but it was a necessary meas-

---

31. Consult an excellent memoir and map by D'Anville, in the *Academy of Inscriptions*. (vol. xxx.)

32. Its former strength is extolled by Procopius, (*Goth. lib. i.* c. 26) yet in the reign of Vitellius, I find only one *cohort* stationed there, (Tacit *Hist. lib. ii.* c. 63.) As to the length of the Via Ostiensis see Wesseling's *Itineraria*, and Cassiodorius *Chronic.* ed. 1729.

ure, as is proved by the after famine of the besieged notwithstanding these precautions. It was also in reality an act of kindness, to withdraw the weaker share of the people from sufferings which their presence would have aggravated, and which even men had scarcely sufficient firmness to endure.

From the arrival of the reinforcements under Martin and Valerian, though far less than those he had expected, Belisarius was enabled, by frequent attacks, to harass the troops of the enemy, and to exercise his own. No deficiencies in the warfare or equipment of the Goths escaped his watchful attention, or were left unimproved by his military skill. Their cavalry, armed with swords and lances, was fitted only for close combat; their archers fought on foot, unprovided with defensive armour, and rarely venturing to quit the ranks of the heavy infantry. In three successive sallies, the loss of the Goths amounted to no less than four thousand of their bravest soldiers; and the Byzantine troops were so much elated with success, as earnestly to press on their commander a general engagement. Well aware how much the barbarians still outnumbered them, Belisarius could not approve of this rash request, and preferred the slower but more secure expedient of gradually wasting the forces of the enemy by well-timed and repeated skirmishes.

Yet, when to the loud clamours of the soldiers was added the impatience of the Roman citizens, eager for a speedy decision of the war in favour of either party, he perceived the necessity of yielding. To have continued his opposition, must have alienated the respect, the affection, and perhaps the obedience, of his soldiers. It was his object, however, in complying with their request, to render it less hurtful, by carefully providing resources for defeat, and enabling the army to withdraw on the first check, and with little loss, beneath the safe shelter of the walls. He fixed on the Salarian gate as the point from whence to sally with all his cavalry, leaving his foot soldiers (they were very few in number) to line the ramparts in his absence. Some of them, however, entreated and obtained permission to share in the battle, having pleaded the ancient glories of the Roman legion.

Since all his forces were thus required for the main attack, Belisarius had no effectual means of restraining the Goths encamped on the opposite shore, and had cause for apprehension lest their numerous squadrons should cross the river, and reinforce the remainder of their countrymen. It being of the utmost consequence to prevent this junction, the general stationed without the walls, near the mole of Hadrian, a large multitude of the newly-enlisted Roman artisans and volunteers, who possessed neither the discipline nor the experience, but who might imitate the array of soldiers. This unwarlike rabble, joined to some Moorish horse, was instructed not to advance beyond the foot of the ramparts, in the hope that its formidable aspect from afar might deceive and delay the barbarians.

Having thus made his dispositions, Belisarius issued forth against the Goths, whom he found prepared to receive him. They encountered his army close in front of their encampments, and the conflict which ensued was long and obstinate. The advantage seemed at first to be on the side of the Romans, and many of the barbarians had fallen, but their place was instantly supplied by a succession of fresh troops, so that their numbers in the field underwent no apparent diminution. On the other side of the Tiber, the stratagem of Belisarius was also successful for a time. The Goths were withheld at a respectful distance, and in momentary expectation of attack from the supposed appearance of a large army marshalled before them.

At length the Roman recruits, emboldened by the hesitation of the enemy, which they foolishly mistook for cowardice, forgot their instructions, and ventured on a charge. The barbarians yielded to the first onset, but soon rallied against such raw and unskilful adversaries, who had wasted the precious moments of surprise in pillage, and who, accordingly, were driven back, with great loss, within the walls. Meanwhile, the forces commanded by Belisarius in person began gradually to yield; their retreat soon grew into a flight; and, according to the observation of Procopius, the battle, which had commenced before the entrenchments of the besiegers, was concluded beneath the ramparts of the city. The Romans were thrown into the utmost disorder, and only preserved from entire defeat by the prudence of Belisarius, who led back within the gates his army, much dispirited and humbled, but not materially impaired.

After this repulse, the Romans, grown wiser by experience, no longer ventured to encounter the barbarians in the field; and, on their part, the besiegers, resigning all immediate thoughts of taking the city by assault, awaited the slow effects of famine. By the prudent banishment of the Roman women and children, all danger of scarcity had been averted for the time; the public granaries afforded regular supplies to the remaining inhabitants, and corn or forage was also sometimes obtained by excursions through the neighbouring country. Detachments of Greek or confederate cavalry (Moors were commonly chosen, from their superior swiftness) often issued forth by night, on the

Campanian side of the city; and if, on these occasions, they obtained no further advantage than that of grazing their horses, the object was still sufficiently important to deserve a sally.

The Goths, at first, careless of such petty inroads, overlooked the intercourse thus carried on between Rome and Campania; but they became alive to its injurious consequences towards the time of the summer solstice, when an officer named Euthalius landed at Terracina from Constantinople, (June, *a.d.* 537), with treasure for the payment of the troops. Intelligence of his arrival was forthwith transmitted to Rome; and Belisarius, by engaging in several skirmishes, and pretending an intention to give a second battle, so skilfully directed the attention of the Goths to another quarter, that he enabled Euthalius and his convoy to enter the city unperceived. Vitiges now determined to cut off all intercourse between Rome and the country. For this purpose, he availed himself of two large aqueducts between the Latin and Appian ways, which, at the distance of seven miles from Rome, surrounded a considerable space, in a double intersection of their high and massy arches.

By filling up the open intervals with stones and clay, the Goths changed this enclosure to a fortress, which they garrisoned with no less than seven thousand men. This measure, assisted by extensive outposts, proved entirely effectual; all further convoys were shut out from Rome; and, within a few months, Belisarius had to contend with the distress, and, its inevitable consequence, the disaffection, of the citizens. The more harmless malcontents sought relief from their calamities by the aid of omens, predictions, and fantastic rites. To superstition, the unfortunate are at all times naturally prone; but it is with regret that we find the Romans still cherishing some remains of attachment to their ancient fables. The Heathen worship had lingered in this city later than in almost any other place. This fact may be explained by the classic recollections of the ground where every relic seemed to plead for Paganism, and by rivalry with the new Byzantine capital which boasted of its Christian purity of faith.

During the siege of Alaric, some senators had proposed to renew the sacrifices in the Capitol;[33] the festival of the *Lupercalia* could not be abolished till the close of the fifth century;[34] and under the command of Belisarius the same spirit was displayed. Not merely were the dark revelations of the Sybil ransacked for a prophecy of approaching

---

33. Sozomen, *Hist. Eccles. lib. ix.* c. 6.
34. Baronius, *Annal. Eccles. a.d.* 496, No. 28.

deliverance,[35] but several heathen zealots secretly endeavoured to appease the Divine displeasure by unbarring, according to former usage in war, the rusty gates of the temple of Janus.

This monument was still standing in the Forum, near the Senate House; it was square in its shape, bronze in its material, and merely of sufficient size to hold the statue of the two-fold deity. The double gates, which corresponded to each aspect of Janus, withstood the superstitious efforts of his votaries, and could not be unclosed, but the very attempt was an offence which might have been actively pursued and severely punished in more tranquil times.

It was, however, in the chief of the opposite religion, that Belisarius detected a far more dangerous breach of the laws. A letter, which he intercepted from several Romans of distinction and especially the Pope Silverius, promised, at an appointed time, to open the Asinarian gate for the secret admission of the Gothic army. This correspondence might appear to require a speedy, and to deserve a rigorous, punishment. The *pontiff* was summoned to the quarters of Belisarius, (Nov. a.d. 537), in the Pincian palace, but his attendant priests were not allowed to pass the antechamber. Silverius found the general seated at the foot of a couch on which Antonina reclined. "Pope Silverius," exclaimed that haughty and imperious woman, "what have we done to you, that you should betray us to the Goths?" It was in vain that the affrighted bishop attempted a denial, respectable witnesses accused, and his own signature convicted him. The ensigns of his dignity were immediately taken from him, he was arrayed in the habit of a monk, and condemned to an exile in the East, for which he embarked without delay; and we may infer from this and other facts, that the Gothic besiegers were almost indifferent to the departures from Rome, and were only anxious to prevent the entrance of supplies.

It was announced by Belisarius to the Roman clergy, that Silverius had forfeited his office, and they accordingly proceeded to a new election, when the deacon Vigilius, by the weight of two hundred pounds of gold, inclined the scale to his side.[36] In his public history, Procopius glides most rapidly over this delicate transaction, and we are reduced to gather its details from the angry invectives and conflicting state-

---

35. Yet the Sybil, from being believed to have foretold the Saviour's coming, was not rejected by several Christians. This superstition continued later than is commonly supposed. Bede records some of her prophetic verses (*Op.* vol. ii. ed. Colon. Agripp. 1688), some Sybilline books appear to have been consulted till the tenth century. (Liutprand ap. Murat. *Script Italic* vol. ii.)

36. This election took place on the twenty-second of November. (Pagi, *Critic*, vol. ii.)

ments of two ecclesiastical writers.[37] The sacrilegious deposition of a Pope has exposed Belisarius to their loud anathema, which is gladly re-echoed by the Roman Catholic annalists of modern times.[38] Yet without denying that the sanctity of the papal tiara may entitle the wearer to peculiar privileges and exemptions, I may observe, that, as to laymen, the military laws, of even the most humane and polished nations, concur in denouncing against such conspiracies the penalty of death. The sentence of Belisarius can hardly be considered too severe, but though we may approve its matter, we must condemn its announcement and its forms.

To give over his authority to a woman, to appear the slave of her displeasure, rather than the minister of justice, to allow her to utter those reproofs which it became only him to speak, were all great infractions of his duty, and must cast a deep blot upon his fame. Much more would that fame be sullied, Were we to believe that he had in reality forged the letter purporting to come from Silverius, in compliance with a request from the Empress Theodora, to find or to make some pretext for removing this obnoxious pontiff. That Theodora possessed great influence over Antonina, and Antonina over Belisarius is undoubted; but the heavy charge of forgery is devoid both of proof and probability, and rather seems a later invention to clear the character of Silverius, and to represent him as an unoffending martyr. His ready violation of his oath of fidelity to Vitiges, renders it not unlikely that he might be capable of a two-fold treason, and might anxiously endeavour, by some service before the expected surrender, to deserve a pardon from the Goths.

Shortly after this event, the calamities of war began to press so heavily on the besieged, as might almost have, justified the treason of anyone not bound by solemn engagements to the imperial cause.

37. Anastasius, *De Vit. Pontif.* 59; and Liberatus, *Breviar.* The latter is the most moderate, and was moreover a contemporary; yet I can place but little reliance on his testimony, since he betrays the utmost ignorance of Italian affairs, and makes Belisarius take Ravenna before Rome.

38. Baronius, *Annal. Eccles.* a.d. 538, No. 4; and 561, No. 7; and Muratori *Annal. d'Ital.* vol. iii. Baronius asserts that Belisarius afterwards repented of his sacrilege, and in expiation of it built a church at Rome. The cardinal adds, that the inscription of this church was still extant in his time, and was as follows:—*HANC VIE PATRICIVS, VILISARIVS VRBIS AMICVS, OB CVLPÆ VENIAM CONDIDIT ECCLESIAM; HANC ICCIRCO PEDEM SACRAM QVI PONIS IN ÆDEM, VT MISERETVR EVM SÆPE PRECARE DEVM.*
But the style of these monkish rhymes seems to belong to a much later period, and I suspect a pious fraud.

The inhabitants still received occasional distributions of corn from Belisarius, but were sometimes reduced to herbs and grasses, and to a preparation from the flesh of the mules, which had died perhaps from disease. Such tainted and insufficient food was the natural forerunner of a pestilence, which diminished still further the remnant of famine and the sword. In this distress the Romans again besought Belisarius to suffer the fate of the war to be quickly determined by a battle, and promised that not a single citizen should withhold his aid on this occasion. "To such a pitch," said they, "has our wretchedness proceeded, that it has already even inspired us with courage, and induced us to take up arms against the barbarians." Could it have been foretold, or believed, some centuries before, that the citizens of Rome would ever make so degrading an avowal?

To these entreaties, Belisarius could give no satisfactory reply. Notwithstanding his earnest solicitations, he was still left without adequate reinforcements from Constantinople; and in these trying circumstances, we may admire the mixture of humanity and firmness which his conduct displayed. When writing to the emperor, he had warmly pleaded in favour of the citizens of Rome; but, in his address to themselves, he descanted on the necessity of patience and subordination, he said:

> Your proposal does not surprise me, I have long expected it. I well know the character of that senseless monster the people, unable either to support the present or to foresee the future, always desirous of attempting the impossible, and of rushing headlong to its ruin. Yet your unthinking folly shall not induce me to permit your own destruction, nor to betray the trust committed to me by my sovereign and yours. Success in war depends less on intrepidity than; on prudence to await, to distinguish, and to seize the decisive moment of fortune. You appear to regard the present contest as a game of hazard, which you might determine by a single throw of the dice; but I, at least, have learnt from experience to prefer security to speed. But it seems that you offer to reinforce my troops, and to march with them against the enemy.
>
> Where then have you acquired your knowledge of war? And what true soldier is not aware that the result of a battle must chiefly rest on the skill and discipline of the combatants? Ours is a real enemy in the field; we march to a battle, and not to a

review. I am, however, willing to praise your courage, to forgive your murmurs, and to prove to you that my present delay is founded on judicious policy. The emperor has collected forces from every part of his dominions, and has already dispatched to our succour a numerous and formidable army. The ships already crowd with their multitude the Ionian and Campanian seas; a few days more and we shall behold these reinforcements amongst us. Their supplies of provisions will speedily put an end to the scarcity, and their valour to the siege.

Not satisfied, however, with patiently awaiting succours which a thousand accidents might defeat or delay, Belisarius made every exertion in his power for relief. The historian Procopius was sent to Naples, to muster the soldiers arriving from Constantinople, or scattered in Campania, and to find means of introducing some convoys of provisions into Rome. He set out by night, through the gate of St. Paul, and passed the Gothic aqueducts without discovery. This facility of departure from the city, was not left unemployed by Belisarius. A few days afterwards he adopted the bold and singular expedient of dismissing a large share of his garrison to seize and maintain some neighbouring strong-holds in flank of the barbarian army, especially Tivoli and Terracina. From this measure, a twofold advantage was anticipated. A larger ration of food might now relieve the wants, and appease the clamours, of the citizens; and, by cutting off the convoys of the Goths, it was expected that they in their turn might experience the miseries of famine. The spirits of the Romans were also greatly raised, when they perceived their garrison resuming the offensive, and, according to the expression of Procopius, from the besieged becoming the besiegers.

Antonina left Rome with the detachment intended for Terracina, having been desired by her husband to proceed to Naples, and there await in tranquillity the uncertain issue of the war; but scarcely had she reached Campania, before she displayed her activity and love of power, by collecting troops, together with Procopius. By their united diligence five hundred soldiers were assembled, ample supplies of corn were prepared, and they soon derived a more important benefit, from the arrival of the Byzantine reinforcements. Nearly two thousand cavalry, having landed at Otranto, proceeded by rapid marches to Campania, and a fleet, with three thousand Isaurians on board, anchored in the bay of Naples. Amongst the chief commanders of these forces was John, the nephew of Vitalian, whose surname of Sanguinary[39] indicates his cruelty, with his avarice and rashness. He was, however, an officer of great energy and daring, well fitted to execute though not to plan an enterprise, and his performance was more rapid than the thoughts of common men.

It was resolved to attempt the relief of Rome by the side of Ostia, and the Isaurian fleet accordingly steered onwards for that port, while the horsemen from Otranto and the Campanian levies proceeded together along the Appian way. They escorted a large train of waggons, laden with corn and wine, and which they intended, according to the Hunnish custom,[40] to range round them as entrenchments in case of attack.

The approach of this expedition was not unknown to the Goths, but Belisarius undertook to employ them by a skirmish, and devised an ingenious stratagem to render it successful. It will be recollected that, at the commencement of the siege, he had closed the Flaminian gate, and the besiegers were therefore quite unsuspicious of any attack from this quarter. By order of Belisarius, the stones piled up against the gate from within, were now removed at night, and he stationed there the flower of his forces. Early the next morning a detachment of one thousand men was directed to issue from the Pincian postern, to insult the camp of the Goths, and, by a pretended flight, allure them to pursuit. This feint produced the desired result.

Both the Goths and the Romans rushed towards the ramparts; the latter with apparent terror, the first with tumultuous triumph. It was then that Belisarius commanded the Flaminian gate to be thrown open, and, sallying forth at the head of his chosen squadron, carried havoc and dismay to the inmost ranks of the barbarians. The imperial troops were hindered from completing their victory, by the smallness of their numbers, and the strength of the enemy's camp; but the slaughter of the Goths was very great, their consternation kept them for some time confined within their entrenchments, and they now began also to feel the effect of the Roman garrisons in the neighbouring fortresses.

Most of their convoys were surprised, many of their communi-

---

39. This epithet, which was of course only applied by his enemies, is omitted by Procopius (*Goth. lib. ii.* c. 5), but recorded by Anastasius (*De Vit Pontif.* c. 60), and copied by Johannes Diaconus (*Chronic.* c. 22). Narses was in favour when Procopius wrote, and Narses was the intimate friend of John. (*Goth. lib. ii.* c. 16.)
40. Jornandes, *De Reb. Getic.* c, 40.

cations interrupted, and the horrors of scarcity were embittered by the progress of disease. Their future prospects seemed to them still more gloomy than their actual sufferings. They fully believed the overcharged accounts of the eastern reinforcements which Belisarius had artfully spread, and imagined that the troops assembling in Campania were but a vanguard to this innumerable army. Under such circumstances, Vitiges thought it politic to attempt negotiation, and dispatched three ambassadors to Rome, whose curious conference with Belisarius is not unworthy of detail. The Gothic spokesman began by recommending, according to the usual practice of the weaker party, the virtues of moderation and forbearance. He declared that his sovereign was guided by a sincere wish of ending the mutual miseries of war, and ready to make sacrifices for this desirable end.

From thence he somewhat inconsistently proceeded to enlarge on. the justice of the Gothic cause; he maintained that the troops of Theodoric had been allowed and authorized by the court of Constantinople to expel the Heruli from Italy, and to possess it in their place; and he concluded by requesting that Belisarius would withdraw his army from their legitimate kingdom. The answer of the Roman general may be easily conjectured;

> You promised to display moderation in your offers, and brevity in your language; but, on the contrary, I have heard a long and presumptuous harangue. Theodoric did not receive the imperial commission against the Herulian monarch, with the view of his seizing on the vacant throne, since how could it matter to Zeno by what foreign usurper Italy was governed? No, it was intended that this country should be entirely freed from barbarian bondage, and re-annexed to the dominion of the empire. For my part, I will never resign the territory of my sovereign; if you have any other terms, propose them.

The Goths resumed:

> Though convinced that even our enemies must inwardly feel the truth of the arguments we have urged, yet we are willing to prove our peaceful intentions, by the cession of Sicily, that fertile and extensive island, so convenient, by its position, for the maintenance of Africa.

Belisarius replied;

> Your generosity, in yielding a province which you have already

lost, requires, and shall receive from us, an adequate return. We will resign to the Goths the whole of Britain, an island much larger than Sicily, and formerly an appendage of the empire.

"But were we," said the Barbarians, "to include Naples and Campania in our cession, would you not agree to a treaty?"

"Far from it," said Belisarius, "we are not empowered to make over the least portion of the rightful imperial dominions."

"Not even," asked the ambassadors, " if we submitted to the payment of a yearly tribute?"

"Not even then," was the answer.

"Allow us at least," rejoined the Goths, "to refer these proposals to the emperor himself, and to conclude a truce with your forces until his pleasure can be known."

To this last request Belisarius gladly agreed. Negotiations for the terms of the truce continued with great activity during several days, and hostages for its conclusion were given on both sides.

Such was the state of things at Rome, when the forces from Campania arrived, by sea and land, at Ostia, their appointed place of meeting, where their position was still one of considerable danger, since a cessation of hostilities had not yet been finally settled. In the darkness of the ensuing night, Belisarius, at the head of only a hundred horse, ventured to sally from Rome, to direct and animate their counsels by his presence. He exhorted them to pursue their march upon the capital, and promised that, in case of any attack from the barbarians, he would advance with his remaining troops to their rescue. The general then remounted, rode back before the dawn to Rome, and had the good fortune, in coming as in going, to pass the Gothic lines undiscovered. In the morning, a council was held at Ostia, in which Antonina presided, to deliberate on the best means of transporting the convoy.

This undertaking appeared to be attended with peculiar difficulties. No waggons could travel safely along the narrow and dilapidated Ostian way; nor could the boats be towed up the river, since the only road along its stream was on the northern bank, in possession of the enemy. Besides, the oxen were worn with fatigue by their rapid journey from Campania, and were lying exhausted on the ground, as if incapable of any further exertion. A new expedient was therefore resorted to: the boats of the Isaurian fleet were filled with the stores of provision, and with rowers, and were then covered by planks, to shield the men from the expected darts of the barbarians. Awaiting a favourable breeze, these boats sailed up the Tiber, and oars were employed whenever the windings of the river rendered unavailing the assistance of the wind. All the forces at Ostia marched along the southern bank, to serve as an escort; but this precaution proved needless.

No attack was attempted by the Goths, who are said to have imagined that this unusual mode of conveyance up the Tiber must be baffled of itself, without any interference of theirs.[41] They were, however, withheld principally by the fear lest an unseasonable skirmish should break off the negotiations for a truce, which was then proceeding to their wish. The convoy, therefore, arrived at Rome without hindrance, and, after months of scarcity and weeks of famine, restored ease and plenty to that afflicted city.

Some days afterwards, (Dec. a.d. 537), the Goths obtained the. reward of their forbearance. A truce was agreed upon, for three months from the winter solstice till the vernal equinox, and the ambassadors of Vitiges were permitted to proceed to Constantinople; but this interval of tranquillity soon became embittered by jealousy and discord. The Gothic garrison of Porto, debarred from maritime supplies by the presence of the Roman fleet, and reduced to great dearth of provisions, quitted its appointed post, and returned to the main forces under Vitiges. Similar distress caused a similar desertion of Albano and Centumcellae or Civita Vecchia,[42] and these important stations were immediately occupied by the Romans, so that the Gothic camps before the city became encompassed on every side by hostile fortresses.

No sooner had the loss of these strong-holds become irreparable, than their value was perceived by Vitiges, who demanded their restoration from Belisarius, and threatened, if his request were denied him, to enforce it by arms. His menaces were received with contempt, but the Gothic monarch thought it prudent to conceal his displeasure for the time. The grounds on which Belisarius acted are censured by Grotius as paltry chicane,[43] and this transaction left in the minds of both parties additional seeds of distrust and resentment.

The Goths considered themselves as morally released from the obligations of the truce, and only awaited a favourable moment for attacking the enemy when most secure and unprepared. Their intention did not escape the discernment of the Roman general; and he

---

41. Procop. *Goth. lib. ii.* c. 7.
42. Wesseling, *Itineraria.*
43. *Droit de la Guerre*, ed. Barbeyrac, vol. ii.

resolved not to imitate their perfidy, but to provide against it. With this view, he dispatched two thousand horse to Alba, on the lake of Celano, under the command of John the Sanguinary. The instructions of this officer were, to refrain from the slightest aggression, and carefully observe the stipulated truce. Belisarius added;

> But if the barbarians should be the first to break through this treaty, then, without a moment's delay, overrun the province of Picenum with your soldiers, and precede the news of your arrival by the rapidity of your movements. Avoid all insult or injury to the Italian inhabitants. Your progress will be easy; the Goths have concentrated their whole force before the walls of Rome, whilst their families and treasures remain undefended. Endeavour, as much as possible, to leave no fortresses behind you in the power of the enemy, and reserve your spoils for a common and impartial division at Rome. Since we are toiling to destroy the drones, you must not claim the sole enjoyment of the honey.

During the short and hollow interval of quiet which ensued, (a.d. 538), the reputation of Belisarius was tarnished by the punishment of one of his most distinguished officers. When, before the siege of Rome, Constantine had been dispatched to occupy Spoleto, he was joined by Presidius, a noble Italian, who, having fallen under the displeasure of the Gothic monarch, had fled in haste from Ravenna. Of all his treasures, he had only been able to save two daggers, whose golden hilts and scabbards were richly studded with jewels. These last relics of his wealth were forcibly seized by Constantine, although Presidius had taken refuge in a church, whose sanctuary would have shielded even the most atrocious felon from justice. Almost immediately afterwards, the advance of the Gothic army sent both Presidius and Constantine headlong on to Rome. In the earlier part of the siege, whilst the imperial cause seemed gloomy and hopeless, Presidius continued silent; but as soon as it began to brighten, he brought forward his complaint. Belisarius repeatedly commanded that his property should be restored to him, but these orders were always baffled and eluded; and the Italian found that Constantine added derision to injury. Provoked beyond all bearing, Presidius ventured to seize the bridle of Belisarius whilst riding through the Roman Forum, and to claim the protection of the laws.

In spite of the threats of the guards, he persisted in his grasp, until the general renewed his promise of speedy satisfaction. Accordingly, on the following day, he convened a council in his palace, and summoned the arrogant and avaricious officer before it. On being once more solemnly required to surrender the stolen daggers, Constantine haughtily replied, that he would sooner fling them into the Tiber.

"Do you then deny my authority?" said Belisarius.

"I do not, on other points," answered Constantine, "but on this I will never obey you."

Justly incensed at this stubborn refusal and public insult, Belisarius now called for his guards.

"No doubt to murder me!" exclaimed Constantine.

"Not so," said the general, "but to compel the restitution of your spoils."

Constantine, still believing that his life was aimed at, and blinded by fury and revenge, resolved to signalise his fall by a memorable crime, and to inflict on his commander the fate which he fancied to be destined for himself. Suddenly drawing his sword, and rushing forwards; he endeavoured to plunge it into the breast of Belisarius. The general avoided the blow, by a rapid movement, and by the interposition of Bessas; and in the meanwhile the guards, who had entered, in obedience to the former call, seized the undaunted assassin. He was dragged into another chamber, and put to death shortly afterwards, by order of his intended victim. Such is the narrative given by Procopius in his public history, and of which he confirms and ratifies the truth in his subsequent libel.[44] In the latter, however, he affirms, in addition to these circumstances, that it was the hatred of Antonina against Constantine which chiefly urged her husband to this hasty sentence; and notwithstanding the just suspicion which always attaches to the *Secret History*, I am disposed, on this point, to credit its testimony to its full extent.

We may, perhaps, judge of this transaction as of the deposition and exile of Silverius, and condemn, not so much the substance as the form. The award on Constantine can hardly be accused of rigour, since a subaltern disobeying the commands and attempting the life of his chief, would, in every age and in every nation, have been deemed deserving of death. But this death should have been deliberate and judicial, and not seem to have proceeded from the impulse of recent injury, for when the punishment too closely follows the offence, it

---

44. See *Goth. lib. ii* c. 8; *Hist. Arcan.* c. i.; and Alemanni, *Not. Hist.* The continuator of Count Marcellinus seems strangely ignorant as to this affair, since he represents Belisarius as just returned from Campania, (*Chronic*, ap. *Sirmond. Op.* vol. ii.)

rather resembles a murder than an execution. Still less should female animosities be allowed weight and influence in a simple question of justice. In this point of view, the affair is most disgraceful to the hero of this narrative, and may serve as an example how the blandishments of some worthless woman may betray even the most honourable men into the least honourable actions.

The King of the Goths had for some time been desirous to violate the truce by a sudden surprise of Rome, and thus at the same moment to commit his perfidy and obtain its reward. For this end, the aqueducts occurred to him, and one [45] near the Pincian postern was explored at night, by some chosen soldiers provided with torches; but their progress was stopped by the buttress which Belisarius had formerly constructed.[46] Detaching a stone from this obstacle, they bore it to the Gothic monarch as a mark of their partial advance, and left him to deliberate by what means their attempt might be more successfully renewed. Yet, in spite of all their precautions, they had not been wholly unobserved by the Romans.

A sentinel on duty near the Pincian outlet had perceived, through a crevice in the wall, a flash of light from their torches; but he and his comrades agreed in ascribing it to the eyes of a wolf glaring in the dark.[47] Such a circumstance was thought too insignificant for a report to Belisarius, and it only reached his ears by some idle conversation it occasioned. Trifling as it seemed, this intelligence was not neglected by the general. He commanded some experienced soldiers to search tile suspected aqueduct, and by this means were discovered not merely the recent removal of a stone, but the droppings of the torches on the ground.

It need scarcely be added, that the numerous guard with which Belisarius thenceforward protected this post compelled Vitig.es to abandon all thoughts of his design; yet it was to the same quarter that the next enterprise of the barbarians was directed. Having observed that, at the time of the mid-day meal, the ramparts were forsaken by the greater number of the sentinels and guards, they at this hour sud-

---

45. This was probably the celebrated Aqua Virgo, which now supplies fountain of Trevi. (Cassiod *Var. lib. vii.* form. 6.) It was conveyed by a subterranean channel to the foot of the Pincian hill. See Pliny, (*Hist. Nat. lib. i.* c. 3.) and Frontinus Fabretti, (ap. Donatum, *Roma Antica*, lib. iii. c. 18.)
46. See earlier in chapter 5.
47. The eyes of several animals are supposed to have the property of shining at night. See a curious adventure which befell Bruce with a hyena. "I saw," he says, "large blue eyes glaring at me in the dark," (*Travels in Abyssinia*, vol. v.)

denly rushed from their encampments towards the neighbouring wall, in hopes of reaching it before the absent soldiers could return. This project was baffled by the valour of Hildiger, who commanded in this station, and who had lately conducted from Africa some further reinforcements to the relief of Rome. He perceived the approach of the Goths, and steadfastly withstood their attack till the arrival of some fresh troops, whose sally completed their discomfiture. By this overt act of hostility, the truce was mutually considered as dissolved.

The fertile invention of Vitiges had now recourse to a third stratagem, more nearly successful than either of the former. In the space between the sepulchre of Hadrian and the Flaminian gate, the limits of Rome were marked by the course of the river; and the walls along its bank were thought to be sufficiently defended by its stream, without needing much strength of their own. Their height was therefore inconsiderable; they were unprotected by towers, and might have been scaled without difficulty, but for the intervention of the Tiber and the vigilance of the garrison. To overcome the former obstacle, Vitiges secretly prepared some boats; against the latter he determined to employ the venal treachery of two Roman citizens, whom he desired to accost the sentinels after dark, to offer them a share of their wine, and, by pouring a strong narcotic into their cups, consign them to profound repose. The two Romans were then to make an appointed signal to the Goths, who hoped to cross the river unobserved, and to climb the defenceless walls with ease.

A project so judiciously concerted was disappointed by the fear or remorse of one of the conspirators, who, like most penitents in similar cases, resolved to atone for one act of perfidy by committing another, and revealed his guilty accomplice. The convicted traitor was sent by Belisarius to the barbarian camp, with his nose slit, his ears cut off, and mounted on an ass; and his appearance announced to Vitiges the ruin of his enterprise. Such repeated reverses broke the spirit of the Goths; they began utterly to despair of taking Rome, and attributed to the special interference of an irritated Deity what the genius of their adversary is perhaps sufficient to explain.

No sooner had the truce been broken through by the Goths before Rome, than a dispatch from Belisarius desired John the Sanguinary to fulfil his instructions. This officer accordingly invaded Picenum, and easily overthrew the feeble forces which the Goths remaining in that quarter could muster against him. He found the cities of Urbino and of Auximum, or Osimo, weakly garrisoned indeed, but very strongly fortified, and was impelled by military ardour to set at naught the orders of his general, and to march onwards, leaving only small detachments before the hostile walls. We find it afterwards stated, that the desire of enriching himself by the pillage of further provinces, was also a principal motive in urging him to disobedience.[48] Fortune, generally propitious to the bold, appeared at first to favour the enterprise of John.

On his approach, the garrison of Rimini, only one day's journey from the Gothic capital, fled with precipitation, alarmed at the disaffection of the Italian inhabitants, and tempted by their neighbourhood to the impregnable ramparts of Ravenna. The Roman officer forthwith took possession of this important city, and his progress, thus far, also enabled Matasontha, the unwilling bride of Vitiges, to send a messenger to his camp, and to concert with him the dethronement and death of her husband. It was warily required, on her part, that John should engage, immediately after the murder of Vitiges, to supply his place with his royal widow.

The news of the surrender of Rimini filled the mind of the Gothic monarch with alarm. All his projects on Rome had been disappointed, his Adriatic capital was menaced with Byzantine troops, and his army weakened by the sufferings of scarcity. However, he remained without taking any decisive measures till the conclusion of the truce, still expecting to receive favourable tidings from Constantinople, and to find the emperor less inexorable than his lieutenant in Italy. As soon as this period had elapsed without the, fulfilment of his hopes, Vitiges reluctantly issued. orders for a general retreat, and one year and nine days from the first commencement of the siege, (Mar. 21, *a.d* 538), the Gothic Army, setting fire to the wooden palisades of its camps, began slowly to repass the Milvian bridge.[49] For some time Belisarius,

---

48. Procop. *Goth. lib. ii.* c. 16.
49. Till the last moment of the truce, the Goths still trusted that their embassy at Constantinople might prove successful, and that the Romans would send them a treaty of peace. To have raised the siege and begun their retreat under such circumstances, would have been impolitic, since Belisarius might have thought himself justified in refusing to ratify with fugitive troops the Byzantine compact, supposed to be concluded with powerful invaders. But when the period fixed for the term of the negotiation was at an end, Vitiges could no longer entertain any hopes of peace. The taking of Rimini, and the danger of Ravenna, then urged them to set off without a moment of unnecessary delay. From these two considerations combined, we may conclude that he raised the siege on the very morning when the term of three months expired, and this is confirmed by the words of Procopius, (*Goth. lib. ii.* c. 10). Now this term expired March 21 , and, as the siege lasted one year and nine days, this date gives us March 12, *a.d.* 537, for its commencement

doubted what course, under such circumstances, it might be proper to pursue. To suffer the barbarians to escape unmolested seemed inglorious, to encounter them fairly in the field was impossible for a garrison diminished by such numerous outposts and detachments from it.

The general, therefore, had recourse to stratagem; and, waiting till one half of the Gothic army had reached the Tuscan bank of the Tiber, he suddenly sallied forth against the remainder with all his troops. A battle ensued, as fiercely contested and as hardly won as any of the preceding engagements. The Romans fought with alacrity and confidence, the Goths with all the courage of despair, but, as Belisarius had expected, the passage of the Milvian bridge soon became encumbered by the runaways from one bank, and the reinforcements from the other, and great numbers were precipitated into the Tiber, whence the weight of their armour prevented them from rising. Thus the troops on the opposite shore could yield but little assistance to their comrades. The victory of Belisarius was complete; a large share of the Gothic rear was cut to pieces, and those who escaped the double dangers of the river and the enemy, hastily joined the rest of the army in retreat. They marched towards Ravenna, on the left of the Flaminian road; and, after so many reverses, their numbers were still sufficiently considerable to allow Vitiges to leave behind him four thousand men for the garrison of Auximum, two thousand for that of Urbino, and above three thousand scattered amongst some smaller fortresses.

While the barbarians thus withdrew, Belisarius dispatched, in the same direction, a thousand horse, commanded by Hildiger and Martin, whose speed might easily outstrip the lingering and impeded march of the Gothic squadrons. He instructed them on their way to draw some infantry from Ancona, which had lately been taken, and was still occupied by a fresh reinforcement from Constantinople.[50] They were then to proceed to John the Sanguinary, at Rimini, and convey to him the orders of Belisarius to quit that fortress with his soldiers, leaving as a garrison the troops they brought him from Ancona.

By this means the general expected that the Goths, on arriving before the walls of Rimini, and finding that it contained no commander of note, nor veteran soldiers, might disdain so inglorious a conquest, and march onwards to Ravenna. Should they, on the con-

---

50. Ancona wm then regarded only as the port of Auximum, which was the capital of Picenum, and a very considerable place. (Procop. *Goth. lib. ii* c. 13.) How complete is the change! Ancona has become one of the most flourishing cities in Italy, and Osimo hardly deserves the name of a town.

trary, undertake the investment, the small numbers of the garrison would be commensurate to the slender store of provisions, and the cavalry of John might, in the meanwhile, be more usefully employed in the field by cutting off the detachments and surrounding the camp of the besiegers.

Accordingly, Hildiger and Martin set out from Rome, successfully avoided the hostile army, and, having forced a passage through the rocky defile of Petra Pertusa,[51] and drawn the requisite troops from Ancona, made known to John the Sanguinary the instructions with which they were charged. But this presumptuous subaltern, whether unable to comprehend the motives, and therefore reluctant to obey the commands of his general, or whether dreading the fatigues and hardships of the adventurous warfare to which he was summoned, refused to comply with the mandate, and remained immovable at Rimini. The consequences of this stubbornness soon set forth the sagacity of Belisarius. Vitiges, allured by the hope of reducing to captivity two thousand chosen horsemen of the enemy, invested the fortress, and pushed his enterprise with the greater ardour, as trusting to retrieve at Rimini the military fame which he had forfeited at Rome.[52]

It must be owned, in justice to John the Sanguinary, that his resolution was as steadfast against the enemy as it had been against his commander, and that he endeavoured, by his courage, to cure the effects of his imprudence. He repulsed the assaults, he deceived the vigilance, he destroyed the engines of the Goths. Yet it appeared equally necessary, and far more difficult, to withstand the pressure of scarcity, which soon began to be severely felt by the besieged, and John must often have admitted the wiser policy of his general, and regretted as pernicious the very numbers of his famished soldiers.

Meanwhile Belisarius was advancing from Rome, (June *a.d.* 538), to carry on hostilities in person. The cities of Tudertia or Todi, and of Clusium or Chiusi, which he had intended to besiege, surrendered on his first approach, to the terror of his name. He was still better pleased on learning the arrival of seven thousand fresh Byzantine troops, which had landed in the March of Ancona, under the com-

---

51. Compare Procop. *Goth. lib. ii* c 11. and *lib. iv.* c. 28. See also a note of Sigonius, (*De Occident. Imp. Op.* vol. i.)

52. It appears that Vitiges, in the siege of Rimini, encamped on the banks of the Rubicon. (Marcellin. *Chron. ap. Sirmond. Op.* vol. ii.) This passage might, perhaps, be useful in deciding between the four rivers to which that celebrated name has been applied in modern times. See Forsyth's *Italy*, Geneva ed.

mand of Narses.[53] This officer, so renowned in later campaigns, was an eunuch, and a domestic of the palace; one of the very few recorded in history who have illustrated either of these characters by military skill. We may justly admire and respect the vigour of a mind which, under every disadvantage of a feeble and dwarfish body.[54] after many years of household cares, of thraldom to female caprices, nay, even of employment in the female tasks of the loom, was found not unequal to the command of armies.

Yet the desire of displaying this remarkable exception to the common rule, has tempted most modern historians to adorn the fame of Narses with a lustre which will be found to diminish and disappear in proportion as it is closely viewed. His talent for war was undoubtedly considerable, but it will be seen in the sequel of this narrative, that his victories were at least as greatly due to his influence over his imperial master, as to his own superiority of tactics. In some respects he only reaped the harvest which Belisarius had already sown. Reinforcements were necessary at that period to carry on the war; they were denied to the hero, they were granted to the favourite. Besides, the avarice[55] and cruelty of Narses were such as would have blackened the most brilliant reputation, and his rapid conquest is nearly outweighed by his harsh and oppressive government.

As subalterns, great men have almost always shown themselves as ready to obey as they afterwards proved able to command; but Narses, till invested with supreme authority, was prone to faction, impatient of control, and careless of the public cause. We are told by an historian, partial to his fame, that on one occasion he deeply lamented the success of the imperial arms, because he himself had foretold and expected a reverse.[56] Nor must we forget, in the consideration of his character, that at the close of his long life he blotted out its glories

---

53. Gibbon observes, (vol. vii.) "the country of Narses is unknown, since he must not be confounded with the Persarmenian." But there were two Persarmenians of the name of Narses, the one who has already been mentioned as deserting to the Romans in the first campaigns of Belisarius, and the other who received that deserter. Now the second is undoubtedly the same as the eunuch, each being called the private imperial treasurer, (Procop. *Pers. lib.* ii. c 15. Goth. *lib. ii.* c. 18.) Moreover the deserter is afterwards mentioned as one of the train of the eunuch in Italy.
54. *Agathias, lib. i.*
55. According to Paul Warnefrid, (*lib. iii.* c 12.) Narses in his second Italian command, concealed many thousand pounds weight of gold in a private cistern, and then put to death the workmen who had constructed it. The secret was disclosed after his own death by his sole confidant.
56. Procop. *Goth. lib.* ii. c. 19. See a warm panegyric on Narses, *lib. iv. c.* 26.

by treason, and called in the national enemy to avenge his private wrongs.[57] Even in his proudest moments, in the day of victory and triumph, we may still discern the habits of falsehood and the petty artifices of the eastern slave. He imposed on the devotion of his soldiers by pretending to the special favour of the Holy Virgin. He asserted that she never failed to apprise him of the most auspicious time for an engagement, nor would he issue his orders for battle until he had received her appointed signal.[58] Such a fraud, were it but once attempted, (and that of Narses was continued for several years) cannot be too strongly condemned.

Even the great discoverer of a new world has been blamed for availing himself of his fore-knowledge of eclipses, to raise the superstitious veneration of the Indians; but Columbus was then in the most pressing danger: his liberty and even his life were at stake, and every other expedient for escape had disappeared.[59] None of these excuses will apply to the Byzantine general.

Narses and Belisarius joined their forces near the town of Fermo, and a council of war was immediately convened by the latter, to deliberate on the best means of relieving Rimini. That its garrison should continue to hold out without some succour was impossible, from the want of provisions, but at the same time it appeared very hazardous for the Romans to advance in that direction, since the large Gothic force, shut up in Osimo, might issue forth and intercept them in the rear. The whole council agreed in deploring the rashness and avarice which had misled John the Sanguinary from the prudent instructions of the general, and some officers even wished to leave him to his fate. Narses, who was bound to John by the closest ties of friendship, without attempting to defend his conduct, urged the necessity of marching to his rescue, and his arguments were enforced by a letter from that chief to Belisarius, announcing that unless relieved before seven days, the pressure of famine must compel him to surrender.

---

57. The invitation to the Lombards by Narses is attested by Paul Warnefrid, (*lib. ii.* c. 5.) and by Anastasius, (*De Vit Pontif.* c. 62.) who are copied by Bede, (Op. vol. ii. ed. 1688.) and Aimoin, (*De Gest Franc, lib. iii.* c 10.) The two last prove at least the popular belief Cardinal Baronius takes the favourite of the Virgin under his protection, and denies his treason; but the weakness of this defence is shown by Muratori, Pagi, &c.
58. Evagrius, *Hist. Eccles. lib. iv.* c. 24. He believes in these miracles.
59. See Robertson's *History of America*, vol. i. 1777, and Mr. Washington Irving's late life of Columbus, (book xvi c. 3.) a work which does justice to its object and honour to its author.

At this intelligence Belisarius hastened to decide and execute his plans. Some troops were left encamped at a short distance from Osimo, in hopes of checking the sallies of its garrison, and the rest proceeded in different divisions to assist their invested comrades. In spite of the new reinforcements, the Roman Army was still far inferior to that of Vitiges, and Belisarius therefore, instead of encountering the barbarians at once, considered it more prudent to employ some stratagem, and to contrive that they should think themselves encompassed by superior squadrons.

One detachment was embarked in the Roman fleet, and committed to the command of Hildiger, and another under Martin was instructed to march along the Flaminian way, and by kindling at night the extended fires of a large army, to create an overcharged impression of its numbers. Belisarius himself, at the head of the main body, proceeded along the rugged ridge of the Apennines. On his approach to Rimini he routed a foraging party of the Goths, and the affrighted runaways, on returning to their camp, announced and magnified the forces of the Roman general. The Goths eagerly prepared for battle, and cast impatient looks towards the mountains from whence they expected the enemy to issue; but their confidence was changed to dismay in the ensuing night, on observing, from another quarter, the numerous lights of the detachments under Martin, and they concluded that two large armies were marching against them.

When the dawn revealed to them, in addition to these, the approach of a Roman fleet, their alarm grew into a panic, they precipitately raised the siege, and the only contest amongst them, says Procopius, was who should arrive the soonest at Ravenna. Had the garrison of Rimini sallied forth against them in these moments of confusion, their defeat might have been decisive; but its exhaustion and discouragement rendered it incapable of any such exertion. Hildiger was the first to enter the deserted camp of the barbarians; he took prisoners the stragglers and the wounded, and seized upon the baggage left behind. The troops of Martin and of Belisarius arrived a few hours later, and the whole of the imperial army was thus reunited beneath the walls of Rimini.

Any views which the Roman general may have entertained for improving and extending this success were baffled by the selfish jealousy of Narses. The friends of this favourite eunuch never ceased from urging to him that having so lately left the sacred presence, and enjoyed the familiar conversation of the emperor, he must be better acquainted with his real wishes than a distant and uncourtly general. They entreated him not to yield to Belisarius the whole glory of the war, but to perplex and thwart his measures by a determined opposition. He was reminded that the greater part of the effective forces at that moment were those under his immediate command, since so many of the veterans of Belisarius were scattered through the garrisons of southern Italy. These perfidious counsels were attentively heard and faithfully obeyed by Narses; he always, on one pretext or another, evaded compliance with the orders of the general, and at length, when commanded to march to the relief of Milan, he openly refused to obey. This orthodox capital of Liguria had borne with impatience the yoke of an Arian monarch, and several of its principal citizens had arrived at Rome towards the end of the siege, requesting some troops from Belisarius to assist their intended revolt.[60]

Amongst these deputies was Datius, the bishop, since canonised by the Catholic Church for his conspiracy against a heretic sovereign, and his more prosperous but less visible warfare against daemons.[61] According to their entreaties, Belisarius, as soon as the Goths had begun to retreat from Rome, ordered a thousand soldiers together with a small detachment of his guards, to embark at Porto, with Mundilas for their commander. Having landed at Genoa,[62] these troops advanced rapidly to Milan, and the insurrection both of that city and of the surrounding districts was effected without difficulty.

But when Vitiges received these adverse tidings he dispatched his nephew, Uraias, at the head of a formidable army, to attempt the reduction of the rebellious province, and on the other side ten thousand Burgundians passed the Alps to uphold the tottering cause of their brother barbarians. These useful auxiliaries came by the secret orders of Theodebert, King of Austrasia, according to the treaty which Vitiges had concluded at the commencement of his reign; and since the Burgundians were the recent and unsettled subjects of Theodebert, he was enabled to disavow all participation in their counsels, and to boast to the emperor of his scrupulous neutrality.

---

60. From the difficulty of accounting for the peaceable passage of these envoys through the Gothic lines, Muratori supposes that they had been banished from Milan. (*Annal. d'Ital.* vol. iii.)

61. Gregor. *Magn. Dial. lib. iii.* c. 4. *ap. Baronium, Annal. Eccles.* a.d. 539. No. 20. The day fixed for the worship of St Datius is the fourteenth of January. (Pagi. *Critic,* vol. ii.)

62. Genoa at this time formed part of the province of Tuscany. (Procop. *Goth. lib. ii* c. 12.)

By the united forces of the Franks and Goths the siege of Milan was forthwith undertaken and vigorously pressed, and the succour of that city became an object of first-rate importance to the Romans. When Belisarius found his private exhortations to Narses unavailing, he tried the effects of a public address in full council. He besought the eunuch not to consider the Goths as already vanquished, nor to imagine that the past successes of the Roman Army might allow it to relax in its exertions. He said:

> Remember that Vitiges is still entrenched at Ravenna with several remaining myriads of soldiers, that Uraias has recovered Liguria, and is now besieging Milan; that a numerous and formidable army defies us from the ramparts of Osimo, and that a chain of fortresses, down to Orvieto, almost in sight of Rome, is defended by barbarian garrisons. The situation of our troops may be considered as more critical than ever, while thus hemmed in by the enemy. Should the report be true that a horde of Burgundians is also marching against us in Liguria these fresh adversaries should likewise raise our apprehensions. Let us not, therefore, remain inactive. Let us send a portion of our troops to the relief of Milan, and with the rest commence the investment of Osimo. The result of these will, of course, determine our further undertakings.

Against self interest most arguments are powerless. Narses declared that he would dispatch no share of the seven thousand men under his personal command, either to Milan or Osimo, and hoping to divide the council, he proposed in opposition to this plan the invasion of the Æmilian province, which nearly corresponds with modern Romagna. To end these mischievous disputes, Belisarius then brought forward the following letter from the emperor to the Roman chief:

> In sending Narses, our private treasurer, to Italy, we have no intention that he should, in any degree, control or direct the war; we desire that Belisarius should still remain invested with supreme authority, and be implicitly obeyed in all his undertakings for the public good.

These words appeared clear and decisive, but the subtle mind of Narses had too long been conversant with the intrigues of the palace not to find or to make a daw. He availed himself of the concluding clause, asserted that the commands of Belisarius in this instance were not really conducive to the public good, and that, therefore, the officers were not required to obey them. It was found impossible to subdue his factious opposition, and Belisarius could only spare from amongst his veterans such slender succours for the relief of Milan, that, as will presently be seen, they proved wholly inadequate to their object. A third proposal, the siege of Urbino, could not, with any plausibility, be likewise withstood by Narses, and the whole army was, therefore, united for this enterprise. The garrison, confiding in the lofty situation and well stored granaries of the city, turned a deaf ear to all terms of surrender, and the investment was begun.

But the jealous spirit of John the Sanguinary, could ill brook that others should succeed in reducing a fortress from whence he himself had been repulsed on his march to Rimini. He appears to have persuaded Narses that the idea of taking Urbino was chimerical and hopeless, and to have held out, as far more fruitful both of wealth and of renown, an inroad into the rich province of Æmilia. Accordingly Narses raised his camp at night, and secretly deserted his general, followed by the troops Under his peculiar orders, and accompanied by John the Sanguinary. The garrison next morning did not fail to observe and to taunt from the ramparts the diminished number of the besiegers. Yet Belisarius resolved to persevere in his undertaking, and the favour of fortune speedily atoned for the secession of his soldiers. The Goths in Urbino were amply supplied with provisions, but possessed only one single spring, and this, from some hidden cause, in spite of the wintry season, (December, a.d. 538), began decreasing, until in three days the water oozing from it was merely sufficient to moisten the adjacent ground.[63]

While therefore the Romans were drawing, with much labour, a military engine against the almost inaccessible walls, they were pleasingly surprised by a signal of surrender from the garrison. The grief of Narses at Rimini, when informed of this unexpected success, was only assuaged by the exploits of John the Sanguinary, who had overrun the Æmilian province with his usual valour, and though beaten back from the walls of Cesena, succeeded in reducing Imola and several other places. Belisarius next directed his arms against Orvieto, which Nature had so strongly fortified as to secure against assault, and which yielded only to the slow but irresistible progress of blockade. While this important bulwark continued in the hands of the Goths the possession

---

63. Such changes in springs were not uncommon in ancient times. See Ovid. *Met. lib. xv.*, v. 272.

of Rome was always considered as precarious.

To the detachment which Belisarius had dispatched towards Milan he had appointed Uliaris and Martin as commanders. These officers advanced by rapid marches to the banks of the Po, where their reflections on the dangers which awaited them on the northern shore detained them in trembling and irresolute suspense. It was in vain that an emissary from Mundilas, the governor of Milan, boldly traversed the lines of the enemy, and swam the river to urge the necessity of their speedily proceeding. The timid chiefs wrote to Belisarius, excusing their delay, and setting forth the formidable and united numbers of the Burgundians and the Goths, and they besought that he would command John the Sanguinary, then stationed in the neighbouring Æmilian province, to join his forces with theirs.

Orders to this effect were instantly dispatched by Belisarius, but John answered by a downright refusal to obey unless with the consent of Narses. To Narses, therefore, who was then peaceably encamped at Rimini, Belisarius at that time engaged in blockading Orvieto, sent a pressing letter. In this document he urges that the scattered battalions of an army, like the limbs of the human frame, should be directed by one pervading spirit, and not attempt various and incompatible movements, he says:

> For my part, I have not at my disposal any troops to spare; but were my force ever so numerous it would still be impossible for me, at this distance, to afford any effectual aid to Milan. Reinforcements from hence would arrive too late, the decisive moment would be lost, and the horses jaded by so long a journey could not on their arrival act with vigour in the field.

Thus admonished, Narses gave the required permission, but it was already too late, and an unseasonable illness of John the Sanguinary occasioned further delay, *(a.d.* 539). Milan had long been reduced to the utmost distress for food; the inhabitants were compelled to subsist on such animals as truth or prejudice represent as loathsome;[64] yet their courage was upheld by the dread of Burgundian fierceness and Gothic revenge.

After Mundilas had made the bravest resistance, and in, vain exhorted his soldiers to attempt a desperate sally. he concluded an ad-

---

64. Mice, for instance, are mentioned, yet the *glires* or dormice were once a favourite dish with the Romans, and even forbidden by an ancient Censorial law as too luxurious. (Plin. *Hist. Nat. lib. xxxvi.* c. 1)

vantageous capitulation for the garrison, but could obtain no terms for the city or the citizens. It is affirmed that Milan was razed to the ground, but as we find it, at no distant period, again commemorated as a flourishing and important city,[65] we may suspect that the destruction was confined to the ramparts, nor is it improbable that all the churches may have been levelled or defaced, the Catholic by the Goths and the Arian by the Franks. St. Datius escaped to Constantinople,[66] but Fidelius, the imperial *prefect*, was less fortunate, he was torn to pieces by the ferocious besiegers, and his mangled limbs were carelessly thrown to the dogs.

While the women were put aside, according to their age and beauty, as concubines or as menials, and bestowed on the Burgundians as the price of their alliance, the men were massacred even at the altars,[67] and the number of the slain has grown in history to three hundred thousand.[68] Such a calculation must appear incredible, yet we are assured that of all the Italian cities at this time, with the exception of Rome, reserved perhaps chiefly from its ancient supremacy, Milan was by far the first in wealth, population, and extent. Its loss deeply afflicted Belisarius, and, on the return of Martin and Uliaris, he showed his indignation by refusing to admit them to his presence. Uliaris was the same soldier by whose hand John the Armenian had fallen.

At nearly the same time, (the winter was drawing to a close—Feb. or March a.d. 539,) the decision of the emperor confirmed the disputed authority of Belisarius in Italy. Narses was recalled to the intimacy of his sovereign, and the administration of his domestic office; but the fierce and intractable tribe of the Heruli, under his personal command, and consisting of two thousand soldiers, seized this pretext for revolt. They marched into Liguria, pillaged the open country, and were concluding a separate treaty with the Goths, when they were checked by one of those sudden changes of purpose to which all barbarous nations are prone, as acting rather from the impulse of the moment, than from systematic principle. Their satiety of plunder, they thought moderation; their regret of the lucrative imperial service, they termed repentance for their mutiny; and, marching back to Constanti-

---

65. Paul Warnefrid, *lib. ii* c. 15 and 25.
66. See the end of Datius in Victor Tunnunensis, (vol. i. ed. 1725.)
67. Marius, *Chronic.* (*Historiens de France*, vol. ii.)
68. Procop. *Goth. lib. ii.* c. 21, perhaps a corruption in the text. This number, absurdly too high, is made as absurdly too low by Cousin, who renders *trois cent*, and the massacre has accordingly been passed over as trifling by some French critics, often apt to depend on translations.

nople under the command of Philimuth, they obtained their pardon.

The departure of Narses left to Belisarius the free and undisputed control of the remaining forces, and the unity of power was soon manifest from the vigour of operations. It was resolved by the general to undertake at once the siege of the two important fortresses of Fiesole and Osimo; the former he committed to a strong detachment under Cyprian and Justin, while he himself marched against the capital of Picenum with eleven thousand men. This city was placed on the summit of an almost inaccessible hill, and defended by an experienced and numerous garrison, which, it may be remembered, Vitiges, on his return from Rome, had augmented with four thousand veterans. It was headed by Visandus, the same who had formerly stood forth as the antagonist of Belisarius in single combat, and had been left for dead upon the field. Several slight skirmishes were fought, at the commencement of the siege, to check the foraging excursions of the Goths; and some confusion was found to attend the Romans in this petty warfare, because the signal of the trumpet equally denoted a charge and a retreat, and the orders of the officers for the one or the other were drowned in the clangour of arms.

It was, therefore, suggested by the historian Procopius, that in future a charge should be made known by the brazen horse-trumpet, and that the trumpet of the infantry, composed only of wood and leather, should announce a retreat. This judicious proposal was readily adopted by Belisarius, but he found it no easy task to bend the spirit of his soldiers to the supposed ignominy of ever retiring before the beleaguered barbarians, he said to them:

> Remember, that even intrepidity must be restrained within certain and moderate limits, and, when it becomes pernicious, ceases to be honourable.

Through these and similar precautions every stratagem of the Gothic troops was baffled, and they in their turn were soon closely pressed by the Romans. It was in vain that they entreated some succour from Vitiges at Ravenna, and reminded him of his former declaration, that in committing Osimo to their defence, he had entrusted them with the keys of his capital and kingdom. The Gothic monarch, instead of bestowing, was reduced to implore protection. In a fruitless embassy, he had solicited the alliance of the Lombards, and he now artfully attempted to divide and overwhelm the Roman forces, by exciting Nushirvan to attack them. Two priests, preferring the interests of their prince to those of their religion, were induced by large presents to traverse secretly the imperial dominions, to the court of the Magian king; and it will be seen in the sequel, that their eloquence and zeal to direct his arms against their brother Christians were attended with success. But this diversion, though powerful, was tardy, and served not to prevent, but only to protract, the final extinction of the Gothic monarchy.

A stronger and less remote alliance was held out in prospect to the Goths, by a formidable army of Franks, which suddenly descended from the Alps, and overspread the fertile plains of Liguria. To the earlier embassies, both of Justinian and Vitiges, Theodebert had given specious promises, but little real support, unwilling either to exalt the power of a dangerous neighbour, or to favour the imperial pretensions upon Italy, which might at some future time be as justly extended to Gaul. The Burgundians whom he had permitted to share in the siege of Milan, consisted of no more than ten thousand men, and returned homewards as soon as this city had surrendered. But, when he perceived both parties weakened by their long and bloody warfare, he fended that it might not be difficult, with his fresh and numerous army, to snatch away the prize for which they were contending. Without declaring his objects, he advanced at the head of forces which have been reckoned at two hundred thousand men, but which more probably amounted to only half the number.[69] Since like time of Brennus, nine centuries before, none of the Gallic chieftains had invaded Italy; but, on the contrary, their territories had been desolated by the arms, and annexed to the dominions of Rome.

The retribution for these conquests, so frequently and so fully paid in the middle ages, now began; and from the days of Theodebert to those of Napoleon the degenerate Italians have often felt, and never withstood but by foreign aid, the attacks of their former province. They have been reduced to deplore the fruitful soil and delicious climate,[70] which age after age allured the barbarians to cross their mountainous barrier, and, by a singular malediction, they are now devoid both of spirit for freedom and of callousness to slavery. A talent for poetry and music, for painting and sculpture, may afford some

---

69. Jornandes states two hundred thousand (*De Regn. Success*), but Procopius one hundred thousand (*Goth. lib. ii.* c. 25.) Aimoin merely says in direct opposition to the assertion of Procopius, that few of the Franks were mounted. (*De Gest Franc, lib. ii* c. 21.) His authority is vey slight.

70. See Filicaja's celebrated sonnet—*Italia, Italia, o tu cui feo la sorte, &c.*

compensation for national disgrace; but it is a singular and striking fact, that of all those illustrious men who hare formed the literature, or revived the arts of modern Italy, not one has been a native of Rome, and that nearly all have sprung from barbarian ancestry in the ancient Cisalpine Gaul.[71] The soil, once so fertile in heroes, seems weary and exhausted with the number.

In two contemporary Greek historians, we find a very different account of the customs and conduct of the Franks in their invasion. The one extols them as models of uncorrupted virtue; be praises their strict execution of the precepts, and their orthodox adherence to the tenets, of the Catholic Church,[72] The other holds them forth as brutal savages, who, with the profession of Christianity, clung to many of their heathen rites, and, who showed at once their cruelty and superstition, by the sacrifice of children to idols.[73] Between such conflicting statements, the truth can hardly be discerned. Yet, if we look to any national chronicle of the Franks, it will appear to turn the balance against them, and to prove that, like most nations in a rude state of society, they seldom distinguished ferocity from valour, or perfidiousness from stratagem. In its equipments their army bore no resemblance to the Roman. None but the king and his immediate attendants rode on horseback, and were armed with lances; the others, on foot, were provided only with swords and bucklers, or wielded a weighty two-edged battle-axe. At the head of these forces, Theodebert was welcomed by the Goths as an ally, and, through their imprudent confidence, he secured the passage of the Po and Tessino near Pavia.

In front of this city were encamped the troops of Uraias, returned from the conquest of Milan; and also an imperial squadron which had been sent by Belisarius to watch their motions, and prevent their advancing into Tuscany. Both these detachments were on the same day

---

71. Guido was of Bologna, Davila of Padua, Tiraboschi of Bergamo, Correggio and Ariosto of Reggio, Bentivoglio of Ferrara, Maffei of Verona, Alfieri of Piedmont, Muratori of Modena, Raphael of Urbino. Fra Paolo, Goldoni, Titian and Canova were Venetians; Petrarch, Guicciardini, Macchiavel, Dante, Michel Angelo, and Boccacio, Florentines. Tasso was born at Sorrento, but his family was from the Milanese. Deduct these, and what remains for southern Italy?
72. Agathias, *lib. i.*
73. Procop. *Goth. lib. i.* c. 25. Cardinal Baronius takes fire at dui imputation on the orthodox Franks (*Annal. Eccles. a.d.* 540, No. 35), and Dom Bouquet endeavours to divert it from his countrymen to the Alamanni, (*Historiens de France*, vol. ii.) From the character given to Theodebert by Gregory of Tours, it seems probable that he, at least, did not authorise these outrages. (*Hist. Franc. lib iii.* c. 25)

surprised and overwhelmed by the attack of Theodebert; the Goths fled in confusion towards Ravenna, and the Romans to their comrades before Fiesole. The whole of Liguria was thus laid open to the Franks, who, like an Alpine avalanche, carried devastation over its extensive plains. Their progress was unopposed by enemies, hut was soon arrested by famine. During the last winter, the tillage of the fields had been neglected amidst the calamities of war, and the scanty crops had withered in the summer, before reaching their full ripeness. In the March of Ancona alone more than fifty thousand persons are stated to have perished from hunger, and the Tuscans were driven to find in acorns an insufficient and unwholesome food. Many fell victims to their eagerness in breaking a long fast; and thus supplies of provisions, if too sudden, became as fatal as the former scarcity.

This disastrous year is forcibly portrayed by Procopius, a personal witness to its horrors. He saw starving wretches fling themselves down upon herbs and grasses, and make a faint attempt to tear them from the ground; but their enfeebled strength often failed them, and they expired in the effort. He saw their bodies left, as they fell, to blacken in the sun, and displaying corruption in its most hideous forms. Yet the ghastly aspect of the dead, was exceeded by that of the survivors. Their livid hue is compared to the colour of an extinguished torch, and their skin seemed closely adhering to their bones. Their haggard features were distorted with a wild and fearful expression, and a gleam of maniac fury shone forth from their hollow eyes. Sometimes their lips were seen to drip with blood, from devouring the severed limbs of their lifeless companions; yet even the birds of prey turned from the carcasses, after seeking in vain for some nourishment in these dry and wasted remains.[74]

As soon as the Roman general was informed of the hostile progress of Theodebert, he dispatched a letter, from before the walls of Osimo, to deter him from advancing, and to threaten the imperial displeasure, he added;

> It would surely be wiser to maintain the tranquil and undisputed enjoyment of your hereditary states, than to endanger their possession in the vain hope of extending their limits.

Such a maxim, which might easily have been retorted on Justinian,

---

[74]. This description is abridged from Procopius (*Goth. lib. ii.* c. 20). See also the testimony of St. Datius in Anastasius (*De Vit. Pontif.* c. 60.), and in the *Historia Miscella* (lib. xvi ap. *Muratori, Script Ital.* vol. i.)

would, doubtless, have been disregarded by Theodebert in a season of prosperity, but it derived importance from the sufferings of his soldiers. Their thoughtless rapacity had soon exhausted the slender stores of provisions, and they were reduced for sustenance to the flesh of a few oxen and the waters of the Po. More than one third of their number was swept away by a disease which unwholesome food and the heat of an Italian summer [75] brought on, and the complaints of the survivors became importunate and loud. Unable to withstand their desire of returning, the king eagerly availed himself of the letter of Belisarius as a plausible pretext, and led back into France his disheartened and diminished forces.

This short episode in the war was attended with no permanent result, and did not interrupt the plans of Belisarius. He had hitherto, with more ardour than success, pushed the siege of Osimo, which was defended by the natural strength of its site, and the disciplined valour of its garrison. When attempting to destroy its cistern for water, the Roman general was baffled by the solidity of ancient architecture,[76] and during a skirmish which ensued, his life had nearly been lost by the deliberate aim of a Gothic archer. One of his guards alone perceived the coming danger, and rushed forward to shield the body of his general by the interposition of his own. In this act of devoted fidelity, his hand was transpierced and disabled, and Unigatus, the name of this brave soldier, is not unworthy of historical record. Finding that he could not divert the stream, the Roman general next determined to render it useless, and accordingly corpses, poisonous herbs and quicklime were thrown into it by his orders.[77]

Thus the besieged could no longer avail themselves of their usual fountain, and a well which they possessed within the ramparts, afforded them only a scanty supply. Their correspondence with Vitiges, which they had hitherto carried on by the secret aid of a Roman soldier, was also discovered and cut off, and Belisarius having left the punishment of the traitor to the discretion of his comrades, he was burnt alive according to a law of Constantine the Great, [78] When Fiesole shortly

---

75. Greg. Turon. *Hist. Franc, lib. ii.* c. 32.
76. This cistern or reservoir, is called an aqueduct by Gibbon, *lib. iii* (vol. vii.).
77. The conduct of Belisarius on this occasion, is quoted and approved by Grotius, after explaining, that the law of nations forbids the secret poisoning of fountains; (*Droit des Gens*, ed. Barbeyrac, vol. ii.). A similar opinion is expressed by Vattel, (vol. ii. ed. 1775.)
78. This law is not mentioned by Procopius, but may be found, *Cod. Theodos. lib. vii.* tit. 1.

afterwards yielded to the Roman arms, and when the principal officers who had defended that city, were shown to the Goths as captives, they no longer refused to treat of a surrender.

It was however demanded on their part, that they should enjoy a free and unmolested passage to Ravenna, and be allowed to carry with them all their public or private treasure. Such terms were heard with unwillingness by Belisarius, and with indignation by his soldiers. They loudly complained that the well-earned rewards of their valour would thus be taken from them; they displayed the wounds they had received, and recounted the exploits they had performed during the progress of the siege. It appeared no easy task to reconcile the pretensions of the Gothic with those of the Roman soldiers, but it was at length agreed that an equal partition of the spoil should be made, and that one-half should remain to the Goths, who consented to acknowledge the emperor as their sovereign.

Ravenna, against which Belisarius now directed his whole army, was surrounded by a twofold barrier of strong ramparts and impervious morasses. This city had first been chosen by Augustus as a principal station for the fleet, and the harbour of Classis or Classe, which he constructed, denotes that object in its name. It would appear as if the sea were slowly receding from each side of the Italian peninsula, at least at the mouth of the rivers. The ancient maritime city of Pisa is now at some distance from the shore, and so early as the fifth century, orchards occupied the harbour of Augustus, at Ravenna.[79] In the time of Procopius, the low sandbanks near Classe, which have since grown part of the land, were every day left dry and exposed by the ebbing of the tide, though the Mediterranean in general has none; and it is remarkable, that this historian should have observed its regular dependence on the phases of the moon.[80]

The great strength of Ravenna needs no further proof than the constant residence of the timid Honorius, who first selected this city for the capital. Even Alaric, in the fullness of his power, had never ventured to invest it, and it had vainly been besieged for nearly three

---

79. Jornandes, *de Reb. Getic.* c. 29. He indulges in some frigid conceits on this occasion. The ancient harbour still displayed trees like masts, but they bore fruits instead of sails, &c. The suburb of Classe was finally destroyed by Liutprand, King of the Lombards, (Paul Warnefrid, *lib. vi.* c. 49) and its site is now overgrown with the pine forests of Chiassi, which Boccacio, Dryden, and Byron have immortalised.
80. *Goth. lib. i.* c. i. Compare this carious approximation to the truth, with the absurd theories collected by Bede. (*Op.* vol. ii. ed. 1688.)

years by Theodoric the Great. Thus therefore the late victories of Belisarius over the Goths, did not altogether insure him certain, or still less, speedy success before Ravenna.

These obstacles were Very rapidly surmounted by the Roman general. On his first approach, he discovered that the spirit of Vitiges was almost broken by repeated failure, and that he might, perhaps, be persuaded to enter into terms. Ambassadors were therefore dispatched to Ravenna, but in the meanwhile every passage, both by sea and land, was guarded by the prudent care of Belisarius, and his prospects of negotiation never induced him to relax his vigilance. During the progress of these parleys, he planned and executed a measure, which enabled him to dictate rather than to treat. He opened a correspondence with Queen Matasontha, and by her secret aid, found means of firing the Gothic granaries and magazines, so that Ravenna became almost devoid of provisions, and unable much longer to hold out.

The co-operation of their queen was suspected by some of the Goths, but a greater number imputed the calamity to lightning, and the first were less terrified by domestic treachery than the latter by so evident a mark of the divine displeasure. All, however, concurred in regarding the immediate downfall of their monarchy as certain and inevitable, either from the rigorous terms of the negotiation, or from the effects of the blockade. But they had not reckoned on their Byzantine allies, the feeble judgment and suspicious temper of Justinian. It has already been mentioned, that during the siege of Rome, some ambassadors from Vitiges bad embarked for Constantinople, to propose the partition of the Gothic kingdom as the terms of peace.

They had been allowed by the imperial court to languish in neglect and contempt, till Nushirvan, roused by Gothic solicitations, and by his own ambitious views, resolved to invade the Roman territories. At this intelligence Justinian trembled, and displayed that inconsiderate rashness, to which the foolhardy and the pusillanimous are equally prone. Without deigning to inquire from his successful general, whether it might not be almost as easy to render the Goths his subjects as his allies, the emperor concluded with the barbarian ambassadors a disgraceful treaty, which left to Vitiges the title of king, the provinces beyond the Po, and a moiety of the treasures at Ravenna.

Accompanied by two Roman senators, the joyful envoys forthwith proceeded to the imperial camp, and from thence to the Gothic capital, which they filled with surprise at their unexpected good fortune. It may well be imagined that Vitiges, who had already thought himself a captive at Constantinople, hastened to ratify a treaty by which his most sanguine expectations were surpassed, and which rather resembled the gift of a benefactor than the stipulations of an enemy. On the other hand, the Roman general heard with indignation of an agreement so pernicious to the public cause, and he called together a council of his principal officers, to consult them on his project of accomplishing the conquest of Italy in spite of the mandate of the emperor.

The men to whom this deliberation was referred, were but little disposed to forward the views of their high-minded leader. Several amongst them were envious of his fame or impatient of his discipline, and a still greater number regretted the pleasures of peace and of home. To a military spirit, the languor of a long blockade is far more hateful than the peril of a siege, and either timidity or weariness might easily be veiled beneath a respectful submission to the imperial commands.

According to the request of Belisarius, who wished to preserve an authentic record of their sentiments, each officer gave in a written opinion, in which the reduction of Ravenna was pronounced to be visionary and impracticable, and the treaty of partition judicious and expedient. Undismayed at this unanimous opposition, the general determined to extinguish the Gothic monarchy, and to present before the throne of Justinian the treasures and the person of Vitiges. He refused to ratify the Byzantine agreement, and his refusal filled the Goths with alarm. Dreading some fraudulent intention on the part of the Romans, they declared that they could place no reliance on the peace proposed to them, unless it were confirmed both by the signature and the oath of Belisarius.

The Roman general, however, persevered in his noble resolution to incur the merit or the guilt of a patriotic disobedience. The infringement of orders by an officer in war, is glorious to him if successful, but fatal in its failure; he renders himself answerable for the uncertain issue of events, while a rigid adherence to his instructions would, even in the greatest reverses, have shielded him from blame. It may therefore be doubted, whether it is necessary for the maintenance of discipline, that such acts of judicious presumption should be capital offences;[81] few men have genius to conceive, and still fewer courage to perform them.

---

81. Amongst the Romans, this disobedience was punished by death. (*Pandect. lib. xlix.* tit. 16, sect. 3.) With us it is so likewise, subject, however, to a discretionary power. (Coleridge's *Blackstone*, vol. i. ed. 1825.)

By the refusal of Belisarius, the brilliant visions of peace and security which had floated before the eyes of the barbarians, vanished almost as rapidly and unexpectedly as they had arisen. To the pangs of disappointment were added those of approaching famine; and their hopeless situation suggested a project which, however singular, is not unparalleled in history, and which may call to the recollection of the reader the wish of the Egyptian *emirs* to choose St. Louis for their king.[82] The Goths resolved to depose a sovereign whom they had always found unfortunate, and to elect as his successor, an enemy whose valour was attested by their overthrow, and whose virtues had extorted their esteem. Under the auspicious command of Belisarius, they trusted to attain a higher pitch of power than that to which even the great Theodoric had raised them, and it was not the title of Gothic king, but of Western emperor which they urged him to assume.[83]

It is probable that their views of conquest passed the bounds of Italy, and extended to France, Africa and Spain. Vitiges himself was forced to acquiesce in this extraordinary scheme, to add his entreaties to those of his subjects, and to place his abdication at the feet of the Roman general. A wider field has rarely been opened to ambition, and it might not have been difficult to obtain the approbation and support of the Roman Army. Though Belisarius had many enemies amongst the officers, every soldier was his devoted partisan; since the same qualities and exploits, which provoked the envy of the one, secured the attachment of the other. For the distant authority of a feeble and unwarlike sovereign, they would have preferred the exaltation of their victorious general, well acquainted with their merit, and by his new dignity enabled to reward it.

On the other part, Belisarius could not be ignorant of the dangers which must attend his continued loyalty, of the secret cabals against him in the palace, where his late disobedience might be magnified into mutiny and treason. Narses also was present with Justinian, Narses who had inflicted too many injuries on Belisarius, to be capable of forgiveness, and who added the merit of a general to the familiar intercourse of a domestic, and the practised cunning of a courtier.

---

82. This curious fact is established by the authority of Joinville, an eyewitness. *Les Admiraulx avoient eu grant envie et par conseil de faire le Roy Souldan de Babilonne*, (ed. 1668.) I need hardly add, that the word Admiral is derived from *Emir*, and is here synonymous with it. See on this title, Ducange (*Observations sur Joinville*), and Gibbon (vol. x.)

83. (Procop. *Goth. lib. ii.* c 29.) To realise this project was reserved for Charlemagne.

But Belisarius was deeply impressed with his oath of allegiance, from which no personal considerations could absolve him, and knew how to despise an usurped and precarious throne. He resolved, however, by a seeming compliance, to hasten the surrender of Ravenna and the captivity of Vitiges.

It is difficult in war to draw an accurate line, and to distinguish with precision where perfidy commences and stratagem should end, and a question may arise, how far the conduct of Belisarius on this occasion is consistent with good faith. Had he of his own accord tendered this proposal to the Goths with a view of deceiving them, his artifice would have been altogether inexcusable, but when an offer was made to him, which insulted his loyalty and honour, he might, perhaps, justly employ it for the advantage of his cause. Those who solicit treachery can hardly complain if treachery be retorted against them. Still, however, though we may excuse, we cannot applaud the duplicity of Belisarius, and it does not appear consistent, either with the integrity of his Roman predecessors, or with the chivalrous spirit which was afterwards kindled in the West.

December a.d. 539, it had been required that Belisarius should solemnly swear to protect from injury the inhabitants of Ravenna, but with regard to his stipulated assumption of the imperial dignity, no promise was exacted by the Goths, who thought his own ambition a sufficient security. A fleet laden with provisions was then permitted to steer into the harbour of Classe,[84] the gates of the Adriatic capital were thrown open to the Romans, and Belisarius triumphantly [85] entered an impregnable fortress, which, for more than two hundred years from this time, proved the firmest bulwark of the eastern empire in Italy. The Goths who still surpassed their victorious enemy in numbers, viewed his scanty battalions with shame and surprise, and the indignant females spitting in the faces of their husbands and brothers, pointed with bitter upbraidings to the pigmy stature of the southern soldiers. In compliance with the oath, and his own maxims of discipline, Belisarius prevented any outrage on the part of his forces, and carefully preserved inviolate the property and persons of the Goths.

On the other hand, Vitiges was detained, though with great respect, a close captive in his palace, the engagement for his safety was

---

84. It appears, that though the ancient harbour of Augustus was now dry land, another had been constructed to supply its place (Procop. *Goth. lib. ii.* c. 29.)

85. The date of this event is ascertained by an ancient document, produced by Muratori in his thirty-second dissertation.

renewed in a church,[86] but his treasures, the accumulated wealth of the great Theodoric, became the spoil of the conqueror. According to the example of the capital, some neighbouring fortresses which still held out, surrendered to the Roman arms, the example of submission extended to the Cottian Alps, and Pavia [87] alone shut her gates, until the reign of Belisarius should be publicly made known. Such hopes were quickly disappointed. As soon as the ramparts of Ravenna were secured, and a share of its barbarian garrison dismissed to the tillage of the neighbouring districts, Belisarius proclaimed his unshaken loyalty, and declared that he would remain, and that the Goths must become the faithful subjects of Justinian.

The reduction of Ravenna, by Belisarius, inflamed still further the jealous animosity of his enemies and rivals at Constantinople, well skilled in the arts to blacken the fame of any general, by representing him, if defeated, as unworthy, if successful, as dangerous. In spite of his recent declaration of fidelity and refusal of empire, Belisarius was secretly accused of aspiring to independent power. Perhaps, however, Justinian might have withstood these perfidious insinuations, had not the invasion of the Persians afforded first a specious pretext, and afterwards an unexpected necessity for recalling the conqueror of Italy.[88] In the letter which commanded his departure, his services were acknowledged and extolled, and a grateful sovereign seemed only anxious to reward his merit, and to employ it on a wider field.

Though it was not difficult for Belisarius to discern the suspicion and displeasure which lurked beneath these courtly professions, he without hesitation determined on obedience. To the Goths, his continued loyalty appeared altogether unaccountable, and the squadron of Uraias at Pavia vainly implored him in another embassy to raise the standard of rebellion, and no longer to prefer the situation of a slave to that of a sovereign. Lamenting his refusal but encouraged by his absence, the feeble garrison of Pavia resolved to make one further effort for the maintenance of the Gothic monarchy, and it will hereafter be seen how, by the recall of Belisarius, and the imbecility

---

86. *Hist. Miscell. ap. Murat. Script Italic,* vol. i. But this wretched compilation is of very slight authority.
87. This city is always called Ticinum by Procopius. In the eighth century, the modern name was equally used, (Paul Warnefrid, *lib.* ii. c. 15,) but in the tenth, it seems to have quite superseded the ancient. (Liutprand, *Hist. lib. iii.* c 1.)
88. That the Persian war was at first a mere pretext on the part of Justinian, is cautiously but clearly stated by Procopius (*Goth. lib. ii.* c. 30,) and more openly by Zonaras (*Annal.* vol. ii.)

of his successors, this slight spark of revolt was blown into a formidable flame, which pervaded once more the whole of Italy, which was again repressed by the hero of this history, and finally extinguished by Narses.

Belisarius embarked at Ravenna with the Gothic captives and treasure, and arrived at Constantinople, (a.d. 540), after five years of warfare from the foot of Etna to the banks of the Po, during which he had subdued nearly the same extent of country as the Romans had acquired in the five first centuries, since the foundation of the city. His prompt unhesitating obedience silenced the voice of envy for a time, and Justinian, urged by the increasing dangers of the east, consented to appoint his faithful servant to that important command. Yet he withheld the well-earned honours of a second triumph, and the spoils of the great Theodoric, placed in the imperial palace, were secluded from public curiosity, and rarely displayed to the wonder and flattery of the senate. The emperor gazed with admiration on the strength and beauty of the Gothic captives, their fair complexions, auburn locks and lofty stature.[89] A great number amongst them enlisted in the guards of Belisarius, which had already been augmented by his victories over the Vandals and the Moors, and which, after this new addition, amounted to no less than seven thousand men.

The captive monarch of the Goths was received by Justinian, with all the generous courtesy which his dignity and misfortunes demanded. An ample estate in Asia, perhaps adjoining to that of Gelimer was allotted to him, and his abjuration of the Arian doctrines was rewarded by the rank of senator and patrician. During two years he continued to enjoy these honours at Constantinople, and ended his eventful life in tranquillity.[90] After his death, Matasontha contracted a second marriage with Germanus the emperor's nephew, and the offspring of these nuptials, Germanus the younger, was the last of the illustrious line of the Amali.

---

89. Compare Procop. *Vandal, lib. i.* c. 2, and *Goth. lib. iii.* c. 1.
90. Jornandes, *De Reb. Getic* c. 60, and Procop. *Pers., lib. ii.* c. 14.

Chapter 6

Chosroes, or Nurshirvan, King of Persia

The peace with Persia, which Justinian had rashly surnamed the Eternal, was soon, in spite of his concessions, distrusted and broken by his rival. Chosroes viewed the conquest of Africa with secret envy, and sent an embassy to Constantinople to demand a share of the spoils, on the plea that his treaty with the emperor had granted leisure for obtaining them. So audacious a request, brought forward beneath the veil of pleasantry, was not slighted by Justinian, and the Persian claimants returned with large presents to their court. But the success of the Roman arms in Italy redoubled the jealous feelings of Nushirvan, who feared lest it should prove the prelude to an invasion of the East. His ambition was artfully worked upon by the Gothic envoys, and by deputies from the Armenians, who had been provoked into rebellion by the tyranny of their Roman governor. It was not difficult to persuade Nushirvan; who was desirous of war, and, according to the usual progress of self-delusion, soon began to consider his wishes as judicious and expedient; nor was he devoid of just grounds for hostilities.

The Byzantine court is admitted to have employed a crooked and insidious policy, in hopes of raising up enemies against him; it had tempted the fidelity of his vassal Almondar, and urged the barbarians of the north to invade his dominions. To resent such injuries as these can hardly be said to merit the reproach of perfidy and falsehood.[1]

---

1. Procop. *Pers. lib. ii.* c. 5. We have hardly any Persian materials to check the Greek account of this campaign. See Herbelot, *Bibliot. Orient.*, and Malcolm's *History*, vol. i. This is the less to be regretted from the extreme inaccuracy with which Oriental historians usually treat of wars. See a very remarkable anecdote on this point in the *Acad. des Inscript.* vol. xxxv.

Early in the spring, and in the eighth year since the conclusion of peace, (*a.d.* 640), Nushirvan invaded the Roman Empire at the head of a formidable army. From the plains of Babylon, where the Persian forces met, they proceeded towards Syria, along the western bank of the Euphrates. Passing onward before the walls of Circesium and Zenobia, the king, in six days march from the frontier, found himself near Sura, of which also he might have neglected the siege had not his stumbling horse conveyed to the Magian priests a promise of success. It is remarkable that such accidents were likewise looked upon as ominous by the ancient Romans, but interpreted in a manner directly opposite.[2]

For one whole day Sura was vainly assaulted by the Persians, and the approach of night constrained Nushirvan to retire with great loss; but he retired with the evident intention of renewing the attack, and the Roman garrison, disheartened by the fall of their gallant commander, forgot that their resistance had already been sufficient to stir up animosity, and was too short to claim respect and generous forbearance. Their bishop was dispatched nest morning to treat of terms, the negotiation into which they entered slackened their vigilance, and afforded an opportunity to the wily Persian of storming the city by surprise. A great number of the inhabitants was put to the sword, the rest were seized as slaves, and their dwellings committed to the flames. It was then amidst the burning ruins and slaughtered inhabitants of a once flourishing city that Nushirvan dismissed Anastasius, the Roman ambassador, commanding him to set off for Constantinople, and to tell his master where and how he had left the King of Persia.

The defence of the eastern frontier had been entrusted by Justinian to a general, named Buzes, who had fixed his headquarters at Hierapolis with considerable forces. His conduct at this place was very characteristic of a modern Greek. First, in an eloquent harangue, he exhorted the citizens and soldiers to a resolute defence, and then collecting his light cavalry took to flight with .the utmost secrecy and speed. Nushirvan was thus enabled to reach Hierapolis without opposition,[3] and nothing seemed to prevent his further progress against Antioch. This city, though partly overthrown by an earthquake fourteen years before,[4] had risen from its ruins through the munificence of Justinian,

2. Tacit. *Annal. lib. xv.* c 7.
3. The testimony of Eutychius on this point (*Annal.* vol.. ii.,) must yield to that of Procopius (*Pers. lib. ii.* c. 6.)
4. Marcellin. *Chron. ap. Sirmond, Op.* vol. ii. The new the name of Theopolis. (Procop. *De Ædif. lib. ii.* c. 10.)

and far outvied any Roman city beyond the Bosphorus in splendour, size and population.

On the earliest rumour of hostilities Justinian had dispatched his nephew, Germanus, to the command of this important station. The new governor immediately surveyed its fortifications, which he found to be in good repair, protected on one side by the stream of the Orontes, and on the others by almost inaccessible cliffs. A single point, however, where a steep hill rose nearly to a level with the ramparts,[5] justly excited his alarm, and he proposed to render it either detached by digging a trench, or defensible by building a tower. Neither design was approved of by the engineers, to whom the subject was referred. They feared that the approach of Nushirvan might be too speedy to allow the completion of the work, and that their unfinished labours at this station would only serve to betray its weakness, and they therefore recommended the miserable policy of trusting to the negligence of their enemies rather than to their own activity.

On his part, Germanus plausibly disguised his regard for his personal safety, and his intention of providing for it in a timely retreat, by observing that the presence at Antioch of one of the imperial family served only to attract the Persians and give them a further inducement to the siege. Such timid counsels, of course, produced general discouragement, and no sooner had Germanus set out for Cilicia[6] than the garrison and citizens sent to treat with Nushirvan.

Their deputy (a bishop) found the monarch employed in the investment of Hierapolis and Beroea, and after much solicitation persuaded him to withdraw from the neighbourhood of Antioch on the payment of one thousand pounds weight of gold. With these terms the *prelate* joyfully returned to his fellow citizens, but he found their disposition no longer the same. Emboldened by the arrival of six thousand fresh troops, and by the harangues of several factious orators, they had rapidly passed from excessive terror to an equally unreasonable degree of security and arrogance; and refusing to purchase their safety by a treaty, they sent back the bishop with a haughty message to the King of Persia.

This wavering caprice offended Nushirvan far more than a steadfast opposition would have done. At the head of his numerous squadrons he now approached and encompassed the capital of the East; yet,

---

5. See an account and a plan of the ancient walls in Pocock's *Description of the East*, vol. ii. pt. 1.
6. Jornandes *de Regn. Success.*

either deterred by its strength, or unwilling to cause its downfall, he renewed his proposal of a ransom. His offer was received with derision and his ambassador with insult; the one was proudly rejected, and the other escaped with difficulty from the hands of the irritated populace. Nushirvan now applied himself, in good earnest, to the siege, he soon discerned the accessible point, and it was there that a general assault was given by his bravest troops under his personal command.

On the other part, the Roman soldiers were not deficient in courage or in zeal, and the youth of Antioch, trained to arms by the daily factions of the Circus, forgot their petty animosities in this pressing danger. The result of the conflict long continued doubtful, until some wooden frames, which had been suspended from the walls to bear a second line of soldiers, gave way as some reinforcements were descending into them.

From the loud crash which this accident occasioned, the Romans at first believed that the wall itself had fallen, and that every thing was lost; the Persians availed themselves of this moment of confusion and dismay, scaling ladders were applied, and the rampart was surmounted.[7] While the Roman garrison escaped through the gate of Daphne, the citizens still maintained, in the streets, a brave but fruitless resistance, which could not repulse, and only served to irritate the enemy. Antioch underwent all the calamities of a city taken by storm. Many of its inhabitants were slaughtered, without distinction of sex or of age; and history has recorded with praise the heroic resolution of two noble matrons, who preserved their chastity by a voluntary death in the waves of the Orontes.[8]

Entering the city, attended by the Roman ambassadors, Nushirvan bewailed the unhappy fate of the Syrians with real or affected pity, and imputed it not untruly to their own stubborn refusal of his terms. He dispatched speedy and effectual orders to prevent any further bloodshed and to save the surviving citizens, but he gave up their wealth to his soldiers and their dwellings to the flames. In a few hours this opulent and extensive capital was reduced to a shapeless mass of ruins, with the exception of the city walls and of an insulated quarter which the conflagration did not reach.

---

7. Antioch was taken in the month of June. (John Malala, vol. ii.)
8. In a siege of Apamea by the Persians, during the reign of Justin the Second, the same story is told of two thousand persons—a somewhat startling number. (Assemann. *Bibliot. Orient,* vol. iii.) Paul Warnefrid relates a very curious artifice, through which some ladies of Friuli escaped both violence and martyrdom. (*lib. iv.* c. 38.)

After this unworthy use of his victory, the king granted a solemn audience to the Byzantine ambassadors, who complained of his invasion, and asserted the upright intentions of their master. In reply, Nushirvan brought forward the intercepted letters from Constantinople to Almondar, and to the Huns; and the ambassadors, confounded by these documents, could only endeavour to throw the blame on the imperial ministers. The conference then turned to the stipulations for a peace. A large yearly payment was demanded by Nushirvan, who offered, at the same time, to lay aside the hateful word of tribute, as if the ignominy consisted not in the deed but in the name. These terms, however degrading, were enforced by his late successes, and a treaty to this effect was reluctantly signed by the ambassadors, but Nushirvan declared that he should not leave the Roman dominions until it had been ratified by the sacred letters of the emperor,[9] and accordingly, he continued to act as if no hopes of peace had been entertained. From Antioch he proceeded to Seleucia, at the mouth of the Orontes, where, in compliance with some national prejudice, he bathed alone in the sea, and solemnly sacrificed to the sun, according to the Magian rites. [10]

He next directed his arms. against Apamea, to which he marched with all his forces, while the inhabitants, headed by their bishop, Thomas, awaited his approach with undaunted confidence. Their courage was not derived from the mere, natural aid of strong bulwarks, a numerous garrison, or the hope of speedy succour, they had none of these; but they possessed, as they believed, a fragment of the True Cross of the Saviour, which was expected to perform some miracle for their deliverance. This relic had been obtained from Jerusalem by the pious theft of a Syrian; the devotion of the Apameans had inlaid its case with a profusion of gems and gold, nor was it offered more than once in the year to the adoration of the people. But in the present danger the bishop drew forth this spiritual weapon for the defence of his flock, and carried it in procession through the church, attended by an innumerable concourse of spectators.

On this occasion a divine manifestation is asserted to have taken place, which Procopus relates on hearsay, but which an ecclesiastical

---

9. A peace was not considered as finally concluded till the emperor had sent letters of ratification, called *Litterae Sacrae*. (Menander, *Excerpt Legat.*)

10. The respect of the Persians for water is mentioned by Herodotus (lib. i. c. 138). See Larcher's note, and also Assemanni (*Bibliot. Orient.* vol. i.). It is remarkable that a superstitious worship of fountains existed in Italy during the dominion of the Lombards, and King Liutprand enacted a severe law against it. (Muratori, *Diss.* 59, vol. v. ed. 1741.)

historian boasts of having witnessed in person.[11]

No sooner had the cross been taken from its case, than a celestial light overspread it, which darted its beams into the furthest recesses of the church, and accompanied the relic as it was moved along. The people of Apamea acknowledged this favourable augury with tears of joy, and derived from it a certain promise of preservation to their city. Yet when Nushirvan arrived, at the head of his army, no miracle was performed to repel him, and he entered the city with no further opposition than the remonstrances of the bishop could afford. Even his sacrilege remained unpunished when he stripped the holy relic of all its precious ornaments; but he was easily induced to restore the bare wood to the fervent entreaties of Thomas. The frequency of such occurrences forms, perhaps, the chief argument against the wonders with which Roman Catholics adorn the middle ages.

These miracles never take place at the time when we should humbly conceive that they would have been most useful, to confute erroneous or settle wavering opinions, but appear only performed in the presence, and attested in the writings of stanch believers, as if they were intended not for proofs but for rewards. Apamea was the term to the progress of Nushlrvan. Satisfied with the easy conquest of Syria, and loaded with its spoils, he commenced a retreat towards his own dominions, but selected a different route and unexhausted country. His numerous squadrons surrounded the city of Chalcis, and a peremptory message informed the inhabitants that they could only escape a siege by the payment of a ransom, and by giving up to his power their Roman governor and garrison.

The terrified citizens gladly yielded the required subsidy; but with regard to the other stipulation, they dreaded lest Justinian should punish their compliance as much as Chosroes their refusal. In this perplexity they sacrificed their religion to their fears, and having first concealed the Roman soldiers in their houses, took a solemn oath that there were none remaining in the town. This stratagem (if so it can be called,) was attended with more success than it deserved, and the king, unsuspicious of deceit, pursued his march to the Euphrates, and constructed a temporary bridge near Barbalissus. To prevent the dispersion of his forces and the pillage of the country, he issued an order that the whole army should effect its passage within three days, and, accordingly, on the fourth, the bridge was broken down. His strict maintenance of discipline and justice, during the whole of this cam-

---

11. Procop. *Pers. lib. ii.* c. 11 . Evagrius, *Hist. Eccles. lib. iv.* c. 26.

paign, has extorted praise even from his enemies, and it was in vain that the citizens of Apamea pleaded for the life of a soldier who had deeply aggrieved them.

Having crossed the Euphrates and entered Mesopotamia, Nushirvan advanced against Edessa. Its inhabitants, secure in an alleged promise of celestial aid,[12] boasted of their city as impregnable, and refused to avoid a siege by payment of a subsidy; but at length, though fully persuaded of the safety of their dwellings from any human attack, they agreed to give two hundred pounds weight of gold, on condition that the Persians should withdraw from their gardens and estates. A more generous motive induced them to contribute in favour of the captives of Antioch, whom Nushirvan had brought in his train, and for whose deliverance a ransom was demanded. Towards this benevolent object every citizen of Edessa gave in a share of his gold and silver, and where these were wanting, of his household effects or implements of trade; all ranks, with different means, showed equal zeal, and the most degraded class of women yielded not only the sums already acquired by their venal charms, but even those jewels and rich dresses, on which their future profits might materially depend.

Yet all this compassion was disappointed through the infamous avarice of Buzes, the same whom we have seen basely deserting his post in danger, and who reappears on this occasion in a still more dishonourable light. With a view of appropriating to himself the treasure thus amassed, he contrived to defeat the treaty for its application, and Chosroes was allowed to lead on his prisoners into Persia. Yet the munificence of the great king rendered them fortunate, and perhaps contented in exile. A city was built for their residence, at one day's journey from Ctesiphon, whose name of Chosroantioch blended their country with their conqueror.[13] Regular supplies of provisions were assigned for their use by their kind or ostentatious founder, and their new structures of a circus and a public bath were enlivened by the skill of charioteers or musicians.

While still encamped near Edessa, the King of Persia received from Constantinople the ratification of the peace, but since its signature at Antioch, his views appear to have greatly changed. The defenceless state of Syria, and his easy progress without meeting a single Roman soldier in the field, suggested to his enterprising spirit the facility of

---

12. See Mosheim, *Eccles. Hist.* vol. i.
13. This place was afterwards called Romia, (*Eutych. Annal.* vol. ii.) and now bears the name of Almahouza. (Herbelot, *Bibliot. Orient.*)

new and more important conquests. He already meditated, in future campaigns, the invasion of both Palestine and Colchos, and might even, without much presumption, look forward to the siege of Constantinople and the downfall of the empire as the ultimate aim of his exertions. Accordingly, with a perfidious disregard of treaties which no considerations of policy can justify, he marched rapidly to Dara, and commenced its siege. From the neighbourhood of this city to the frontier, its fortifications had always been an object of much consequence to Rome and jealousy to Persia. It was protected by a double wall of great strength, the inner one being no less than sixty feet in height, with towers of one hundred; and it contained a numerous garrison, headed by Martin, who had served with distinction under Belisarius in Africa and Italy, and had been dispatched to the East on the first rumour of hostilities.

After an unsuccessful attack, the Persians had recourse to stratagem, and laboured at a mine with silent and unsuspected activity, but the important secret was revealed to the garrison by a friend, or, as they believed, by an angel; and a countermine, which they judiciously began, proved fatal to the Persian pioneers and to the hopes of their monarch. Impatient of further delay, and urged by the approach of winter, he entered into terms with the besieged, and, according to his usual practice in this war, agreed to retire for a stipulated sum. On being informed of this aggression, Justinian, as must have been expected, declared the treaty with the Persians at an end; and both parties awaited with anxiety the fate of the next campaign.[14]

At this critical juncture, the mind of Justinian was distracted by twofold apprehensions, since his suspicious temper rendered him almost as fearful of his generals as of his enemies. Although Belisarius had been hastily recalled from Ravenna, on the ground that his immediate presence was necessary in the East, he was detained the whole summer , (a.d. 541), and ensuing winter at Constantinople, and only dispatched to the frontier late in the spring; so that little leisure was allowed him to collect and discipline his forces. Antonina did not accompany her husband, but he was attended by several of his veteran officers, and by nearly all the Gothic captives, who were thus, like the Vandals, condemned in a distant country to march beneath the same banners they had formerly met in battle.

---

14. The Persian historians, in their account of this expedition, confound Nushirvan with Sapor. The former is said by them to have made a Roman emperor prisoner. (Malcolm's *Hist*. Vol. i.

On his arrival at Dara, Belisarius, instead of regular forces, found only a confused assemblage of soldiers; many without arms, still more without the spirit to wield them, and, according' to their own national historian, trembling at the very name of Persia.[15] He was joined by numerous Saracen auxiliaries, under Arethas; but little reliance could be placed on the co-operation of these fickle savages, attracted only by the hopes of booty.

While busily employed in equipping and distributing his army, and in expectation of a speedy attack from the Persians, the Roman general sent some spies to obtain intelligence of their movements and designs. By such means, he soon became informed that no invasion was preparing in this quarter, and that Chosroes himself was engaged by a distant expedition of the Huns; a report which it will presently be teen had been spread by that wily monarch, to conceal his real intentions. A project was then formed by Belisarius, for resuming the offensive and entering the Persian territories; and having tried the resolution of his officers in a public Council, he found their opinions favourable to his views.

But the leaders of those troops commonly stationed in Syria, (June, a.d. 541), expressed their apprehensions lest their absence should enable Almondar to desolate their province. In reply, the general reminded them that the time of the summer solstice was at hand, when religious rites withheld these Arabs from any act of hostility during two months;[16] and he promised to dismiss the Syrian soldiers to their post before this term should have expired. Having thus overcome their opposition, Belisarius crossed the frontier with all his forces, and marched upon Nisibis.

Meanwhile Nushirvan, in another quarter, was aiming a well-directed and successful blow at the Roman power in Asia. It was the remark of Agrippa, that the jealous weakness of most princes leads them to undertake easy objects in person, and to commit those which appear difficult and doubtful to their generals.[17] Such was not the character of the King of Persia: he was always present where the stake seemed greatest and the throw most hazardous. The ancient Colchos,

---

15. Procop. *Pers. lib. ii.* c 16.
16. The total number of these sacred months was four in each year. See the ninth chapter of the *Koran*, and the seventh section of Sale's *Preliminary Discourse.* "This is the right religion," says Mahomet; "but attack the idolaters in all the months, as they attack you in all."
17. Dion Cassius, *lib. xlix.* c. 4.

the modern Mingrelia, bore at this period the name of Lazica, from one of its tribes which had usurped a sovereignty above the rest,[18] and it was governed by monarchs of its own, who continued for a considerable time vassals of Persia, until at last the introduction of Christianity throughout their dominions, and their consequent horror of the Magian rites, induced them to transfer their allegiance to the Romans. Yet they paid no tribute; the King of Lazica, when invested with the ensigns of his dignity by the emperor, only stipulated to guard the defiles of Caucasus on his frontier against the inroads of the Huns; and the two nations derived mutual advantage from a commerce in which the Lazi exchanged their slaves and hides for a supply of salt and of corn.

This useful connexion was dissolved through the tyranny and rashness of Justinian, who, while striving to reduce the Colchians to subjects, lost them as allies. A numerous body of troops had been stationed in their country, headed by a worthless officer named Zibus. Securely nestled in a fortress built by him at Petra, he decreed from this strong hold the most shameless and unbounded exactions, and, above all, a ruinous monopoly of trade. Such treatment was equally galling to the pride or to the poverty of the Lazi, and they resolved in a secret embassy to renounce their Roman masters, and entreat the protection of Chosroes. Their deputies represented to the great king, in glowing colours, all the advantages which Colchos might afford him, that a torrent of barbarians from the Caucasus could at his pleasure be poured upon the empire, that his fleets might command the *euxine*, and sail without obstacle to the very palace of his Byzantine enemy.[19]

Had even these grounds not been solid, they would have appeared so to the ambition of Nushirvan. He immediately granted this welcome request; and having collected a large army on the pretext of a Hunnish war, commenced his march with the Colchian ambassadors for his guides. His path led through a lonely tract of forests and mountains; it was narrow, precipitous, and in. secure, but the diligence of his pioneers soon rendered it easy.[20] On his arrival in Lazica, its king, Gubazes, hastened to make his submission; the people crowded round the

---

18. This name still prevails near Trebizond. (Chardin, *Voyages*, vol. i.) According to Mr. Hope, the Lazi are chiefly employed near Constantinople in garden-work. See a note to Anastasius vol. i., third ed.

19. See the projects of Chosroes for reaching Constantinople, in Procopius (*Goth. lib. iv.* c. 7.) and Agathias, (*lib. ii.* p. 36.)

20. By the new road, even elephants could be brought with an army, (Procop. *Goth. lib. iv.* c. 13.)

standards of their deliverer, and Zibus found himself encompassed and besieged in Petra. No city could be stronger in position: it crowned the summit of a steep and insulated cape, and on this occasion withstood several assaults of the Persians, until the death of the governor disheartened the Roman soldiers, and induced them to surrender.

All the ill-gotten treasure of Zibus, hoarded in this fortress, fell into the hands of Nushirvan; but he wanted time to complete and consolidate his conquests. Having received intelligence of the invasion of Belisarius and the engagement near Nisibis, he hastily ordered a retreat towards his own dominions, leaving, however, a sufficient garrison at Petra. Such was the commencement of the Lazic war, of which the later operations, inconclusive in result, and confused in narrative, are detailed with most tedious accuracy through many a long page of the Byzantine historians.

On crossing the Persian frontier, Belisarius, as was stated before, had directed his course towards Nisibis; but, at the distance of seven miles from that city, he suddenly turned to the right, and encamped in a spacious plain, supplied, even at that season (it was midsummer), with plentiful fountains. By unremitting exertions, he had brought the discordant materials of his army into some degree of discipline and order; but neither his rank, his merit, nor his fame, could secure the deference of Buzes and the other Eastern officers, as impatient of control as they had shown themselves unfitted for authority. With loud clamours they complained of his apparent caprice, in desisting from his march, and many of them openly refused obedience to his orders. Belisarius, however unwillingly, found himself compelled to justify his measures, and thereby diminish the chance of their success, he said:

> It was not my intention, thus publicly to disclose my designs. When every chief is imprudently entrusted with the plans for a campaign, they soon become whispered through the camp, and, even passing its limits, often reach the ears of an enemy. But, since I perceive among you so wayward and turbulent a spirit, each aspiring to become the controller and judge of our military operations, instead of their passive instrument, I will break through the silence which good policy enjoins. My views, under present circumstances, are as follows. I do not believe that Chosroes, though himself employed in repelling a barbarian invasion elsewhere, has by any means withdrawn all his forces from this frontier, and least of all from Nisibis, the

first and most important city in the province, and the bulwark of his kingdom.

On the contrary, I have received certain information that it contains a body of troops so considerable in their numbers, and so highly distinguished for discipline and valour, as to be fully enabled to meet us in the field. As a further proof of the strength of this garrison, you may observe that its command has been committed to Nabedes, yielding to none but to the king himself in rank and estimation with the Persians. I am convinced that this officer will not allow an undisputed passage, that he will offer us battle; and it is only by defeating him that we shall find ourselves at liberty to pursue our expedition. Now if this battle were given close under the walls of Nisibis, we could not contend with the enemy on equal terms. Issuing from their strong hold, and with reinforcements in their rear, they might follow up any advantages with vigour; and should they, on the contrary, be worsted, their ramparts would afford them a secure and speedy refuge.

Our pursuit would be checked by these solid barriers, against which, while they continue to be manned by an army not inferior to ours, every effort must be vain. But if, on the other hand, awaiting the Persian forces at this spot, we should be victorious, then, my comrades, I entertain the most confident hope of reducing the fortress which they are appointed to defend. By the disorder of their flight, we may either mingle in their ranks and enter the gates together, or we may cut off their retreat in that direction, and, compelling them to escape elsewhere, may easily overcome the resistance of a city thus forsaken by its garrison.

The policy of the Roman general was approved by all the officers to whom it was thus openly revealed, with the exception of two, named Nicetas and Peter, who persisted in their first impatience, and, slighting the orders of Belisarius, marched forward with the troops under their personal command, till only a mile from Nisibis. Belisarius sent them an earnest injunction to hold themselves at least ready for engaging, and to await his signal, and they were also admonished to be particularly on their guard at noon, since the Persians, knowing this to be the usual hour for meals in the Roman army, might probably select it as the time of their attack. Such judicious commands were likewise set at nought by these stubborn mutineers. Oppressed with the unwonted glare of an Assyrian sun, the soldiers laid aside the cumbrous weight of their arms at mid-day, and dispersed to gather fruit, through the adjoining groves of fig-trees. From the ramparts of Nisibis the Persian governor perceived their careless security, and suddenly sallied forth with the greater part of his garrison, to surprise and overwhelm them. On beholding the enemy in full career from the gates, the Roman soldiers, terrified and helpless, ran to their arms, hastily equipped themselves for battle, and formed in mingled and irregular squadrons, while a messenger was dispatched, beseeching the aid of Belisarius.

Even before he received their request, this vigilant general was already on his march, having conjectured, from the cloud of dust which he saw arising in the direction of Nisibis, that the Persians had advanced; but, in spite of his activity, he could not save the detachments of Peter and Nicetas from the consequences of their own imprudence. The Persians had scattered them on the very first onset, taken their standard, and pursued them with considerable slaughter, till the arrival of Belisarius and his veterans changed the fortune of the day. An iron barrier was presented to the enemy by the long lances of the Gothic confederates, and the Byzantine forces vied with them in valour. A pitched engagement ensued, the Romans caught the spirit of their leader, and the troops of Nabedes were entirely defeated; yet, as Belisarius had foreseen, the neighbourhood of Nisibis shielded them against any heavy loss, and no more than one hundred and fifty could be slain in their headlong flight. Next day they displayed, in triumph from the ramparts, the standard they had gained, and, according to Procopius, covered it with sausages as a mark of their contempt.

The minds of both Nicetas and Peter were impressed by their disaster; they felt their folly, and thenceforth yielded a cheerful obedience to the commands of Belisarius. But his plan for the campaign was altogether baffled, since the Persians, having found their inferiority in the field, no longer ventured to sally from Nisibis, and confined themselves to the keep of their impregnable fortifications. As it therefore became necessary for the Roman general to devise some other project, he resolved to give up all hopes of Nisibis, and to carry his arms beyond that city into Persia. A march of thirty miles brought the Roman Army before the town of Sisauranum, defended by the strongest ramparts and most warlike citizens, besides whom it contained a chosen band of eight hundred Persian horsemen, and a governor of tried courage and conduct, named Bleschanes.

Having closely approached the walls, Belisarius gave directions for a general assault, but his troops were beaten back with considerable loss. After this failure, Belisarius, to guard against the danger of fresh misgivings and complaints among his officers, thought it advisable to entrust them with his further designs, and while appearing to consult, in reality to guide their judgment. Having therefore summoned them to his presence, he thus addressed them:

> Your long experience of war, my comrades, must have taught you with how much peril an army advances through a hostile country, when leaving behind it, in the power of the enemy, fortresses filled with numerous brave and enterprising soldiers. Such is our present situation. For should we penetrate any further into Persia, the garrisons both of Nisibis and Sisauranum would doubtless hover on our rear, and close upon us on the first favourable opportunity. Were another army to encounter us in front, we should have to contend with two-fold adversaries, in defiles where success might be hopeless, and valour unavailing. I need not allude to the disastrous results which, in such circumstances, would attend an overthrow, nor tell you that our retreat to the Roman frontier might be utterly and irretrievably cut off.
>
> Let us, therefore, encamp before Sisauranum, and make every exertion for its capture, while Arethas, with his cavalry, is dispatched into Assyria. The Saracens are as unfit for sieges as they are well adapted to inroads through an open country. To these light troops let us add a body of our bravest soldiers. Should they find no army prepared to oppose them, they may retaliate on the Persians the havoc of their late invasion; and if, on the contrary, any hostile force should appear, let them return, without hazarding an engagement, and bring us this intelligence, which will serve to direct us when we march beyond the Tigris. The Persian garrison at Nisibis will then be kept in check by ours at Sisauranum, and we shall proceed, secure of resources in the rear, and apprised by our Saracen detachments of the real state of the provinces beyond us.

The speech of Belisarius convinced his hearers of the soundness of his views, and, in conformity to them, Arethas was ordered to pass the Tigris, accompanied by a detachment of twelve hundred Romans. These were chiefly selected from amongst the guards of Belisarius, and were placed at the full disposal of the Arab chieftain, though under the immediate command of Trajan and another officer. Arethas accepted with pleasure a task so congenial to his temper, and found a wide career for his rapacity in the fertile plains of Assyria, which had long remained untouched by invasion, and were then unprepared to withstand it. Meanwhile Belisarius actively pressed the siege of Sisauranum, cheered by the report of some Persian prisoners that the garrison and citizens possessed but a scanty store of provisions. Not having expected an attack, they had neglected to fill their granaries and magazines, and were only furnished with such supplies as they could speedily bring together on the news that the enemy was at hand, while the crowd of peasants, who had flocked to their walls for shelter, still further hastened the approach of scarcity.

It was not, therefore, very difficult for an envoy of Belisarius to persuade the besieged to surrender, merely stipulating that their lives should be spared. This condition was strictly observed by the Romans, and every kindness was moreover shown to the citizens, whose adherence to Christianity, and whose Roman descent, were natural grounds for friendship and favour: but Bleschanes and his troops were sent as captives to Constantinople, and soon afterwards transferred to Italy, where, according to the practice of the sixth century, they became enrolled as imperial mercenaries, and served against the Goths. Such a system, however singular, appears to have been constantly successful; but its success may be ascribed to the degeneracy of the age. To make a high-minded soldier fight in the ranks of his national enemies is no easy undertaking, and it would certainly have failed with an ancient Roman or a modern Spaniard.

The ramparts of Sisauranum were razed to the ground, and Belisarius, having thus far made good his project, impatiently awaited the return of Arethas, in order to pursue his march. The zeal of the Saracen, however, had abated in proportion as his object of pillage was attained, and he dreaded lest, on arriving once more at the Roman encampment, he should be called upon for a partition of the spoils. He resolved not merely to continue alone and unrestrained, but even to withhold all tidings of his movements, and, for this purpose, to prevent the junction of Trajan and his colleague with the main army of their countrymen. By his orders some pretended spies brought them accounts of a formidable Persian army intercepting them from Sisauranum, and the crafty Arab availed himself of this forged intelligence to make them effect their retreat in another direction. They accordingly repassed the Tigris lower down, and returned to the Roman territories along the left bank of the Euphrates, so as to be entirely shut out from any further share in this campaign.

The prolonged absence of Arethas, and the want of all information respecting him, raised of course to the highest pitch the suspicion and alarm of Belisarius and of his officers, and as it was impossible to march onwards in this uncertainty, his skilful plans for the prosecution of the war were thus for a second time baffled by the fault of subalterns. During the delay thus occasioned, the burning heat of the climate exhausted the strength and patience of the European soldiers, who were either almost stifled in close and sultry tents, or scorched by the rays of the sun. A contagious fever spread throughout the camp, nearly one third of the army was disabled from disease, and the remainder were impatient for home. The troops drawn from Syria, above all, disguised their own weariness and timidity under the specious pretext of solicitude for their defenceless province, and they loudly complained that the two months appointed for their service were already at an end. A council of war was summoned by the general, where Nicetas expressed the wishes of the soldiers and his own. He urged, that thus enfeebled and disheartened, they could undertake no enterprise against the enemy, that a battle might not leave a single Roman survivor to relate the mournful tale, and that nothing but the most effectual means for self-preservation remained to be considered.

His arguments were enforced by the clamour of the other officers, who, with tumultuous cries, demanded the signal for retreat. Late experience had taught Belisarius that any opposition to their wishes would be fruitless, and he therefore yielded to necessity. The sick were transported on beasts of burthen, the weary soldiers found their strength revived by the direction of their march, and the Roman dominions were attained without accident or molestation. Scarcely had Belisarius passed the frontier, before he be came informed of the real fate of Arethas, but the distance of this perfidious ally shielded him from the punishment which otherwise would doubtless have followed his detection.[21]

Thus ended a campaign in which, through untoward circumstances and the misconduct of others, Belisarius was debarred from equalling his own former achievements, and fulfilling the expectations of his countrymen. The Byzantine citizens, who had weighed rather

---

21. Yet Arethas was some years afterwards created a patrician, and honourably received at Constantinople. (*Hist. Miscell. lib.* xvi. Murat *Script Ital.* vol. i., and Zonaras, *Annal.* vol. ii.)

the fame and merit of the general than the obstacles with which he had to contend, had already seen him in fancy entering Ctesiphon in triumph, and leading Nushirvan, as Gelimer and Vitiges, a captive, before the throne of Justinian. They therefore beheld, with surprise and disappointment, their favourite hero returning, without any decisive advantage or memorable exploit, to Constantinople, having been recalled by the emperor as soon as he had stationed the army in its winter quarters.

This expedition, though lame and abortive, was however attended by one important result, the recall of Nushirvan from the unfinished conquest of Lazica. On his arrival in the Persian dominions, he found that Belisarius had already left them, and the lateness of the season compelled him to defer till another year his schemes of ambition and revenge. Early in the ensuing spring, (a.d. 542), he took the field, at the head of the most numerous and most formidable army which he ever yet had mustered in his wars against the Romans. He chose the same course which, in his first invasion, he had so successfully pursued, keeping the Euphrates on his right, and advancing towards Syria by rapid marches.

It was his intention from thence to carry his arms into Palestine, and undertake the siege of Jerusalem, which allured his avarice by its treasures, and of which the sanctity, in the eyes of an adverse sect, might inflame his Magian hostility. Since the fall of Antioch, Jerusalem might again be considered, as in the time of Pliny,[22] the first city of the east, and the pious zeal of successive crowds of pilgrims had enriched its shrine by offerings, and its inhabitants by the purchase of relics. [23] In his progress, Nushirvan prudently left unattempted those towns which had delayed him in his former invasion, and whose wealth was already drained by his demands at that period; but he made an exception with regard to Sergiopolis. The bishop of that city had failed to discharge a debt then contracted for the ransom of the prisoners of Sura, and, if we may believe the partial evidence of the Greek historians, Nushirvan showed such unrelenting rigour on this occasion, as appears utterly at variance with his Persian surname of The Just. It was in vain that the luckless *prelate* pleaded the poverty of his diocese, and declared that he had made a most earnest but fruitless application to

22. Plin. *Hist. Nat. lib. v.* c. 1.
23. An active commerce was carried on at Jerusalem in fragments of the True Cross. The monks maintained that this relic possessed a miraculous power of growth and vegetation, so that the supply in the market never ceased. (Baronius, *Annal. Eccles.* a.d. 326, No. 50.)

the emperor; he was, nevertheless, imprisoned and put to the torture, until he consented to purchase his freedom, by yielding the consecrated gold of his cathedral.

But the people of Sergiopolis shut their gates against the rapacious envoys of Nushirvan; they were immediately invested by a detachment of six thousand Persians, while their walls were manned with no more than two hundred regular soldiers. Reduced to extremity, and hopeless of relief, they had already determined to capitulate, when a friendly Christian, serving in the ranks of the enemy, privately informed them that the besiegers had exhausted their supply of water, and must within two days be compelled to retire. These joyful tidings were confirmed by the event; the King of Persia would not suspend or turn aside his march, to reduce an insignificant fortress, and the inhabitants, freed from this imminent peril, returned their grateful thanks to their patron saint for his seasonable aid. An ecclesiastical historian has not blushed even to affirm, that, at the intercession of Sergius, the city was garrisoned during the siege by a legion of angels, protected against human assault by shields and armour.[24]

After the recall of Belisarius, the defence of the Roman frontier had been entrusted to several chiefs, amongst whom were Buzes, and a nephew of the emperor, named Justus;[25] but they neither ventured to encounter Nushirvan in the open field, nor determined upon, any combined plan of defensive operations. Each of them, with the troops under his personal command, hastily betook himself to some fortress or stronghold, which might afford at least a temporary shelter. Such a system would have left the King of Persia at full liberty, either to pursue his march unmolested, or to attack and overwhelm every squadron in its turn. But, in this pressing danger, Justinian, struck with alarm, had summoned once more to his confidence and councils the only man whose genius could avert the impending storm. Belisarius, unattended by supplies or reinforcements, and with no resources but those of his genius, was reappointed general of the east, and dispatched with post-horses to the scene of action.

On his arrival in Syria, Buzes and Justus, who had prudently retreated beyond the reach of present danger to the walls of Hierapolis, and had drawn with them the greater part of the Roman troops, represented to him, in a letter, the doubtful plans and irresistible force of Nushirvan, and urged that Belisarius could not better provide for the

---
24. Evagrius, *Hist. Eccles. lib. iv.* c, 28.
25. See Ducange, *Fam. Aug. Byz.*

public safety and for his own, than by confining himself with them in the fortifications they had chosen. The answer of Belisarius has been recorded by his secretary:[26]

> Your advice might be just and salutary, if the people now at the mercy of Chosroes were subjects to some foreign state, instead of living under the dominion of Rome. Could we, in that case, while continuing inactive, hope to escape uninjured, it would be folly to rush into needless and voluntary dangers. But if the Persian monarch now directs his desolating course through the adjoining provinces of the empire, whose wealth and whose weakness equally invite him, I must tell you that it would be far better for us to perish bravely in their defence, than to purchase our personal security by remaining cold and indifferent spectators of their ruin. Such conduct would not deserve the mere name of timidity—it would be treason. My orders are, therefore, that you should join me as speedily as possible at Europus, where it is my intention to collect all the forces in my power, and where I trust that God will enable me to strike some decisive blow at the barbarians.

Animated by this resolution of their chief, Buzes and other officers hastened with their troops to the spot he had assigned. Justus, on the other hand, forgetting that one of the noblest privileges of royal birth is to be foremost in the field, preferred the easy and inglorious task of commanding the small detachment left behind for the garrison of Hierapolis.

Europus, where the Roman army now encamped, was a small open town on the Euphrates, one of those which Nushirvan had neglected to seize in his rapid march from Assyria. By taking this central and exposed position, Belisarius cut off the communication of the invaders with Persia, and displayed an apparent purpose of opposing their return. We cannot but remark, that such was precisely the stratagem attempted by Napoleon at the close of the adventurous and brilliant campaign of Paris, when, finding himself unable with his few remaining veterans to make head against the enemy, he left his capital open to them, and threw himself upon their rear. And though his plan was not attended with success, nor therefore with public praise, it has been considered by tacticians as a bold and masterly manoeuvre. A vague report of the supposed designs of Belisarius filled the mind of Nu-

---
26. Procop. *Pers. lib. ii.* c. 20.

shirvan with doubts and misgivings, while more accurate intelligence would have shown him that his power of marching homewards at his pleasure could never be seriously affected by such scanty battalions as his adversary could bring forward. In the opinion of the Roman commander himself, as stated by Procopius, an army even of one hundred thousand men would hardly have been sufficient for that object.[27]

The King of Persia ordered his troops to stop short in their progress towards Palestine, while one of his most trusty attendants was dispatched to the imperial camp, with the ostensible mission of complaining that Justinian had never sent ambassadors to conclude a peace, but with secret instructions to observe and report the real strength of the army, and views of the general.

Abandanes (such was the name of the envoy) found Belisarius apprised of his approach, and prepared to baffle Nushirvan by retorting his own artifice against him. Under the pretence of a hunting excursion, he had advanced to some distance before his camp with six thousand chosen soldiers, remarkable for their mien and stature, who formed a considerable part, but who appeared only a small detachment of his army. On the opposite shore of the Euphrates the watchful envoy might discern a squadron of Armenian cavalry, ready to dispute the passage of the river, and whose unknown numbers were magnified a hundred fold by his startled imagination.

The troops around him, as if secure of victory, looked upon him with careless or disdainful eyes, and seemed only intent on enjoying the pleasures of the chase. They had laid aside their heavy arms, and even their military dress, and each soldier bore only some single weapon, a sword, a bow, or a battle axe. In the first rank around the station of the general, were seen the natives of Thrace and Illyria,—beyond them stood the Goths and Heruli, while the Vandals and Moors formed the outer circle, and the aspect of so many barbarian captives now changed into zealous auxiliaries, must have forcibly recalled to the awestruck Persian the late conquest of Africa and Italy. Belisarius received the ambassador in a tent of the coarsest canvass, not unworthy the ancient simplicity of Rome, his countenance was cheerful, and his answer to the message of Nushirvan haughty and undaunted, he said:

> It is not, by the system which the King of Persia now pursues, that treaties can be formed or upheld. Other sovereigns, if any

---

27. Procop. Pers. lib. ii. c. 21.

cause of dissension arise between them and some neighbouring state, first send an embassy to urge their claims, and only have recourse to arms when their remonstrances have proved unavailing. Chosroes on the contrary, after having carried hostilities into the very heart of the Roman Empire, begins to speak of conferences and negotiations for a peace.

Dismayed by this tone of superiority, and by the confident demeanour which the Roman battalions had artfully assumed, Abandanes hastened to assure his royal master that he would have to contend with the most skilful and courageous commander of the age, and with troops of extraordinary discipline and determination. He urged moreover, that under existing circumstances the Persians could not engage on equal terms. Should the king be victorious, he could hope for no higher renown than that of overcoming a subject and slave of Justinian, and must find himself debarred from reaping the common fruits of success, by the neighbourhood of so many fortified cities, which would immediately afford shelter and protection to the vanquished Romans. If on the contrary, the event of the battle should prove unfavourable to him, the honour and majesty of Persia would receive a fatal wound, no refuge or resource would await the invading army, and not one of its soldiers might ever reach his country to tell the disaster of the rest. Nushirvan, persuaded by these arguments, consented to give, up all thoughts of Palestine; but he found even the choice of a route for his return a source of much perplexity.

The districts which he had already traversed, were exhausted and destitute of provisions, and should he on the other hand direct his march towards Europus, he feared much opposition to his passage of the river. After having wavered for some time, he selected the latter alternative, and his retreat was hastened by another able manoeuvre of the Roman general. The Armenian auxiliaries who appeared to guard the opposite bank were withdrawn, as if only for some temporary object, so that Nushirvan considered it necessary to employ with unwearied activity the precious moments of their absence.

The passage of the troops was soon effected by the labours of the engineers, who were always provided with portable iron clasps to connect and support large wooden beams for the construction of a bridge, and by this means a river seldom delayed the progress of a Persian army. Having entered Mesopotamia, the king protested, in an embassy to Belisarius, that his only motive for retreating was to give a proof of his friendship for the Romans, and to place no obstacles in the way of reconciliation. The general replied by a request that, such being the case, he might treat with moderation and forbearance the imperial province, which still lay between him and his own dominions.

Thus was the great Nushirvan, the conqueror of the East, driven back towards Persia by the stratagems and the name of Belisarius, who could only muster an army very far inferior in numbers, and wholly incapable of hazarding a battle. Though some unwarlike and ignorant citizens might complain that the invaders had been quietly permitted to escape, it seems that the reputation of Belisarius amongst statesmen and soldiers was greatly enhanced by this achievement, and they even extolled it as surpassing the glory of the Vandal or Gothic wars.[28] If, in fact, it be less honourable to conquer with the loss of lives than to gain a bloodless and unpolluted victory, or if the greatest proof of military genius be to carry any fixed object with the smallest exertion and waste of means, then we shall hardly consider these praises as unjust or overcharged.

Scarcely was this campaign at an end before Belisarius was again recalled by the emperor to Constantinople, and his departure from the East disclosed how entirely his late success had been due to his own unassisted talents. After the loss of his pervading spirit the Roman army sunk, as it were, into a dull, lifeless, and corrupted mass: Reinforced till it amounted to nearly thirty thousand men, but headed by no less than fifteen generals, of unequal merit and discordant views, it was routed in the valley of Dubis by a squadron of four thousand Persians, and Procopius doubts whether a defeat, so total and decisive, had been undergone by the Romans at any previous period of their annals. The chiefs, who before the day of conflict had allowed and imitated the rapine of the soldiers, now vied with them in quickness of flight, and scattered their useless arms, and (more unwillingly perhaps) the fruits of their pillage, along the encumbered roads.

A groundless apprehension of a rally or an ambuscade withheld Nabedes, the Persian general, from following the runaways, but their fears urged them to hurry onwards from a fancied pursuit; they did not stop till their expiring horses sunk beneath them from fatigue, and this engagement, like that of Guinegate in modern times, might deserve to be called the Battle of the Spurs. So great a disaster might perhaps have decided the fate of all the Roman provinces in Asia, had not

---

28. Compare Procop. *Pers. lib. ii.* c. 21. *Hist. Arcan.* c. 3.

a new and unexpected enemy now arisen against both Chosroes and Justinian, and raged with equal fury at Constantinople and at Ctesiphon. This enemy was the plague. A more destructive and extended pestilence than the world had seen for many centuries carried havoc through the most fertile regions of Asia, while Europe suffered far less severely from this fearful scourge. Through its calamities the forces of the Persians were lessened and their ambitious designs laid aside, and after an obstinate but unsuccessful siege of Edessa they narrowed their views to languid and desultory hostilities in Colchos.[29]

During the two last Persian campaigns the political security, as well as the domestic happiness of Belisarius, were shaken by the misconduct of his wife. It will be recollected that on the departure of the African expedition, (a.d. 533), a soldier, newly baptised, was embarked as an auspicious omen in the galley of the general.[30] This soldier's name was Theodosius, he had been brought up in the Eunomian heresy, which he abjured on this occasion, and was, according to a custom of the age, adopted by Belisarius as a spiritual son. This favour was but ill requited. In the progress of the voyage the young proselyte became deeply enamoured of Antonina, who returned his passion, and their intercourse was seen or suspected by all except the injured husband. The zeal of friends, which usually supplies such defects of vision, and kindly allows no man to remain ignorant of his misfortunes or his faults, was withheld in this case by the knowledge of Antonina's influence with the empress, and of her own vindictive temper.

At length, nearly three years afterwards, when Belisarius was wintering at Syracuse, (a.d. 536), Macedonia, a female attendant of his wife, stung by some petty injury, revealed the dangerous secret. In his first transport of indignation the Roman general decreed the death of Theodosius, and the terrified youth only escaped by forthwith embarking for Asia, but Antonina was not so easily detected, she loudly avouched her innocence, and exerted her extraordinary power of fascination, or, according to popular credulity, of witchcraft. Her tears were admitted as arguments, her blandishments as proofs, and she succeeded in convincing Belisarius of her perfect innocence. He delivered over to her mercy Macedonia, whom he now regarded as a perjured and malignant accuser, and he also gave up two witnesses

---

29. Some fresh materials for the wars between Rome and Persia, in the latter years of Nushirvan, may be found in Joannes *Epiphaniensis*, in the volume published by M. Hase, in 1819 from the inedited MS. of the Royal Library at Paris.
30. Procop. *Vandal, lib. i.* c. 12. *Hist. Arcan.* c. i

brought forward by that woman; an act which will deserve the severest censure if we believe, with the secret historian, that he had previously pledged an oath for their safety. By order of Antonina their tongues were cut out, their bodies torn limb from limb, and the mangled fragments cast into the sea.

Meanwhile a letter of recall was dispatched by Belisarius to his adopted son, but a personal quarrel between Photius and that youth for some time delayed the arrival of the latter in Italy. He was received with fatherly affection by Belisarius, by Antonina with passionate love; he took the direction of the household, was employed as one of the envoys to Ravenna,[31] and found many opportunities of amassing wealth. But on the return of the general to Constantinople, (a.d. 540), Theodosius perceived the danger of his situation, and was tempted to secure the advantages which he had 540. already gained. The busy rumours of a capital, or the unguarded fondness of Antonina, might any moment betray his secret to Belisarius, and expose himself to some summary and dreadful punishment, and he therefore considered it advisable to withdraw to Ephesus, where he shaved his head, and assumed the habit of a monk.

The indiscreet despair of Antonina at his departure sufficiently showed its prudence; she wept, she raved, she tore her hair, she appealed to Justinian and Theodora for their intercession, and artfully impelled her unsuspicious husband to solicit the return of his son. In reply to these commands or entreaties Theodosius pleaded fervent devotion and taste for the monastic life, but he secretly promised to revisit Constantinople as soon as his fears of discovery should be lessened by the departure of Belisarius for the Persian war. This was the real reason why Antonina did not follow her husband in this as in his earlier campaigns, and the precious moments of his absence were devoted to her lover.

During this period of pleasure, (a.d. 541), Antonina, however, found means to strengthen and secure her influence over the empress, by rendering her an important service. This anecdote, which we derive from a far more authentic source than the foregoing,[32] clearly sets forth the subtle, unprincipled, and daring character of the wife of Belisarius. An open enmity had subsisted for some time between Theodora and John of Cappadocia, the first minister of state, and they mutually balanced and divided the imperial favour, but neither could

---

31. Observe a cursory notice in the public history. (*Goth. lib. ii.* c. 28.)
32. Procop. *Pers. lib. i.* c. 25. He relates this whole with extraordinary freedom.

gain sufficient ascendancy to bring about the downfall of the other. Well knowing how flagitious was the woman with whom he had to deal, John was carefully on his guard against her emissaries, and, above all, bewared of nightly assassination, and it therefore became necessary to employ some stratagem against him.

Antonina began by winning the friendship of his daughter, Euphemia, a young and artless girl, and secretly complained to her of the suspicions and injustice which Belisarius had undergone from the emperor, even whispering some threats of rebellion, which were reported by Euphemia to her father. No intelligence could have been more welcome to the *prefect*. Like many other sceptics on religion, he was prone to the most childish superstitions, and firmly believed a prophecy made to him, that he should one day ascend the imperial throne.[33]

As the moment of this exaltation now seemed to him at hand by the co-operation of Belisarius, he entered into negotiation with Antonina, and was easily allured to a treasonable conference in her palace, near Constantinople. The emperor, when apprised of this transaction, dispatched the eunuch Narses, and some other officers, to ascertain its truth, and, with orders, should the charge of Antonina be well founded, to kill the *prefect* on the spot. They were placed by Antonina in ambush, and were secret witnesses to her interview with John: they heard the minister avow his designs of rebellion, and rushed forwards with drawn swords upon the convicted traitor; but the valour of his servants (there were several in waiting) allowed John some moments of leisure for escape, and he took shelter in a church at Constantinople from the sanctity of this asylum his life was spared, but he was compelled to shave his head and to take the vows as a priest, in order to disable him from holding in future any civil office. He was banished from the capital, and Theodora thus freed from his presence reigned without a rival in the councils of the emperor.

It was not long before the wife of Belisarius found it necessary to implore the imperial protection, upon which this intrigue had given her a claim. She had long nourished a bitter hatred against her son, as the enemy of her lover. Photius had accompanied Belisarius to the Persian war; but, at the distance of a thousand miles, he still felt the

---

33. It had been foretold to him that he should be invested with the robe of Augustus. By a singular accident he was, when compelled to assume the priesthood in his degradation, clad in the sacerdotal garments of a priest named Augustus, and thus the people considered the prophecy as fulfilled. (Procop. *Pers. lib. ii.* c. 30.)

effects of her unforgiving resentment, and was encountered by her persecutions at every turn. Provoked beyond bearing, he at length determined, as the surest means of revenge, to reveal her dishonour to her husband. The Roman general received this disclosure with the utmost surprise and indignation; he entreated Photius to remember his ties of obligation rather than of kindred, and they cemented their union by a mutual vow of vengeance. At the close of the campaign, Antonina joined Belisarius on the frontier: she was forthwith imprisoned, and threatened with death by her husband, whilst Photius was dispatched towards Ephesus to inflict a still more summary punishment upon her paramour.

Apprised of his danger, Theodosius sought the sanctuary of the altar; but on a seasonable gift of money from Photius to the bishop, the suppliant was yielded to his enemy, and Photius bore him away as a captive to Cilicia. But the watchful gratitude of the empress interfered in behalf of a frailty for which, moreover, her own character and conduct so strongly pleaded. Positive injunctions were sent to Cilicia; both Photius and Theodosius were brought to Constantinople: the one was cast into a dungeon and tortured at the rack, the other was received with distinction in the imperial palace, where, however, he expired from illness shortly after his arrival. The author of the *Anecdotes* asserts that Photius, having twice made his escape to a sanctuary, was twice dragged from the altar back to prison; yet such a violation of religious privileges seems altogether at variance with the spirit of the age.

This spirit was displayed in the belief that the third escape of Photius, some years afterwards, was effected by the aid of the prophet Zachariah.[34] On this last occasion, Photius proceeded to Jerusalem, where he was suffered to reside in the habit of a monk, and where he afterwards attained the rank of abbot.[35] Such was the long train of calamities which his mother's vices entailed upon this gallant young soldier.

At the same time that emissaries had been dispatched to seize Photius in Cilicia, a peremptory mandate had summoned Belisarius and Antonina from the Persian frontier. The empress commanded the injured husband to refrain from the punishment of his wife: he obeyed the order of his sovereign; she next required a reconciliation at his hands, but he refused a demand which no sovereign had a right to

---

34. Zachariah had become a principal object of public devotion, from the supposed discovery of his remains. (*Sozomen, lib. ix.* c 17.)
35. See Alemanni, *Not. Hist.*

make.³⁶ He therefore remained at Constantinople, under the secret displeasure of Theodora and Justinian, and they only wanted some plausible pretext to accomplish his ruin. The invasion of Nushirvan, in the ensuing spring, impelled the terrified emperor to lay aside his animosity, and restore to the hero the direction of the eastern armies; but in this campaign his former offence was aggravated, and the glory of saving the East outweighed by the guilt of frankness.

Justinian was recovering from a dangerous illness; (*a.d.* 542), a rumour of his death had reached the Roman camp; and Belisarius seems to have given an opinion in favour of the emperor's nearest kinsman as his successor, instead of acknowledging the pretensions of Theodora to the throne.³⁷ This declaration inflamed with equal anger the aspiring wife and the uxorious husband. Buzes, the second in command, who had concurred in these views, was confined in a subterranean dungeon, so dark that the difference of day or night was never apparent to its inmate.

Belisarius himself was recalled, with flattering professions of confidence and friendship, lest resentment should urge him to rebellion; but on his arrival at Constantinople, the mask was thrown aside; he was degraded from the rank of general of the East; a commission was dispatched into Asia to seize his treasures; and his personal guards, who had followed his standard through so many battles, were removed from his command. Even the eunuchs of the palace did not blush to cast lots for the distribution of these valiant veterans. His friends kept aloof, by order of Justinian, or from their own prudent aversion to the fallen. A statesman in disgrace has often no enemies so dangerous, bitter, and unsparing, as his former friends; because their friendship has become a crime in the eyes of the ruling powers, and must be atoned for by proportional animosity against him.

It was with feelings of mingled compassion and surprise, that the people beheld the forlorn appearance of the general as he rode along the streets with a small and squalid train. He was received by the emperor and Theodora with angry disdain, and was exposed during the whole day, without protection, to the insults and scoffings of the rabble at the gates. The public and himself were persuaded that his

36. This refusal, which is overlooked by Gibbon (vol. vii.), is established by a subsequent passage in the *Secret History*: (c. 4.) This fact alters the whole complexion of the narrative, and explains the letter of the emperor.
37. Besides the doubtful authority of the secret historian, the pretensions of Theodora are apparent from the unusual form of the oath of allegiance, which was jointly to Justinian and to her. See the eighth novel and Alemanni, *Not. Hist.*

death had been resolved upon; and as he withdrew in the evening to his lonely palace, he frequently turned round, as if expecting the appointed assassins to advance, but the empress had determined to take this opportunity of rewarding Antonina's services, by clearing her fame, and effecting her reconciliation with her husband. After sunset, a messenger from the palace brought Belisarius the tidings of his fate in a letter from Theodora. She declared that his life was granted him, and that a portion of his fortune should be spared, solely at the intercession of his wife; and she trusted that his future conduct would show forth his gratitude to his deliverer.

The death of Theodosius, and the lapse of a year, had already in some degree calmed his indignation, his former fondness was beginning to revive, and the favourable moments of surprise and gratitude were improved by Antonina with her usual skill. The uxorious hero consented to disbelieve or to forgive her former infidelity, and once more to become her affectionate, confiding, and submissive husband. Such he ever afterwards continued; and on her part, Antonina, who had now attained the ripe age of forty-three, became less abandoned, or at least more cautious, in her conduct. A fine of three thousand pounds weight of gold was levied on the property of Belisarius, and he was suffered for many months to languish in obscurity. At length, however, (*a.d.* 544), he was named to the command of the war in Italy, with the title of Count of the Imperial Stables;[38] yet from the overpowering force of the Goths at that period, and the smallness or rather the nothingness of the means placed at his disposal, this appointment might be considered at least as much an exile as a trust.[39]

It was generally believed, at Constantinople, that Belisarius only accepted this mission as an opportunity of speedy rebellion and revenge; but his patient loyalty was proof against all personal injuries, and he never allowed the wrongs of the subject to pervert the power or to interrupt the duties of the soldier. If, before his departure, the general made no attempt to draw Photius from his dungeon, and to appease the hatred of his mother,—if he did not strain every nerve to rescue a friend who had suffered solely in his cause, we must deplore, in these transactions, not merely the weakness but the guilt of Belisarius.

---

38. On this office see a law of *a.d.* 413, (Cod. Justinian. *lib. xii* tit. 11.) The *Comes Stabuli* was likewise a high office amongst the Franks of this age. (Greg. Turon. *lib. x.* c. 5.)
39. Procop. *Goth. lib. iii.* c. 10.

CHAPTER 7

Italy After the Departure of Belisarius

At the departure of Belisarius from Ravenna, in obedience to the commands of his sovereign, the conquest of Italy might be considered as almost entirely achieved. The Gothic monarchy lay powerless and prostrate, and the faint opposition of a handful of soldiers in Liguria, appeared only, as it were, the last convulsion of its expiring agonies. The single city of Pavia, which still delayed its submission, would doubtless soon have followed the example of the rest, when the hopes of its garrison were raised by the recall of Belisarius, (*a.d.* 540), and still more by the faults of his successors. Justinian had rashly appointed to the vacant command eleven generals of equal rank,[1] neither respected by the soldiers, nor united amongst themselves, and who seemed only to value their high office as affording superior facilities for spoliation.

The administration of the revenue had been entrusted to Alexander, a crafty scribe, who, from a slender patrimony, had risen, by the most nefarious means, to the possession of enormous wealth. Deeply skilled in every refinement of chicane, no pity or remorse ever checked his rapine; and, from his skill in diminishing the size without altering the appearance of gold coin, he was commonly known at Constantinople by the by-word of *psallidion*, or the Scissars. On his arrival at Ravenna, he found Italy exhausted by the calamities of war; but this consideration was far from restraining his active ingenuity. Heavy taxes were imposed on all classes, and confiscations levied from the estates of the wealthy, on the plea of pretended debts to Theodoric and the other Gothic Kings. Under this oppressive yoke, they might

---

1. The testimony of Procopius (*Goth. lib. iii.* c. 3) outweighs that of the continuator of Marcellinus, who names Constantine as chief general. (*Chron. ap. Sirmond. Op.* vol. ii.)

derive some consolation from the perfect impartiality of Alexander, who defrauded the Byzantine soldiers no less than the Italian subjects. Instead of fixed and regular payments, the money for their subsistence was partly withheld and partly doled out in scanty and uncertain remittances; and the veterans found no other reward for the perils they had encountered, and the wounds they might display, than neglect and destitution.

According to the strong expression of Procopius, the troops were reduced to beggars; all sense of honour was relaxed, all subordination destroyed; some forsook their encampments for the pillage of the neighbouring country, while others in disgust deserted to the enemy. The Italians, groaning beneath the tyranny of those whom they had hailed as friends and deliverers, turned an eye of regret to the happy reign of Theodoric, and looked with hope and favour to the reviving strength of the Goths at Pavia.

This squadron at first could not muster above one thousand men, but was gradually recruited by some scattered detachments. The royal title was offered to Uraias, the brave nephew of Vitiges; but he considered the ill fortune of his kinsman as a sufficient motive for his own exclusion, and generously directed the choice of the council to Hildibald, whose relationship to the King of the Visigoths in Spain,[2] might acquire for his new subjects that powerful alliance. But base minds can still less forgive a favour than an injury. Hildibald nourished a secret hostility against his benefactor, and yielded to the entreaties of his queen, whose hatred, like most female enmities, was frivolous in its origin, and dreadful in its vengeance. She had been deeply incensed, on some public occasion, by the richer dress and more numerous attendants of the wife of Uraias, who had moreover aggravated this offence by her haughty demeanour.

Uraias fell a victim to the ingratitude of his friend, (*a.d.* 541), and to the wounded vanity of a woman; but his murder roused the anger of the Goths, and soon met with its just reward. A soldier named Vilas, having been bereaved of his bride by Hildibald, gratified the public resentment and his own, by striking off the head of the tyrant, when seated at a solemn banquet in the midst of his nobles. The Rugians, a separate tribe, who had joined the victorious standards of Theodoric, and remained amongst his subjects, determined the new election in favour of their countryman Eraric. This choice was of course unwel-

---

2. This was Theudes, who was an Ostrogoth by birth, and who reigned till *a.d.* 548. See Mariana, *Hist. Hisp. lib. v.* c. 8.

come and displeasing to Tidel,[3] or, as the Greeks have termed him, Totila, nephew of the late king, who commanded a detachment at the small town of Treviso, and he immediately offered to join the Roman standards.

A day had already been fixed for the surrender of Treviso, when the Goths became sensible that their Rugian monarch was ill fitted by his talents, or by his courage, to retrieve their ruined affairs. In a secret embassy, they offered the crown to Totila, and the ambitious youth gladly consented to assume that dangerous honour, provided Eraric were dispatched before the time for executing his treaty with the Romans should arrive. The usurper was accordingly put to death by his discontented subjects, and the nephew of Hildibald triumphantly entered the palace of Pavia.[4]

In the character of Totila, we cannot by any means, as in that of Theodoric, his illustrious predecessor, admire a perfect example of barbarian virtue. His military merit is indeed attested by the confession of his enemies, and still more clearly by the rapid progress of his arms. But his temper was fierce, vindictive, and unsparing; and though his policy enjoined clemency to the Italians, in hopes of gaining their affection, and a liberal treatment of his captives, in order to allure them to his service, yet, where he had no such object to restrain him, we behold the tyrant unveiled. As an instance of his capricious cruelty, it may be sufficient to mention, that one of his favourite officers, having been wounded in battle by a Roman commander, who was afterwards himself taken prisoner, the Gothic monarch suspended his decision during the lingering illness of his friend, and finding that it ended in death, commanded the immediate execution of his captive.[5]

A more generous enemy would have acknowledged that the Roman had only done his duty in the conflict, and that at all events his guilt could never depend on the accident whether or not the wound he had inflicted proved ultimately fatal. On the first occasion when the name of Totila appears in history, we find him a traitor to his countrymen, ready to sacrifice their cause to the gratification of his private animosity; and in the sequel of my narrative it will be seen that, in his conduct, passion frequently triumphed even over interest.

Yet in some respects we may applaud his character. His promises

---

3. Ludewig, *Vit. Justinian*. Grotius makes the original *Tot-las* (*Hist. Goth.*)
4. This palace had been built by the great Theodoric. Paul Warnefrid, *lib. ii.* c 27. and *Anonym. Vales.*
5. Procop. *Goth. lib. iii.* c. 19.

were sacred and inviolable, the terms of his stipulations with his adversaries were always observed with fidelity, and the discipline of the victorious army was strictly established and enforced. By his offers he attracted, by his justice he retained, deserters from the Roman Army; and the captives whom he made in battle were often tempted to renounce the thankless service of Justinian. No sooner had he been chosen king by his countrymen, than he justified their choice by the vigour of his government; he led his forces, now augmented to five thousand soldiers, through Liguria, and seems to have reduced several important cities, and more especially Verona.[6]

The Byzantine generals remained, at Ravenna, tranquil spectators of these conquests, until the upbraidings of the emperor awakened their dormant courage. In a council of war, (a.d 542), it was resolved by Bessas, John the Sanguinary, and the other chiefs, first to direct their arms against Verona, and afterwards against Pavia, to crush the last remnant of the Goths. Accordingly they took the field at the head of twelve thousand men, including the Persian garrison of Sisauranum, lately dispatched by Belisarius from the East, and they encamped at nine miles from Verona, where a Goth, appointed to the command of one of the city gates, privately promised to betray his station. The generals determined that, without hazarding the whole army, a detachment should make the doubtful and dangerous attempt, and as every Roman officer shrunk from this command, it devolved on Artabazes, one of the Persian captives. In the dead of night, the gate was opened to him, and to one hundred chosen soldiers; the city was surprised, and the affrighted Goths escaped by another outlet.

But they rallied on a neighbouring hill; the break of day, and the high ground which they occupied, enabled them to discern the small number of the enemy; and the Roman generals, on their march to the support of Artabazes, had halted, while disputing with each other the partition of the expected spoil. By their delay, the subject of their quarrel was irrecoverably lost to them. The handful of soldiers in Verona was speedily overpowered by the superior force of the barbarians, and only a few (amongst them Artabazes himself) preserved their life and liberty, by leaping from the walls, and breaking through the Gothic ranks. After this inglorious expedition, which served merely to betray their weakness and discord to the enemy, the Roman gener-

---

6. This is no where positively stated; but the Goths are said by Procopius *(Goth. lib. iii.* c. 1.) to have possessed no other city than Pavia, and yet (c 3.) we find Verona in their hands.

als hastened to repass the Po, and fixed their encampment at Faenza. They were followed by the forces of Totila, and it was in vain that Artabazes urged the expediency of defending against the Goths the passage of the river. On the approach of the hostile army, this brave Persian again signalised himself above his Roman comrades, by accepting a challenge to single combat from a Goth of gigantic stature and experienced skill.

The valour of Artabazes prevailed; the barbarian was unhorsed and slain, but an accidental thrust from the lance of his expiring enemy, struck the victor with a mortal wound, and the loss of this distinguished officer was deeply felt by the Romans in the battle which ensued. Animated by an harangue from Totila, the Goths advanced to the charge with all the generous boldness which a national cause inspires, while the Romans displayed the voluntary cowardice of hirelings, whose pay has been withheld. The engagement was not long undecided. A squadron of three hundred barbarians, artfully posted by Totila in ambush, suddenly appeared in the rear of the imperial forces, and was magnified by their terrors into a second Gothic Army. Chiefs and subalterns fled in disorder from the field; many prisoners were made in the pursuit, and all the standards taken, a disgrace which, according to Procopius, had never befallen the Romans on any previous occasion.

The result of the Battle of Faenza, was the total dispersion of the Byzantine troops. Each of the eleven generals led the squadron under his personal command to the shelter of some different fortress, so that the whole of Italy now lay open and exposed to Totila, with many cities to reduce, but no army to encounter. The victorious monarch was not slow in availing himself of the advantages which his merit and good fortune had acquired. While he himself reduced the cities of Pesaro and Fano, a share of his forces was dispatched to form the siege of Florence, and might have succeeded in this enterprise, had not the garrison received a large reinforcement from Ravenna, headed by John the Sanguinary. These troops, confiding in their far superior numbers, sallied forth against the barbarians, who retreated towards the Appennine, and entrenched themselves on a hill near Mugello.[7]

Here they repulsed their assailants with loss, and, assisted by a false report that the Byzantine chief had fallen, produced a panic rout. The Romans of this detachment were scattered, not, as lately, party by party, but man by man, and a great number who fell into the hands of

---
7. See Sigonius, *De Imp. Occident, lib. xix.*

the enemy were persuaded to enlist in his service. This second victory induced Totila to form a project, bold and adventurous in appearance, but of which the soundness was shown by the event. Had he attempted the regular siege of the neighbouring cities, he would have found them ready for a long, and perhaps successful, resistance; he would have left the open country in possession of the Romans, and given them leisure to recover from their consternation.

He, therefore, meditated to carry his arms into the furthest part of Italy, where no attack was looked for, and no defence prepared. In pursuance of this plan, he marched through Æmilia and Picenum, and having reduced the forts of Cesena and Petra in his way, passed the Tiber, and advanced into Campania. The city of Benevento, though a place of strength, yielded to his unforeseen attack, and he razed its ramparts to the ground.

From thence he proceeded to Naples, which, as no danger had been apprehended, was garrisoned by only one thousand soldiers, but which possessed in Conon a firm and faithful governor. The place was invested by the king in person; but considerable detachments of his army were sent into the adjoining provinces, which, from the total want of Roman troops, they overran with ease. Lucania and Bruttium, the Apulians and Calabrians, were successively subdued, and almost the whole of southern Italy once more acknowledged the Goths as sovereigns, while, in another quarter, the fort of Cumae enriched them with its hoards of treasure. Some ladies, of senatorial rank, who had been surprised in their Campanian villas, were sent back to their husbands without ransom, and the generous or politic forbearance of Totila was rewarded by his growing popularity.

The progress of the Gothic monarch filled the Byzantine court with just alarm. Troops were hastily collected and dispatched. The supreme command in Italy, with the title of Praetorian Prated, were bestowed on Maximinus, a senator, not merely ignorant of war, but deficient in the first and most common requisite for a soldier, personal courage.[8] He had left Constantinople at the head of a formidable fleet, and a large body of Thracian and Illyrian soldiers, together with some Hunnish horse; yet, instead of proceeding at once to the object of his expedition, he timidly lingered on the coast of Epirus. Demetrius, one of his officers, landed with a handful of men in Sicily, where he learned that the garrison of Naples was reduced to extreme distress, and required immediate succour. For this purpose he gathered to-

---

8. Compare Procop. *Goth. lib. ii*: c. 29, *lib. iii.* c. 6.

gether as many vessels as possible from every port in the island; and it appears that Totila, apprised of the large number of these ships, and not aware by how few soldiers they were manned, would not, in all likelihood, have ventured to attack them had they steered directly for the bay of Naples.[9]

Instead of such judicious boldness, Demetrius, like most weak men, mistook delay for prudence, and sailed first to Porto, at the mouth of the Tiber, where he hoped to obtain some reinforcements. But the imperial troops in Italy were disheartened by their late defeats, they refused to quit the protection of their ramparts, and the Byzantine officer was compelled to proceed alone when the favourable moment for action had already passed. Totila had discovered the real weakness of the convoy, and suddenly assailed it with some light brigantines as it lay at anchor near the coast. A few soldiers, and Demetrius himself, escaped, by having at the first onset betaken themselves to their boats, but all the ships fell into the hands of the enemy, and all the Romans on board were either killed or made prisoners.

Amongst the latter was the *epitrope*, or civil governor of Naples, who had secretly travelled to Porto in order to hasten the expected supplies, and who, in the earlier part of the siege, had imprudently manifested his loyalty to the emperor by taunts and invectives against the Gothic invader. For these he was now destined to undergo a most rigorous punishment. The vindictive barbarian commanded his hands and his tongue to be cut off, and then, in derision, restored the mutilated wretch to freedom.

On the return of Demetrius almost alone to Sicily he found Maximinus, at length arrived with all his forces, and distracted by the twofold apprehension of either encountering the enemy, or suffering the displeasure of Justinian. To guard equally against these opposite grounds of fear the trembling general resolved to fix his own station at Syracuse, and to dispatch his ships and soldiers to the relief of Naples, under the command of Demetrius and other officers. But the winter was now so far advanced that a naval expedition, could no longer be undertaken with security. A furious tempest assailed the Roman fleet off the coast of Naples, and by a singular fatality the wind drove the ships straight against the Gothic encampment. The imperial troops made no resistance, but the barbarians were not appeased by their ready submission, and did not receive any as captives until they had glutted their animosity by hurling a great number into the sea.

---

9. Procop. *Goth, lib. iii. c.* 6,

Some few ships were enabled to weather the storm and escape to Sicily, but the strength of the Byzantine squadron was thoroughly broken by this second disaster, and, Demetrius, less fortunate on this than on the former occasion, was amongst the prisoners. With a rope round his neck he was, by order of Totila, dragged to the foot of the Neapolitan ramparts, and commanded to announce his own ill-fortune, and to exhort the besieged to capitulate. In another age the example of Regulus might perhaps have been remembered and renewed, but Demetrius passively spoke the lesson which his conqueror enjoined, and the Neapolitans were still less strongly moved by his words than by seeing in captivity before them the officer on whom their chief hope of succour had been placed. They entered into parleys with Totila, and it was agreed that the imperial troops should surrender the city and be honourably dismissed to Rome if no auxiliaries should arrive before the end of thirty days.

To cut short these lingering expectations of relief Totila offered to prolong this term from one month to three, and the garrison, dismayed at this apparent security, and urged by famine, opened their gates forthwith. The terms of capitulation were observed by the Gothic monarch with justice, (*a.d.* 543), and even generosity. It was in vain that his principal officers pleaded for the life of a soldier whom a Neapolitan citizen accused of the violation of his daughter, and Totila sternly replied to their entreaties that he who could commit so base an outrage must needs be a coward in the field. The imperial troops who had embarked for Rome, but been withheld by contrary winds, received horses and provisions to make the journey by land, and officers were appointed to attend them on their road, and secure them against any insult or delay. Fearing lest a sudden and plentiful supply of food might prove fatal to the famished Neapolitans, Totila adopted the most humane and salutary precautions.

Guards were stationed at the gates, none of the inhabitants were permitted to leave the city, and a daily pittance was allotted to them, which small at first and increasing by degrees restored without oppressing their exhausted strength. The greater part of the ramparts was afterwards levelled to the ground, in order to deprive the Romans in future of this convenient strong-hold, and to save the citizens from the calamities of another siege. Such was the policy pursued by Totila with respect to almost every fortress which fell into his power.

On leaving Naples the king divided his army, and having dispatched one share to form the siege of Otranto, marched with the other towards Rome. In a letter to the senators he appealed to their memory of the paternal reign of Theodoric, and, like all new monarchs, abounded in professions for his own. Nor were his efforts fruitless; several senators, and especially their chief Cethegus,[10] became his secret partisans. His proclamations were found each morning affixed in the principal streets of Rome; in these he solemnly promised, and even swore, his forgiveness of all past injuries, and modestly ascribed his victories not to any prowess of his own, but to the general indignation which the tyranny of the Romans had aroused. The imperial governors of the city, perplexed and angry at the publication of these manifestos, knew not whom to accuse or to punish, and only embittered the public discontent by the exile of all the Arian priests at Rome. That these men were ill-wishers to the established Catholic Government is sufficiently probable, but there are some enmities which it is wiser to bear than to repel, and this impolitic measure spread over Italy a number of zealous and active ringleaders, who might else have assisted their party no further than by masses and prayers.

The ulterior progress of Totila this year was checked by the havoc of that plague, to which I have already adverted at the close of the Persian war, and which now exerted its baneful influence over western Europe.[11] In this quarter it was not, however, of very long continuance, and after its cessation the imperial prospects in Italy seemed more than ever cheerless, declining, and forlorn. The Byzantine *armada* had been annihilated by the forces of the Goths or the storms of the Mediterranean. All the open country was possessed by Totila. The public revenues were intercepted, and the troops still maintaining some separate cities became every day more turbulent and ungovernable from their increasing arrears.

Under the dominion of an insolent soldiery the Italian citizens endured rapacity and outrage in every form, their household effects were plundered, their daily food was snatched from them, and their complaints were answered with blows. Accordingly their disaffection to the Romans, and wishes for the restoration of the Gothic monarchy grew more and more ardent and decided, especially when they

---

10. The ancient Cethegi were amongst the first of all the noble families (Sallust. *Bell. Catil.* c 17.), but it is probable that they had long been extinct. I find one of this name mentioned by Victor Tunnunensis and others, as Consul for the year a.d. 504. (*Chron.* ed, Canisii, vol. i.). The identity of this Cethegus, with the partisan of Totila, is confidently affirmed by Sigonius, yet there is an interval of almost forty years between the two. (*Imp. Occident lib. xix.*)
11. See Muratori, *Annal. d'It*al. vol. iii.

observed the generous conduct and fair promises of Totila. In their letters to the emperor the Roman generals did not dissemble their despondency, they gave up every thing as lost, and unanimously declared their utter inability to carry on the war.

Embarrassed and dismayed by these reports Justinian once more summoned Belisarius to the post of danger, (a.d. 544), but neglected to supply any sufficient forces, and even withheld the domestic guards of which the general had lately been bereaved. Attended only by a handful of his veterans Belisarius traversed Thrace, where, by lavish donatives, he succeeded in mustering four thousand youthful volunteers, and these he forthwith conducted to Salona. With such forces it was clearly impossible to meet the enemy in battle, or even to venture forth from the shelter of fortresses. Belisarius therefore determined, after sailing round the Adriatic, to disembark at Ravenna, there to fix his first Italian headquarters, and issue his orders to the governors of the inland cities. His earliest care, however, on arriving at Salona was the relief of Otranto, which the barbarians were closely blockading, and whose garrison was reduced to extremity by famine and disease.

The general dispatched to its succour a squadron of his fleet, with sufficient provisions for one year, and some troops, commanded by Valentine. Their voyage was favoured by the winds, nor was there any time to lose, since the besieged had agreed to surrender should no supplies arrive before a stipulated period, and the Roman convoy came in sight only four days before this term. Its arrival changed the aspect of affairs. The enfeebled garrison embarked, it was replaced by fresh and vigorous soldiers, new stores filled the public granaries and magazines, and the Goths, in despair, desisted from their enterprise. Thus successful, the Roman ships set sail for Salona, where Belisarius awaited their return to pursue his progress. At Pola, his next station, he remained some time, employed in regulating the discordant materials of his little army, and preparing it for immediate service.

The news that Belisarius was at hand greatly alarmed the Gothic monarch, who well knew his talents, and was ignorant of the smallness of his force on this occasion. To ascertain the real fact Totila had recourse to an ingenious stratagem. He forged a letter, purporting to come from the Roman governor of Genoa, and dispatched it to the camp at Pola by some trusty messengers, who were enjoined to observe as narrowly as possible the strength and numbers of the enemy. These spies were received by Belisarius without suspicion, they were desired to assure the Genoese of speedy succour, and having found full opportunity for executing the secret object of their mission, they hastened to inform their sovereign that the Byzantine troops were few, and altogether despicable.

They found the king engaged in the siege of Tivoli, which was soon afterwards betrayed to him by its inhabitants, but these had reason to repent their perfidy. Totila was desirous of intimidating Rome by some striking example of rigour in its neighbourhood, and accordingly put every citizen of Tivoli to the sword, under circumstances of such barbarity that Procopius forbears to detail them, lest he should furnish a mischievous example to succeeding ages. His testimony to these cruelties is the more unimpeachable, since on other occasions he loudly extols the character of Totila, and endeavours by its virtues to excuse the defeats or to heighten the achievements of his countrymen.[12]

Meanwhile Belisarius, having arrived at Ravenna, immediately after landing addressed both the Romans and Goths in a public harangue, he said:

> The dominion, of the emperor in Italy has been endangered by the guilt or imbecility of his lieutenants. Anxious to render these provinces tranquil and contented as before he has postponed his projects of conquest against Persia, and has sent me to redress your wrongs. Let it be your part to assist the execution of his generous designs. Let those amongst you who have friends or kinsmen amongst the rebellious troops of Totila forthwith recall them from that guilty cause, by announcing to them the imperial promises and pardon. Spare me, I beseech you, the painful duty of entering the field against fellow-countrymen, misled from their allegiance.

These, and many similar exhortations, proved wholly unavailing, not a single soldier was allured from the Gothic ranks, and Belisarius soon perceived that he could trust only to his own resources for success. He was now not far distant from the Gothic army, for the king, after the reduction of Tivoli, had crossed the Appennine and undertaken the siege of Osimo. It was the first object of Belisarius to relieve this important city. One of his outposts surprised a barbarian squadron near Bologna; another, of a thousand men, succeeded in reaching Osimo; but it was worsted in a sally, and, either from panic

---

12. Procop. *Goth. lib. iii.* c 10. As to the motive of Totila I follow the probable conjecture of Le Beau, (*Bas Emp. lib. xlvii.*)

or mistaken policy, again quitted the city, and was driven back with loss to Rimini.

Disappointed in this quarter, Belisarius next planned a bold attempt upon Pesaro, which he considered to be advantageously placed for grazing and forage, and therefore a station useful for his cavalry. When Totila had taken that city, after the Battle of Faenza, he had, according to his usual system, torn away the gates and lowered the walls, hoping thus effectually to prevent the enemy from defending them again. But Belisarius dispatched some trusty emissaries to take, by night, the exact measure of the open intervals; and according to their report, strong iron barricades, of the necessary size and number, were constructed at Ravenna, and forwarded in boats to Rimini.

By order of the general, some troops, with Thorimuth for their leader, now threw themselves into Pesaro, and, having fixed the new bulwarks brought with them in the place of gates, unremittingly laboured with the citizens to repair the ruined walls. The Gothic king, at the news of this singular enterprise, hastened with his army to hinder its completion; but the rising fortifications were already capable of withstanding an attack; and after a long and obstinate blockade, he found it necessary to abandon his undertaking, and return to his camp before Osimo.

This capital of Picenum surrendered to him in the course of the winter, (*a.d.* 545). Early in the ensuing campaign he again took the field, reduced Ascoli and Fermo, and finding the Roman forces altogether unable to oppose him, meditated no less a project than the siege of Rome. Accordingly, he began his march through Tuscany, pausing in his progress to invest Assisi, Perugia, and Spoleto. The former city was defended by Siegfried, a Goth in the imperial service, whose fidelity disdained the offers, and whose valour repulsed the assaults, of Totila; nor was it till this intrepid barbarian had fallen, that his terrified garrison consented to surrender. His example may be contrasted with that of Herodian, governor of Spoleto, far less devoted to his natural than Siegfried to his adopted country, and who, fearing the punishment of his previous rapine and malversation, gladly availed himself of this opportunity to escape the justice of Belisarius, by yielding to the arms of Totila.[13]

At Perugia, the governor, Cyprian turned a deaf ear to all the offers of the Gothic king, who hereupon contrived the assassination of that stubborn and troublesome loyalist. This expedient proved as useless as

---

13. Compare Procop. *Goth. lib. iii.* c. 12. and *Hist. Arcan.* c. 5.

it was infamous; the garrison persevered in its resistance after the death of its chief; and Totila, impatient of further delay, raised the siege and pursued his march along the Tiber.

To the fortresses thus attacked by the barbarians, Belisarius found it impossible to afford the slightest aid. As a last resource, he dispatched John the Sanguinary with a letter to Justinian, in which his forlorn situation is described with the natural eloquence of truth.

> Great prince, I am arrived in Italy, unprovided with men or money, with horses or with arms, nor can any spirit bear up against such disadvantages as these. In my progress through Thrace and Illyria, I collected, by great exertions, a handful of raw and undisciplined recruits, whom I can hardly furnish with weapons, and whom I find unfit for almost every purpose of war. The troops already stationed in Italy are deficient both in numbers and in courage. Their minds have been debased and enslaved by their frequent defeats; and no sooner do the barbarians approach, than they relinquish their horses, and cast their arms on the ground.
>
> To raise any taxes is impracticable, since the provinces are in possession of the enemy; and the long arrear of pay which our soldiers vainly claim loosens every tie of discipline and duty. A debtor is but ill able to command.
>
> Be assured, my sovereign, that the best part of your army has already gone over to the Goths. Were it sufficient for success that Belisarius should appear in Italy, your aim would be accomplished: I am now in the midst of the Italians. But if you desire to conquer, far greater preparations must be made; and the title of general dwindles to a shadow, where there is no army to uphold it. My own personal guards and veteran soldiers should, in the first place, be permitted to rejoin me; and it is only by full and ready payments, that you can secure the useful service of the Huns and other barbarian mercenaries.[14]

Before the departure of John the Sanguinary with this letter, he had bound himself by the most solemn oaths to execute his commission with zeal, and return with promptitude; yet on his arrival at Constantinople, he neglected the public interests, and prolonged his stay for an advantageous marriage with the grand-niece of the

---

14. See on this letter the remarks of the Count de Buat, who thence launches out into a defence of the feudal system. (*Hist. des Peuples*, vol. x.)

emperor.[15] Much precious time was lost; and Belisarius, finding his presence at Ravenna grown fruitless, since the scene of action had been transferred beneath the walls of Rome, resolved to meet the expected reinforcements, and afterwards lead them to the relief of the capital. Leaving, therefore, merely the necessary garrison in Ravenna, he sailed with his remaining troops to Dyrrachium on the coast of Epirus, where he impatiently awaited the lingering supplies; and, in repeated letters, laboured with more zeal than success to awaken the attention and obtain the active interference of the emperor.

After a long period of delay, John the Sanguinary and some other chiefs gradually brought up troops collected from different quarters of the empire; while the eunuch Narses, who had proceeded on a mission to the Heruli, sent some mercenaries from amongst that warlike people. But the slowness and languor of these preparations left Totila at full leisure to accomplish his designs; and in behalf of the western capital, Belisarius at first could only dispatch to Porto a body of one thousand men, headed by Valentine and Phocas.

Remembering the former failure of Vitiges at the head of one hundred and fifty thousand men, Totila, whose forces did not probably exceed as yet one-fifth of that number, declined the siege of Rome, and applied himself to the more easy and promising task of a close blockade. No supplies from the neighbouring country were allowed to enter the gates, and a fleet was stationed at the Lipari islands to intercept the usual convoys of Sicilian corn. The defence of the city had been entrusted to Bessas, the same whose avarice and valour were displayed in the first Italian war; and the garrison, after all its losses from death or desertion, could still muster three thousand soldiers. Besides these, a detachment from the guards of Belisarius had succeeded in safely traversing the country from Ravenna; and their general had seized this opportunity of transmitting instructions, and expressly desiring Bessas not to hazard his scanty force in skirmishes or sallies, but to confine himself to the protection of the walls. This injunction was transgressed by the thoughtless courage of those very officers who had conveyed it to Rome. In spite of every remonstrance, they attacked the vanguard of Totila, and justified the prudence of their general by their overthrow and death.

Bessas was warned by their example; and through a singular fatality, his too strict and unbending adherence to the commands of Belisarius produced, as great an evil as had resulted from rashly disobeying

---

15. Her name was Justina, she was a daughter of Germanus by his first wife Passara. See *Hist. Arcan.* c. 5. and Ducange, *Fam. Aug. Byz.*

them. On he arrival of Valentine and Phocas at Porto, they entreated Bessas to second, by a sally, their enterprise against one of the Gothic encampments; but the Roman garrison remained immovably fixed on the ramparts, and most of the Byzantine auxiliaries were accordingly slain or dispersed in their unassisted attack.

Some time before the beginning of the siege, Pope Vigilius had been summoned to the presence of the emperor, and had already arrived in Sicily, on his way to Constantinople, when he learnt that Rome was encompassed by the Goths, and threatened with all the calamities of famine. His generous charity collected a great number of ships, (*a.d.* 546), and stored them with abundant provision; they succeeded in eluding the vigilance of the Gothic fleet, and were already on the very point of reaching Porto, when the approaching squadron was unfortunately discerned by the barbarians on shore. A strong party of the enemy concealed themselves in the outworks at the mouth of the harbour, in order to surprise and seize the crews immediately on their landing; and the Roman garrison, too feeble to sally forth and dislodge these artful adversaries, could only, by waving their cloaks from the rampart, give their friends a signal to beware.

But the Sicilians, mistaking these equivocal gestures for marks of exultation at the unexpected arrival of supplies, availed themselves of a favourable breeze, and sailed headlong into the hostile snare. Not a single ship escaped; all the stores were taken, and the Romans on board were massacred to a man, with the exception of a bishop, reserved for a personal interview with Totila. This *prelate*, however, had but little cause to rejoice in his reprieve. When the Gothic monarch found his questions with regard to the forces and intentions of the Byzantine army either skilfully evaded or answered by patriotic falsehoods, he in a transport of savage anger ordered his attendants to strike off the hands of his captive.

From this time forward no hope of supplies from Sicily could be entertained by the inhabitants or the garrison of Rome, and they began to undergo more and more the hardships of a scarcity. It was therefore resolved to enter into terms with Totila, and to propose a truce with the promise of surrendering the city, should no Byzantine reinforcements speedily arrive. For this important mission they chose the archdeacon Pelagius, whose talents some years afterwards raised him to the papal throne,[16] and whose liberality during the prevailing

---

16. Victor Tunnunensis *Chron.* ed. Canisii, vol. i. but his date is faulty, and we must read xxviii. for xxxviii. See Muratori, *Script Ital.* vol. iii.

distress had greatly endeared him to the people. The reverend envoy was graciously received by Totila, who even declared himself willing to grant any request he might make, provided it did not relate to the Sicilians. On these ungrateful islanders he owned himself determined to wreak the severest vengeance for their ready welcome and aid to Belisarius, at the outset of the war.

The wary priest replied:

If such be your fixed intention with regard to Sicily, and that your resentment is thus implacable for injuries neither personal nor recent, what degree of reliance can the Romans place on your mercy, after having actually borne arms against yourself?

With this answer Pelagius left the Gothic camp, and returned to share the sufferings of his fellow-citizens. Their wretchedness was embittered by the unfeeling avarice of Bessas, who hoarded his supplies of corn until the increasing scarcity enabled him to dole it forth at an extravagant price. Each *medimnus* [17] of grain was now commonly sold for seven pieces of gold, an ox (some few were occasionally captured) produced no less than fifty, and the soldiers were tempted by the prospect of enormous gain, to deny themselves a part of their scanty rations. Thus the fortunes of the wealthy Romans were quickly drained, and they found it necessary to appease the pangs of hunger by yielding their plate and furniture to the rapacious cruelty of Bessas. The poor were happy if they succeeded in obtaining a tasteless mixture, in which one quarter of flour was added to three quarters of bran.

Amongst them the possession of a dead horse, or any other carcase, was looked upon as a sort of treasure, and furnished a meal of unusual luxury; but the greater number of the citizens only sustained existence by the herbs they could collect. In each ruin, which the degenerate Italians had never prized or spared for its own magnificence, or as a memorial of their forefathers, they now discovered a real value from the abundance of grass and nettles which it bore.[18] To this miserable food both citizens and soldiers were finally reduced, when no other resource remained, when even dogs, cats, and mice, had already been devoured. The conduct of a Roman father in this utmost need affords

---

17. The *medimnus* consisted of six *modii*, and was equal to about a bushel and a half English. *Cic. in Verr. iii.* c. 45. and Adam's *Antiquities.*
18. The indifference of the Romans in the fifth century to the works of their ancestors, is apparent from an edict of Majorian, (*ad calc Cod. Theod.* ed. 1607.) Some degree of pride in these edifices was revived by the respectful care of Theodoric the Great. (Procop. *Goth. lib. iv.* c. 22.)

a sad example how misfortune may be goaded into madness. His five children were surrounding him with piteous cries for bread; he veiled his face in silent anguish, and their little hands then drew his robe to attract his attention to their prayers.

At length, rising with all the calmness of despair, he bid them follow, directed his steps to the bridge of Hadrian, and threw himself headlong into the stream below. Day after day a famished crowd encompassed the palace of Bessas, beseeching that he would either unlock his granaries, or permit their departure from Rome, or that if neither alternative were allowed them, he would at least, by a speedy execution, save them from the lingering tortures they endured. His attendants [19] coolly replied, that to feed them was impossible, to dismiss them dangerous, and to kill them unlawful.

To the rich, however, the avarice of Bessas readily sold the permission of leaving the city, but many found their strength too much broken for the journey, and expired on the road, whilst the fierceness of the Gothic troops proved equally fatal to those who fell into their hands. Such is the gloomy picture which Procopius has drawn of this period. Yet he had not beheld it in person, and there are two circumstances which lead me to believe that the accounts he received of it may have been overcharged, from the silly proneness of mankind to pride themselves on past calamities. In the first place, we find [20] that at the conclusion of the siege many Roman nobles were still possessed of horses, whereas these would doubtless have been killed for food, if their owners had been urged by such utter famine.

Secondly, Procopius, after asserting that nearly all the besieged were at last constrained to subsist entirely on wild herbs, describes the wan and ghost-like aspect to which this spare diet had reduced them. Now it may be observed, that this wretched resource of hunger is attended with directly opposite effects, rendering the body bloated, with many of the symptoms of dropsy.[21] Some allowance should therefore be made in the narrative of the Greek historian, yet enough will remain to prove the deplorable condition to which at this time the ancient capital had fallen.

---

19. Procop. *Goth. lib. iii.* c. 17. The Latin version of Maltret ascribes this answer to Bessas himself, and has misled several modern writers.
20. Procop. *Goth. lib. iii.* c. 20.
21. See for instance De Thou's account of the siege of Paris in 1590, by Henry IV. (*Histoire*, vol. xi.) I find in Gregory of Tours the same result from a famine about one thousand years before, where the sufferers were likewise obliged to feed on herbs. The people, he says, *tumefacti deficebant* (*Hist. Franc, lib.* vol. c. 45.)

The last hope which the wretched inhabitants could entertain of succour or deliverance, was drawn from the well-known skill of Belisarius. We have left that general at Dyrrachium, vainly labouring to hasten the promised reinforcements from Constantinople. After the tardy junction of all the troops, and when their employment became matter for deliberation, it was proposed by John the Sanguinary to disembark on the opposite coast of Italy, and march straight to Rome; but several considerations restrained Belisarius from approving this adventurous design. His forces were still very far inferior to those of Totila, and could not, without the most desperate rashness, run the hazard of a battle. The growing distress of Rome required that not a moment should be lost in affording it relief, but a journey by land might be retarded by many unforeseen occurrences, and at all events would consume no less than forty days, whilst a favourable wind might waft the fleet in five. The general, therefore, thought it most prudent to proceed by sea, with the main part of his army, at the same time dispatching John with his best light cavalry, to scatter the handful of barbarians which garrisoned Apulia, and then rejoin him in the neighbourhood of Rome.

By this means the same extent of territory would be subdued, as if the whole army had traversed it; and, on the other hand, the squadron of John, free from all encumbrances, and protected by its very smallness, might both arrive more speedily at its destination, and more easily elude pursuit. Having left John with sufficient forces and full instructions for this enterprise, Belisarius sailed from Dyrrachium with the remainder of his fleet. It had not been his intention to touch on any part of the southern coast of Italy, but a storm constrained the pilots to enter the port of Otranto. This city was now again invested by some Gothic troops, who, on beholding the Roman ships, precipitately raised the siege, and fled towards the unwalled town of Brindisi. They had trembled at the approach of Belisarius, but when they learnt that his fleet had again put to sea, and was steering round the Cape of Leuca, they imagined all personal danger to be past. Their careless security proved advantageous to John the Sanguinary, who had crossed the Straits unperceived, and who was guided by the treachery of a captive to the camp of the barbarians, before they were apprised even of his landing. Being wholly unsuspicious of attack, they were ill prepared for resistance, and the Romans had no other toil than to slaughter the helpless, or pursue the fugitive soldiers.

From hence the Byzantine officer proceeded to Canusium or Canosa, within four miles of the field of Cannae,[22] where he found himself welcomed as a friend and deliverer. The fickle populace thinking as usual the present hardships the most intolerable, had forgot the late tyranny and oppression of their Roman rulers, and were now only alive to the disgrace that they, orthodox Catholics, should obey an Arian monarch. A great part of Apulia, and of the neighbouring provinces, seized this occasion for revolt, and John encountered no opposition whatever, till at Capua [23] he found a body of three hundred chosen soldiers, which Totila had sent with instructions to hover on the rear of the invaders, and not to close upon them until other forces should assail them in front. John was apprehensive of being surrounded and cut off, and, without attempting to reach the station of Belisarius, undertook the easy enterprise of overwhelming the Gothic bands in Lucania.

Belisarius, who, meanwhile, had reached Porto with his armament, and was impatiently awaiting the junction of his officer, loudly complained of the cowardice which had withheld the flower of the Roman Army from charging and dispersing three hundred barbarians. That John was really deficient in bravery, might be presumed from his proposal at Dyrrachium, since the same men commonly unite foolhardiness in council with fears in the field, and endeavour by the one to avert all suspicion of the other. But the practical courage of John had been proved in many hazardous encounters, and we may more justly ascribe his retreat at Capua to his preferring the profits and the independence of a separate command. Finding it useless to expect any longer the co-operation of his lieutenant, Belisarius applied himself singly to the difficult but necessary task of relieving Rome.

In the long and laborious preparations which Totila had made against attack, he had prudently considered the genius rather than the force of his antagonist He had availed himself of the changes in the channel of the Tiber, which by no means displays a regular and progressive augmentation as it advances towards the sea, but appears for

---

22. The distance of twenty-five *stadia* is assigned by Procopius. (*Goth. lib. iii.* c. 18.) It is singular that Mr. Keppel Craven, in the journey which he has so ably described, should have failed to see the two most interesting objects in his way, the field of Cannae and the only temple yet standing in Magna Graecia.

23. This celebrated city appears in the sixth century as only a small provincial town. In the time of Paul Warnefrid it might again deserve the name of *urbs opulentissima*. (*De Gest. Langobard. lib. ii.* c. 17.) The ancient Capua was consumed by fire a.d. 842, and the present city founded three miles from it on the banks of the Volturno. (Wesseling, *Itineraria*.)

example much less broad near the castle of St. Angelo than near the Ponte Molle. At a spot about thirteen miles below the city, where the two banks approach most nearly together, Totila joined them by massy beams in the manner of a bridge, flanked at each end by a solid wooden tower. The summit of these towers was lined with detachments of his bravest soldiers; at a certain distance in front a strong iron chain was drawn across the river, and other troops were stationed at the side of this additional defence. Such precautions seemed to render utterly impracticable the navigation of the Tiber, more especially against the stream; but as Belisarius could not venture a battle on shore, no other choice remained, and his enterprise against these formidable barriers was one of the boldest of that or indeed of any age.

By pretended deserters from his camp, who joined the Goths only to report their proceedings, he ascertained the precise position and admeasurements of the bulwarks they had raised. In consequence of this information, he fastened two of his largest boats compactly together, and constructed on their united surface a tower surpassing in height those of the hostile bridge, and containing an ample supply of sulphur, bitumen, and other similar combustibles. Two hundred boats were laden with provisions, and manned with chosen soldiers, who were protected by a covering of thick planks from the darts of the enemy, while a great number of small apertures enabled them to discharge their own.

At Porto itself Belisarius left only a single squadron, which he entrusted to Isaac, with the strictest injunctions to maintain his appointed station as the last and only fortress still possessed by the Romans on this coast, and not to be drawn from the ramparts by any motive whatever, not even should intelligence arrive that the general had fallen. The remaining troops were posted in strong and well-chosen positions on each bank of the Tiber, to protect the approach of the port and keep the forces of Totila at bay; and orders were at the same time dispatched to Bessas to second the attack of his countrymen by a vigorous and seasonable sally.

Belisarius in person undertook the command of this adventurous expedition. By dint of sails and oars the loaded vessels slowly but successfully ascended the adverse stream. With their missiles, which from the decking of the ships the enemy had no effectual means of returning, the Romans slew or scattered the outposts near the iron chain, forced this weighty barrier, and arrived close upon the Gothic bridge. The barbarians in this quarter made a brave and persevering resistance, and new reinforcements were pouring in from the neighbouring camp, when Belisarius directed his floating castle against them. The combustibles he had provided were thrown into the Gothic tower on the northern bank, its wooden materials assisted their effect, it almost instantly appeared in full blaze, and of the two hundred soldiers it contained, every one perished in the flames.

Appalled at this sudden and unexpected disaster, the barbarians fled, the bridge was abandoned to the exulting assailants, and no further obstacle seemed to intervene between them and the capital. At this moment of triumph the fruits of victory were snatched from Belisarius by the double disobedience of his officers. The opposite vices of youth and of age appeared to have conspired against him. Bessas had found in the famine of Rome such ample gratification for his avarice that he rejoiced in the continuance of the siege, and was unwilling to see its close until the last remains of wealth had been wrung from the chap, wretched inhabitants.

On the other hand, the martial spirit of Isaac was roused by the news of the success; he forgot his orders, he advanced with all his troops against a Gothic encampment, and, after a first advantage from surprise, was defeated and taken prisoner with his followers. Some fugitive horsemen announced this overthrow to Belisarius, who trusted too hastily their exaggerated statement, and, believing the ramparts of Porto to be now utterly defenceless, gave the signal for retreat. On his arrival he found that fear had, as usual, greatly magnified the evil, and that a more steady adherence to his first design might perhaps have saved the capital, in spite of the misconduct of his subalterns. The value of Porto to the Romans would furnish excuses to a panegyrist or a poet; but the historian will suspect that Belisarius was misled by an instant of dismay, and appeared for once deficient in firmness and decision. A dangerous and almost fatal fever was the result of his grief and disappointment; and his illness unfortunately prevented any further attempt for the deliverance of Rome.

At the time when Bessas had withheld the required assistance from the general, he had probably expected that a capitulation might always, at his pleasure, end the siege and secure his riches. By a just retribution, the treachery of some of his soldiers baffled this selfish policy. Engrossed by his thirst for gold, he had neglected the discipline of his garrison, the nightly rounds on the walls were discontinued, and four Isaurian sentinels availed themselves of the slumber of their comrades and the absence of their chiefs, to reach the hostile encampment unperceived. Their offer of opening a gate to the barbarians was received with suspicion or indifference; thrice they found it necessary to renew their proposal to Totila, and thrice the place was inspected by his officers, before he would consent to hazard the experiment. By such delay the rumour of their project spread amongst the Gothic army, and some captives taken by the Romans in a sally spoke of this conspiracy to Bessas, but the useful warning was despised. At length, in the night of December 17, a.d. 546, almost precisely ten years since Rome had first yielded to Belisarius, the treacherous Isaurians assisted four Gothic soldiers in scaling the walls. By their united labour the Asinarian gate was hewed down, and the troops of Totila marched into the city.

A prudent fear of ambuscade induced them to await in close and compact order the break of day; but the Byzantine garrison attempted no further resistance, and escaped on the opposite side. Some Gothic officers pressed Totila to intercept their retreat. "What event," replied the monarch, "can be more welcome than the flight of an enemy?" Many of the Patricians who were still provided with horses followed Bessas from Rome, and the remainder took refuge at St. Peter's shrine. The number of citizens must no doubt have been considerably thinned by the calamities of the siege, as well as by the many cases of voluntary exile it occasioned; but we should surely disregard the corrupted text of Procopius, which tells us that no more than fire hundred inhabitants remained. This error, attributable rather to the copyist than to the author, appears the more glaring, since we find the population of Rome, later in the same century, termed a countless multitude by another historian of authority.[24]

No sooner were the Goths in full and secure possession of the city, than their monarch hastened to offer thanksgiving at the church of St. Peter; but, during his devotions, twenty-six Byzantine soldiers, and sixty Roman citizens, were slain by his attendants in the porch. Totila was received by Pelagius, who, stretching forth the Gospels in his hand, besought the conqueror to spare him. "Now at length, Pelagius, you appear before me as a suppliant," said Totila, with a scornful smile.

"I am a suppliant," replied the archdeacon, "God has made us your subjects, and, as such, we expect your mercy and forbearance."

In compliance with his earnest entreaties, no further bloodshed was allowed, and the wives and daughters of the citizens were saved from the violence of the soldiers, who, on the other hand, obtained

---

24. *Inaestimabilis multitudo* (Paul Warnefrid, *lib. iii.* c. 23.)

an unbounded permission of pillage, as soon as the most precious effects had been reserved for the share of their sovereign. Large treasures were still found amassed in the patrician palaces, and the coffers of Bessas, filled by so much cruelty and rapine, now served to enrich his enemies. Through the spoliation of the Goths, many of the most illustrious senatorial families were driven to utter ruin, were compelled in the meanest garb to wander from house to house, imploring often unsuccessfully a morsel of bread; and their noble birth, or hereditary opulence, afforded them only an additional plea for pity. Amongst them might be observed Rusticiana, the daughter of Symmachus, and widow of Boethius,[25] whose income had been bountifully lavished on the poor, and who was now reduced to solicit the same charity which she had so often bestowed. Her death was loudly called for by the barbarians, who accused her of having overthrown the statues of the great Theodoric, but she was protected by the seasonable and generous interposition of Totila.

On the ensuing day he admonished his troops, in a public harangue, to strengthen and uphold, by moderation, the conquests which their valour had gained. Yet the king appeared strangely deficient in the virtue which he recommended, when, immediately afterwards, he convened the Roman Senate, and addressed that assembly, says Procopius, as an angry master might revile his slave. He extolled the paternal reign of Theodoric, descanted on the ingratitude with which the Roman nobles had requited it, and urged them to declare what benefits their treachery had purchased from Justinian, he said:

> Have not you been stripped of your rights and privileges,— have not rapacious accountants insulted you with forged and fraudulent demands,—have not oppressive taxes been claimed with equally unsparing rigour in peace and in war? To you I am not indebted even for the smallest spot of desert ground; but these men, (and here he pointed to the four Isaurian sentinels, and to Herodian, who stood beside him), these men have admitted me into Spoleto and Rome. You therefore shall in future be regarded as the vilest of my slaves, and they, the friends and allies of the Goths, shall enjoy the dignities and honours which at present you unworthily possess.

The senators, terrified and downcast, heard these upbraidings in

---

25. On Rusticiana see a note of Sigonius, (*Imp. Occident lib.* 19.) and Muratori, (*Annal. d'Ital.* vol. iii.)

silence, and did not venture to plead for themselves; but the eloquence of Pelagius was again exerted over the stern barbarian, and wrung from him, if not a pardon, at least a reprieve. The indefatigable archdeacon then set out, by desire of Totila, on an embassy to the Byzantine Court, having first pledged himself, by the most solemn oaths, to return as soon as possible, and to execute his. commission with good faith. He was the bearer of proposals of peace and alliance on the same terms as had formerly subsisted between Theodoric and Anastasius; and in case of refusal the Gothic monarch threatened to invade the empire through Illyria, after putting the whole senate to the sword, and razing the Western capital to the ground.

On the arrival of Pelagius at Constantinople, and his delivering the letter entrusted to his care, Justinian only replied that he had given Belisarius an uncontrolled direction of the war, and the power of concluding peace whenever it might appear advantageous to the public interest. To him, therefore, the emperor referred the question; but before Pelagius could convey this answer, the conditional menace of subverting Rome had nearly been accomplished.

Provoked by the success of John the Sanguinary in Southern Italy, Totila resolved to march against him, first wreaking a fearful vengeance on the city which had dared for so many months to withstand and detain his arms. Different parts of the wall, amounting altogether to one third of its circumference, had already been overthrown by his orders, and several private dwellings had been burned,[26] but now a fierce decree was issued that this birth-place of empire should be levelled to a sheep-walk. Accordingly the Goths were preparing to consume by fire, or by violence, the most precious edifices of antiquity, when Belisarius, having been apprised of their mischievous design, dispatched to his antagonist a letter which his secretary has preserved.

> The most mighty heroes and the wisest statesmen have always considered it their pride to adorn a city with new and stately buildings, while, on the other hand, to destroy those which already exist, has been reserved for the dull ferocity of savages, careless of the sentence which posterity will pass upon them. Of all the cities which the sun beholds in his course, none can vie with Rome in size, splendour, or renown. It has not been reared by the genius of one man, by the labour of a single age. The august assembly of the republican senate, and a long train

---

26. Marcellin. *Chron. ap. Sirmond. Op.* vol. ii.; and Procop. *Goth. lib. iii.* c. 22.

of munificent emperors have, by the progressive and accumulated toil of centuries, and by the most lavish expenditure of wealth, brought this capital to its present high and acknowledged pre-eminence.

Every foreign country has furnished architects for its construction, artists for its ornament, and the slow result of their joint exertions has bequeathed to us the noblest monument of ancient glory. A blow aimed at these venerable fabrics will resound equally through past and future ages. It will rob the illustrious dead of the trophies of their fame, it will rob unborn generations of the proud and cheering prospect which these trophies would afford them. Consider, also, that one of two events must needs occur. You will in this war either obtain a final victory over the imperial forces, or yourself be subdued. Should your cause prevail, you would, by the havoc which you meditate, overthrow not a hostile city but your own, while your present forbearance would preserve for you the first and fairest possession of your crown.

If, on the contrary, fortune should declare against you, your mercy to Rome will be rewarded by the mercy of the conqueror to you; but none could be expected from Justinian, after the desolation of his ancient capital. What benefit can, therefore, in any case accrue to you from so barbarous an outrage? All mankind have now their eyes turned towards you: your fame is in the balance, and will incline to one scale or to the other, according to your conduct on this decisive occasion; for such as are the deeds of princes, such will be their character in history.

After long reflection and repeated perusals of this letter, Totila yielded to its arguments, and dismissed the envoys of Belisarius with a promise of forbearance, which from this time forwards he faithfully observed.

The next military operation of Totila was to station several squadrons of his army at Mount Algidus, about eighteen miles to the southward of the capital. Around this central camp, he placed outposts at considerable distances, in order to prevent any sally from his enemies at Porto, and keep them as it were imprisoned within their walls. His remaining forces then marched, under his personal command, to attack the Byzantine troops and Italian insurgents in the southern provinces; and nearly all the citizens of Rome, with their wives and children, were led captive in his train. The lower classes of the Romans were dispersed through the plains of Campania, and those of senatorial rank guarded in the town's, whence they were directed to send in secret some of their domestics through Lucania and Calabria, enjoining their vassals to quit the Byzantine standards, and again betake themselves, as usual, to the occupations of husbandry.

This order was obeyed by many of the Calabrian peasantry; but their co-operation had already afforded great advantages to John the Sanguinary. He had become master of Taranto; and, finding that city of considerable extent and ill provided with bulwarks, he was fearful of defending, yet unwilling to abandon, so important a position. He therefore judiciously insulated by a deep trench, and lined with ramparts, a narrow neck of land which projects into the bay, and which by this means answered every purpose of a citadel.[27] At the time when Totila marched against him, the Roman officer was far northward in Apulia, but did not await the enemy's approach, and precipitately fled to Otranto.

Seeing no enemies to encounter in the field, Totila fixed his head-quarters upon Gargano, a mountainous promontory of the Adriatic, chiefly remarkable in modern times for the city founded by Manfred the usurper, and the miracles attributed to Michael the archangel.[28] From this station the Gothic monarch sent detachments, which overrun a great extent of open country, and reduced the fortress of Acherontis, now called Acerenza, the strongest in Lucania. To counterbalance this success, he here received intelligence that Spoleto had been surprised by the Romans. It was lost as it had been won, through treachery.

A Byzantine officer, one of the followers of Bessas, had, by permission of Belisarius, assumed the part of a deserter, in hopes of recovering his captive family, and afterwards striking some sudden blow in favour of his countrymen. Martian (such was his name) had hastened to Rome, had been favourably received by Totila, and been appointed to a military command in the garrison of Spoleto. The wall of that city had been razed after its capture by the Goths, but they had converted a neighbouring amphitheatre into a strong hold, by closing the

---

27. See a plan of the internal harbour in Swinburne's *Travels*, vol. ii. ed. 1790.
28. For the foundation of Manfredonia, at the foot of Gargano, see Muratori (*Annal. d'Ital.* vol. vii.) The first alleged apparition of St. Michael was towards the end of the fifth century. (Baronius *Annal. Eccles. a.d.* 493. No. 42.) In the middle ages it was a place of frequent pilgrimages, and is so still. (Craven's *Tour*.)

lower arches and defending the higher as ramparts.[29] A large share of the troops at Spoleto consisted of Roman deserters, who were urged by the promises and arguments of Martian to return to their former standards after redeeming their treachery by some signal service. This active agent also entered into correspondence with the Byzantine garrison of Perugia; and, by the joint attack of repentant deserters and advancing auxiliaries, easily overpowered the Gothic forces, put the greater number to the sword, and led captive the survivors to the camp of Belisarius.

Elated with the capture of Rome and the flight of John the Sanguinary, and justly considering the reduction of Otranto as a secondary object, Totila resolved to turn his arms against Ravenna, the centre and the citadel of the Byzantine force in Italy. He had already begun his march along the Adriatic coast, when a splendid exploit of Belisarius recalled him with precipitation to the banks of the Tiber. So bold and adventurous does this scheme appear in its conception, so unlikely seems the success with which it was attended, that were it not upheld by the most unquestionable testimony, we might be inclined to rank it with the fabulous achievements of King Agramant or Amadis of Gaul. It was, as Procopius tells us, declared by everyone at first to be impracticable and insane; nor does history anywhere display a like attempt to this of Belisarius, excepting his own former enterprise at Pesaro, which he now repeated on a larger scale and more illustrious scene. He meditated to throw himself into Rome with the few thousand men at his disposal, to repair the demolished ramparts as much as a few days might allow, and to stand the desperate siege which Totila would doubtless undertake.

In order to ascertain how far this project might be feasible, and to view in person the state of the Eternal city, Belisarius sallied forth with a chosen squadron of one thousand soldiers. The Gothic officers at Algidus, having been apprised through treachery of this intended excursion, did not fail to station several bodies of troops in ambush on the road, who suddenly assailed the inferior force of Belisarius. The barbarians fought with spirit, but the Romans were animated by the presence and example of their leader, and, after a long and obstinate engagement, repelled the enemy with great slaughter; nor were they any further molested in returning to Porto. So decisive, indeed, was

---

29. This is the earliest example of a practice which became very common in the middle ages. Thus, for instance, the Coliseum at Rome was fortified by the Frangipani, &c. See Mr. Hobhouse's *Historical Illustrations*, sec. ed.

this skirmish, that the barbarian army appears from this time to have confined itself within its camp of Algidus, and offered no opposition to the Roman general, when shortly afterwards he began to execute his enterprise. He marched to Rome with the greater part of his forces, (February, *a.d.* 547), leaving only one small squadron as the garrison of Porto. Since the retreat of Totila, the capital had for forty days remained desolate and lonely, nearly all the inhabitants had forsaken it, and beasts of prey were seen to prowl round the tenantless dwellings.

This silent and solitary scene was animated by the arrival of Belisarius, and by the unwearied activity with which he laboured to fortify and maintain his station. The Sicilian corn and other supplies, which he had amassed at Porto for the relief of Bessas, were now conveyed, without hindrance, by numerous vessels on the Tiber, and served to replenish the public granaries and magazines. Those citizens who had fled to the neighbouring villages were recalled by the love of their birthplace, and the villagers themselves were attracted to Rome by a liberal distribution of food. It was impossible, in so short an interval, to attempt a complete repair of the demolished portions of the walls; no material from the quarry was provided for construction, no mortar for cement; but the united and incessant toil of the whole garrison raised in the breaches a rude pile of broken fragments and irregular stones, resembling less a rampart than a ruin.

Even in the present age the practised eye of the antiquarian discerns, or fancies it discerns, in several places of the Roman walls, the hasty repairs of Belisarius and the fragments of ancient edifices inserted in the structure.[30] To protect these shapeless bulwarks, the ditch which Belisarius had deepened in the former siege was cleared from fallen rubbish, and bristled on every side with pointed stakes. From the absence of workmen, the general found himself unable to restore the city gates, which Totila had torn away; but, employing the expedient by which the Spartans had supplied their want of walls, he carefully selected some of his most undaunted soldiers to line the vacant space. And thus, by a singular revolution of the wheel of fortune, Belisarius, after the lapse of ten years and so many unavailing victories, was again reduced to his former situation, enclosed in Rome with far inferior forces, and awaiting the aggression of a Gothic king.

No more than twenty-five days were allowed the general for these various and necessary preparations. On the twenty-sixth, Totila, who at the first intelligence of the audacious project of his enemy had has-

---

30. Nardini, *lib. i.* c 8. Consult, also, the *Memoir of Flaminius Vacca*, No. 13

tened by forced marches from the Adriatic, appeared in sight of Rome, and encamped on the banks of the Tiber. Enraged at the sudden loss of a city so lately and so laboriously subdued, he did not delay the onset beyond the morning after his arrival; and during the few hours which he allotted for repose, his army was augmented by the Goths from Algidus. At the earliest dawn of day, the barbarians advanced to the charge, and the steadfast resistance of the garrison redoubled the animosity of their attack.

Goaded by a sense of shame and disappointment, they displayed the most determined valour; while, on the other hand, the spirit of the Romans was upheld by the very urgency of the dangers around them. They fought, says Procopius, with far greater resolution than could have been expected from them; and this courageous conduct of troops whom, on so many other occasions, we have seen terrified fugitives or unwarlike mutineers, may show how great is the ascendant which the pervading mind of a hero can exert. Their station on the ramparts enabled them to pour down a thick shower of missiles, which the Goths could not as effectually return, and a great slaughter of the latter accordingly ensued.

Yet they did not desist from their assault till night, when the prolonged engagement had rendered both armies alike faint and breathless with fatigue. Returning to their former encampment, the Goths spent the hours of darkness in dressing their wounds and refreshing themselves with food and sleep, but their unwearied antagonist continued watchful against nocturnal surprise, and provident for the next encounter. By his care sentinels were posted on the walls, the guard of the gates was entrusted in rotation to detachments from the bravest of his soldiers, whilst others rendered each entrance less accessible in future, by fixing a great number of *tribuli* or fourfold iron spikes before it.[31] Next day the Gothic monarch led his forces to a second assault; they were again beaten back; and Belisarius seized the moment when they appeared with their ranks disordered and their strength impaired, to charge them in a vigorous sally. A great number of the Goths were put to the sword, the remainder fled in confusion, and the hope of Totila to enclose and cut off the Roman troops in their pursuit was baffled by the prudence of Belisarius, in supporting them with fresh reinforcements and securing their return.

The result of this double disaster compelled Totila to remain inac-

---

31. For the *Tribuli,* see Procopius, Goth. lib. iii. c. 24. and a note of Chilmead *ad Malalam,* vol. *ii.*

tive for a considerable time; he had lost his bravest warriors, and the rest were disabled with wounds or dispirited by failure, while their shattered armour and broken weapons bore testimony to the fierceness of the combat. After an interval of many days, the barbarians, recruited by repose, once more issued from their camp to renew their enterprise; but the result of this attempt proved still more unfavourable to them than either of the former. Even before they reached the ramparts, the troops of Belisarius came forward to meet them in the field, and an obstinate engagement immediately began.

In the course of the conflict, the officer bearing the royal standard of Totila fell from his horse pierced by a mortal wound; it was with difficulty that the Goths could rescue this precious trophy; and to leave the enemy no cause for exultation, they hastily severed the left arm of the corpse, and secured a massy bracelet of gold with which it was adorned. Later in the day the Goths were completely routed, and, giving up all hope of storming the city, they commenced their retreat upon Tivoli. Amidst the crowd and confusion of their flight, we are assured that a greater number perished in the river than had fallen in the field.[32]

To prevent pursuit, and intercept the communication of the Romans, they broke down all the adjacent bridges on the Tiber, except the Milvian, which was protected by its neighbourhood to Rome.[33] Hence it appears that their encampment must have been upon the Tuscan bank, as otherwise the river would not have interposed between them and their destination. Their departure enabled Belisarius to complete and improve his measures for defence; new gates were constructed and affixed, and the keys of Rome were for the second time sent in triumph to Justinian.

Meanwhile the Goths entrenched themselves upon the rugged heights of Tivoli, and in their consternation began rebuilding the walls of that city which they themselves had recently demolished. The late reverses had been most injurious to Totila, not merely from the loss they occasioned, but from the consequent decline of his influence and popularity. The rapid succession of regicides and usurpers on the Gothic throne had abated the respect of the people for prerogative, and made the power of the sovereign dependent chiefly on the pros-

---

32. Jornandes, *De Regn. Success.*
33. These bridges were afterwards repaired by Narses, and the inscriptions which he placed on the Salarian have been found in modern times. They are transcribed by Giphanius (*Comment.*

perity and splendour of his reign.[34]

While Totila had been victorious, the Goths, enriched by pillage and elated with success, had loudly celebrated his genius and military skill, but now with equal eagerness exclaimed against his policy as short-sighted and unreasonable. He ought either, they said, to have levelled Rome to the ground, according to his original purpose, or taken effectual means to secure its possession to himself. In a long and elaborate harangue, the king endeavoured to regain their esteem and to dissipate the awe and misgivings which the late exploit of Belisarius had struck into their minds.[35] Being well aware that discontent is often caused and always increased by inactivity, he did not allow his soldiers to linger long at Tivoli, but led them to the siege of Perugia, as to an useful and easy undertaking.

Scarcely, however, had the city been invested, before Totila received intelligence of another mischance, less hurtful to his interests than humiliating to his pride. His hasty march against Belisarius from southern Italy, and the defenceless state of that country, had suggested to John the Sanguinary a project to free the Roman senators and their families from the thraldom to which the Gothic monarch had consigned them. Setting off, accordingly, with a body of chosen horsemen, he proceeded towards Campania with the utmost secrecy and speed. On the other hand, Totila, apprehensive of some such scheme, had, before leaving Tivoli, detached a share of his cavalry to secure his captives against rescue. It so chanced that the vanguard of this squadron entered Capua precisely at the same time with the troops of John the Sanguinary; a conflict ensued; the barbarians were worsted, and, tumultuously retreating upon their comrades, involved them in their flight.

Thus the field was left open to the Byzantine officer. He found in the Campanian cities the wives of nearly all the Roman senators, but a smaller number of their husbands, since many of the latter had provided for their personal safety by following Bessas from the capital, leaving their families at the mercy of the Goths. These illustrious exiles were respectfully dismissed by John, to await, in the tranquil and luxurious province of Sicily, the final event of the war. In the mean time the Gothic cavalry, continuing their retreat after the skirmish of Capua, appeared in the presence of their king before Perugia, and,

---

34. (Greg. *Turon. lib. iii.* c. 30.) This remark is as true of the Ostrogoths as of their brethren in Spain.
35. Speech of Totila (or Procopius) (Procop. *Goth. lib. iii.* c. 25)

hoping to palliate their own cowardly behaviour, brought him false and overcharged accounts of the numbers of the enemy.

Their partial statements would probably have been suspected and disbelieved by the calmer judgment of this wary monarch; but, inflamed with anger at the disappointment of his scheme and the release of his prisoners, he was not unwilling to regard the forces of John as considerable, in order to justify to himself and to his army his wish of indulging his resentment by a personal expedition against them. With a body of ten thousand men, the best part of his troops, he marched into southern Italy, and, on approaching the station of his enemy, quitted the level road and advanced through a mountainous and almost impassable track; thus eluding the observation of those outposts which, as he rightly conjectured, had been placed by John the Sanguinary to provide against surprise.

By such means the Roman squadron, of far inferior strength, was surrounded one evening by the troops of Totila, before it had received the slightest intelligence of their progress.[36] Had the king deferred his attack till next day, every Byzantine soldier, at least according to the opinion of Procopius, would have been taken as in a snare; but his headlong animosity prompted him to give the signal for an immediate onset. The Byzantine troops were overthrown and scattered at the first charge, but the darkness favoured their flight; and John himself, with the greater part of his followers, soon found himself secure within the ramparts of Otranto.

The victories of Belisarius at Rome seemed to afford the most favourable prospect of closing this war, like his first Italian campaigns, by the thorough subjection of the Goths and the captivity of their sovereign. But his forces, originally small, had gradually melted away and diminished by success; and after providing for the necessary garrisons of Rome, Civita Vecchia, and Porto, he found that the troops remaining for active service in the field amounted to no more than two hundred infantry and seven hundred horsemen. With such a handful of soldiers, it was impossible for the most practised skill and undaunted courage to achieve, or even to attempt, any decisive undertaking. He received from Constantinople neither men for the reinforcement nor money for the pay of his troops; and as the least touch is galling to a wound, so even the smallest taxes on the impoverished Italians proved

---

36. This is the account of Procopius, but the continuator of Count Marcellinus ascribes the surprise to the treachery of some Bulgarian soldiers. (*Chron. ap. Sirmond, Op.* vo. ii.)

both unproductive and hateful.

In urgent and repeated letters, Belisarius besought the emperor to improve this advantageous opportunity, and, by a short but vigorous effort, to spare himself a long train of languid and fruitless hostilities. But it appeared more easy to overcome the valour of Totila than the indolence and procrastination of Justinian. For a long time he remained deaf to the entreaties of his general, and at length dispatched, in different bands, a small and insufficient force, of which the greater part lingered in Epirus; and which, had it even been united, would not have mustered fifteen hundred men.[37]

Taranto was fixed upon as the place of general meeting; John the Sanguinary moved thither with his forces, and orders were sent by the emperor to Belisarius to assume the command of this army, and to augment it by all the troops at his disposal. Belisarius accordingly made his preparations for departure, and having appointed Conon, the late governor of Naples, as chief of above three thousand men, whom he left for the garrison of Rome, bid farewell to that city for ever. He embarked at Porto, and passed through the Straights of Messina with a favourable breeze, but was assailed by a sudden tempest on the eastern coast of Calabria. So violent and lasting was the storm, that he found it necessary to steer into the port of Crotona, now Cotrone, the only harbour between Taranto and the Straights of Sicily[38] and here he disembarked his forces, until calmer weather should allow the prosecution of his voyage. He found at Cotrone neither food to maintain, nor walls to defend, his followers; the Gothic Army was not far distant; and while these circumstances endangered his stay, an adverse wind continued to oppose his departure.

But his genius, fertile in resources, soon devised an expedient to obtain, at the same time, subsistence and security. A rugged chain of mountains forms a natural barrier to the district of Cotrone, interrupted only by two steep and narrow defiles; of which the one bore the name of Labula, and the other was known by the popular byword of Bloody Rock, either from an unusual colour in the surrounding precipices, or from some traditional tale of slaughter. Retaining only his two hundred foot-soldiers with him, the general dismissed his cavalry to guard these ravines, whose neighbourhood abounded in forage and provisions, and whose watchful maintenance would render Cotrone altogether inaccessible. So advantageous, indeed, did this po-

---

37. Observe the remark of Muratori on Justinian's conduct. (*Annal. d'Ital.* vol. iii.)
38. Keppel Craven's *Tour*.

sition appear to Belisarius, that he formed a project to transfer the headquarters from Taranto, and, instead of proceeding on his voyage, summon his officers to join him.

This scheme was baffled by an unforeseen disaster, (a.d. 548). The Roman horsemen, whom the presence and authority of their general had kept in excellent discipline, relaxed from their duty as soon as his piercing eye was no longer fixed upon them: they forsook their allotted post, they listlessly strolled through the adjacent fields, and did not even place outposts and sentinels to apprise them of approaching danger. Their careless security proved auspicious to the designs of Totila, who marched against them at the head of three thousand chosen cavalry, and fell upon them when least prepared for resistance. The generous self-devotion of Phazas, an Iberian confederate, through the sacrifice of himself and of his gallant followers, afforded the means of escape to some of his companions; but the flower of the Roman army was put to the sword on this occasion, and a few scared fugitives, closely pressed by the barbarians, brought the first tidings of their defeat to Belisarius.

No time was to be lost, or the captivity of the general and of the surviving soldiers might have completed and adorned the triumph of the enemy. Belisarius gave orders for instant embarkation; the Roman ships set sail, and, committing themselves to the same gale which had withheld their progress towards Taranto, were wafted by its violence in one day to Messina, a distance of one hundred miles.

Immediately after his victory, the Gothic monarch proceeded to invest Ruscianum or Rossano, a fortress important from its position in the centre of the Tarentine gulph, and from the presence of many Italian nobles who had chosen it as their surest place of refuge. On his part, the Roman general availed himself of the first fair wind to undertake another voyage with the scanty remnant of his army, and two thousand fresh troops received in Sicily. Having arrived at Otranto without further accident, he from thence dispatched Antonina to Constantinople, to exert her influence with the empress in obtaining some succours, and to represent his utter inability of acting without them. But before Antonina could complete her journey, Theodora had already fallen a victim to a loathsome and incurable disease;[39] and her death, (June, a.d. 548), at this juncture proved, perhaps, as unfortunate for Belisarius as her life had been before.

As soon as the landing of the general was known, John the San-

---

39. Theodora Augusta Chalced. (Victor Tunnunensis ed. Canis. vol. i.)

guinary and the other officers at Taranto hastened to range themselves beneath his banner; and a fleet and army were thus collected, which, however inadequate to the conquest of Italy, appeared sufficient to attempt the relief of Rossano. This city was valiantly defended by three hundred Illyrian confederates, who had been left as a garrison by John, and whom Belisarius had reinforced from Cotrone with one hundred additional soldiers; but the want of provisions now began to be severely felt amongst them. Belisarius sailed from Otranto with all the ships in his power; and they were steering towards Rossano, when they became scattered by a fearful hurricane, the more dangerous from the want of harbours on this coast.

At length the fleet was reunited in the bay of Cotrone, and led by Belisarius within sight of the invested city. But on his approach he beheld the shore lined with the troops of the barbarians, in close and embattled order; successive ranks of lancers and bowmen were ready to overwhelm their enemy on landing with a shower of darts, and their ardour was directed by the skill of Totila himself. With deep regret Belisarius found himself constrained to desist from his hopeless enterprise, and once again return to Cotrone, where he discussed with his officers in council by what means his few and disheartened soldiers might still become available in this unequal contest.[40] After due deliberation, it was unanimously declared most advantageous that Belisarius should proceed once more to Rome, in order, at all events, to defend that important station to the last, and sustain the siege which Totila doubtless intended to renew; while John the Sanguinary and another officer should assume the command of two light squadrons of cavalry in the southern provinces, and endeavour, by harassing the rear of Totila, to draw him from the investment of Rossano. To such slender resources and miserable shifts had the want of reinforcements from Constantinople reduced the former conquerors of Italy!

From the dark and cheerless prospect around him, the eyes of Belisarius turned with eager impatience to the negotiations of Antonina at Constantinople. His first wish was to receive such supplies as might enable him to serve the state with effect, and to maintain his ancient reputation; his second was, to be recalled from his command if he was designed to continue a passive spectator of barbarian conquests, without the power to dispute or even to delay them. During this interval of suspense, his active spirit appears to have employed itself in render-

---

40. All these reverses are ascribed by Cardinal Baronius to the former deposition of the Pope. *Annal. Eccles. a.d.* 549. No. 3.

ing Cotrone an useful military station by the building of ramparts.[41] It was found impossible to draw from the emperor the least exertion in support of his general: he was at that time engrossed by religious quarrels, determining some of the most subtle refinements of the schoolmen, and actively persecuting heretics. From this pious occupation no entreaties, no arguments could rouse him; and their voice was almost drowned amidst the din of conflicting theologians. Antonina, therefore, applied herself to obtain the recall of her husband; and this favour, at least, was granted to her prayers.

By this measure the defence of Italy was, in fact, tacitly abandoned; and I cannot but pause for a moment, to reflect on all the misery and bloodshed produced by the fickle temper of Justinian. The fairest regions of the world would not have been exposed, in this age, to constant and unavailing desolation, had either timidity withheld the emperor from war, or had he been animated with constancy and courage in its progress. As a pretext for the departure of his general from Italy, Justinian appears to have alleged the warfare of the Persians on the Lazic frontier; but it may be doubted whether he really entertained the least intention of dispatching Belisarius to that languid and desultory contest. With feelings such as those which Hannibal must have experienced on embarking from Italy, Belisarius now took an everlasting farewell of that country which he had first beheld twelve years before, in the strength of his age and the meridian of his glory, which had been the scene of his greatest but least permanent exploits, and which, at his departure, had nearly reverted to the dominion under which he found it.

Like the Carthaginian hero, his victories had been due to his own genius and exertions; while exterior circumstances, over which he possessed no control, were the causes that had snatched away the prize of the combat from his hands. Yet the five last campaigns of Belisarius lowered his military fame in the eyes of his contemporaries. His enemies (and merit always makes many), overlooking the scantiness of the force at his disposal, did not fail to point out that he never once had offered battle nor forced his way inland, but had wandered like a runaway from harbour to harbour, and from fortress to fortress.[42]

---

41. This construction by Belisarius is no where expressly mentioned; but Cotrone was unwalled at his firs arrival, and yet I find it afterwards sustaining a siege. Compare Procop. *Goth. lib. iii.* c. 28. *lib. iv.* c. 26. The present fortifications of Cotrone date no higher than Charles the Fifth (Swinburne's *Travels*, vol. ii. ed. 1790.)

42. Compare Procop. *Goth. lib. iii.* c. 35, and *Hist. Arcan.* c 5.

Amidst their undeserved upbraidings and presumptuous ignorance, Belisarius doubtless looked forward with cheering confidence to the judgment of posterity, and posterity has answered his appeal.[43]

After the second departure of Belisarius from Italy, the connexion of his biographer with that country is also at an end; yet having already traced the war from its first commencement, I shall briefly pursue its fate till the final extinction of the Goths. The recall of Belisarius hastened and completed the ruin of the imperial cause in Italy. Rossano and Perugia, which had long been objects of ambition to the barbarian monarch, surrendered without further resistance, and no obstacle appeared to withhold him from renewing the siege of Rome. That city was now invested by Totila, for the third time, but with feelings very different from those which he had formerly displayed. Having asked a princess of France in marriage, he was stung by the contemptuous answer, that Italy could not justly be considered as the kingdom of him who had shown himself desirous of destroying, and unable to maintain, its capital.

Totila, therefore, resolved in future not merely to observe the forbearance which Belisarius had enjoined, but to follow the footsteps of the great Theodoric, and apply himself to repeople and protect the Eternal city whenever it should again have yielded to his arms. It has already been mentioned, that the garrison left at Rome by Belisarius amounted to three thousand men. Soon after he had sailed from the Tiber, these soldiers, in a mutiny, had murdered their governor Conon, and forthwith dispatched some priests to the Byzantine court, not merely to obtain their pardon, but to claim their long arrears of pay. In case either demand should be refused, they threatened instantly to surrender their station, and enlist in the troops of Totila; nor did the emperor find it possible to withstand so persuasive an argument. Their offence was forgiven, some hopes of speedy payment were held out to them, and these concessions induced them to submit with implicit obedience to Diogenes, whom Belisarius had named the second in command.

This officer belonged to the personal guard of the general, and had served with credit and distinction in the first Italian war, and on this occasion, his conduct equally deserves the praise of prudence and of

---

43. "In these campaigns," says Gibbon, "he appears a more consummate master of the art of war than in the season of his prosperity, when he presented two captive kings before the throne of Justinian," (vol. vii.) See also the opinion of Le Beau, Muratori, &c.

valour. The reduction of Porto by the barbarians, and the consequent loss of maritime convoys, were supplied by his provident care in having sown an ample harvest within the Roman walls; and this fact should be precious to the antiquary, as denoting that large tracts of desolate and open ground then existed in the city. Several assaults of the Gothic army were repulsed; and Rome might have prolonged its defence, however uselessly, for a considerable time, had not some Isaurian soldiers unfortunately recollected with how much liberality the former treachery of their comrades was rewarded. At their instigation, Totila, on an appointed night, embarked some Gothic trumpeters in two boats on the Tiber, with orders to approach as closely as possible to the Roman walls, and draw the attention of the garrison by a loud flourish of their instruments. While the soldiers appointed to watch on the ramparts rushed to the quarter where they heard the sound, and where they expected an attack, the gate of St Paul was opened to the army of Totila by the perfidious Isaurians.

Surprised and dismayed, the Byzantine troops fled towards Civita Vecchia, the only fortress which they still retained in the neighbouring country; but Totila, having foreseen that their retreat would take place in this direction, had stationed an ambush on the road. The greater part of the garrison fell in the skirmish which ensued; and Diogenes, disabled by a wound, could hardly escape with a handful of survivors. Four hundred other soldiers sought sanctuary in churches, where they were protected by the compassion or the piety of Totila; and an equal number headed by Paul the Cilician, a veteran officer of Belisarius, maintained the tomb of Hadrian. This massy pile had, as we have seen, already served as a tower and bulwark to the outward wall; but this is the earliest of the many instances when it answered the purpose of a citadel, and continued to hold out after the city around it was subdued.[44] It had been designed for this object by Totila; and at the time that he demolished a large share of the city wall, he had on the contrary built one along the side where this monument was unprotected by the outer ramparts, so as to render it defensible in every quarter.

As, however, the Goths never made the slightest resistance in this place when the city was entered by the Romans, it seems probable that the structure had merely been commenced, and that it was afterwards completed by the care of Belisarius. A project whence the inventor had never drawn any advantage or support was now turned against himself. An assault of the victorious Goths was repulsed by Paul of

---

44. Compare *Goth. lib. iii.* c. 36. *lib. iv.* c. 33,

Cilicia; but the want of provisions hindered his troops from sustaining a long blockade, and their horror of horseflesh urged them to attempt a headlong and almost hopeless sally. Dreading the disastrous effects of their despair, Totila proposed to them either to return to Constantinople, forfeiting the possession of their steeds and weapons, or to retain it by enlisting in his service; they accepted the first alternative; but a shame of proceeding homewards unarmed and despoiled, and the tempting offer of regular payments, afterwards determined the greater number for the second. In his treatment of the Roman citizens on this occasion, Totila displayed great clemency and moderation; the few senators still confined in their Campanian prison were reinstated in their former homes, and his conduct towards the whole people has been favourably compared to that of a father with his children.[45]

The private buildings which his late animosity had levelled to the ground were rapidly restored at his command, and magazines of provisions were appointed for the use of the returning population. The monarch himself presided at the celebration of equestrian games in the amphitheatre, for which the Romans still retained their hereditary fondness; but all these employments could hardly for a moment distract Totila from the prosecution of the war. Above four hundred vessels were collected to transport his troops to Sicily; and while some Gothic detachments entered Taranto and Rimini, the king, at the head of his principal forces, was reducing Reggio. From thence he passed over into Sicily, where the Roman garrisons of Syracuse, Messina, and Palermo appear alone to have withstood his arms; and he wreaked his long-deferred resentment upon the islanders, by pillage of the lesser cities and devastation of the open country.

Such success emboldened him to undertake more distant enterprises. A small squadron subdued, with great ease, the islands of Corsica and Sardinia, and a fleet of three hundred sail conveyed a barbarian army to lay waste the opposite shores of the Adriatic. Bat the Goths were unskilled in maritime warfare, and the growing strength of their navy was checked and broken by a defeat near the Bay of Ancona, when no more than eleven galleys out of forty-seven effected their escape.

During these transactions, which occupied a space of four years, (*a.d* 548-552), Justinian viewed at first the loss of Italy without concern. His zeal against; the Arians was, however, artfully inflamed by Pope Vigilius, and he consented to renew the Gothic war, yet, as formerly,

---

45. *Hist. Miscell. ap. Murat. Script. Italic*, vol. i. & Anastasius, *De Vit. Pontif.* c. 60.

he provided no sufficient forces; and his rapid revocation of generals clearly marks his feeble and vacillating judgment. After selecting his nephew Germanus, he suddenly changed in favour of Liberius, a civilian unfitted for so important a command by the infirmities of age and want of experience in the field.[46] No sooner had the new general sailed for Sicily, than he was supplanted by Artaban, who in his turn yielded to Germanus, appointed for the second time. Great expectations were entertained of the latter, his former victories over the Sclavonian invaders and rebels in Africa were remembered, his flight from Antioch was forgotten—(such is the favour shown to princes), and his marriage with Matasontha gave him friends and partisans amongst the Goths themselves.

But all these hopes were disappointed by his early death; and his son Justinian, who, with John the Sanguinary, succeeded him as joint commanders, were soon afterwards removed. The emperor now cast his eyes upon Narses, whose ambition for military honours had not cooled during twelve years of inactivity or of diplomatic employment, but whose judgment was not dazzled by the tempting proposal. The late example of Belisarius clearly showed the inefficiency of the greatest personal exertions, when unsupported by sufficient forces; and Narses resolutely declined the direction of the war, unless he received such supplies, both of men and money, as might enable him to conduct it with advantage to his country and glory to himself. This favour, which the hero had solicited in vain, was granted to the courtier. The public treasury was placed at his disposal; large sums were laid aside to tempt the fidelity of deserters from the Gothic standards; and while the payment of arrears gratified the ancient soldiers, the liberality of Narses attracted new. Alboin, King of the Lombards, was induced by great presents to execute a former treaty with the empire; and he dispatched, as auxiliaries, two thousand five hundred of his bravest soldiers,[47] besides more than three thousand of less note.

A squadron of Persian refugees was collected, levies were made

---

46. Liberius was extremely old, (Procop. Goth. lib. iii. cap. 39.) Yet Gibbon complains of his youth, and Cousin(*ad Goth. lib. iv.* c. 24,) confounds him with the Pope of that name, who died two centuries before.

47. This number is stated by Gibbon at two thousand two hundred (vol. vii.) He has blindly followed the translation of Maltret; not the original Greek (*Goth. lib. iv.* c. 36.) In like manner, he draws volunteers from Germany, on the authority of Cousin, who in one place (*ad Goth. lib. iii* c. 39) has mistaken Germanus for Germania. Yet, only a few pages further, we find Gibbon loudly condemning the "French and Latin readers of Procopius."

in Thrace and Illyria, and the Roman standards were joined by three thousand Herulian horsemen, to whom Narses had peculiarly endeared himself by his former largesses in Italy. The total number of the troops assembled is not recorded, but cannot be estimated at less than thirty thousand men;[48] and while the preceding Byzantine armies in this war, from their extreme inferiority of numbers, had on no occasion been able to encounter Totila in the open country, and accept the battle which he constantly was offering, we find that the force of Narses greatly exceeded that which his antagonist could muster.[49] Thus the advantage of numbers was suddenly retorted on the Goths.

When acting under Belisarius in the earlier Italian campaigns, we have seen Narses in the most disadvantageous colours, careless of the public interest, struggling against legitimate authority, and always ready to hinder the prosecution of the war through private jealousies and cabals. But by an unusual transition, the turbulent subaltern had become a skilful, judicious, and discerning general, and ever since he held the supreme command had diligently recommended and enforced the duties of subordination. As soon as his arrangements were completed, he led his troops to Salona, and from thence to the head of the Adriatic Gulf. In order to avoid the Franks, who, during the distracted state of Italy, had usurped several of its northern districts, Narses marched along the morasses and lagoons of the Venetian shore, reached Ravenna without hindrance, and allowed nine days for the refreshment of his soldiers.

In his further progress, some molestation was experienced from the garrison of Rimini, which had cut through the stately marble bridge constructed by Augustus, and still remaining to attest his munificence. But Narses effected a passage higher up the stream, and, avoiding the fortress of Petra Pertusa, diverged to the mountains on his right, and rejoined the Flaminian road a few miles below that dangerous defile. Confiding in his superior force, and doubtful how long he might be able to control and unite the jarring elements of which it was composed, Narses postponed the siege of cities, and was anxious to avail himself of his advantages in a pitched and decisive battle.

---

48. I derive this computation from the numbers at the Battle of Tagina, when, however, the army had been reinforced by a detachment from the garrison of Ravenna. On that day, each of the wings amounted to eight thousand; there was a squadron, at the left wing, of fifteen hundred; and the Lombards and Heruli, in the centre, made eight thousand five hundred more. The Persians, the Huns, and other confederates, are mentioned, but not computed.

49. See, especially, *Goth. lib. iv. c.* 50.

On the other hand, the martial and impetuous spirit of Totila rendered him no less impatient for a prompt conclusion of the war; and having mustered all his troops at Rome, he led them by hasty marches against the enemy, (June, a.d. 552). The two armies came in presence in the field of Tagina, near the modern town of Gualdo, a level space surrounded on almost every side by the rugged heights of the Appennine. This spot had already been rendered famous by a defeat of the Gauls, and seemed to present an inauspicious augury to the barbarians.[50] Totila was not dismayed by the formidable aspect of the hostile army, and haughtily dismissed the envoys of Narses, who represented the folly of attempting to contend with such overwhelming numbers, and urged him to anticipate defeat by capitulation. "On the eighth day," said the wily monarch, "we will meet in battle," but these words did not deceive his vigilant antagonist; and when, next morning, he suddenly drew out his troops in array, he found the Romans fully prepared for an engagement.

Under these circumstances, the onset was delayed by the barbarian, until two thousand Goths, his last reinforcements, should arrive; and he availed himself of the interval to display before both armies his personal activity and strength. Gold shone upon his armour, the royal purple was conspicuous in a streamer from his spear, and his spirited steed was made to prance and curvet in the most skilful evolutions. He hurled his lance into the air, he caught it in its fall, he threw himself backwards on his saddle and suddenly recovered his seat, and, in short, observes the admiring historian,[51] it was apparent that from his earliest youth he had been well instructed in the art of dancing.

Meanwhile the Roman general, rode along the line, exhorting his troops to overwhelm the scanty battalions of the Goths, and displaying golden bracelets, collars, and other precious trappings, as the destined rewards of valour. It was late in the afternoon before Totila received his expected succours, and having then exchanged his glittering cuirass for some less splendid and conspicuous armour, he gave the signal for battle. The engagement was short, but decisive. A headlong charge of the Gothic horsemen was steadfastly encountered by the Roman line, and they were assailed in flank by distant volleys of arrows; whilst the lance, their only weapon, could neither avert nor retaliate this attack.

They were driven back in confusion and dismay, and, pressing against the Gothic infantry, broke its ranks and involved it in their

---

50. Liv. *lib. x.* c.28. Procop. *Goth. lib. iv.* c. 29.
51. Procop. *Goth. lib. iv,* c. 31 .

flight. The runaways were pursued in all directions by the relentless conquerors; no quarter was given; and the loss of the barbarians, on this occasion, exceeded six thousand men. Protected by the approach of night, Totila had fled from the field, followed by only five of his train: he was overtaken by some Roman soldiers, headed by Asbad, of the tribe of the Gepidae; but they were yet ignorant of the importance of their prize. The dangerous secret was revealed by the inconsiderate exclamation of a Goth: "Do you dare to strike the king?" and Asbad, instructed by these words, raised his lance and pierced Totila with a mortal wound. A blow which he himself immediately received from a brave barbarian, disabled him from further conflict or pursuit; his soldiers remained in attendance on their chief, and the Goths bore off their prince at full speed, in spite of the anguish which he suffered from such rapidity of movement.

After a progress of twelve miles, they halted at the village of Capra.[52] The expiring monarch was lifted from his horse, and the fidelity of his subjects soothed his latest moments, but the humble tomb to which their pious care consigned him was, a few hours afterwards, revealed by Gothic treachery and rifled by Roman curiosity and avarice. The remains of Totila were exposed to the exulting gaze of the soldiery, whilst his bloody garments and hat adorned with jewels were dispatched, as trophies of victory, to the emperor, and laid before his throne at a solemn meeting of his court.[53] Such, after reigning eleven years, was the end of Totila, a prince whose death left his countrymen in almost as desperate a condition as he had found them on his first accession.

From the field of Tagina Narses now pursued his march towards the capital; nor could the towns of Spoleto and Narni, which Totila had dismantled, offer any obstacle to his progress. The Eternal city yielded to his first assault. The Gothic garrison, entrenching itself on the mole of Hadrian, protracted its resistance a few days longer; but Narses was enabled to send once more to Justinian the keys of Rome, which had thus been taken and retaken five times in less than twenty years. Each successive capture had been oppressive to the people, but this last was fatal to the senate. The Barbarian confederates in the Byzantine army never failed to represent the wealthy as traitors to the emperor, and often committed murder as an excuse for robbery, while

---

52. The site of Capra is investigated by Sigonius, but he seems to place it too far to the northward, near Arezzo. (*De Occident. Imp, Op.* vol. i.)
53. John Malala, vol. ii. Theophanes *Chronograph.*

on the other hand, the senators in Sicily, who had begun to hasten homewards, were intercepted in Campania by the despair and vengeance of the Goths, and three hundred high-born hostages from Rome were butchered to the northward of the Po.

The death of so many nobles appears to have occasioned the downfall and cessation of their order in the state, and thus almost the same epoch, though from very different causes, beheld the Roman senate and the Roman consulship extinguished. From this time forwards, till the new institution by Arnold of Brescia, in the twelfth century, the annals of history seldom contain the words of Consul or Senator, and even then these classic titles are only used for Count or *Seigneur*.[54]

After the death of Totila, as after the captivity of Vitiges, the surviving remnant of the Goths assembled within the ramparts of Pavia, where Teias, one of their principal officers, was unanimously proclaimed their king. That the new monarch was worthy of the throne may be presumed from his accepting it so readily, at a moment when it only promised a career of peril, toil, and probable destruction. On learning that the troops of Narses had invested Cumae he resolved, without delay, to relieve that important fortress, which was defended by his brother Aligern, and contained the greater part of the treasures of Totila. Putting himself therefore at the head of his slender force, he advanced by hasty marches into Southern Italy, (a.d. 553), eluded the Roman detachments stationed to arrest his progress, and arrived in safety at the foot of Mount Vesuvius.

Here he entrenched himself along the river called Sarnus by the ancient Romans, and Draco in the middle ages, and which at present has again reverted to the name of Sarno. The opposite bank of the stream was occupied by Narses, and, for two whole months, these armies continued in presence, apparently desirous of exhausting each other's patience, and only engaged by occasional single combats or distant skirmishes of archers. At the end of this period the fleet of Teias, on which he depended for the subsistence of his soldiers, deserted to the Romans, and the barbarians, struck with consternation, fled from their advantageous position towards the neighbouring mountain of Lactarius.

On this commanding height the Goths might be secure from attack but not from famine, and instead of awaiting its lingering tortures,

---

54. See Du Cange, *Gloss. Med. Lat.* vol. i *et iii. sub voc. Consul et Senator*, and Gibbon, vol. xii. The word senator was used for nobles or principal citizens as early as the time of Gregory of Tours. See his history, especially *lib i.* c. 29.

they resolved to meet a prompt and glorious death in battle. Descending therefore into the plain, they dismissed their horses that no means of escape might allure them from their purpose, and charged the Roman Army without a hope of victory, but with all the courage of despair. Hitherto the Gothic monarch had displayed the skill of a chief; he was now remarkable for the personal prowess of a soldier. Conspicuous at the van of his little army, he expected and parried the blows which were aimed from every quarter at so important a mark, while his weighty lance seldom failed in transfixing his assailants.

Neither danger nor fatigue could move him from his station, and he seemed, says Procopius, as if rooted in the ground. At length, when calling on his armbearer [55] for a fresh buckler, and laying aside his own, encumbered by the weight of twelve hostile javelins, his breast, uncovered by this incautious movement, was struck with a mortal blow. His severed head was raised on a spear by the troops of Narses, but the barbarians were rather animated than disheartened by the example of their leader. They continued the engagement till the night, they renewed it on the ensuing day with their strength enfeebled, but their spirit unimpaired, and it was only when darkness again divided the combatants that the few survivors proposed, and Narses accepted, a capitulation. It was agreed that the remaining Goths should either wander forth from Italy, or live in future the peaceful and loyal subjects of Justinian.[56] Still, however, in spite of this treaty, Aligern, nestled on the lofty rock of Cumae, continued to hold out, and the Roman general was compelled to employ the most protracted and laborious expedients against him.

The Sybil's grotto (no doubt the same which now, returned to its original size, is displayed to the inquiring traveller by Italian antiquaries) was scooped and widened to an enormous cavern, and drew down in its fall a rampart and gate of Cumae which surmounted it.[57] Yet the undaunted Goth still maintained the summit of the crumbling precipice, nor was it till he perceived the entire dispersion of his countrymen, and hopelessness of his cause, that he consented to surrender. He was received with all the courtesy and respect which

---

55. The name of an armbearer amongst the Northern barbarians appears to have been Schilpor, in which we may trace the origin of Schildführer, in modern German. (Paul Warnefrid, *lib. ii. c.* 28.)
56. Compare Agathias, *lib. i.*, and Procopius, *Goth. lib. ii. c.* 35. By supposing an alternative, we can easily reconcile their conflicting statements.
57. Agath. *lib. i.*

so high-minded an enemy deserved, and forthwith appointed to an honourable post in the Roman Army.

With this capitulation, the Gothic war may be considered as ended, and the Gothic name as altogether extinguished. It is true that an embassy which Teias had previously dispatched to the Franks and Alamanni, obtained from them a promise of assistance, and that next autumn a large horde of these barbarians descended from the Alps. But it arrived too late; defeat had thinned, and emigration scattered the Goths: they could no longer claim any political importance, and were a pretext rather than a party to the ensuing war. Having thus brought their monarchy to its final overthrow, I shall now bid farewell to Italian history, which I have already carried beyond the strict limits of my subject.

CHAPTER 8

Conspiracy to Murder

In the first Italian war a precipitate recall had hindered Belisarius from completing and securing his triumphs; in the second he had been denied any effective means for upholding his ancient . reputation. At Constantinople he had suffered the most unjust and ignominious treatment, yet in circumstances where resistance would have been as easy, and perhaps more safe, the loyalty of Belisarius had always patiently submitted. This well-known loyalty was now destined to expose him to the first brunt of a treasonable enterprise, directed against the person and the empire of Justinian, for on the same principle that the attack of a rampart should be preceded by the overthrow of its bulwarks, the conspirators had resolved to aim their earliest blow at Belisarius, as the firmest pillar of the throne. To explain the views and motives of the parties to this plot, some previous details are requisite.

A marriage with Praejecta, the emperor's niece,[1] had obtained for the patrician Areobindus the important government of Africa. In the eyes of his sovereign, this alliance might supply the want of military skill and even of personal courage, but the new *exarch* found it of little avail in gaining the esteem or commanding the obedience of his subjects. His weakness was speedily discovered and as speedily abused. An artful officer, named Gonthar, who had originally served in the guards of Solomon,[2] discerned with the keen glance of ambition, an opportunity so favourable to a rebel.

By his *cabals* the Moors were excited to hostilities and the Roman troops to mutiny; a conflict arose, (a.d. 546), in the very streets of Carthage, and though a great number of faithful adherents still supported the lieutenant of the emperor, they were disheartened and

---
1. Ducange, *Fam. Aug. Byz.*
2. Procop. *Vandal, lib. ii.* c. 19.

defeated by his cowardly flight. Areobindus had escaped to the sanctuary of a convent in Carthage, which Solomon had lately built and surrounded with strong walls, for the twofold purpose of monastic seclusion or military strength.

The Bishop of Carthage was dispatched, by the victorious Gonthar to draw his rival from that sacred retreat, under the most solemn promises of safety, and the trembling Areobindus returned to the palace, clad in the habit of a slave, and stretching forth in his hands the gospels and an infant newly baptized, yet neither these religious restraints, nor his abject entreaties for life, could disarm the vengeance of the tyrant. He was welcomed with smiling courtesy and specious promises, and at supper the highest place was assigned him, but at the close of the entertainment he was murdered.[3] Thus Gonthar became, for awhile, the sovereign of Africa; and, hoping to allay the indignation of the emperor, he drew Praejecta from captivity, allotted to her an apartment in the palace, and openly aspired to her hand. But the daring usurper did not enjoy the fruits of his treason beyond thirty days.

Amongst the officers who had attended Areobindus at his departure from Constantinople, was Artaban, an Armenian, of the noble race of the Arsacides, who had lately headed an insurrection of his countrymen against the troops of Justinian, and had transfixed with his lance their general Sittas, the colleague of Belisarius, in his first military expedition.[4] His subsequent desertion to the Romans, of which the motive is not explained, was rewarded by an appointment in the Byzantine Army, and under his direction a conspiracy was now formed against the African tyrant. The unguarded hour of a banquet was fixed upon as the fittest for assassination, and Artasires, one of the followers of the Armenian prince, was chosen to strike the first blow, said this intrepid soldier to his chief:

> If my attempt should fail, kill me on the spot with my own sword, to torn aside all suspicion from yourself, and lest the rack should wring from me the names of my accomplices.

An enterprise, undertaken with such heroic determination, could hardly prove otherwise than successful. Gonthar was slain, and Carthage once more acknowledged the sway of Justinian, who showed his gratitude by naming Artaban *exarch* of the province he had saved.[5]

---

3. Procop. *Vandal.* lib. ii. c. 26.
4. Procop. *Pers. lib. ii.* c. 3.
5. Procop. *Vandal, lib. ii. c.* . 28.

But this recompense, however ample, did not satisfy his aspiring spirit. He had become enamoured of the widow of Areobindus, who, on her part, was not unmindful of the debt due to her deliverer; nor did she set out for Constantinople until she had bound herself to him by a solemn promise of marriage. After her departure Africa appeared wearisome and tasteless to her lover, who solicited his recall from Justinian, and hastened to the capital, where it is probable that he might have succeeded in his wishes, had not an unforeseen hindrance interposed. In his early youth he had contracted a marriage which was afterwards dissolved, according to some of the legal grounds established in that age. As long as Artaban had continued poor and unfortunate, his wife had cheerfully admitted the legality of the divorce; but his rise to wealth, prosperity, and power, suddenly awakened her pious scruples and conjugal affection. Quitting her retreat for Constantinople, she threw herself at the feet of the empress, and implored her intercession for restoring her beloved and rightful husband.

The compassion of Theodora was excited, her devotion was alarmed, she compelled the unwilling Artaban to take back again his former spouse, and Praejecta became the bride of another suitor.[6] It is true that soon afterwards the death of the empress left Artaban at liberty to obtain a second divorce, but his mind still brooded deeply over his disappointed passion, and was intent on some project of revenge, and his resentment was inflamed by the solicitations of his kinsman Arsaces, lately exasperated against Justinian by detected treachery and ignominious punishment, (a.d. 548). It was resolved by these two Armenians to assassinate the emperor, and to raise to the throne his nephew Germanus, whose valour and virtue had greatly endeared him to the people. They well knew, however, the inflexible fidelity of Belisarius, now on his return from Italy, and dreaded lest, instead of patiently acquiescing in the projected usurpation, he should, on the first intelligence of it, collect an army in Thrace, and lead it to punish the conspirators.

They therefore considered it more prudent to defer the execution of their design till the arrival of the hero at Constantinople, when a single thrust of a dagger might free them from all future apprehensions of his loyalty. Little doubt was entertained by the traitors of the concurrence of Germanus, whose feelings of attachment to Justinian, both as a subject and as a kinsman, must, in their opinion, long since have yielded to the injustice and neglect which his merit had experienced. But the honest and high-minded prince recoiled with horror

---

6. Procop. *Goth. lib. iii.* c. 31.

from their infamous proposal; and, far from engaging in their enterprise, was anxious, on the contrary, to disclose it to the emperor. To obtain, however, more certain evidence than his own unsupported assertion, he employed the stratagem of pretended compliance. A trusty friend concealed beneath a curtain was the witness of a private interview, and his testimony, when brought forward before Justinian, served to arraign the conspirators, and to vindicate Germanus. The plot was revealed to the emperor at almost the very time when Belisarius was entering the suburbs of Constantinople, and thus a few days of earlier departure from Otranto, or of greater speed in his journey, would probably have cost him his life.

Through the warning of Germanus, it was easy to avert the threatened danger; a meeting of the senate was convened for the trial, the persons of Artaban and Arsaces were secured, and the rack extorted from them the confession of their crime. The only remaining question, therefore, was the sentence to be passed upon them, and on this point we may, according to our various dispositions, either admire the clemency, or deplore the weakness of Justinian, who merely degraded Artaban from his dignities, and confined him in an apartment of the palace.[7] A readiness to pardon is certainly the more popular and shining quality in princes, yet it may be doubted whether we ought not to prefer a just severity which shields the innocent by seldom sparing the guilty, and strikes the minds of hesitating rebels with salutary terror.

But if the mere forgiveness of Justinian seem rash and inconsiderate, what shall we say of his once more raising Artaban to a high and honourable trust?[8] The convicted conspirator was one amongst the many generals whom the caprice of the imperial councils, after the return of Belisarius, appointed in rapid succession to die supreme authority in the Gothic war. He is afterwards mentioned as obtaining some success against the troops of Totila in Sicily,[9] but his further fate is not recorded, and I look in vain for the termination of his singular and adventurous career.

Such were the public transactions which attended the return of Belisarius from Italy. Another of a private nature seems to have occurred, which is however transmitted to us by a testimony neither as authentic nor as ample.[10] It had been a favourite object of the late

---

7. Procop. *Goth. lib. iii.* c. 32.
8. *Esprit des Loix, lib. viii.* c. 7.
9. Procop. *Goth. lib. iv.* c 24.
10. *Hist. Arcan.* c. 6.

empress to conclude a marriage between Anastasius, her nephew, or perhaps one of her illegitimate descendants,[11] and Joannina, the only child of Belisarius, and therefore sole heiress of his wealth. Joannina had been left at Constantinople when her parents set out for the Italian war, and they were far from approving of the proposed alliance; but fearful of offending, by an open refusal, a woman of such exalted rank and vindictive temper, they merely deferred their consent till their return, probably expecting, from the lingering disease of Theodora, that she might then be no more. The empress was not however to be so easily baffled. She employed the last few months of her life in rendering, as she imagined, this marriage necessary, by prevailing on the intended bride to sacrifice her honour, and it was not till half a year from this time that Antonina arrived at Constantinople.

Regardless of the virtue, the fame, and perhaps the affections of her daughter, she broke off the intended nuptials, and Belisarius, on his return, submitted as usual to the wishes of his wife. Whether Joannina ever contracted any other marriage, or whether the family of Belisarius was extinct at her death, has not been recorded. From this time forwards, during the next eleven years, (*a.d.* 548-559, the life of Belisarius affords no remarkable occurrence. He remained at Constantinople in the tranquil enjoyment of opulence and dignities. Besides his ancient post of general of the East, Justinian had named him chief of the imperial guards, and though the older senators and patricians might have claimed superior rank, they unanimously yielded to his precedency of merit.[12]

In this well-earned repose Belisarius might probably have continued till his death, had not the calamities and danger of his country once more summoned the veteran to arms. During the last years of this reign the apparent quiet of the empire was not that healthful repose which a nation expects and requires at the close a victorious war, but the faintness of utter exhaustion and decay. The glaring faults and the pernicious consequences of Justinian's military system have already been exposed elsewhere, and the emperor, who even in his youth had displayed the timidity and vacillation of old age, daily became more suspicious of his soldiers and fearful of his enemies.[13]

---

11. There is great difficulty as to the precise relationship of Anastasius to the empress. Alemanni and Ducange, on the faith of the *Historia Arcana*, make him her grandson, but the three objections of Gibbon are insurmountable, (vol. vii.)

12. Compare Procop. *Goth. lib. iii.* c. 35. *lib. iv.* c. 21. We must now bid farewell to this accurate and judicious historian.

13. Agathias, *lib. v.* His testimony is confirmed by that of Menander. (*Excerpt. Legat.*)

In order to restrain the one without employing the other, he adopted the dangerous plan of paying yearly subsidies to bribe the peace of the barbarians, and endeavoured, by subtle negotiations, to stir up their separate tribes to mutual war.[14]

Such an expedient may sometimes be successfully employed but can never be safely relied on; yet the emperor, says Agathias, treated the army as if he expected to have no further occasion for its services. Thus the Roman troops rapidly melted away, the few remaining squadrons were stationed in distant provinces, and nothing was left for the protection of the capital but the corrupt and unwarlike Scholarians. Various tribes beyond the Danube, whose uncouth names may be comprised in the general appellation of Bulgarians,[15] desolated the European provinces by many a predatory inroad, each terminated rather by their own satiety of plunder, than by any opposition they encountered.

At length, in the thirty-second winter of the reign of Justinian, (a.d. 559), a more important and decisive expedition was attempted. Zabergan,[16] their enterprising and ambitious leader, passed the frozen Danube, at the head of his cavalry, and advanced by rapid marches into the midst of Thrace, where he divided his forces, and having detached the one share to the conquest or rather the pillage of Greece, led the other against the capital.[17] Under his personal command Zabergan retained no more than seven thousand horsemen; but their number appeared multiplied by the extent of their devastations, and by the terror of the Greeks. As heathens, they were ignorant or careless of the sanctity of churches and of convents, and freely despoiled the first of wealth and the second of beauty. Crowds of captives were hurried along in their train, without regard to sickness, pregnancy, or age, and the new-born infants were left like corpses on a field of battle to the dogs and birds of prey.

The Long Wall of Anastasius might have arrested the progress of Zabergan, but its solidity had already yielded to time and decay, and it is compared by Agathias, in his usual rhetorical style, to an unprotected sheepfold, where the prowling wolf, far from encountering a

---

14. *Hist. Arcan.* c. 11., and an extract from Joannes Antiochenus ap. *Alemann.*
15. I most observe that the word Bulgarian does not occur in the narrative of Agathias, but I am induced to employ it by the example and arguments of Gibbon, (vol. vii.)
16. Agathias calls this chieftain sometimes Zamergan and sometimes Zabergan, but Menander turns the scale in favour of the latter. (*Excerpt. Logat.*)
17. For the proceedings of the army in Greece, compare Agathias, *lib. v.*

bite, is not even threatened by a bark. There were no troops to man it; no military machines to play upon the enemy, nor any engineers to direct their use, several breaches were open and accessible, and other parts were demolished by the assailants with as little hindrance, says the historian, as any private dwelling could be razed. Continuing his march from hence, the savage chief pitched his camp at the village of Melantias, on the banks of the River Athyras, and no more than twenty miles from the capital. It is remarkable that this was also the spot which, in the reign of Zeno, bounded the progress of Theodoric the Great.[18]

So bold and successful an aggression filled Constantinople with helpless and despairing terror. The public places were encumbered by a growing multitude of villagers and peasants, some escaped from the actual presence of Zabergan, and others merely from the fear of his approach. The citizens listened with consternation to their dismal tales, and already beheld in fancy the sufferings of a siege, ending only in the conflagration of their dwellings, and the murder of their families; and their dismay could hardly have been greater had the Bulgarians already penetrated into the midst of the city. Nor were these feelings confined to the populace alone; the senators and nobles were seen to mingle with it, under the usual levelling influence of fear, and the emperor himself sat trembling in his palace. By his orders all the churches in the European confines of the capital, from the *propontis* to the *euxine*, were hastily stripped of their most precious ornaments, and the sea was covered with barges, and each road with chariots, conveying these and other treasures to the shelter of the walls. Near the Golden Gate,[19] where the attack of the enemy was expected to take place, an useless crowd of officers issued their contradictory and unheeded orders,[20] and some of the unwarlike Scholarians seemed (such is the significant expression of Agathias) to guard the neighbouring ramparts.

In this general confusion and affright, Justinian and his subjects turned with hope to the illustrious conqueror of Africa and Italy, whose strength was broken by old age and military labours, but whose heart was still alive to the call of loyalty and honour. The struggle was no longer for increase of territory or dominion over foreign nations, but for the very existence of the Roman empire, and Belisarius prepared to crown his glorious life by a last and decisive battle. He

---

18. Marcellin. *Chron. ap. Sirmond Op.* vol. ii.
19. For the Golden Gate see Ducange *Const. Christ. lib. i.*
20. Tacit. *Hist. lib. iii.* c. 73.

resumed his rusty armour, he collected a handful of his scattered veterans, and his contemporaries were astonished at observing, amidst the weakness of decrepitude, all the martial spirit and buoyancy of youth.[21] The recklessness of personal danger which is recorded of him in this short campaign would be less deserving of praise if experience did not show that we cling to life with increasing fondness in proportion as our infirmities render it painful and precarious. The first object of Belisarius was to find means for mounting his cavalry, and the horses of the imperial stables and of the amphitheatre were added to those which a compulsory requisition obtained from private citizens.[22]

With every exertion he could only muster three hundred effective soldiers; they were veterans who had served under him in his former campaigns, and they were augmented in numbers, not in force, by a multitude of raw recruits, devoid of experience, of valour, and even of weapons, and whom their own countrymen represent as intending to remain spectators, rather than parties in a conflict. The Roman standards were also joined by a crowd of peasants, who sought protection from the rapine and outrage of the enemy, but were both unwilling and unable to encounter him. At the head of this mob of soldiers Belisarius undauntedly advanced from the ramparts to the village of Chettos, in front of the barbarians. To deter the enemy from any immediate attack, and thus obtain time for the fortification of his camp, he was desirous of creating an exaggerated impression of his numbers, and therefore dispatched outposts along the plain, to kindle fires and beacons, according to a stratagem of the ancient Lombards.[23] During the day the place of fires was supplied by artificial clouds of dust, and Zabergan, deluded by their aspect, refrained from advancing any further against so extended a line.

Meanwhile the Roman general was not inactive; he sent secret spies to ascertain the real strength of the enemy, of which none but vague popular rumours had been hitherto received, and by employing the peasants of his army in an occupation more suitable to their habits than warfare, his encampment was speedily surrounded by a ditch and rampart. He laboured with unremitting assiduity to establish some degree of order in the Roman ranks, but found himself opposed by

---

21. Agathias, *lib. v.*
22. Theophanes *Chronograph.*
23. See Paul Warnefrid, *lib. i.* c. 11., with a note of Lindenbrogius. For the practice of estimating the numbers of the enemy by their fires at night, see Caesar's *Commentaries.* (*De Bell. Gallic lib. ii.* c. 7.)

two different and conflicting obstacles. No courage, as we have already seen, inspired the great mass of his army, while on the other hand his three hundred veterans were flushed with arrogant and overweening confidence. Like most soldiers retired from active service, they had probably boasted of their past campaigns, and from imposing upon others had, by a curious but common progress of the human mind, gradually imposed upon themselves, so that at length they grew almost invincible in their own opinion, and fancied that no barbarians, however numerous, could withstand their disciplined valour. They were impatient both of stratagem and of delay, and rendered necessary a public admonition from the general, he said:

> In remembering your ancient achievements, do not forget the calm and cautious demeanour which secured them. Judgment, and not headlong courage, is the true arbiter of war. How else durst I, with my hair already whitened by old age, and my failing limbs grown unfitted for fatigue, plunge into the toil and tumult of another campaign, unless I relied on those faculties which continue unimpaired amidst bodily decay? If, therefore, prudence and good council can correct the infirmities of declining years, how much more will they not avail when you join them to the full strength and vigour of manhood? These barbarians are accustomed to predatory inroads, like robbers they know how to rush forth unexpectedly on their prey, but they are little practised in the art of disposing a battle with skill or awaiting it with firmness. Let us only observe the military discipline of our forefathers, and restrain our rashness, and we shall teach these invaders how much a small but well trained squadron surpasses a newly levied and tumultuous horde.

Having thus endeavoured to curb the impatience of his ancient comrades, Belisarius patiently awaited the attack of the barbarians. His stratagem had succeeded in gaining time for marshalling his forces, but Zabergan soon became aware how small a number of effective soldiers was in reality opposed to him. Against three hundred men he did not consider it necessary to lead his whole army at once, but taking with him no more than two thousand horse, he trusted at the first onset to disperse his antagonists and pursue them to the capital. By secret emissaries the Roman general was informed of the approach of the Bulgarians, and enabled to prepare accordingly. He chose an advantageous position behind a thick and extensive wood, and concealed a hundred of his veteran cavalry on each side of the narrow defile through which he expected Zabergan to pass, with instructions for them to remain in ambush until his appointed signal should be heard. From the peasants and citizens in his army he found it useless to expect any military aid, but he had provided them with stakes, which, when brandished and struck together, might resemble arms in appearance and in sound, and he directed them by their shouts to animate their countrymen and distract the enemy.

Unsuspicious of danger the Bulgarians pressed forwards with dissonant cries, and in full confidence of victory. They were boldly charged by Belisarius in front, while fresh enemies suddenly rose upon their rear, and the dust which clouded the air from the trampling of the horse concealed the real weakness of the assailants from their view. On every side they heard the voice of multitudes, on every side they felt the arm of valour. Their practice in archery and their rapidity in evolution were rendered unavailing by their confined position, and they found themselves helpless, encompassed, and cut off. In the first ranks the Roman hero was conspicuous, performing the duties and displaying the prowess of a soldier, and thus, by his united skill and intrepidity, succeeded in vanquishing two thousand with three hundred men.

The Bulgarians were driven back in the utmost disorder; four hundred fell in the battle or the pursuit, and it was with difficulty that Zabergan himself effected his escape. The alarm of the fugitives spread throughout the army at Melantias with the usual rapid contagion of fear; and the soldiers testified their sorrow and dismay by the savage rite of cutting deep gashes in their cheeks. Raising their camp with precipitation, they began retreating towards the north, and Belisarius prepared, by a close pursuit, to renew and complete his triumph.

But this patriotic satisfaction was denied him; his military enterprises were checked in the midst of their career, and the same causes which had so often already tried his virtue and obedience, again exerted over him their baneful influence. His public services once more received, in the councils of the emperor, the customary rewards of slander and suspicion. At the news of his victory and of their deliverance, the citizens of Constantinople had gratefully extolled his merit, and proclaimed Belisarius as the saviour of his country. His intrepid conduct at the head of his three hundred veterans was compared to that of the same number of Spartans at Thermopylae, and his former battles against the Persians, Goths, and Vandals, were declared inferior to this last achievement. Such praises were imputed as a crime to Belisarius by an envious multitude of courtiers and domestics, and the general was accused of aiming at popular favour with ambitious and disloyal designs.

A sentence of recall was hastily pronounced and submissively obeyed. Belisarius was received at the palace with coldness and disparagement, his late service was buried in silence, and instead of following up his victory against the troops of Zabergan, Justinian preferred the less glorious task of bribing their departure. On learning that Belisarius was recalled, the Bulgarians had stopped short in their retreat, and lingered during the whole summer in Thrace, but at length the liberality of the emperor, and the dread of being intercepted by armed vessels on the Danube, induced them to retire homewards for a stipulated sum. The Byzantine people were loud in their murmurs at this treaty, expressing the strongest indignation that these barbarians, after pillaging the provinces, threatening the capital, and insulting the majesty of the empire, should be afterwards paid and rewarded by Justinian for their friendly visit.[24] On his part the emperor showed his sense of such ignominy and his desire to avert it in future, by his anxious diligence in fortifying the Long Wall, and he even stationed himself for sometime at Selybria, to superintend and hasten its repairs.

With the defeat of the Bulgarians we must bid farewell to contemporary evidence, and the disgrace and death of Belisarius are only to be gathered from the obscure and contradictory records of later ages. An inquiry into the real facts will unavoidably lead me into such minute and tedious details, that I shall postpone it till the conclusion of my narrative, and merely state, in this place, the general results at which I have arrived.

Nearly four years from the Battle of Chettos, a conspiracy was formed by Marcellus, Sergius, and some other illustrious senators, (a.d. 563), for the murder of Justinian. It is no small proof how much the natural faults of Justinian were aggravated by old age, and how intolerable his government had grown, that the disaffected should not have patiently expected the death of an octogenarian. The conspirators were detected, torture was used to wring from them the names of their accomplices, and some domestics of Belisarius ventured to accuse their master.[25] Since the Bulgarian victory, the hero had remained under the displeasure of Justinian; but it required the very

---

24. Agathias, *lib. v.*
25. It must be observed that the Roman laws limited the use of torture to slaves, except in cases of treason. See the Pandects, *lib. lxviii.* tit. 18.

extremity of jealous dotage to believe that he, who in the full vigour of manhood had refused a crown, and preserved his loyalty amidst the strongest temptations to rebellion, should now, at the close of life, assume the part of an assassin. Such considerations were overlooked by his sovereign, or suppressed by his enemies.

In the month of December, Belisarius was ignominiously deprived of his guards and domestics; his fortunes were sequestered, and he was detained a close prisoner in his palace. The trial of the true and supposed conspirators took place in the ensuing year,(a.d. 564), when a sentence of death was probably pronounced on all and executed on the greater number. The past services of Belisarius, which might have proved his innocence, served at least to mitigate his fate; and, according to a frequent practice of the Byzantine court with eminent stateprisoners, the decree of death was relaxed into one of blindness, and his eyes were accordingly put out. It was then that, restored to liberty, but deprived of all means of subsidence by the preceding confiscation of his property, Belisarius was reduced to beg his bread before the gates of the convent of Laurus. The platter of wood or earthenware which he held out for charity, and his exclamation "Give a penny to Belisarius the general," remained for many years impressed on the recollection of the people. It would seem that this spectacle of persecuted merit, aroused some dangerous feelings of indignation and pity, and was therefore speedily removed from public view.

Belisarius was brought back, most probably as a prisoner, to his former palace, a portion of his treasures was allotted for his use, and these circumstances may have given some colour for the assertion two or three centuries afterwards, of his having been restored to honours and to freedom. His death, which perhaps was hastened by the grief or the hardships of captivity, ensued in the course of next spring, (a.d. 565), and Antonina, who survived him, devoted to the cloister the remains of her life and fortune. Such, in all likelihood, is the authentic narrative of the fall of Belisarius.

In person Belisarius was tall and commanding, and presented a remarkable contrast to the dwarfish and ungainly aspect of his rival Narses.[26] His features were regular and noble, and his appearance in the streets of Constantinople, after the Vandal and Gothic victories, never failed to attract the admiration of the people. His character may not unaptly be compared to that of Marlborough, whom he equalled in talents and closely resembled in his faults of luxuriousness and love

---

26. Procop. *Goth. lib. iii.* c. 1. Agathias, *lib. i.*

of money. As a military leader, he was enterprising, firm, and fearless; his conception was clear, and his judgment rapid and decisive. His conquests were achieved with smaller means than any other of like extent recorded in history. He frequently experienced reverses in the field, but in no case did he fail without some strong and sufficient reason for his failure, such as the mutiny of his soldiers, the overwhelming numbers of his antagonists, or his total want of necessary supplies; and it may also be observed of him, as of Arminius, that though sometimes beaten in battle, he was never overcome in war.[27] His superior tactics covered his defeats, retrieved his losses, and prevented his enemies from reaping the fruits of victory; and it is particularly mentioned, that even in the most desperate emergencies, he never lost his courage or presence of mind.

Amongst the circumstances which contributed most strongly to his success, were the kindness which his adversaries met with at his hands, and the strict discipline which he maintained amongst his soldiers. This moderation of Belisarius appears the more entitled to praise from the fierceness and disorder usual in his age.[28] It was his first care after every victory to extend mercy and protection to the vanquished, and to shield their persons, and, if possible, their property from injury. During a march the trampling of the cornfields by the cavalry was carefully avoided, and the troops, as Procopius tells us, seldom ventured even to gather an apple from the trees, while a ready payment to the villagers for any provisions they brought, made them bless the name of Belisarius, and secured to the Roman camp a constant and cheerful supply.

To the soldiers who transgressed these rules, the general was stern and unforgiving; no rank could defy, no obscurity elude his justice, and because he punished severely, he had to punish seldom. He knew how to despise those shallow declaimers who cry out against any rigour In the law because they can more easily compute the penalties it inflicts than the crimes it has prevented. But while the licentious and the turbulent were repressed by the strong arm of Belisarius, his liberality cheered and animated the deserving. The gift of a golden bracelet or collar rewarded any achievement in battle, the loss of a horse or weapon was immediately supplied from his private funds,[29]

---

27. Tacit. *Annal. lib. ii.* c. 88.
28. See, for instance an incidental remark of Procopius, (*Vandal, lib. i.* c. 21.)
29. Compare Procop. *Goth. lib. i.* c. 28. and *lib. iii.* c. 1. In another passage, the historian alludes to his mildness of manner, (lib. ii. c. 8)

and the wounded found in him a father and a friend. To all he was open and easy of access, and by his courteous demeanour often comforted where he could not relieve. From his generosity, says Procopius, you would have deemed him very rich, from his manners very poor. His private virtues promoted and confirmed the discipline of his soldiers; none in all his campaigns ever saw him flushed with wine, and the charms of the fairest captives from the Goths or Vandals could not overcome his conjugal fidelity.

But the most striking and peculiar feature in the character of Belisarius, as distinguished from other illustrious generals, was his enduring and unconquerable loyalty. He was doubtless bound to Justinian by many ties of gratitude, and the suspicions entertained of him in Africa may be considered as fully counterbalanced by the triumph and other honours which attended his return. But from the siege of Ravenna till his final departure from Italy, he was, almost without intermission, exposed to the most galling and unworthy treatment; he was insulted, degraded; and despised; he was even attacked in his fame when restored to an important station, without any means for discharging its duties, and for sustaining his former reputation. It would be difficult to produce another instance of such signal and repeated ingratitude, unless in republics, where, from the very nature of the government, no crime is so dangerous or so severely punished, as serving the state too well.

When we consider the frequency, and therefore the ease of revolutions in this age, the want of hereditary right in the imperial family, the strong attachment of the soldiers to their victorious general, while the person of Justinian was hateful even to his own domestic guards, it will, I think, be admitted, that a rebellion by Belisarius must have proved successful and secure. The same conclusion is likewise apparent, from the offer of proclaiming him Emperor of the West at Ravenna,[30] yet on no one occasion was he roused into the slightest mark of disobedience or resentment; he bore every injury with unchanged submission; he resisted the feelings of indignation, of revenge, of self-interest, and even the thirst for glory, which, according to Tacitus, is of all frailties the longest retained by the wise.[31] I say nothing of his subsequent beggary and blindness, because it might fairly be objected that he then had no longer any means of rebellion in his power; but his whole previous life is still more remarkable for magnanimity

---

30. Procop. *Goth. lib. ii.* c. 89.
31. Tacit. *Hist. lib. iv.* c. 6.

in suffering than for excellence in action. Besides him no more than six generals have been named, by one of our most judicious critics, as having deserved without having worn a crown [32] and the smallness of this number should display the difficulty of withstanding this brilliant temptation, and enhance the reputation of those few who have withstood it.

The chief fault of Belisarius seems to have been his unbounded deference and submission to his wife, which rendered him first strangely blind, and afterwards weakly forgiving, to her infidelity. But its mischievous effects were not confined to private life, and nearly all the errors which can be charged upon his public career are imputed to this cause. It was Antonina who assumed the principal part in the deposition of the Pope, who urged the death of Constantine, who promoted the persecution of Photius, and in his whole conduct with regard to that worthless woman, Belisarius appears alternately the object of censure or of ridicule. His confidence in her must have tended to lower his official character, to fetter and mislead his judgment, and to prevent his justice and impartiality wherever her passions were concerned.

The second reproach to which the character of Belisarius appears liable, is that of rapacity in the latter part of his career. His unimpeachable integrity in early life is proved by the most undoubted testimony, the, silence of the Secret Historian. Possessing an ample patrimony, and receiving from the emperor no small share of the Gothic or Vandal treasures, in addition to the usual emoluments of his office, he was enabled to defray his gifts and largesses to the soldiers of his army, and to maintain a personal guard which, at the close of his first Gothic campaigns, amounted to no less than seven thousand men. But, after his last command in the East, his wealth had been almost exhausted by an enormous fine; there was no public booty to share in his second Italian war; and yet, on his return from it, we find him again in possession of considerable property.

This fact is in itself strong presumptive evidence of corruption, and adds weight and certainty to the charge of the author of the *Anecdotes*, who informs us that Belisarius, in his last Italian campaigns, was compelled, by the total want of supplies from Constantinople, to levy taxes for the prosecution of the war; but was, at the same time,

---

32. See Sir William Temple, (*Works*, vol. ii. ed. 1705.) The seven chiefs he mentions are as follows: Belisarius, Ætius, Huniades, Gonsalo of Cordova, Scanderbeg, Alexander Duke of Parma, and the great Prince of Orange.

meanly solicitous to repair his shattered fortunes.[33] It is probable that on this, as on other occasions, the submissive hero was influenced by Antonina, in whose breast, through a common succession, the passion of love had been followed by that of avarice. How ill did Belisarius understand his real interests! How highly would his fame have been exalted by an honourable poverty, and how much would the animosity of his enemies at court have abated, had they seen no spoils to gather from his fall!

The life of Belisarius produced most important effects on the political and religious revolutions of the world. I have already endeavoured to show that his reduction of Africa probably contributed to the rapid progress of the Mussulmans, but this and his other victories certainly saved his country from impending ruin. During the fifth century, more than half the provinces of the ancient empire had been usurped by the barbarians, and the rising tide of their conquests must soon have overwhelmed the remainder. The decline of the Byzantine Romans was threatened by the youthful vigour of the Vandal and Ostrogoth kingdoms. Although the founders of these mighty monarchies had been wisely solicitous for peace, they left their successors fully able to undertake any projects of invasion; and an alliance of these states against the Romans must have proved fatal to the latter. The strength of the empire had been tried singly against Genseric by Basiliscus, against Theodoric the Great by Sabinian, and both had miserably failed.

On the opposite frontier, it required the presence or the reputation of a hero to deter the able and ambitious Chosroes from advancing. An attentive consideration of the empire in the reigns of Zeno and Anastasius, will display all the symptoms of increasing weakness and approaching dissolution; while the barbarians were flushed and impelled by recent victory. Had not Belisarius arisen at this particular juncture, the Vandals, Goths, and Persians would in all likelihood have divided the imperial provinces amongst them. The Arian doctrines, of which the two former were zealous partisans, would then probably have prevailed in the Christian world, the whole balance of power in Europe would have undergone incalculable changes, and the treasures of Greek and Roman genius would never have enlightened modern times.

Not only did Belisarius rescue his country from immediate downfall, but his conquests gave it resources for the future. The barbarians,

---

33. *Hist. Arcan.* c. 5.

who soon filled the vacant interval left by the Ostrogoths from the Danube to the Rhone, were far inferior to them in number, in spirit, and in policy, and the possession of southern Italy, which Belisarius re-annexed to the empire, served for upwards of five centuries as its most important outpost and bulwark. Under the *catapans* or Greek governors (a title still to be traced in the province of Capitanata), the troops were inured to war, and the Lombards or Normans were encountered with little danger from defeat. The battles which might else have been fought beneath the walls of Constantinople, were decided near those of Ban or Taranto.

★★★★★★

It now remains for me to explain my grounds for adhering to the original narrative of the blindness and beggary of Belisarius. The reader may perhaps be inclined to forgive the length and tediousness of this inquiry, when he recollects that the truth can only be discerned by carefully weighing the authority, and comparing the opposite statements of the testimonies on this subject.

I must in the first place maintain that a popular report so confidently stated and so universally current as this, is in itself a very strong presumption of truth. Even Gibbon, who in this instance speaks so slightingly of tradition, has elsewhere expressed great deference for its "honest voice,"[34] and the accurate Niebuhr conceives the recollection of Tarpeia to have been verbally transmitted for twenty centuries, amidst all the manifold vicissitudes of Rome.[35] There is perhaps little danger of the authority of tradition being undervalued in a country where men of sense and judgment on other subjects have seriously believed that whole epic poems could be preserved by its means for above a thousand years. But without proceeding to these extravagant lengths, it will, I think, be found that local tradition, however defective in minute or intermediate circumstances, is almost always correct in the general and more striking results.

Thus I should not expect, from the memory of the people, any exact account of the campaigns of Belisarius, but it seems well adapted for retaining the two extreme points of his triumph and his beggary. Let it be considered, also, that in this case there was no interest of national vanity to serve by falsehood, and that his ignominious treatment contributed neither to his own glory nor to that of the empire. It is surely not presuming too much on the veracity of any man, not

---

34. Vol. xi.
35. *Römische Geschichte, erster Theil*, 1827.

even of a modern Greek, to suppose that he may speak the truth when there is no motive for a lie.

To explain why so general and positive a tradition should have arisen if unfounded, its antagonists have supposed that it was invented as a strange example of the vicissitudes of fortune.[36] Such a theory might, perhaps, be admissible if it related to a period of profound peace and regular succession, which afforded no remarkable changes, and where fancy was called in to supply the place of extraordinary facts. But the Byzantine history above all others abounds in revolutions and capricious turns of destiny, where we find the most lowborn individuals acknowledged as sovereigns from accident as often from merit, and the most powerful monarchs overthrown by foreign arms or domestic treason.

In the very first century after the death of Justinian, what was the fate of the Emperors Maurice, Phocas, Heracleonas, and Constans? With us such names may, perhaps, appear obscure or insignificant, but to a Byzantine ear would not the downfall of any one of these monarchs seem more striking than that of any subject, however illustrious for his station or his merit? Or if it was absolutely necessary that this example of vicissitude should be taken from amongst the contemporaries of Justinian, there were surely sufficient real instances to render forgery superfluous. Were not the kings of the Vandals and the Ostrogoths, perhaps the most powerful sovereigns of the age, led as captives and suppliants to kneel before the throne of Justinian? As an instance of an opposite change from low to high, was not Justinian himself raised from a cottage to the palace?

And amongst his subjects we should not overlook the fate of John the Cappadocian, a man at that time of great and widely-extended reputation, who filled the place of prime minister for more, than ten years, and whose influence and power far exceeded that of Belisarius, since it spread over the whole empire, while that of the victorious general was bounded to the immediate scene of war. This able but worthless statesman was hurled from his dignity, and reduced to such poverty that he found himself constrained to beg his bread from province to province. Each city which had groaned beneath his oppression, successively enjoyed a view of his degradation and distress.[37] Here then are examples of the strangest and most undoubted vicissitudes, and why should the Greeks, with these examples before their eyes,

---

36. Gibbon, vol. *vii.* Lebeau, *lib. xlix.* c. 65, &c.
37. Procop. *Pers. lib. i.* c. 25.

devise a new and groundless legend respecting the end of Belisarius?

Besides, is it so easy to establish a fable? Could an event be thus imposed upon the people of the very capital where it is stated to have happened? With regard to foreign countries or distant provinces, indeed, the vulgar is always ready to believe any tale which may flatter its prejudices, or gratify its love of wonders. A Mandeville or Marco Polo may dazzle our eyes with the wealth of Cipango and Cathay, and European credulity may raise the coffin of Mahomet into the air, or people the coasts of Patagonia with imaginary giants. But when on the other hand Our own district is in question, the power of fiction is confined to narrow bounds; it may sometimes pervert or discolour, but can hardly invent a fact, and though for instance national vanity might transform a doubtful battle into a victory, it must yield where there was a manifest defeat or no conflict whatever. A great number of examples might be brought forwards to show the length of time and the fidelity with which these domestic traditions are preserved. Our modern annals derive many precious facts from this source, and it is well known how greatly a most numerous sect (the Roman Catholic) relies on traditional records of religion.

On every field of battle, however lonely or remote, the peasant will still point to the scene of action, and relate what his forefathers beheld. Now the memory of the disgrace of Belisarius is precisely similar. It was preserved amongst his fellow-citizens, of whom some must have seen him in his degradation, and even relieved him by their alms, and it therefore, I conceive, deserves the name and the authority of a local tradition. To put this part of the subject in a still stronger point of view, let anyone only consider for a moment by what means he could attempt to deceive his countrymen in a point of their own early history? Were he to assert, for example, that the Black Prince, the first Earl of Shrewsbury, or any other of our national heroes, had been blinded and reduced to beg his bread through the streets of London, what credit does he think that this "strange example of the vicissitudes of fortune" would be likely to receive? It may be answered, that the superior civilization of modern England to Constantinople renders this parallel unfair.

But the Byzantine Empire was never devoid either of literature or learning, although it is true that the one was spiritless and servile, and the other abstract, barren, and obscure. Not merely were there the voluminous histories which stilt instruct and fatigue posterity, but many others of which the name alone survives, and of which the originals have either perished, or lie concealed amidst the learned rubbish of some Grecian convent.

Having said thus much of the credit to which local traditions are entitled, let us next examine the probability of the event which they have here transmitted; that is, how far it may appear conformable to the general manners of Constantinople, or to the supposed exigencies of this particular case. It is well known that the Roman Emperors, from Diocletian downwards, borrowed many institutions and customs from Persia. Not only were Eastern objects introduced, but the Eastern name was also frequently retained, and thus for example a Roman squadron of " immortals" was established under the reign of Michael Ducas. Thus, also, the Persian Castle of Oblivion was imitated at Constantinople,[38] and under Justinian we are forcibly reminded of Oriental manners, when we find a convicted traitor mounted on a camel, and led round the streets of the capital.[39] Now in Persia a very ancient and regular practice has prevailed with regard to those persons whom the king may dread as rivals, but whom he still respects for their closeness of kindred or eminence of merit.

By depriving them of sight, he reduces them to the same harmlessness and inefficiency as if he sentenced them to death, while at the same time he avoids the more harsh and hateful nature of that punishment.[40] It seems that this policy, amongst others, was adopted by the sovereigns of Constantinople, and the Byzantine history affords numerous instances of its application. Within twenty years from the blinding of Belisarius, the same punishment from a similar motive was inflicted by the Emperor Tiberius on a Lombard chief.[41] It was not of his life but of his eyes that Constantine the Sixth was deprived by his exemplary mother St. Irene;[42] the Emperor Romanus Diogenes underwent a similar fate from his victorious rival,[43] and in the reign of Nicephorus Botaniates, the rebellion of Bryennius was also thus rewarded.[44] Leo Grammaticus records the instance of Symbatius, son-in-law of Michael the Third, who was condemned to blindness and

---

38. Procop. *Pers. lib. i.* c.6., Theophylact Simocatta, *lib. iv.* c. 6, and Gibbon, vol. iii.
39. Procop. *Goth. lib. iii.* c. 32.
40. Procop. Pers. *lib. i.* c. 6. *Voyages de Chardin*, vol. ii.
41. Paul Warnefrid, *lib. ii.* c. 30.)
42. Theophanes, *Chronograph*. Near his own times this writer becomes better authority.
43. Nicephor. Bryenn. *lib, i.* c. 25.
44. This Bryennius was the father of the historian Nicephorus Bryennius, a fact which, from the dryness of his narrative in this place, would hardly be supposed. See *lib. iv.* c. 17.

reduced to beg his bread by the confiscation of his fortune. [45]

Of such examples several others might be added, but these are already, I conceive, more than sufficient to establish my position. Now the case of Belisarius was precisely one where the exercise of this Oriental policy might be expected. After forty years of faithful service, could the moat servile courtier have advised, or the most angry feeling have impelled Justinian to command his execution? While convinced of his late treacherous enterprise and ambitious views, and dreading his future vengeance, would the emperor, whose natural timidity was augmented by old age, have restored him to freedom and power? It must be remembered that we are to consider here not our own opinion of the integrity of Belisarius, but the firm belief which the emperor entertained at this period, that his general had formed and directed a dangerous conspiracy against his life.

In this dilemma can anything be more probable than that Justinian, according to his favourite system, should have steered a middle course, and by blinding the hero have secured himself against all future fears without incurring unnecessary blame? This sentence, like those to which I have already referred, was no doubt designed and represented as a mitigation of the capital punishment inflicted upon the other conspirators, even upon those of senatorial rank. According to our usual error of estimating ancient events by the standard of our principles and feelings in modern times, the blindness of Belisarius may indeed appear romantic and incredible, but I think that an impartial consideration of the foregoing arguments will show that it was completely in unison with the temper of Justinian and the customs of the Greeks.

From these preliminary observations I how proceed to consider the direct historical testimonies on the disgrace of Belisarius. It is not denied in any quarter that he was closely imprisoned for several months by command of the emperor. Till the moment of his release there is no disagreement, but from that time the narrative now universally admitted represents him as restored to his former honours, while others confirm the popular account of his beggary and blindness. Before we draw these opposite statements in array against each other, it will be proper to clear the ground for the conflict, by removing those volumes of vague declamation or servile copy which, without affording any authority on either side, serve only to clog and embarrass the discussion.

---

45. See Ducange *Not. Hist, ad. Zonar.*

In the first place, it is allowed on all hands that the anonymous chronicle known by the name of the *Historia Miscella*, and published by Muratori in the first volume of his useful collection, can claim no weight on this subject, nor is it so much as noticed by Gibbon.[46] This work, which comprehends the whole history of Rome, is a mere transcript from other writers, more especially Eutropius and Theophanes, and was even supposed by Cardinal Baronius to have been compiled by the latter.[47] It is valuable only in those cases when the writers whom it copies have been lost, but confers no additional authority on those facts, which we still can derive from the fountain head. In the *Historia Miscella* the disgrace of Belisarius is merely abridged from Theophanes,[48] and we must therefore discard it as any original testimony.

The same principle, which is not disputed in the case of the *Historia Miscella*, may also be applied, and must also be admitted, in that of Cedrenus. Of this author's birth or station, nothing certain is known, although he is supposed to have been a monk, and to have lived in the eleventh century.[49] His annals extend from the creation till the reign. of Isaac Comnenus, (*a.d* 1057), and are, as might be expected, barren and meagre in proportion to the richness of the subject. During the whole work Cedrenus is the copyist of some other writer for each particular period, and during several centuries his master is Theophanes, to whom he owns his obligations at his outset. I have collated many passages of these two historians, more especially all those relating to the reign of Justinian, and I can confidently pledge myself to the fact that Cedrenus merely abridges from his predecessor. He often transcribes whole sentences word by word, and implicitly follows his model, even in the grossest errors and omissions.

Thus, for example, Theophanes, from a reason which I shall afterwards explain, devotes many pages to an account of the African expedition and of the Persian wars, but comprises all the Gothic campaigns of Belisarius in a single sentence, although it is evident that they do not yield in interest or importance to any other transactions of the time; and Cedrenus, having no other guide, does not and cannot supply this deficiency. Not merely does be relate the same facts, but he preserves the same arrangement and the same expressions, and as his

---

46. Vol. vii.
47. Muratori, *Praefat. ad Hist. Miscell.*
48. Compare *Hist. Miscell. lib. xvi.* and Theophanes, *Chronograph.*
49. Xylandrus in *Praefat.*

object is conciseness, he generally shortens the original narrative, and only in a very few cases enlarges a little on the topics which Theophanes had introduced. It is needless to quote particular instances, since a reference to any parallel passages will confirm this, observation. So thorough is the dependence of Cedrenus on Theophanes, that the learned Pagi rejects the former in corroboration of a date.[50] With regard to my present subject, on which Cedrenus follows Theophanes as usual.[51] I must maintain that he has no claim to be regarded as a separate and additional authority, and that the credit due to any statement is no more increased by the number of compilations and abridgments than by the printing of another edition. Did anyone ever consider the assertion of a witness, as confirmed by hearing its echoes?

In the twelfth century,[52] Constantine Manasses wrote, in Greek verse, a history of the world from the time of the Creation. The more recent date of his poem (if, indeed, it deserve that name) is not less apparent from the list of the emperors whom he records, than from the swelling and empty style in which he writes. Each circumstance, instead of being distinctly expressed, is buried beneath insipid ornaments; and it is hardly possible, unless through collateral aid, to distinguish his facts from his metaphors.

Thus, without clearly stating the injuries which Belisarius underwent, he merely tells us that this matchless general received the treatment of a fugitive slave, exhausted the goblet of calamity, and was rendered more naked than a pestle.[53] He then breaks forth into a long and tiresome invective against the envy which had brought the hero to this state, and which he laboriously compares to almost every hateful and noxious object in the world. It will be observed, that from the strong terms which he employs, and from his making no mention whatever of any restoration of Belisarius to liberty and wealth, he seems to confirm the popular tradition; yet I think that no reliance can be placed on this rhetorical declaimer, whose vague expressions are not incompatible with either theory, and I would therefore exclude altogether his testimony from this question. The same remark is also applicable to Glycas, whose annals extend forty years further than those of Manasses, but who is supposed to have lived about the same

---

50. *Critica*, vol. ii. Cedrenus, observes Vossius, (*De Hist. Graec. lib, ii.*) See, also a remark of Gibbon to the same effect, (vol. viii.)
51. Cedrenus, vol. i.
52. *Labbe de Script. Byz*.
53. *Constant. Manass*.

period.⁵⁴ His account of the disgrace of Belisarius seems abridged from that of Manasses, who has expressed it in six lines, of which three are almost literally transcribed by Glycas. They are therefore of course entitled to no greater weight than the original testimony of that wretched versifier.

Still less can we derive any information on this point from Suidas. In the article *Belisarius* of his Lexicon, he gives no account of the life or actions of that general, and merely transcribes his character from a passage in Procopius. ⁵⁵

The chronicle of John Malala likewise disappoints us on the present occasion, not so much from any fault in the writer as from the ravages of time. Antioch was his birthplace, but his era is by no means equally certain; and while some critics suppose him to have lived shortly after the reign of Justinian, others have placed him three centuries later.⁵⁶ His annals, which commence at the Creation, are not thought to bear very considerable weight;⁵⁷ yet still, from the want of original evidence on the disgrace of Belisarius, they would probably he almost decisive of the question.

But the latter part of his history has unfortunately perished, and his narrative, through the failure of the manuscript, breaks off abruptly a few months before the release of Belisarius from captivity. It is impossible for us at present to ascertain, or even to conjecture, whether the progress of his work represented Belisarius as driven to beggary and deprived of sight, or as restored to wealth and freedom, yet, from one of his expressions, there may perhaps be some slight reason to imagine that his statement was the former, ⁵⁸ In relating the imprisonment of Belisarius, Malala concludes by telling us, that the veteran general remained beneath the displeasure of his sovereign. Now I cannot, but conceive that if the historian bad intended, shortly afterwards, to commemorate his restoration to imperial favour, he would hardly have spoken in so absolute a sense, and would have qualified the word "re-

---

54. I can find no ground for the conjecture of Fabricius, that the work of Glycas appeared the first, (*Bibliot. Graec.* vol. vi.)
55. See Suidas, vol. i. ed. 1619, and Procop. *Goth. lib. iii.* c. 1.
56. Compare the opinions of Dr. Hody (*Prolegom. ad Malal.*) Jortin (*Eccles. Hist.* vol. iv.), Gibbon (vol. vii.), and Fabricius (*Bibliot. Graec* vol. vi.).
57. See the remark of Gibbon (vol. ii.) "The authority of that ignorant Greek is very slight." And again, (vol. iv.) "John Malala is a writer whose merit and authority are within the limits of his native city."
58. *Annal* vol. ii.

mained" by some limitation of time. I am, however, unwilling to place any reliance on such grammatical niceties of phrase, and must dismiss the Antiochian as an inconclusive witness on either side.

Having excluded those passages from which no original information appears to be derivable, we may endeavour to trace the real fate of Belisarius from the remaining testimonies, with a feeling of regret that we should not find them more ample and authentic. This period was, in fact, one of those unrecorded intervals of time not uncommon in the middle ages, when we are devoid of any certain light from contemporary evidence, and are reduced to the faint and doubtful gleams which later annalists impart. The disgrace of Belisarius occurred after the conclusion of the histories' of Procopius, Agathias, Marcellinus, and Jornandes; and before those of Simocatta, Corippus,[59] and the patriarch Nicephorus, began. Our earliest authority is derived from a writer born almost two hundred years after the event; and when possessing only such scanty and imperfect materials. I do not think that I have insisted too strongly on the weight to which local traditions are entitled. I shall now proceed to show that the restoration of Belisarius to his former rank is maintained only by one original writer, and is opposed by no less than three, of whom two assert his loss of sight and his appeal to public charity.

It will already have been perceived that the single testimony to which I am alluding is that of Theophanes; and since there is no other voucher for his tale, our judgment must materially depend on the question of his credibility. The question resolves itself into these: whether his life and character were fitted to inspire confidence, whether his narrative in general be faithful and correct, and whether in this particular case there was any likelihood of error or temptation to imposture? Of his life we possess a very full account, which Hanckius has laboriously compiled. Theophanes was born in the year 758, and it is only by a conjectural emendation in the test of an ancient biographer that some writers represent him as ten years older.[60] From early youth he manifested a strong taste for the monastic profession; and though the importunity of his parents prevailed on him to contract a marriage, he soon afterwards resigned himself entirely to his inclination for the cloister, and employed his ample inheritance in the building of a monastery, of which he justly became the abbot.

---

59. I call the poems of Corippus history, since they afford many of the most important hints for the reign of Justin the Second, and are interesting in no other respect.
60. Hanckius, *De Script. Byz.* part i. c. xi. sect. 8.

At the second council of Nice, the fervent recluse distinguished himself in the cause of images, and obtained, in after life, the surname of Confessor, from his persevering adherence to their worship. He died in the island of Samothrace, towards the year 818; and since his favourite tenet has triumphed both in the Greek and Latin churches, he has been promoted to the rank of Saint by their grateful attachment.[61] Thus far Theophanes appears only as an honest, though perhaps mistaken, partisan, but his character must assume a very different aspect when we find that he endeavoured to forward and assist his arguments by pretending to the gift of miracles. On one occasion, for example, Theophanes asserted that the disembarkation of the patriarch Nicephorus in another part of his island had at the same instant been made known to him by the Holy Spirit.[62]

Here there is but one alternative: we must pronounce Theophanes either a prophet or an impostor; and those who deny him to have been the latter, must be prepared to revere him as the former. Now I think it not unreasonable to conclude, that he whose whole life is a lie cannot be trusted in his writings; that he who for the interest of his sect commits a fraud upon the living will not scruple to misrepresent the dead, whenever the same interest demands it; and thus the single fact of his pretended inspiration appears sufficient to overthrow his authority as an historian.

If, from the consideration of his character, we pass to the perusal of his chronicle, we shall find the presumption which we drew from the imposture of the one confirmed by the inaccuracy of the other. His work is little more than a panegyric on orthodox and a philippic against pagan or schismatic sovereigns; and in the whole period of five hundred years, from Diocletian to Leo the Fifth, it would be difficult to prove from his pages that the merit of a true believer was ever sullied by a fault, or that any virtue could adorn the errors of a heretic. For this end, not merely are facts distorted, but they are invented or suppressed according to the object of the writer. To select only a single instance from those which almost every passage might afford, he relates the death of Crispus, one of the most memorable and most melancholy events in the reign of Constantine the Great, without the slightest intimation that the emperor was anywise concerned in it;[63] and on the same principle that this partial annalist omits the frailties of the first, imperial convert, he is

---

61. Hanckius, *ecclesià Graecâ*, sect. 52.
62. Hanckius. *ut suprà* sect. 53.
63. *Chronograph.*

desirous to exalt the reputation of Justinian.

Both that emperor and his uncle Justin the First were firm pillars of the Catholic church and though the former in his dotage diverged into some heretical tenets, and even endeavoured to enforce them, this fault, in; the eyes of Theophanes, appeared diminished by its shortness of duration, and atoned for by the orthodox persecutions of almost forty years. Accordingly, Theophanes very gently touches upon and rapidly passes over this error [64] while, on the other hand, he exultingly proclaims that the heretics and Pagans were deprived of their places of worship, which were given to the prevailing party; that their property was confiscated, and. their persons exposed to punishment. The emperor receives from him the rare epithet of *eusebestados*, or most holy; nor do the vices of Theodora restrain the unblushing historian, from bestowing the same title upon her.[65]

Now does it seem improbable, judging from analogy, that this bigoted monk in his obscure retreat, ignorant or careless of the traditions of the capital and the writings of profane historians, should venture to invent or to admit, on the slightest authority, any tale respecting the disgrace' of Belisarius, which would exempt the pious emperor from the imputation of harshness and ingratitude? It is true that this is only a conjecture, but it is a conjecture warranted by the whole spirit of his principles; the tenor of his narrative, and the inconsistencies in this particular story. We know from Agathias. and Menander that the timid temper of Justinian was still, further weakened by old age.

Now, after carrying his suspicion so far as to insult his most ancient and most faithful servant, to seize his property and confine his person, is it likely that the emperor would expose himself to the chance of his resentment by restoring him to liberty and power? If his fears could urge him to the imprisonment, would they have permitted the release without some precaution, such as that of blindness, to render ineffectual any projects of rebellion and revenge? Or, again, if Justinian had really restored Belisarius to his former favour, on what pretext could he, immediately after the death of that general, again sequester his treasures from his widow or his daughter? The exactness of dates, which Theophanes affects, may be only a mark of that experienced cunning which labours to make a falsehood credited by making it circumstantial.

In addition to the foregoing remarks, I may observe, that Theophanes, even when his religious feelings are not concerned, is some-

---
64. *Chronograph.*
65. *Ibid.*

times grossly inaccurate. Thus, for instance, he confounds the persons or the nations of Odoacer and Theodoric, the successive sovereigns of Italy,[66] and attributes to Belisarius, in his first Persian campaign, the reverses which several years before had followed the surrender of Amida. [67] His reading was not extensive, nor was it well applied; and even the fond partiality of a commentator does not hinder Goar from admitting that Theophanes sometimes asserts contradictions by his undistinguishing recital of opposite statements.[68]

He was acquainted with the two books of the Vandal expedition, and the second book of the Persian war by Procopius, of which he has accordingly given a very ample abridgment;[69] often transcribing whole sentences, and never adding any original remarks or further information; but he does not appear to have known the other writings of that author, and dispatches the conquest of Italy by Belisarius in a single sentence. Is this the conduct of an historian, carefully referring to each authentic record in his reach, and assigning to every object its just proportion in his narrative? It may perhaps be thought surprising, that with all these faults, Theophanes should ever have been followed and transcribed by the later Byzantines; but their deference is easily explained, by his honours as a saint and their own superstitious devotion. A fervent partisan of images impresses the modern Greeks with at least as much respect as their forefathers ever paid to sages or to heroes.

Having thus weighed the statement of Theophanes, let us proceed to the consideration of the rest I shall first allege the authority of Zonaras, a monk who lived at nearly the same period as Cedrenus. Like Cedrenus, also, he is sometimes a mere transcriber;[70] but his copy bears greater importance, since in many cases we no longer possess the originals from which it is derived. Several new and authentic facts

---

66. *Chronograph.*
67. *Ibid.*
68. See Hanckius, part i. c xi. sect. 63. The opinions of Gibbon, as to the merits of Theophanes, are almost as contradictory as the author of whom he speaks. When supporting his story of the restoration of Belisarius to wealth and honours, he praises his "exact *Chronicle*," (vol. vii.) Yet in the same volume he informs us, that Theophanes is "full of strange blunders." Elsewhere he remarks, that "his chronology is loose and inaccurate" (vol. ix.), and that he is "the father of many a lie."
69. *Chronograph.* Ludewig justly speaks of the writer with disregard, as of a mere "*epitomator Procopii,*" (*Vita Justiniani.*)
70. Yet the general character of his history is very far superior to that of Cedrenus. See the opinion of Fabricius, (*Bibliot. Graec.* vol. x.) "Zonaras says Gibbon, "had read with care, and thought without prejudice," (vol. vii.) Niebuhr quotes him as an authority for the reign of Tarquinius Superbus, (*Römische Geschichte.*)

relative to the reign of Justinian may be gathered from his work, having probably been taken from the lost histories of Theophanes Byzantius, or Menander.

With regard to the disgrace and death of Belisarius, which he comprises in a single sentence,[71] he evidently contradicts the story of Theophanes, and intimates that the Roman general was never re-established in his forfeited honours and possessions. His silence respecting the blindness of Belisarius may be considered as a strong argument against it; but it must be recollected that Zonaras was above all things studious of brevity, and that a compiler who begins at the Creation has but little space to spare. In his dry and lifeless narrative, we only view as it were the skeletons of great events. I must also remark that Zonaras, with the true servility of a Byzantine Greek, measures the importance of every object by its reference to the sacred person of the sovereign.

Such a feeling is conspicuous in the whole progress of his narrative; and thus he might probably consider the enrichment of the treasury by a large confiscation as far more interesting to his readers than the fate of the disgraced and forsaken hero. This principle may, I think, afford a full and satisfactory explanation why Zonaras should pass over the blindness and beggary of Belisarius; although he found them recorded in the earlier and more circumstantial histories which he has unskilfully abridged.

The next writer to whom I shall advert, John Tzetzes (erroneously called a monk by Gibbon)[72] is supposed to have died at the close of the twelfth century, and has left behind him several "*Chiliads*" or *Cantos* of a thousand lines of "political" or popular verses, in which the most striking events of former times, or the most curious facts in natural history, are commemorated, and, among others, he brings forward the fate of Belisarius, deprived of sight by order of the emperor, and compelled to solicit from public charity a scanty and degrading subsistence.[73] The circumstance of his not writing in plain sober prose may, in the judgment of some persons, create a prejudice against his testimony; but it must be recollected that poetry is precious to the historian whenever it does not claim the privilege of fiction. If it professes to relate events without adorning them, it is entitled to precisely the same credit as the author would have received in the more com-

---

71. *Annal.* vol. ii.
72. Vol. vii.
73. Chil. iii. v. 339

mon style of narrative.

Thus the conquests of the Normans in Italy are chiefly to be gathered from the rude lines of William the Apulian; and the harmonious numbers of Ferdousi afford the best materials for the early annals of Persia; and if I may venture to employ a sacred instance, I shall urge that the authority of the *Book of Job* is not lessened by the metre in which the original is written.[74] The accuracy of John Tzetzes, on this occasion, may therefore be fairly measured by that which the rest of his narrative displays; and, with regard to this point, I cannot do better than allege the testimony of so eminent a scholar as Fabricius, he remarks:

> Tzetzes was acquainted with many tongues, even with the Syriac and Hebrew; he had deeply studied the poets, the historians, the mathematicians, and the philosophers of every age; and his writings show various and extraordinary erudition.[75]

A painful perusal of the whole twelve thousand and some hundred lines may perhaps have earned me some right of stating an opinion, and I think Tzetzes entitled to no small share of the praises which he so frequently and so lavishly bestows upon himself.[76] It should always be borne in mind, that the same degree of learning which appears common and familiar in the nineteenth century, must excite surprise and admiration when we find it in the twelfth. Tzetzes manifests considerable ingenuity in discovering the real events, which lie concealed beneath the fables of mythology; and he quotes from above two hundred ancient authors, many of whom have not been preserved till modern times.

His inaccuracies, which are by no means numerous, refer very seldom to facts, but rather to circumstances of time and place, and may be probably ascribed to the practice in which he glories, of writing from memory instead of consulting his originals as he proceeds.[77] Thus, for instance, he transfers to the Battle of Cannae the unheeded earthquake which occurred during that of Thrasimene.[78] His two principal blunders are relative to the British islands;[79] but still greater ignorance

---

74. See Dom Calmet's Dictionary, vol. i.
75. *Bibliot. Graec.* vol. x.
76. The conceit of Tzetzes is not a little ludicrous, and breaks out on every occasion. "If anyone," he says, "wishes to behold so exact representation of Cato, both in mind and person, let him look at me." See Chiliad III. v. 170, and XI. v. 22. In the latter passage he also compares himself to Epaminondas
77. *Chil.* VIII. v. 182, and XII. v. 13.
78. See *Chil.* I. v. 769, and *Liv. lib. xxii.* c. 5.

is displayed in the other Byzantine writers who mention them, not excepting even the discerning and exact Procopius.[80] With regard to the case of Belisarius, there is one circumstance which strongly tends to prove that Tzetzes did not speak from mere popular report, and had not formed his judgment without authentic and convincing documents.

After relating the beggary and blindness of the hero, he tells us that other chronicles, on the contrary, assert his restoration to opulence and honours. From this remark, it seems natural to conclude that Tzetzes had read the annals of Cedrenus and Theophanes, but was induced to reject their testimony by the superior credit of other histories which have since unfortunately perished. Now, devoid as we are, on this point, of all contemporary information, ought we not to value and to trust the dispassionate opinion of a judicious writer, upon evidence which we have no longer the power of producing fully or therefore of accurately weighing?

It is at present generally held, on the authority of Pagi, Gibbon, and Ducange, that Tzetzes is the earliest writer extant who attests the mendicity and loss of sight of Belisarius. I am now about to bring forward a new and authentic testimony, to which public attention has never yet been called, and by which this story may be traced nearly one century higher. The work in question, which was not printed till the year 1711, could not be known to Pagi, whose first volume appeared in 1689, nor to Ducange, who died in 1688; but it ought not to have escaped the discerning eyes of Gibbon or Lebeau. It consists of a description, in four books, of the city of Constantinople, and is inserted in Banduri's *Imperium Orientale*. The era as well as the rank of the author, are shown by his dedication to the Emperor Alexius Comnenus, who ascended the throne in the year 1081, but we are ignorant of his name.

This omission may, at first sight, be considered as lessening the value of his testimony; but reflection will convince us that, though anonymous assertions should always be received with doubt and distrust, the case is very different when the disguise of a writer has arisen, not from any wilful concealment on his part, but from the deficiency of records. It is seldom that an historian has occasion to speak of himself in the progress of his work, and his name, when confined to the title-page, is more exposed to the injuries of time than any other

---

79. *Chil.* VIII. v. 719, and X. v. 651.
80. *Goth. lib. iv.* c. 20.

portion of the manuscript. Its preservation, therefore, is less frequently due to the author than to the information of the copyist and the care of the librarian. Several of the most interesting and important ancient documents are nameless; nor do the ablest critics appear to consider their credit as impaired, provided that the time and place of their composition can be ascertained by other means.

Is not the ninth panegyric admitted as excellent authority for the times of Constantine the Great; and do we not owe to the Valesian Fragment our best materials for the reign of Theodoric in Italy? If we only knew of Procopius that he was a fellow-soldier of the hero whose campaigns he has related, should not we think his claim on our confidence sufficiently established without any mention of his name? In like manner, I conceive that the writer of this description of Constantinople, notwithstanding his involuntary mask, is entitled, when he relates [81] the mendicity and loss of sight of Belisarius, to all the credit which his undisputed accuracy on other points seems justly to deserve.

The acceptance of his work by the emperor (in that age a very unusual honour) may also be admitted as some proof of his merit and exactness. It is true that his evidence dates only from the end of the eleventh century; but it will assume a higher and more authentic character, and approach more nearly to the time of action, if we believe, with Banduri,[82] that this work consists chiefly of compilations from earlier historians. This opinion he maintains on two, grounds: first, the inequalities of the style; and secondly, the collation of some passages taken from those chronicles which are still preserved; so that other extracts may be concluded to have been likewise made from the greater number which have perished. I must remark that the judgment of Banduri on this point is entirely unbiased, since it seems, from a subsequent passage in his writings, that he adhered to the other accounts of the fate of Belisarius. [83] He did not consider it his duty, as a commentator, to investigate the subject for himself, but borrowed his decision from Ducange, as is proved by his blindly following that learned Frenchman in a strange mistake regarding Agathias.

Ducange, who on this occasion departs from his usual admirable and unerring accuracy, rests his denial of the popular tradition principally on the ground that Agathias, a contemporary writer, records the

---

81. See *Imp. Orient*, vol. i.
82. *Praefat.*
83. *Imp. Orient*, vol. ii.

imprisonment of Belisarius without mentioning his mendicity and loss of sight.[84] Now there is not one word of this imprisonment in the Greek historian, nor could we expect to find it in his pages, since it is believed to have occurred nearly four years after the conclusion of his narrative.[85]

Thus, then, stands the case. The mendicity of Belisarius is contradicted by one original writer of the ninth century,[86] and asserted by two of the eleventh or the twelfth.[87] It remains for the reader to determine whether the force of tradition, the little dependence that can be placed on the fidelity of the former historian, and the other grounds which have been stated, do not more than counterbalance and outweigh this difference of time.

Although on this subject no further original evidence appears to be attainable, there is one other collateral consideration which may serve to guide and assist our judgment. I have already had occasion to allude to those Byzantine historians whose works are no longer preserved, but whose names and subjects may still be gathered from the casual mention of other writers. A list of them has been drawn out by Fabricius, with his usual laborious skill; and, exclusive of such compilers and abridgers as we still possess in Cedrenus and Zonaras, they amount to no less than thirty-three, a number exceeding those extant.[88] It must likewise be recollected, that at the revival of literature and learning in the fifteenth century, several ancient compositions still existed, of which the present age is unhappily deprived. Thus, for instance, the treatise of Cicero De Gloria was in the hands of Petrarch;[89] and many Grecian manuscripts were brought into the West after the taking of Constantinople by Mahomet the Second.

From hence it seems natural to conclude that the great scholars of that or the succeeding age may have had access to documents Which

---

84. *Not. Hist, ad Zonar.*
85. Agathias, *lib. v.* and Pagi, *Critic,* vol. ii.
86. As the chronicle of Theophanes extends till the year 813, it was not completed, and probably was not begun, till the ninth century, (Hanckius *De Script Byz.* part i c. xi. sect. 60.)
87. That Tzetzes did not copy the anonymous author of the eleventh century, and should therefore be considered a separate authority, is proved by a slight difference between them. The one represents the bowl which Belisarius held out for charity as of wood, and the other as of earthenware.
88. *Bibliot. Graec.*, vol. vi.
89. Petrarch. *Epist. lib. xv.* I am indebted for this quotation to Middleton's *Life of Cicero.*

are now denied us, and that their opinion on any point of history should therefore carry considerable weight At that time, when every branch of science, literature, or legislation was in its infancy, men applied themselves to classic studies with a degree of undivided attention and persevering industry, which has produced the most advantageous consequences, which has cleared away the brambles and the thorns from the path of their successors, and thereby enabled them to pursue it to a greater distance. The present age is doubtless better skilled in the knowledge of antiquity, but we are deeply indebted to their labours for that knowledge; and, if I may borrow the lively illustration of Crousaz, it is only by climbing on their shoulders that we see further than they.[90]

Now nearly all these eminent scholars, Crinitus, Volaterranus, Pontanus, and Egnatius, concur in their belief of the blindness of Belisarius; although, according to the classic model, they do not quote the authority which guided them.[91] To this general agreement there is only one single exception. Alciat dissents from the received opinion respecting Belisarius;[92] but Alciat is an author whose own ignorance may be justly presumed from his venturing to charge Tacitus with ignorance of Latin.[93] He was urged to the defence of Justinian by a blind admiration for the compiler of the Pandects;[94] and almost his only argument for denying the alleged fate of the Byzantine hero is drawn from the silence of Agathias and Procopius, and is grounded on the supposition that their histories extended sufficiently far to have comprehended this memorable event, had it really taken place.

I need not remark, that as they conclude some years before the disgrace of Belisarius, the silence of Thucydides or Livy on the subject would be just as conclusive an objection. Dismissing Alciat, therefore, with merited contempt, I am disposed to place great reliance on the unanimity of his more learned brethren, who, from possessing more full and perfect evidence, could perhaps more justly estimate the merits of the cause. Amongst those who, at a later period, adhered to that opinion, I might mention Baronius and Fiorelli, but the cardinal is biased by his wish to inflict a judgment on Belisarius for his arbitrary

---

90. Crousaz, *Logique*, vol. i.
91. See Crinitus, *De Honestâ Disciplinâ, lib. ix.* c. 6. Volaterranu, *Anhiropol. lib. xxiii.* ed. 1552. Pontanus *De Fortitudine, lib. ii. Op.* vol. i. ed. 1556. and Egnatius *De Exempl. Ill. Vir. lib. iv.* Ed. 1554.
92. Parergon, *lib. iv.* c. 24.
93. See La Mothe Le Vayer, *Œuvres* vol. iii.
94. This motive of Alciat is admitted by Gibbon, (vol. vii.)

deposition of a Pope;[95] and Fiorelli is only anxious to display his own Italian tinsel eloquence.[96]

Before I conclude, it may be proper to make some mention of a statue which lately formed part of Prince Borghese's collection at Rome, but which at present is placed in the Louvre. It clearly represents the act of begging, and, till the middle of the last century, was unanimously ascribed to the Byzantine general.[97] By the aid of a passage in *Suetonius*, Winkelman most ingeniously devised another explanation, and supposed the figure to represent Augustus propitiating

Nemesis, according to his yearly custom. This theory, however, has not proved altogether satisfactory; the statue has since been attributed to Chrisippus, and is at present inscribed with the name of Posidonius. The original opinion, which called it Belisarius, is in perfect accordance with its attitude, but is attended with two great, and I think decisive, objections. Its skilful sculpture seems incompatible with the decline of the arts in the sixth century, nor is it easy to imagine by what monarch it could have been raised. The immediate successors of Justinian were bound to the memory of that emperor by ties of family respect and gratitude, and would hardly have insulted it by such a monument as this; nor would other nations have been desirous to display the image of their conqueror.

---

95. *Annal. Eccles. a.d.* 561. No. 7.)
96. *Monarch. d'Orient*, ed. 1679. He is speaking of the glory of Justinian.
97. See Sandrart, *De Sculpt. Vet.*

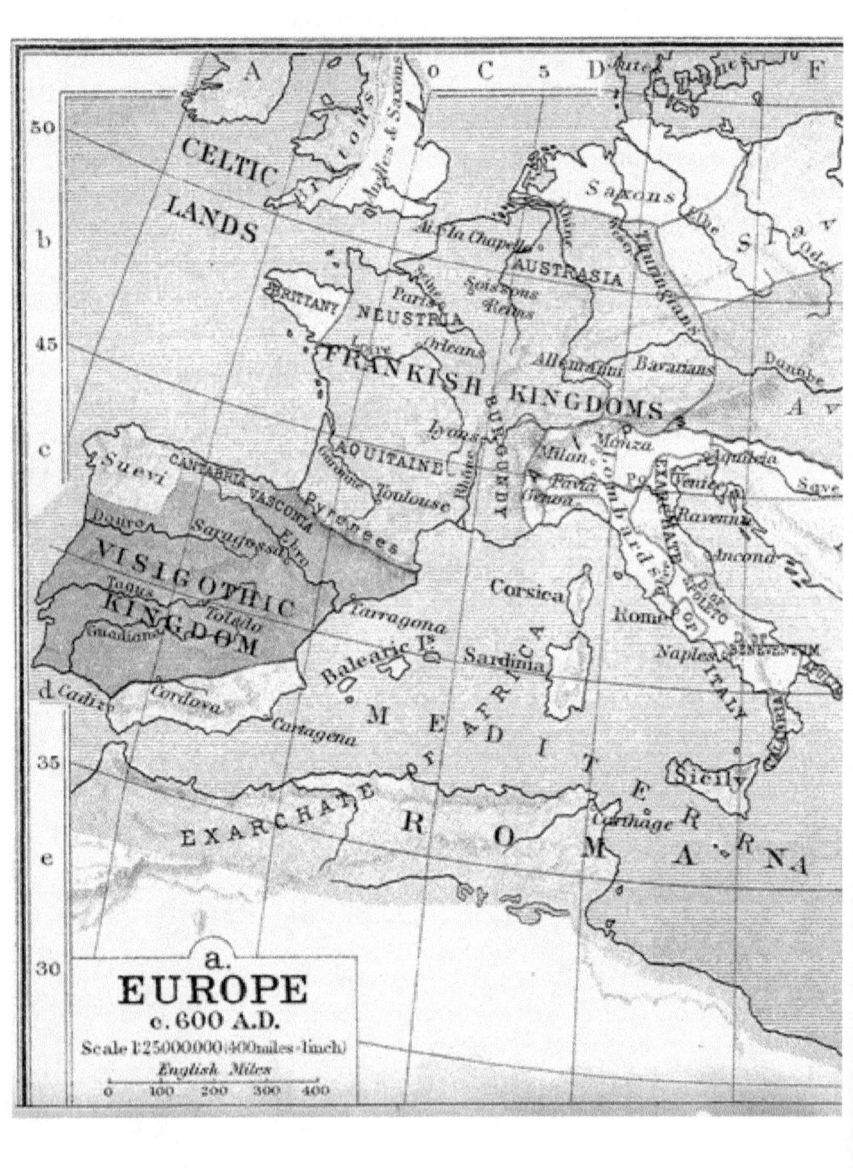

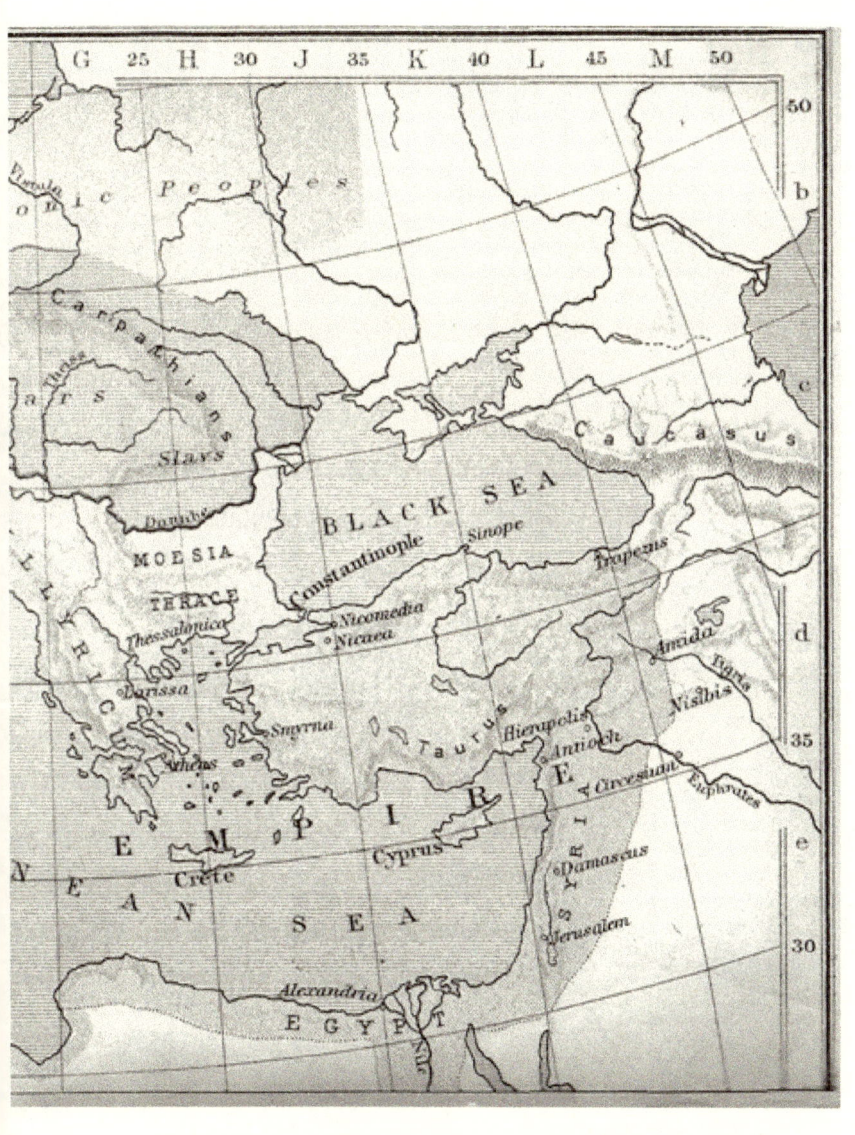

Belisarius: A Short Biography
By S. G. Goodrich

This celebrated general, to whom the emperor Justinian is chiefly indebted for the glory of his reign, was a native of Germania, on the confines of Thrace, and was born about the year 505. It is probable that he was of noble descent, liberally educated, and a professor of the Christian faith. The first step in his military career was an appointment in the personal guard of Justinian, while that prince was yet heir apparent to the throne,

The Roman or Byzantine Empire, at this period, embraced almost exactly the present territory of the Turkish dominions in Europe and Asia Minor, with the addition of Greece—Constantinople being its capital. Italy was held by the Goths; Corsica, Sardinia and Barbary in Africa, by the Vandals.

Justin I., an Illyrian peasant, having distinguished himself as a soldier, had become emperor. His education was of course neglected, and such was his ignorance, that his signature could only be obtained by means of a wooden case, which directed his pen through the four first letters of his name. From his accession, the chief administration of affairs devolved on Justinian, his nephew and intended heir, whom he was reluctantly compelled to raise from office to office, and at length to acknowledge as his partner on the throne. His death, after a languid reign of nine years and a life of nearly fourscore, left Justinian sole sovereign in name, as well as in fact.

In order to appreciate the life and actions of Belisarius, it is necessary to understand the character of the new emperor, during whose long reign his great exploits were performed. The first act of Justinian on ascending the throne, was to marry a dissolute actress, named Theodora, who, though licentious, avaricious, cruel and vindictive, soon acquired an almost complete control over him. His mind was essentially feeble and inconstant, and, though his Christian faith was doubtless sincere, it was less fruitful of virtues than of rites and forms. At his accession his treasury was full; but it was soon exhausted by his profuseness, and heavy taxes were imposed, offices put to sale, charities suppressed, private fortunes seized, and, in short, every act of rapacity, injustice and oppression, practised by his ministers, to support the wasteful magnificence of the court.

The troops of the empire at this period were by no means what they had been in the time of Scipio and Caesar. They consisted, to a great extent, of foreign mercenaries, and were divided into squadrons according to their country; thus destroying all unity of feeling, and annihilating that national spirit which once made the Roman arms the terror of the world. These hired troops, which greatly outnumbered the native soldiers, marched under their own national banner, were commanded by their own officers, and usually followed their own military regulations. The inefficiency of such mingled and discordant forces, is obvious; yet it was under such a system that Belisarius entered upon his military career.

With a feeble and corrupt government, an ill-appointed and trustless army, the Roman Empire was still surrounded with powerful enemies. It is scarcely possible to conceive of a great nation in a condition of more complete debility and helplessness, than was the kingdom of the Caesars, at the period in which Belisarius appears upon the active stage of life.

Kobad, King of Persia, after a long cessation of hostilities, renewed the war toward the close of Justin's reign, by the invasion of Iberia, which claimed the protection of the emperor. At this period, Belisarius, being about twenty years of age, had the command of a squadron of horse, and was engaged in some of the conflicts with the Persian forces, on the borders of Armenia. In conjunction with an officer named Sittas, he ravaged a large extent of territory, and brought back a considerable number of prisoners.

On a second incursion, however, they were less fortunate; for. being suddenly attacked by the Persian forces, they were entirely defeated. It appears that Belisarius incurred no blame, for he was soon after promoted to the post of Governor of Dara, and the command of the forces stationed there. It was at this place that he chose Procopius, the historian, as his secretary, and who afterwards repaid his kindness by a vain attempt to brand his name with enduring infamy.

Soon after Belisarius obtained the command of Dara, Justinian came to the throne, and enjoined it upon his generals to strengthen the defences of the empire in that quarter. This was attempted, but the Persians baffled the effort. Belisarius was now appointed general of the East, being commander-in-chief of the whole line of the Asiatic frontier. Foreseeing that a formidable struggle was soon to ensue, he applied himself to the raising and disciplining an army. He traversed the neighbouring provinces in person, and at last succeeded in mustering five and twenty thousand men. These, however, were without discipline, and their spirit was depressed by the ill success that had long attended the Roman arms.

In this state of things, the news suddenly came, that 40,000 men, the flower of the Persian Army, commanded by Firouz, was marching upon Dara. Confident of victory, the Persian general announced his approach, by the haughty message that a bath should be ready for him at Dara the next evening. Belisarius made no other reply than preparations for battle. Fortifying himself in the best manner he was able, he awaited the onset; exhorting his men, however, by every stimulating motive he could suggest, to do honour to the name and fame of Rome.

The battle began by a mutual discharge of arrows, so numerous as to darken the air. When the quivers were exhausted, they came to closer combat. The struggle was obstinate and bloody; and the Persians were already about to win the victory, when a body of horse, judiciously stationed behind a hill by Belisarius, rushed forward, and turned the tide of success. The Persians fled, and the triumph of Belisarius was complete. They left their royal standard upon the field of battle, with 8000 slain. This victory had a powerful effect, and decided the fate of the campaign.

The aged Kobad, who had conceived a profound contempt for the Romans, was greatly irritated by the defeat of his troops. He determined upon a still more powerful effort, and the next season sent a formidable army to invade Syria. Belisarius, with a promptitude that astounded he enemy, proceeded to the defence of this province, and, with an inferior force, compelled the Persian army to retreat. Obliged at length, by his soldiers, against his own judgment, to give battle to the enemy, he suffered severely, and only avoided total defeat by the greatest coolness and address. Even the partial victory of the enemy was without advantage to them, for they were obliged to retreat, and abandon their enterprise. Soon after this event, Kobad died, in his eighty-third year, and his successor, Nushirvan, concluded a treaty of peace with Justinian.

The war being thus terminated, Belisarius took up his residence at Constantinople, and here became the second husband of Antonina, who, though the child of an actress, had contracted an exalted marriage on account of her beauty, and having filled a high office, enjoyed the rank and honours of a patrician. While thus raised above the dangerous profession of her mother, she still adhered to the morals of the stage. Though openly licentious, she obtained through her bold, decided, and intriguing character, aided by remarkable powers of fascination, a complete ascendancy over Belisarius. It is seldom that a man is great in all respects, and the weakness of the general whose history we are delineating, was exhibited in a blind and submissive attachment to this profligate woman.

A singular outbreak of popular violence occurred about this period, which stained the streets of Constantinople with blood, and threatened for a time to hurl Justinian from his throne. The fondness of the Romans for the amusements of the circus, had in no degree abated. Indeed, as the gladiatorial combats had been suppressed, these games were frequented with redoubled ardour. The charioteers were distinguished by the various colours of red, white, blue, and green, intending to represent the four seasons. Those of each colour, especially the blue and green, possessed numerous and devoted partisans, which became at last connected with civil and religious prejudices.

Justinian favoured the Blues, who became for that reason the emblem of royalty; on the other hand, the Greens became the type of disaffection. Though these dangerous factions were denounced by the statutes, still, at the period of which we speak, each party were ready to lavish their fortunes, risk their lives, and brave the severest sentence of the laws, in support of their darling colour. At the commencement of the year 532, by one of those sudden caprices which are often displayed by the populace, the two factions united, and turned their vengeance against Justinian. The prisons were forced, and the guards massacred. The city was then fired in various parts, the cathedral of St. Sophia, a part of the imperial palace, and a great number of public and private buildings, were wrapped in conflagration. The cry of "*Nika! Nika!*" Vanquish! Vanquish! ran through every part of the capital.

The principal citizens hurried to the opposite shore of the Bosphorus, and the emperor entrenched himself within his palace. In the mean time, Hypatius, nephew of the emperor Anastatius, was declared emperor by the rioters, and so formidable had the insurrection now become, that Justinian was ready to abdicate his crown. For the first and last time, Theodora seemed worthy of the throne, for she withstood the pusillanimity of her husband, and, through her animated exhortations, it was determined to take the chance of victory or death.

Justinian's chief hope now rested on Belisarius Assisted by Mundus, the governor of Illyria, who chanced to be in the capital, he now called upon the guards to rally in defence of the emperor; but these refused to obey him. Meanwhile, by another caprice the party of the Blues, becoming ashamed of their conduct, shrunk one by one away, and left Hypatius to be sustained by the Greens alone.

These were dismayed at seeing Belisarius, issuing with a few troops which he had collected, from the smoking ruins of the palace. Drawing his sword, and commanding his veterans to follow, he fell upon them like a thunderbolt. Mundus, with another division of soldiers, rushed upon them from the opposite direction. The insurgents were panic-struck, and dispersed in every quarter. Hypatius was dragged from the throne which he had ascended a few hours before, and was soon after executed in prison. The Blues now emerged from their concealment, and, falling upon their antagonists, glutted their merciless and ungovernable vengeance. No less than thirty thousand persons were slain in this fearful convulsion.

We must now turn our attention to Africa, in which the next exploits of Belisarius were performed. The northern portion of this part of the world, known to us by the merited byword of Barbary, hardly retains a trace of the most formidable rival and opulent province of Rome. After the fall of Jugurtha, at the commencement of the second century, it had enjoyed a long period of prosperity and peace—having escaped the sufferings which had fallen upon every other portion of the empire. The Africans in the fifth century were abounding in wealth, population, and resources. During the minority of Valentinian, Boniface was appointed governor of Africa. Deceived by Ætius into a belief of ingratitude on the part of the government a home, he determined upon resistance, and, with this view, concluded a treaty with the Vandals in the southern portion of Spain.

These, embarking from Andalusia, whose name still denotes their former residence, landed at the opposite cape of Ceuta, *a. d.* 429. Their leader was the far-famed Genseric, one of the most able, but most lawless and bloody monarchs recorded in history. Of a middle stature, and lamed by a fall from his horse, his demeanour was thoughtful and silent; he was contemptuous of luxury, sudden in anger, and boundless in ambition. Yet his impetuosity was always guided and restrained by cunning. He well knew how to tempt the allegiance of a foreign nation, to cast the seeds of future discord, or to rear them to maturity.

The barbarians on their passage to Africa consisted of 50,000 fighting men, with a great crowd of women and children. Their progress through the African province was rapid and unopposed, till Boniface, discovering the artifices of Ætius, and the favourable disposition of the government of Rome, bitterly repented the effects of his hasty resentment. He now endeavoured to withdraw his Vandal allies; but he found it less easy to allay, than it had been to raise, the storm. His proposals were haughtily rejected, and both parties had recourse to arms. Boniface was defeated, and in the event, Genseric obtained entire possession of the Roman provinces in Africa.

Carthage, which had risen from its ruins at the command of Julius Caesar and been embellished by Diocletian, had regained a large share of its former opulence and pride, and might be considered, at the time of which we speak, the second city in the western empire. Making this his capital, Genseric proceeded to adopt various measures to power, and, among others, determined upon the creation of a naval force. With him, project and performance were never far asunder. His ships soon rode m the Mediterranean, and carried terror and destruction in their train. He annexed to his kingdom the Balearic islands, Corsica and Sardinia; the last of which was afterwards allotted by the Vandals as a place of exile or imprisonment for captive Moors: and during many years, the ports of Africa were what they became in more recent days, the abode of fierce and unpunished pirates.

With every returning spring, the fleet of Genseric ravaged the coasts of Italy and Sicily, and even of Greece and Illyria, sometimes bearing off the inhabitants to slavery, and sometimes levelling their cities to the ground. Emboldened by long impunity, he attacked every government alike. On one occasion, when sailing from Carthage, he was asked by the pilot of his vessel to what coast he desired to steer— "Leave the guidance to God," exclaimed the stern barbarian; "God will doubtless lead us against the guilty objects of his anger!"

The most memorable achievement of Genseric, the sack of Rome in 455, is an event too much out of the track of our narrative to be detailed here. We can only pause to state, that, after spending a fortnight in that great metropolis, and loading his fleets with its spoils, he returned to Africa, bearing the Empress Eudccia thither, as his captive. She was, at length, released, but one of her daughters was compelled by Genseric to accept his son in marriage.

The repeated outrages of the Vandal king at length aroused the tardy resentment of the court of Constantinople, and Leo I., then emperor, despatched an army against him, consisting of nearly one hundred thousand men, attended by the most formidable fleet that had ever been launched by the Romans. The commander was a weak man, and being cheated into a truce of five days by Genseric, the latter took advantage of a moment of security, and, in the middle of the night, caused a number of small vessels, filled with combustibles, to be introduced among the Roman ships. A conflagration speedily ensued; and the Romans, starting from their slumbers, found themselves encompassed by fire and the Vandals. The wild shrieks of the perishing multitude mingled with the crackling of the flames and the roaring of the winds; and the enemy proved as unrelenting as the elements. The greater part of the fleet was destroyed, and only a few shattered ships, and a small number of survivors, found their way back to Constantinople.

A peace soon followed this event, which continued I uninterrupted till the time of Justinian. Genseric died in 477, leaving his kingdom to his son Hunneric. About the year 530, Gelimer being upon the Vandal throne, Justinian began to meditate an expedition against him. His generals, with the exception of Belisarius, were averse to the undertaking. The same feeling was shared by many of the leading men about the court, and in an assembly, in which the subject was under discussion, Justinian was about to yield to the opposition, when a bishop from the east earnestly begged admission to his presence.

On entering the council chamber he exhorted the emperor to stand forth as the champion of the church, and, in order to confirm him in the enterprise, he declared that the Lord had appeared to him in a vision, saying, "I will march before him in his battles, and make him sovereign of Africa." Men seldom reject a tale, however fantastic, which coincides with their wishes or their prepossessions. All the doubts of Justinian were at once removed; he commanded a fleet and army to be forthwith equipped for this sacred enterprise, and endeavoured still further to insure its success by his austerity in fasts and vigils. Belisarius was named supreme commander, still retaining his title as General of the East.

In the month of June, *a. d.* 533, the Roman armament, consisting of five hundred transports, with twenty thousand sailors, and nearly the same number of soldiers, became ready for departure. The general embarked, attended on this occasion by Antonina and his secretary, the historian Procopius, who, at first, had shared in the popular fear and distaste of the enterprise, but had afterwards been induced to join it by a hopeful dream. The galley of Belisarius was moored near the shore, in front of the imperial palace, where it received a last visit from Justinian, and a solemn blessing from the patriarch of the city, A soldier recently baptised was placed on board, to secure its prosperous voyage; its sails were then unfurled, and, with the other ships in its train, it glided down the straits of the Bosphorus, and gradually disappeared from the lingering gaze of the assembled multitude.

With a force scarcely one fourth as strong as that which was annihilated by Genseric, about seventy years before, Belisarius proceeded upon his expedition. Having touched at Sicily and Malta, he proceeded to the coast of Africa, where he landed in September, about one hundred and fifty miles from Carthage, and began his march upon that city. He took several towns, but enforcing the most rigid discipline upon his troops, and treating the inhabitants with moderation and courtesy, he entirely gained their confidence and good will. They brought ample provisions to his camp, and gave him such a reception as might be expected rather by a native than a hostile army.

When the intelligence of the landing and progress of the Romans reached Gelimer, who was then at Hermione, he was roused to revenge, and took his measures with promptitude and skill. He had an army of eighty thousand men, the greater part of whom were soon assembled, and posted in a defile about ten miles from Carthage, directly in the route by which Belisarius was approaching. Several severe skirmishes soon followed, in which the Vandals were defeated.

The main army now advanced, and a general engagement immediately ensued. In the outset, the Vandals prevailed, and the Romans were on the eve of flying, defeated, from the field. A pause on the part of Gelimer was, however, seized upon by Belisarius to collect and rally his forces, and with a united effort he now charged the Vandal Army. The conflict was fierce, but brief: Gelimer was totally defeated, and, with a few faithful adherents, he sought safety in flight. Knowing that the ruinous walls of Carthage could not sustain a siege, he took his way to the deserts of Numidia.

All idea of resistance was abandoned; the gates of Carthage were thrown open, and the chains across the entrance of the port were removed. The Roman fleet soon after arrived, and was safely anchored in the harbour. On the 16th September, Belisarius made a solemn entry into the capital. Having taken every precaution against violence and rapacity, not a single instance of tumult or outrage occurred, save that a captain of one of the vessels plundered some of the inhabitants, but was obliged to restore the spoil he had taken. The soldiers marched peaceably to their quarters; the inhabitants continued to pursue their avocations; the shops remained open, and, in spite of the change of sovereigns, public business was not for a moment interrupted! Belisarius took up his quarters in the palace of Gelimer, and in the evening held a sumptuous banquet there, being attended by the same servants who had so lately been employed by the Vandal king.

With his usual activity, Belisarius immediately applied himself to the restoration of the ruinous ramparts of the city. The ditch was deepened, the breaches filled, the walls strengthened, and the whole was completed in so short a space as to strike the Vandals with amazement. Meanwhile, Gelimer was collecting a powerful army at Bulla, on the borders of Numidia at the distance of four days' journey from Carthage.

Having placed the capital in a proper state for defence, at the end of three months from its capture, Belisarius led forth his army, leaving only five hundred, troops to guard the city. Gelimer was now within twenty miles of the capital, having raised an army of one hundred thousand men. No sooner had the Romans taken up their march toward his camp, than they prepared for battle.

The armies soon met, and Belisarius, having determined to direct all his endeavours against the centre of the Vandal force, caused a charge to be made by some squadrons of the horse guards. These were repulsed, and a second onset, also, proved unsuccessful.

But a third prevailed, after an obstinate resistance. The ranks of the enemy were broken; Zazo, the king's brother, was slain, and consternation now completed the rout of the Vandals. Gelimer, under the influence of panic, betook himself to flight; his absence was perceived, and his conduct imitated. The soldiers dispersed in all directions, leaving their camp, their goods, their families, all in the hands of the Romans. Belisarius seized upon the royal treasure in behalf of his sovereign, and in spite of his commands, the licentious soldiers spent the night in debauchery, violence and plunder.

Gelimer fled to the mountains of Papua, inhabited by a savage but friendly tribe of Moors. He sought refuge in the small town of Medenus, which presented a craggy precipice on all sides Belisarius returned to Carthage, and sent out various detachments, which rapidly subdued the most remote portions of the Vandal kingdom.

Immediately after the capture of Carthage, he had despatched one of his principal officers to Justinian, announcing these prosperous events. The intelligence arrived about the time that the emperor had completed his *pandects*.[1] The exultation of the monarch is evinced by the swelling titles he assumes in the preamble of these laws. All mention of the general by whom his conquests had been achieved, is carefully avoided; while the emperor is spoken of as the "pious," "happy," "victorious," and "triumphant!" He even boasts, in his Institutes, of the warlike fatigues he had borne, though he had never quitted the luxurious palace of Constantinople, except for recreation m some of his neighbouring villas.

While the Roman general was actively employed at Carthage, Pharus was proceeding in the siege of Medenus, which had been begun immediately after the flight of Gelimer. Pent up in this narrow retreat, the sufferings of the Vandal monarch were great, from the want of supplies and the savage habits of the Moors. His lot was likewise embittered by the recollection of the soft and luxurious life to which he had lately been accustomed.

During their dominion in Africa, the Vandals had declined from their former hardihood, and yielded to the enervating influence of climate, security and success. Their arms were laid aside; gold embroidery shone upon their silken robes, and every dainty from the sea and land were combined in their rich repasts. Reclining in the shade of delicious gardens, their careless hours were amused by dancers and musicians, and no exertion beyond the chase, interrupted their voluptuous repose.

The Moors of Papua, on the contrary, dwelt in narrow huts, sultry in summer, and pervious to the snows of winter. They most frequently slept upon the bare ground, and a sheepskin for a couch was a rare refinement. The same dress, a cloak and a tunic, clothed them at every season, and they were strangers to the use of both bread and wine. Their grain was devoured in its crude state, or at best was coarsely pounded and baked, with little skill, into an unleavened paste.

Compelled to share this savage mode of life, Gelimer and his attendants began to consider captivity, or even death, as better than the

---

1. These were a digest of the civil law of Rome, made by the order of Justinian, and have been preserved to our lime. They contained five hundred and thirty-four decisions or judgments of lawyers, to which the emperor gave the force of law. The compilation consists of fifty books, and has contributed to save Justinian's name from the contemps and reproach which had otherwise been heaped upon it.

daily hardships they endured. To avail himself of this favourable disposition, Pharus, in a friendly letter, proposed a capitulation, and assured Gelimer of generous treatment from Belisarius and Justinian. The spirit of the Vandal prince, however, was still not wholly broken, and he refused the offers, while acknowledging the kindness of his enemy. In his answer he entreated the gifts of a lyre, a loaf of bread, and a sponge, and his messenger explained the grounds of this singular petition. At Medenus, he had never tasted the food of civilized nations, he wished to sing to music an ode on his misfortunes written by himself, and a swelling on his eyes needed a sponge for its cure. The brave Roman, touched with pity that such wants should be felt by the grandson and successor of Genseric, forthwith sent these presents up the mountain, but by no means abated the watchfulness of his blockade.

The siege had already continued for upwards of three months, and several Vandals had sunk beneath its hardships, but Gelimer still displayed the stubborn inflexibility usual to despotic rulers, when the sight of a domestic affliction suddenly induced him to yield In the hovel where he sat gloomily brooding over his hopeless fortunes, a Moorish woman was preparing, at the fire, some coarse dough. Two children, her son and the nephew of Gelimer, were watching her progress with the eager anxiety of famine. The young Vandal was the first to seize the precious morsel, still glowing with heat, and blackened with ashes, when the Moor, by blows and violence, forced it from his mouth.

So fierce a struggle for food, at such an age, overcame the sternness of Gelimer. He agreed to surrender on the same terms lately held out to him, and the promises of Pharus were confirmed by the Roman general, who sent Cyprian as his envoy to Papua. The late sovereign of Africa re-entered his capital as a suppliant and a prisoner, and at the suburb of Aclas, beheld his conqueror for the first time.

With the capitulation of Gelimer, the Vandal war was at an end. There now remained to Belisarius but the important task of making the conquered countries permanently useful to the Romans. But, while occupied in this design, his glory having provoked envy, he was accused to Justinian of the intention of making himself king over the territories he had conquered. With the weakness of a little mind, the emperor so far yielded to the base accusation as to send a message to Belisarius, indicating his suspicions. The latter immediately departed from Carthage, and, taking with him his spoils and captives, proceeded to Constantinople.

This ready obedience dissipated the suspicions of the emperor, and he made ample and prompt reparation for his unfounded jealousy. Medals were struck by his orders, bearing on one side the effigy of the emperor, and on the other that of the victorious general, encircled by the inscription, *Belisarius, the glory of the Romans*. Beside this, the honours of a triumph were decreed him, the first ever witnessed in the Eastern capital.

The ceremony was in the highest degree imposing. The triumphal procession marched from the house of Belisarius to the hippodrome,[2] filled with exulting thousands, where Justinian and Theodora sat enthroned. Among the Vandal captives, Gelimer was distinguished by the purple of a sovereign. He shed no tears, but frequently repeated the words of Solomon, "*Vanity of vanities: all is vanity.*" When he reached the imperial throne, and was commanded to cast aside the ensigns of royalty, Belisarius hastened to do the same, to show him that he was to undergo no insult as a prisoner, but only to yield the customary homage of a subject. We may pause for a moment to reflect upon the caprices of fortune, which had raised a comedian, in the person of Theodora, to see the successor of Genseric and Scipio prostrate as slaves before her footstool.

Both the conqueror and captive experienced the effects of imperial generosity. The former received a large share of the spoil as his reward, and was named consul for the ensuing year. To the Vandal monarch, an extensive estate in Galatia was assigned, to which he retired, and, in peaceful obscurity, spent the remainder of his days.

We must now turn our attention to Italy. Theodoric the Great, the natural son of Theodomir, King of the Ostrogoths, became the master of Italy toward the close of the fifth century. The Gothic dominion was thus established in the ancient seat of the Roman Empire, and the King of the Goths was seated upon the throne of the Caesars,

Theodoric has furnished one of the few instances in which a successful soldier has abandoned warlike pursuits for the duties of civil administration, and, instead of seeking power by his arms, has devoted himself to the improvement of his kingdom by a peaceful policy. Upright and active in his conduct, he enforced discipline among his soldiers, and so tempered his general kindness by acts of salutary rigor, that he was loved as if indulgent, yet obeyed as if severe. He applied himself to the revival of trade, the support of manufactures, and the encouragement of agriculture.

---

2. A space where the chariot races were exhibited.

At the death of this great monarch, in 526, his grandson, Athalaric, then only ten years of age, became king. After a nominal reign of eight years he died in consequence of his dissipations, and was succeeded by Theodatus, the nephew of Theodoric. This prince having attained the throne by the murder of Amalasontha, the widow of Theodoric, Justinian regarded him as an usurper stained with an atrocious crime, and therefore determined to drive him from his throne.

Accordingly, a force of twelve thousand men was despatched to Italy under Belisarius. Landing at Catania, in Sicily, they surprised the Goths, and had little difficulty in reducing the island. Fixing his head quarters at Syracuse, he was making preparations to enter the heart of Italy, when a messenger came to inform him that a serious insurrection had broken out at Carthage. He immediately set out for that place. On his arrival the insurgents fled, but Belisarius pursued them, overtook them, and, though their force was four times as great as his own, they were completely defeated in a pitched battle. Returning to Carthage, the Roman general was informed by a messenger from Sicily that a formidable mutiny had broken out in his army there. He immediately embarked, and soon restored his troops to order and discipline.

The rapid conquest of Sicily by Belisarius struck terror into the heart of king Theodatus, who was weak by nature, and depressed by age. He was therefore included to subscribe an ignominious treaty with Justinian, some of the conditions of which forcibly display the pusillanimity of one emperor, and the vanity of the other. Theodatus promised that no statue should be raised to his honour, without another of Justinian at his right hand, and that the imperial name should always precede his own in the acclamations of the people, at public games and festivals: as if the shouts of the rabble were matter for a treaty!

But even this humiliating compact was not sufficient for the grasping avarice of Justinian. He required of Theodatus the surrender of his throne, which the latter promised; but before the compact could be carried into effect, he was driven from his throne, and Vitiges, a soldier of humble birth, but great energy and experience, was declared his successor. Establishing his headquarters at Ravenna, the Gothic king was making preparations to sustain his cause, when Belisarius, who had taken Naples, was invited to Rome by Pope Sylverius. Taking advantage of this opportunity, he immediately advanced, and triumphantly entered the "eternal city."

Rome had now been under the dominion of its Gothic conquerors for sixty years, during which it had enjoyed the advantages of peace and prosperity. It had been the object of peculiar care, attention, and munificence, and had received the respect due to the ancient mistress of the world. Still, the people at large looked upon their rulers as foreigners and barbarians, and desired the return of the imperial sway, seeming to forget that they were preferring a foreign to a native government.

Belisarius lost no time in repairing the fortifications of Rome, while he actively extended his conquests in the southern parts of Italy. His military fame was new a host, and most of the towns submitted, either from a preference of the Byzantine Government, or respect for the military prowess of the Roman general.

The great achievements of Belisarius strike us with wonder, when we consider the feeble means will which they were accomplished. His force at the outset of his invasion of Italy did not exceed 12.000 men. These were now much reduced by the bloody siege of Naples, and by his subsequent successes, which made it necessary to supply garrisons for the captured towns.

Vitiges, in his Adriatic capital, had spent the winter in preparations, and when the spring arrived, he set forth with a powerful army. Knowing the small force of Belisarius, he hurried forward towards Rome, fearing only that his enemy should escape by flight. The genius of Belisarius never shone with greater lustre than at this moment. By numerous device? he contrived to harass the Gothic army in their march, but owing to the flight of a detachment of his troops whom he had stationed at one of the towers, to delay their progress, they at last came up in him by surprise.

He was at the moment without the city, attended by only a thousand of his guards, when suddenly he found himself surrounded by the van of the Gothic cavalry. He now displayed not only the skill of a general, but the personal courage and prowess of a soldier. Distinguished by the charger whom he had often rode in battle—a bay with a white face—he was seen in the foremost ranks, animating his men to the conflict. "That is Belisarius," exclaimed some Italian deserters, who knew him. "Aim at the bay!" was forthwith the cry through the Gothic squadrons and a cloud of arrows was soon aimed at the conspicuous mark. It seemed as if the fate of Italy was felt to be suspended upon a single life—so fierce was the struggle to kill or capture the Roman leader.

Amid the deadly strife, however, Belisarius remained unhurt; and it is said that more of the army fell that day by his single arm, than by that of any other Roman. His guards displayed the utmost courage and devotion to his person, rallying around him, and raising their bucklers on every side, to ward off the showers of missiles that flew with deadly aim at his breast. Not less than a thousand of the enemy fell in the conflict—a number equal to the whole Roman troop engaged in the battle. The Goths at length gave way, and Belisarius, with his guards, re-entered the city.

On the morrow, March 12th, *a. d.* 537, the memorable siege of Rome began. Finding it impossible, even with their vast army, to encircle the entire walls of the city, which were twelve miles in length, the Goths selected five of the fourteen gates, and invested them. They now cut through the aqueducts, in order to stop the supply of water, and several of them, having never been repaired, remain to this day, extending into the country, and seeming like the " outstretched and broken limbs of an expiring giant."

Though the baths of the city were stopped, the Tiber supplied the people with water for all needful purposes. The resources and activity of Belisarius knew no bounds: yet he had abundant occasion for all the advantages these could supply. The relative smallness of his force, the feebleness of the defences the fickleness and final disaffection of the people, the intrigues of Vitiges, and his vastly superior army constituted a web of difficulties which would have overwhelmed any other than a man whose genius could extort good from evil, and convert weakness into strength.

For a whole year, the encircling walls of Rome were the scenes of almost incessant attack and defence. The fertile genius of Vitiges suggested a thousand expedients, and the number as well as courage of his troops enabled him to plan and execute n variety of daring schemes. Yet he was always baffled by his vigilant rival, and his most elaborate devices were rendered fruitless by the superior genius of the Roman general. At last, on the 21st of March. *a. d.* 538, foreseeing that Belisarius was about to receive reinforcements, and despairing of success in the siege, Vitiges withdrew his army, suffering in his retreat a fearful massacre, from a sally of the Roman troops.

Vitiges retired to Ravenna, and Belisarius soon invested it. While he was pressing the siege, Justinian, probably alarmed by the threats of the Persian king, entered into a treaty with the ambassadors of Vitiges, by which he agreed to a partition of Italy, taking one half himself, and allowing the Gothic king to retain the other portion. Belisarius refused to ratify this treaty, and soon after, was pressed by the Goths to become their king. Vitiges even joined in this request, and Belisarius had now the easy opportunity of making himself the emperor of the West, without the remotest fear of failure. But he was too deeply impressed with his oath of allegiance, to allow him to entertain a treacherous design toward his sovereign, and he rejected the tempting offer. The merit of his fidelity under these circumstances, is heightened by the consideration that he had refused the ratification of the treaty, and was well aware that reproach, or even hostility, might await him at Constantinople.

Soon after these events, Ravenna capitulated, and Belisarius became its master. His fame was now at its height; but this only served to inflame the envy of his rivals at Constantinople. These, insidiously working upon the suspicious temper of Justinian, induced him to command the return of Belisarius to Constantinople. With prompt obedience, he embarked at Ravenna, carrying with him his Gothic captives and treasure. After five years of warfare, from the foot of Etna to the banks of the Po, during which he had subdued nearly the same extent of country which had been acquired by the Romans in the first five centuries from the building of that city, he arrived at Constantinople.

The voice of envy was silenced for a time, and Belisarius was appointed to the command of the army now about to proceed against the Persians. The captive monarch of the Goths was received with generous courtesy by the emperor, and an ample estate was allotted to him in Asia. Justinian gazed with admiration on the strength and beauty of the Gothic captives—their fair complexions, auburn locks, and lofty stature. A great number of these, attracted by the fame and character of Belisarius, enlisted in his guards.

In the spring of the year 540, Chosroes or Nushirvan, the Persian king, invaded the Roman provinces in the east. The next year Belisarius proceeded against him, and took his station at Dara. Here, instead of a well-appointed army, he found only a confused and discordant mass of undisciplined men. After various operations, being baffled by the treachery or incapacity of his subalterns, he was obliged to retreat, and closed a fruitless campaign, by placing his men in winter quarters.

Being recalled to Constantinople, he went thither, but took the field early in the spring, with the most powerful army he had ever commanded. Nushirvan advanced into Syria, but, thwarted by the masterly manoeuvres of Belisarius, he was at last obliged to retreat. Soon after, the Roman general being again recalled by Justinian, the most fatal disasters befell the Roman Army.

During these Persian campaigns, the political security, as well as the domestic happiness of Belisarius, were shaken by the misconduct of his wife. She had long been engaged in an intrigue with Theodosius, the young soldier newly baptized as an auspicious omen in the galley of the general, upon his departure for Africa. Though told of this, Belisarius had been pacified by the protestations and artifices of Antonina; but while he was absent in Asia Minor, she, being left in Constantinople, pursued her licentious career with little scruple.

Her son Photius, a gallant young soldier, being a check upon her conduct, became the object of her haired. While at the distance of a thousand miles, during the Persian campaign, he still experienced the malignant influence of her intrigues, and, urged by a sense of duty to his stepfather, made him acquainted with his mother's depravity. When she afterwards joined her husband on the frontier, he caused her to be imprisoned, and sent Photius towards Ephesus to Inflict summary punishment upon Theodosius. The latter was taken captive by Photius. and borne to Cilicia.

Antonina, by her convenient intrigues in behalf of Theodora, had laid her under great obligations, and obtained the greatest influence over her. The empress, therefore, now interfered to save her friend. Positive injunctions were sent to Cilicia, and both Photius and Theodosius were brought to Constantinople. The former was cast into a dungeon and tortured at the rack; the latter was received with distinction; but he soon expired from illness. Photius, after a third escape from prison, proceeded to Jerusalem, where he took the habit of a monk, and finally attained the rank of abbot.

Belisarius and Antonina were summoned to Constantinople, and the empress commanded the injured husband to abstain from the punishment of his wife. He obeyed this order of his sovereign. She next required a reconciliation at his hands; but he refused to comply with a demand which no sovereign had a right to make. He, therefore, remained at Constantinople, under the secret displeasure of Theodora and Justinian, who only wanted some plausible pretext to accomplish his ruin.

The invasion of Nushirvan, in the ensuing spring impelled the terrified emperor to lay aside his animosity, and restore the hero to the direction of the eastern armies; but in this campaign, his former offence was aggravated, and the glory of saving the East was outweighed by the guilt of frankness. Justinian was recovering from a dangerous illness; a rumour of his death had reached the Roman camp, and Belisarius gave an opinion in favour of the emperor's nearest kinsman as his successor, instead of acknowledging the pretensions of Theodora to the throne. This declaration inflamed with equal anger the aspiring wife and the uxorious husband.

Buzes, the second in command, who had concurred in these views, was confined in a subterranean dungeon, so dark that the difference of day and night was never apparent to its inmate. Belisarius himself was recalled, with flattering professions of confidence and friendship, lest resentment should urge him to rebellion; but on his arrival at Constantinople, the mask was thrown aside; he was degraded from the rank of general of the East; a commission was despatched into Asia to seize his treasures; and his personal guards, who had followed his standard through so many battles, were removed from his command.

It was with mingled feelings of compassion and surprise, that the people beheld the forlorn appearance of the general as he entered Constantinople, and rode along the streets, with a small and squalid train. Proceeding to the gates of the palace, he was exposed during the whole day to the scoffs and insults of the rabble. He was received by the emperor and Theodora with angry disdain, and when he withdrew, in the evening, to his lonely palace, he frequently turned round, expecting to see the appointed assassins advancing upon him

In the evening, after sunset, a letter was brought him from Theodora, declaring that his life was granted and a portion of his fortune spared at the intercession of his wife, and she trusted that his future conduct would manifest his gratitude to his deliverer. The favourable moments of surprise and gratitude were improved by Antonina with her usual skill. Thus, by the artifices of two designing women, the conqueror of armies was subdued, and Belisarius once more became the duped and submissive husband.

A fine of three hundred pounds weight of gold was levied upon the property of Belisarius, and he was suffered for many months to languish in obscurity. In 544, however, he was appointed to the command of the war in Italy, whither he soon proceeded. Here, in his operations against far superior forces, he displayed the same genius as before, and in February, 547, he again entered Rome. He pursued the war with various fortune; but at last, finding his means entirely inadequate to the necessities of the contest, he begged of the emperor either reinforcements or recall. Engrossed by religious quarrels, Justinian took the easier course, and adopted the latter. Thus, after having desolated Italy with all the horrors of war for several years, he now abandoned it, from mere weakness and caprice.

Belisarius returned to Constantinople, and for several years his life affords no remarkable occurrence. He continued in the tranquil enjoyment of opulence and dignities; but, in the year 559, various warlike tribes beyond the Danube, known under the general name of Bulgarians, marched southward, and desolated several provinces by sword, fire, and plunder. Zabergan, their enterprising leader, having passed the frozen Danube in the winter, detached one portion of his army for the pillage of Greece, and the other against the capital.

So sudden and bold an aggression filled Constantinople with helpless and despairing terror. The people and the senators were agitated with fear, and the emperor sat trembling in his palace. In this general confusion and affright, all eyes were turned with hope to the conqueror of Africa and Italy. Though his constitution was broken by his military labours, his heart was alive to the call of his country, and Belisarius prepared to crown his glorious life by a last and decisive battle. He resumed his rusty armour, collected a handful of his scattered veterans, and in the return of martial spirit he seemed to shake off the weakness of decrepitude.

Sallying from the city with three hundred mounted men, he met Zabergan at the head of two thousand cavalry. Selecting a favourable position, he withstood the onset, and, seeming to recover the powers of his youth, he astonished all around him by his intrepidity and skill. After a severe and bloody struggle, the Bulgarians were driven back in the utmost disorder; four hundred fell on the field, and Zabergan himself escaped with difficulty. The whole army of barbarians, amounting to many thousands, were seized with contagious fear, raised their camp, and retreated to the north.

Belisarius was preparing for a close pursuit, when again his enemies awaked the suspicions of Justinian by suggesting that he was aiming at popular favour with disloyal views. The enthusiastic praises of his heroic conduct, by the people, turned even the emperor's heart to jealousy, and he chose rather to purchase the departure of the barbarians by tribute, than to permit Belisarius to obtain new laurels by chastising their audacity.

From this period, Belisarius continued under the displeasure of

Justinian, whose suspicious temper seemed to grow more virulent as his faculties sunk in the dotage of years. In 563, several conspiracies against the life of Justinian were detected, and under torture, some of the domestics of Belisarius accused their master of participation. This testimony, disproved by the long life and the habitually submissive loyalty of Belisarius, was sufficient for his conviction. He was stripped of his fortune, deprived of his guards, and detained as a close prisoner in his palace.

The other conspirators were condemned and executed; but, in consideration of the past services of Belisarius, the decree of death was changed for that of blindness, and his eyes were accordingly put out.[3] He was now restored to liberty, but, deprived of all means of subsistence, he was compelled to beg his bread before the gates of the convent of Laurus. There he stood with a wooden platter which he held out for charity, exclaiming to the passersby, "Give a penny to Belisarius the general!"

The affecting scene was long impressed upon the recollection of the people; and it would seem that this spectacle of persecuted merit aroused some dangerous feelings of indignation and pity, and he was, therefore, removed from public view. Belisarius was brought back to his former palace, and a portion of his treasures was allotted for his use. His death, which was doubtless hastened by the grief and hardships of his lot, occurred in 565; and Antonina, who survived him, devoted the remains of her life and fortune to the cloister.

In person, Belisarius was tall and commanding; his features regular and noble. When he appeared in the streets of Constantinople, he never failed to attract the admiration of the people. As a military leader, he was enterprising, firm, and fearless. His conception was clear, and his judgment rapid and decisive. His conquests were achieved with smaller means than any other of like extent recorded in history. He experienced reverses in the field; but never did he fail without strong and sufficient reason. His superior tactics covered his defeats, retrieved his losses, and prevented his enemies from reaping the fruits of victory. Never, even in the most desperate emergencies, was he known to lose his courage or presence of mind.

---

3. This portion of the story of Belisarius has been the subject of controversy. It has been doubted by Gibbon and other historians, whether the infliction of blindness upon Belisarius and his beggary, were not mere traditional fables. But Lord Mahon, in his excellent life of the great Roman general from which we have drawn the preceding account, appears to have established their authenticity. The beautiful tale of Belisarius by Marmontel, is fictitious in many of its details.

Though living in a barbarous and dissolute age, Belisarius possessed many shining virtues. In the march of his armies, he would avoid the trampling of the cornfields, nor would he allow his soldiers even to gather apples from the trees without making payment to the villagers. After a victory, it was his first care to extend mercy and protection to the vanquished. The gift of a golden bracelet or collar rewarded any valorous achievement among his troops; the loss of a horse or weapon was immediately supplied from his private funds; the wounded ever found in him a father and a friend. To all, he was open and easy of access, and by his courteous demeanour often comforted, where he could not relieve. From his generosity, one would have deemed him rich; from his manners, poor. His private virtues promoted and confirmed the discipline of his soldiers. None ever saw him flushed with wine, nor could the charms of his fairest captives overcome his conjugal fidelity.

But the most remarkable feature in the character of Belisarius is his steadfast loyalty, and the noble magnanimity with which he overlooked the suspicious meanness and ingratitude of his sovereign. It is impossible to find in history another instance of an individual so strongly induced to rebellion by treacherous treatment or the part of his country, and the opportunity of placing a crown upon his head without the risk of effectual opposition, who refused, from patriotic motives, the double temptation.

That Belisarius had faults, is not to be denied. His blind submission to his wife displayed great weakness, and led him into most of the errors which are charged upon his public career. In his last campaign in Italy, his wealth having been exhausted by an enormous fine, he endeavoured to repair his losses by imitating the rapacity universally practised by other commanders of that period. He thus inflicted upon his memory a serious stain, and showed that, however he was exalted above the age, he was still a man. His whole career affords a striking moral, coinciding with the emphatic language of Scripture, "*Put not thy trust in princes.*"

ALSO FROM LEONAUR
AVAILABLE IN SOFTCOVER OR HARDCOVER WITH DUST JACKET

THE 2ND MAORI WAR: 1860-1861 *by Robert Carey*—The Second Maori War, or First Taranaki War, one more bloody instalment of the conflicts between European settlers and the indigenous Maori people.

A JOURNAL OF THE SECOND SIKH WAR *by Daniel A. Sandford*—The Experiences of an Ensign of the 2nd Bengal European Regiment During the Campaign in the Punjab, India, 1848-49.

THE LIGHT INFANTRY OFFICER *by John H. Cooke*—The Experiences of an Officer of the 43rd Light Infantry in America During the War of 1812.

BUSHVELDT CARBINEERS *by George Witton*—The War Against the Boers in South Africa and the 'Breaker' Morant Incident.

LAKE'S CAMPAIGNS IN INDIA *by Hugh Pearse*—The Second Anglo Maratha War, 1803-1807.

BRITAIN IN AFGHANISTAN 1: THE FIRST AFGHAN WAR 1839-42 *by Archibald Forbes*—From invasion to destruction-a British military disaster.

BRITAIN IN AFGHANISTAN 2: THE SECOND AFGHAN WAR 1878-80 *by Archibald Forbes*—This is the history of the Second Afghan War-another episode of British military history typified by savagery, massacre, siege and battles.

UP AMONG THE PANDIES *by Vivian Dering Majendie*—Experiences of a British Officer on Campaign During the Indian Mutiny, 1857-1858.

MUTINY: 1857 *by James Humphries*—Authentic Voices from the Indian Mutiny-First Hand Accounts of Battles, Sieges and Personal Hardships.

BLOW THE BUGLE, DRAW THE SWORD *by W. H. G. Kingston*—The Wars, Campaigns, Regiments and Soldiers of the British & Indian Armies During the Victorian Era, 1839-1898.

WAR BEYOND THE DRAGON PAGODA *by Major J. J. Snodgrass*—A Personal Narrative of the First Anglo-Burmese War 1824 - 1826.

THE HERO OF ALIWAL *by James Humphries*—The Campaigns of Sir Harry Smith in India, 1843-1846, During the Gwalior War & the First Sikh War.

ALL FOR A SHILLING A DAY *by Donald F. Featherstone*—The story of H.M. 16th, the Queen's Lancers During the first Sikh War 1845-1846.

AVAILABLE ONLINE AT **www.leonaur.com**
AND FROM ALL GOOD BOOK STORES

ALSO FROM LEONAUR
AVAILABLE IN SOFTCOVER OR HARDCOVER WITH DUST JACKET

THE FALL OF THE MOGHUL EMPIRE OF HINDUSTAN by H. G. Keene—By the beginning of the nineteenth century, as British and Indian armies under Lake and Wellesley dominated the scene, a little over half a century of conflict brought the Moghul Empire to its knees.

LADY SALE'S AFGHANISTAN by Florentia Sale—An Indomitable Victorian Lady's Account of the Retreat from Kabul During the First Afghan War.

THE CAMPAIGN OF MAGENTA AND SOLFERINO 1859 by Harold Carmichael Wylly—The Decisive Conflict for the Unification of Italy.

FRENCH'S CAVALRY CAMPAIGN by J. G. Maydon—A Special Correspondent's View of British Army Mounted Troops During the Boer War.

CAVALRY AT WATERLOO by Sir Evelyn Wood—British Mounted Troops During the Campaign of 1815.

THE SUBALTERN by George Robert Gleig—The Experiences of an Officer of the 85th Light Infantry During the Peninsular War.

NAPOLEON AT BAY, 1814 by F. Loraine Petre—The Campaigns to the Fall of the First Empire.

NAPOLEON AND THE CAMPAIGN OF 1806 by Colonel Vachée—The Napoleonic Method of Organisation and Command to the Battles of Jena & Auerstädt.

THE COMPLETE ADVENTURES IN THE CONNAUGHT RANGERS by William Grattan—The 88th Regiment during the Napoleonic Wars by a Serving Officer.

BUGLER AND OFFICER OF THE RIFLES by William Green & Harry Smith—With the 95th (Rifles) during the Peninsular & Waterloo Campaigns of the Napoleonic Wars.

NAPOLEONIC WAR STORIES by Sir Arthur Quiller-Couch—Tales of soldiers, spies, battles & sieges from the Peninsular & Waterloo campaigns.

CAPTAIN OF THE 95TH (RIFLES) by Jonathan Leach—An officer of Wellington's sharpshooters during the Peninsular, South of France and Waterloo campaigns of the Napoleonic wars.

RIFLEMAN COSTELLO by Edward Costello—The adventures of a soldier of the 95th (Rifles) in the Peninsular & Waterloo Campaigns of the Napoleonic wars.

AVAILABLE ONLINE AT **www.leonaur.com**
AND FROM ALL GOOD BOOK STORES

ALSO FROM LEONAUR
AVAILABLE IN SOFTCOVER OR HARDCOVER WITH DUST JACKET

AT THEM WITH THE BAYONET *by Donald F. Featherstone*—The first Anglo-Sikh War 1845-1846.

STEPHEN CRANE'S BATTLES *by Stephen Crane*—Nine Decisive Battles Recounted by the Author of 'The Red Badge of Courage'.

THE GURKHA WAR *by H. T. Prinsep*—The Anglo-Nepalese Conflict in North East India 1814-1816.

FIRE & BLOOD *by G. R. Gleig*—The burning of Washington & the battle of New Orleans, 1814, through the eyes of a young British soldier.

SOUND ADVANCE! *by Joseph Anderson*—Experiences of an officer of HM 50th regiment in Australia, Burma & the Gwalior war.

THE CAMPAIGN OF THE INDUS *by Thomas Holdsworth*—Experiences of a British Officer of the 2nd (Queen's Royal) Regiment in the Campaign to Place Shah Shuja on the Throne of Afghanistan 1838 - 1840.

WITH THE MADRAS EUROPEAN REGIMENT IN BURMA *by John Butler*—The Experiences of an Officer of the Honourable East India Company's Army During the First Anglo-Burmese War 1824 - 1826.

IN ZULULAND WITH THE BRITISH ARMY *by Charles L. Norris-Newman*—The Anglo-Zulu war of 1879 through the first-hand experiences of a special correspondent.

BESIEGED IN LUCKNOW *by Martin Richard Gubbins*—The first Anglo-Sikh War 1845-1846.

A TIGER ON HORSEBACK *by L. March Phillips*—The Experiences of a Trooper & Officer of Rimington's Guides - The Tigers - during the Anglo-Boer war 1899 - 1902.

SEPOYS, SIEGE & STORM *by Charles John Griffiths*—The Experiences of a young officer of H.M.'s 61st Regiment at Ferozepore, Delhi ridge and at the fall of Delhi during the Indian mutiny 1857.

CAMPAIGNING IN ZULULAND *by W. E. Montague*—Experiences on campaign during the Zulu war of 1879 with the 94th Regiment.

THE STORY OF THE GUIDES *by G.J. Younghusband*—The Exploits of the Soldiers of the famous Indian Army Regiment from the northwest frontier 1847 - 1900.

AVAILABLE ONLINE AT **www.leonaur.com**
AND FROM ALL GOOD BOOK STORES

www.ingramcontent.com/pod-product-compliance
Lightning Source LLC
Chambersburg PA
CBHW031616160426
43196CB00006B/153